Introduction to Public Law:

A Comparative Study

Elisabeth Zoller

MARTINUS NIJHOFF PUBLISHERS

This book is printed on acid-free paper.

Library of Congress Cataloging-in-Publication Data

Zoller, Elisabeth.
Introduction to public law: a comparative study / Elisabeth Zoller.
p. cm.
Includes bibliographical references and index.
ISBN 978-90-04-16147-4
1. Rule of law—History. 2. State, The—History. 3. Public law—History. 4. Public law (Roman law) I. Title.

K3171.Z65 2007
342—dc22

2007045540

This paperback was originally published in hardback under ISBN 978 90 04 16147 4.

ISBN 978 90 04 20584 0

CONTENTS

Foreword

This book is about public law, in the sense first defined by the Romans, that is, the law of the *res publica*—literally ''the public thing''—the public interest or common good, predicated on a differentiation between the State and the government. Today, that definition has fallen into oblivion, largely replaced by more formalistic concerns, with public law governing the relations between the citizen and the State, and private law defined as the law that applies between the citizens themselves. This shift in definition would not be objectionable if the word ''State'' still meant what it did in the republican age, that is, the thing of the people, the common wealth, the common good—or, precisely, the *res publica*. But this is not the case. In most countries, the State is not differentiated from the government. The consequences of this amalgam are pervasively negative.

When the State is understood as nothing more than a group of people in power, public law is necessarily assimilated to the rules it enacts—thus the bedrock principle of a government by men, rather than by law. Viewed this way, public law is strongly opposed to the rule of law, even incompatible with it, or twisted in such a way that it becomes the law that protects the individual against public power. Under these conditions, its object is no longer the *res publica*, the public interest, but rather the private interest, under which all legal rules and institutions can be subsumed.

But law is not concerned with private interests only. Law is concerned with justice, and justice implies both public and private interests. That the law is concerned with the protection of everyone's rights is a self-evident truth. Modern law began with this premise, both in the United States, where the Declaration of Independence of 1776 asserted, with ''respect to the opinions of mankind,'' that ''to secure [certain unalienable] rights, governments are instituted among men,'' and, in France, where the Declaration of the Rights of Man of 1789 proclaimed ''in the presence and under the auspices of the Supreme Being'' that ''[t]he aim of all political association is the preservation of the natural and imprescriptible rights of man.'' Regardless of its common law or civil law foundations, then, law is always deeply interested in dispensing justice among private interests. These private interests include relations between landlords and tenants, debtors and creditors, victims and tortfeasors, and employers and employees, to name just a few examples.

If law is primarily concerned with private interests, and is thus intrinsically private, what do we need public law for? The answer, I believe, is this: We need a yardstick to evaluate the respective legitimacy of private interests and to distinguish among them whenever they come into conflict. To adjudicate between private interests, we must have rules with appropriate guidelines, so that each is given its due and just share. There is no possibility of doing that fairly in our contemporary democratic societies except in accordance with the *res publica*, the enduring common interests of a people: in other words, the object and purpose of public law. Otherwise, "the government of the people, by the people and for the people" would become meaningless.

* * *

The present book is the English version of a work first written in French and published by the Éditions Dalloz in the collection "Précis Dalloz" under the title *Introduction au droit public* in 2006. I acknowledge with gratitude the permission given to me by the Éditions Dalloz for writing the English version of that work.

The English version closely follows the initial French version, without however being a word-for-word translation. On several occasions, I departed from the French text, whenever public law concepts called for more or different explanations. One of the greatest difficulties I encountered was how to convey in English the positive meaning that the word "*loi*" (statute) has in the French language, as opposed to its somewhat inferior, if not negative, connotation in the English language, where a statute is not to be confused with the law. The French language, unlike English, possesses two words to talk about law, *droit* and *loi*. The sum of "*lois*" forms the "*législation*" (legislation), which is distinct from "*droit*" (law). This distinction was explained by Portalis in the Preliminary Address on the *First Draft of the Civil Code* (1799) as follows: "Law (*droit*) is universal reason, supreme reason based on the very nature of things. Statutes (*lois*) are, or ought to be, law reduced to positive rules, to specific precepts. Law is morally imperative, but in itself not constraining. It guides; statutes command. It is the map; and statutes, the compass." What Portalis means here by "*loi,*" is the statute no more, no less, that is, a "law" enacted by a legislative body. "*Loi*" is absolutely central to a proper understanding of public law, because *loi* is the act of public law, par excellence. To avoid any confusion between "*loi*" and law, I have used the English words "statute," or "statutory law" or "legislation" to translate the French concept of "*loi.*"

* * *

This book has benefited from many comments and explanations made by foreign colleagues on the status of public law in the common law world. My intellectual debt goes in particular to Alfred C. Aman, Jr., Patrick L. Baude, Yvonne Cripps, Robert C. Post, Lauren K. Robel, Cheryl A. Saunders, Michael Taggart, David C. Williams, and Susan Hoffman Williams. The usual disclaimer applies.

I am also much indebted to Rebecca Bertoloni-Meli and Ralph Gaebler of Indiana University Law Library at Bloomington for having made my long-term research project an experiment in academic joy and intellectual rewards.

Recognition and gratitude are due to Leora J. Baude who gave me great assistance in revising my initial draft. Unless otherwise indicated, all translations are mine. Grateful thanks go to Maria Angelini and Maxine Idakus for rare professionalism in editing the manuscript.

Last but not least, this book would never have come into being without the exchange of ideas about law and society pursued for so many years with my dear friends Lucile Tallineau (Paris X-Nanterre) and Carol J. Greenhouse (Princeton). It owes to them more than I can say. Only errors are mine in this work; the good, if any, is always the result of a sharing of thoughts with them.

About the Author

Elisabeth Zoller (*Docteur en droit, Agrégée de droit public*) is Professor of Public Law in the Law School at the University of Paris II (Panthéon-Assas) where she is Director of the Center for American Law and Director of the Doctorate Program on the Common Law System. She joined the Law School of Paris II in 1995 where she teaches constitutional law and comparative public law. In France, she taught international law and constitutional law at the Universities of Angers and Nantes (1979-1983) and Strasbourg (1989-1994).

She has authored several books in French and English on international law, constitutional law, and more recently comparative law. Her English publications include *Peacetime Unilateral Remedies: An Analysis of Countermeasures* (1984) and *Enforcing International Law through United States Legislation* (1985). Her award-winning French publications include *De Nixon à Clinton, Malentendus juridiques transatlantiques* (1999), which won the Prix Charles Lyon-Caen in 1999, and *Grands arrêts de la Cour suprême des États-Unis* (2000), which won the 2001 Prix Maurice Travers (both prizes of the Académie des sciences morales et politiques (Institut de France)).

In the United States, she was a visiting professor at Cornell University (1984), Rutgers University (1987-1988), and Tulane University (1994). Since 1996, she regularly visits Indiana University Law School-Bloomington where she teaches and researches in comparative constitutional law. She is a Senior Fellow in the Law School of the University of Melbourne where she teaches comparative constitutional law.

Elisabeth Zoller was Counsel and Advocate for the Government of the United States of America before the International Court of Justice in the Case concerning Questions of Interpretation and Application of the 1971 Montreal Convention arising from the Aerial Incident at *Lockerbie* (1998) and in the Case concerning Avena and Other Mexican Nationals (2004).

Abbreviations

AC	Appeal Court (United Kingdom)
AJCL	American Journal of Comparative Law
AJDA	Actualité juridique de droit administratif
AP	Archives parlementaires de 1787 à 1860, Assemblée nationale constituante (1789-1791)
APD	Archives de philosophie du droit
Cahiers CC	Les cahiers du Conseil constitutionnel
Cambridge L. J.	Cambridge Law Journal
Cleveland St. L. Rev.	Cleveland State Law Review
CMLR	Common Market Law Reports
Columbia L. Rev.	Columbia Law Review
Cornell L. J.	Cornell Law Journal
Cornell L. Q.	Cornell Law Quarterly
D.	Recueil Dalloz
DAR	Dictionnaire de l'Ancien Régime [L. Bély (Dir.)], PUF, Quadrige, 2002
DCJ	Dictionnaire de la culture juridique [D. Alland & S. Rials (Dirs.)], Lamy / PUF, 2003
DCRF	Dictionnaire critique de la Révolution française [Furet & Ozouf (Dirs.)], Coll. Champs no. 264-267, Flammarion, 1992, 4 volumes: Acteurs, Institutions et créations, Événements, Idées
DPP	Dictionnaire de philosophie politique [Ph. Raynaud & S. Rials (Dirs.)], PUF, 3rd ed. 2003
ECSC	European Coal and Steel Community
EEC	European Economic Community
EJIL	European Journal of International Law
Harv. L. Rev.	Harvard Law Review
Hastings Int'l & Comp. L. Rev.	Hastings International and Comparative Law Review
Hastings L. J.	Hasting Law Review
IJGLS	Indiana Journal of Global Legal Studies
JCP	Juris-classeur périodique (Lexis-Nexis)
Mich. L. Rev.	Michigan Law Review

N.Y.U. L. Rev.	New York University Law Review
PPS	Problèmes politiques et sociaux (La Documentation française)
RA	Revue administrative
RCADI	Recueil des cours de l'Académie de droit international de La Haye
RDP	Revue du droit public en France et à l'étranger
Rec.	Recueil des décisions du Conseil constitutionnel
Rec. Lebon	Recueil des décisions du Conseil d'État
RFDC	Revue française de droit constitutionnel
RFDA	Revue française de droit administratif
RUDH	Revue universelle des droits de l'homme
South Calif. L. Rev.	South California Law Review
Stanford L. Rev.	Stanford Law Review
Syracuse J. Int'l L. & Comm.	Syracuse Journal of International Law and Commerce
Texas L. Rev.	Texas L. Review
U. Penn. L. Rev.	University of Pennsylvania Law Review
US	United States Reports
Virginia L. Rev.	Virginia Law Review
Wm. & Mary Q.	William & Mary Quarterly
Wm. & Mary L. Rev.	William & Mary Law Review
Yale L. J.	Yale Law Journal

Introduction
Thinking About Public Law

Public law in national legal systems. No matter the diversity of legal systems, they all take into account, in one way or another, a necessary distinction between public law and private law. Every country has its own way of conceptualizing this distinction and putting it into practice. In general, the manner in which they do so bears witness to the ''prejudices, habits, dominating passions, of all that finally composes what is called national character.''[1]

In some legal systems, the distinction is blurred or barely discernible; it can be intuited only from specific rules or particular institutions embedded in the larger body of the law in force. Such is the case in England and in the United States. Both countries possess some public law rules or institutions—for instance, in England, the so-called ''public law remedies'' which are distinct from those available in private law[2] or in the United States, the ''cases of private right and those [of public rights] which arise between the government and

[1] A. de Tocqueville, *Democracy in America* [Translated by Harvey C. Mansfield and Delba Winthrop], 2000, University of Chicago Press, I, I, chap. 2, p. 28

[2] *O'Reilly* v. *Mackman*, [1983] 2 AC 237, 255-6 (Lord Denning, J.):

> In modern times we have come to recognise two separate fields of law: one of private law, the other of public law. Private law regulates the affairs of subjects as between themselves. Public law regulates the affairs of subjects vis-à-vis public authorities. For centuries there were special remedies available in public law. They were the prerogative writs of certiorari, mandamus and prohibition. As I have shown, they were taken in the name of the sovereign against a public authority which had failed to perform its duty to the public at large or had performed it wrongly. Any subject could complain to the sovereign: and then the King's courts, at their discretion, would give him leave to issue such one of the prerogative writs as was appropriate to meet his case. But these writs, as their names show, only gave the remedies of quashing, commanding or prohibiting. They did not enable a subject to recover damages against a public authority, nor a declaration, nor an injunction. [. . .] But now we have witnessed a break-through in our public law. It is done by Section 31 of the Supreme Court Act [. . .]. Now [. . .] judicial review is available to give every kind of remedy.

persons subject to its authority in connection with the performance of the constitutional functions of the executive or legislative departments.''[3] In both countries, however, cases concerning these remedies or rights are adjudicated in the last resort by ordinary courts, remaining within their jurisdiction rather than withheld for another court's purview on account of their public law component.

Sometimes, though, the distinction between public law and private law is glaring. Rather than being deduced in the legal system through various rules or institutions, the distinction structures the whole legal system, constituting its very backbone.[4] Such is the case in France, where public law is radically separate from private law: Two different high courts exist, one to adjudicate private law disputes (*Cour de cassation*) and one to hear public law cases (*Conseil d'État*). This division between two court systems has important consequences for French legal education. All students take common courses during the first three years of their legal studies, but then the curriculum splits,[5] and the students graduate from law school with a specialization in either private or public law.

---

[3] *Crowell* v. *Benson*, 285 US 22, 50 (1932); *Murray's Lessee* v. *Hoboken Land & Improvement Company*, 18 How (59 US) 272 (1855). Another example of public law institutions is the so-called *public law litigation*, an expression coined by Abram Chayes, which refers to cases in which the federal courts are no longer called upon to resolve private disputes between private individuals according to the principles of private law, but instead, they are asked to deal with grievances over the administration of some public or quasi-public program and to vindicate the public policies embodied in the governing statutes or constitutional provisions, A. Chayes, ''The Role of the Judge in Public Law Litigation,'' 89 *Harv. L. Rev.* 1281 (1976); A. Chayes, ''Public Law Litigation and the Burger Court,'' 96 *Harv. L. Rev.* 4 (1982). On the public/private distinction in the United States, see Morton J. Horowitz, ''The History of the Public/ Private Distinction,'' 130 *U. Penn. L. Rev.* 1423 (1981-1982).

[4] On the distinction between private law and public law in French law, see J.-B. Auby (Ed.), *The Public Law / Private Law Divide: Une entente assez cordiale*, Oxford; Portland, Or., Hart, 2006 [previously published in 2004 by LGDJ, Paris]; G. Chevrier, ''Remarques sur l'introduction et les vicissitudes de la distinction du '*jus privatum*' et du '*jus publicum*' dans les œuvres des anciens juristes français,'' *APD* (1952), p. 5; O. Beaud, ''La distinction entre droit public et droit public: un dualisme qui résiste aux critiques'' in J.-B. Auby & M. Friedland [Eds.], *La distinction du droit public et du droit privé: regards français et britanniques*, Ed. Panthéon-Assas, 2004, p. 29; J. Caillosse, ''Droit public—droit privé: sens et portée d'un partage académique,'' *AJDA* 1996, p. 955; E. Desmons, ''Droit privé, droit public,'' *DCC*, p. 520; D. Truchet, *Le droit public*, PUF, Coll. Que Sais-je?, 2003.

[5] After three years, students earn a ''licence,'' or undergraduate diploma. In order to practice, they must earn at least a master's degree, which takes another two years. A doctorate requires at least three years further study.

These preliminary notes yield a first observation: Public law is to be found everywhere. There are no States without *some* public law.

Public law as law of the res publica. Notwithstanding the diversity with which the various legal systems of the world apply the distinction between public and private law, some generalizations are in order. For instance, everywhere, civil or commercial law regulates social relationships by taking into account the fact that the state may be a party to such relationships; nowhere are provinces, counties, or cities legally considered mere associations of citizens; nowhere may a creditor of the State attach the funds held by a tax collector.[6] Everywhere, special rules have been developed to deal with such situations because, everywhere, common sense supports a *res publica*, a "public thing," a common wealth, existing alongside, or even above, the multitude of private things. Each country has special rules to deal with situations that are of concern for the "public thing," the *res publica*. These rules form public law.

A. THE ROMAN FOUNDATIONS OF PUBLIC LAW

The Roman origin of the res publica. The concept of *res publica* is the *raison d'être* of public law. Without a "public thing," there would be no need for legal rules to protect and develop the wealth of physical resources (territory, population) and spiritual values (liberty, human rights) that a people inherits from its ancestors and wishes to bequeath to its descendants.[7]

The *res publica* was created by the Romans to solve problems arising from Roman domination of the Mediterranean basin. Rome's urban institutions were modeled after those of the ancient cities; it had a Senate and an assembly of citizens that elected the magistrates. With the legions' conquests, these institutions became inadequate. Actually, they were already out of date when the republic extended its government over the Italian peninsula. In order to avoid a return to the Oriental tradition of power personified in a single man, such as the Egyptian Pharaoh, the Romans invented the notion of *res publica*—the goods,

---

[6] R. David, "Introduction," *International Encyclopedia of Comparative Law*, Vol. II: The Legal Systems of the World, Chapter 2: Structure and the Divisions of the Law, JCB Mohr / Mouton, Tübingen / Paris, 2-19, p. 11.

[7] To that extent, the *res publica* is the other side of the public good and it is felt instinctively by the citizen. See R. N. Bellah, R. Madsen, W. M. Sullivan, A. Swindler, S. M. Tipton, *Habits of the Heart, Individualism and Commitment in American Life*, University of California Press, 1985, p. 193: "What is the content of the public good? [T]he public good is based on the responsibility of one generation to the next, and [. . .] an awareness of such a responsibility is a sine qua non for an understanding of the public good."

affairs, and institutions that are the "thing of the people," a sort of property held in common. The power of the people over their property is abstract and general; no one possesses or exercises it personally or exclusively. The foundation of the power is distinct from its exercise; the *res publica* belongs to everyone in general and to no one in particular; everyone participates in it, but no one has ownership of it.[8]

Cicero was the first author who defined the public thing as the thing common to all, the thing of the people, a notion that eventually would turn into the common good or the public good: *res publica, res populi.* "The public thing is the thing of the people; and by people, I mean not just any gathering of people, but a large group of people forming a society and united by their adherence to a pact of justice and the sharing of common interests: *juris consensu et utilitatis communione sociatus.*"[9] This "pact of justice" and the "community of interests" born of the solidarities between men are the two pillars of the "public thing"—the thing of the people, which later was viewed as the common or public good, or the general interest, all these terms being different expressions of the *res publica.* There is no polity without a "public thing" because, as Sieyès put it in 1788 on the eve of the French Revolution: "It is impossible to conceive of a legitimate association whose objects are not common security, common liberty, in a word, the *res publica* (*chose publique*)."[10] The *res publica* is what ties the people together; it forms the raison d'être of their will to live together, in short, to form a society.

---

[8] On the discovery of the *res publica* by the Romans, see J. Ellul, *Histoire des institutions, Le moyen âge*, PUF, Quadrige, 1999, p. 19.

[9] Cicero, *De la République*, edited by A. Fouillée, Paris, Delagrave, 1868, p. 12.

[10] E. Sieyès, *Qu'est-ce que le Tiers État?* PUF, Quadrige, 1989, p. 85. Sieyès's phrase in French reads as follows: "Il est impossible de concevoir une association légitime qui n'ait pas pour objet la sécurité commune, la liberté commune, enfin la chose publique." The English translation for "*chose publique*" (literally "public thing") is no easy matter. Neither "common welfare" [E.-J. Sieyès, *What Is the Third Estate*? [Translated by M. Blondel and edited, with historical notes, by S.E. Finer], Praeger Publishers, New York,1964 pp. 156-57: "It is impossible to imagine a legitimate association whose object would not be the common security, the common liberty, and, finally, the common welfare"], nor "public establishment" [E.-J. Sieyès, *Political Writings: including the debate between Sieyès and Tom Paine in 1791* [Translated by M. Sonenscher], Indianapolis / Cambridge, 2003, p. 153: "It is impossible to conceive of a legitimate association whose objects are not common security, common liberty, and a public establishment"] conveys the real meaning of *chose publique*, the French expression for *res publica*, that is, according to Webster's Dictionary, "the commonwealth, the State." Instead of an impossible translation, I have chosen to keep the Latin expression as the best word to convey the object of public law.

Treatment of the res publica *in Rome.* Romans not only identified the "public thing." Experts in legal matters, they also understood that the survival of the "public thing" depends on its distinction from private things. The "public thing" must be subject to special rules, because it deals with things that are common to all. There is, on the one hand, what is useful to one person (*singulorum utilitas*) and, on the other, what is useful to a multitude of people. What is useful to a multitude of people forms the "public thing," the thing collectively owned by the people, the *res publica*. It is distinct from the multitude of other things that are privately owned and useful only to one person or a small group of people such as a family or an enterprise. Notwithstanding the variety of the criteria advanced to justify a distinction between public law and private law, the fundamental criterion remains that of the persons and situations to which the general notion of *utilitas* (utility) applies.[11] Private utility

---

[11] N. Bobbio, *Democracy and Dictatorship* [Translated by P. Kennedy], Minneapolis, University of Minnesota Press, 1989, p. 3. Max Weber in his treatise *Economy and Society*, particularly in the section on Sociology of Law, offered another criterion of distinction between public law and private law [*Economy and Society*, Edited by G. Roth & C. Wittich, University of California Press, 1978, vol. II, p. 642]. He suggested: "[P]rivate law might be contrasted with public law as the law of coordination as distinguished from that of subordination." As Bobbio noted (*supra,* at pp. 3-9), this distinction between two types of social relationships (between equals and between unequals) is often used as a template for supporting other academic oppositions such as law and contract, the State and the market, the citizen and the bourgeois, natural law (private law), and positive law (public law), the commutative justice that governs exchange (private law), and the distributive justice that guides public authority in the distribution of honors and duties (public law). These oppositions have to be handled with care; they do not describe reality with exactitude if only because they are not mutually exclusive and often overlap; rather they must be viewed as signposts that help to organize reality without ever explaining it completely. Two criticisms have been articulated against the dichotomy between the private and the public viewed as an opposition between consent and coercion, coordination and subordination, agreement and domination. On the one hand, "in the first third of the twentieth century, American legal realists argued that private rights between individuals should always be conceptualized as state legal interventions designed to serve ends of public policy" [R. Post, "The Challenge of Globalization to American Public Law Scholarship," 2 *Theoretical Inquiries in Law*, 323, 324 (2001)]. Under a legal realist approach, all law, at the end of the day, may be viewed as "coercive"; it always carries with it elements of subordination because it may always be enforced by the state apparatus. As Post rightly puts it: "We might reformulate the difference between public and private law as one of enforcement; as a question of whether the state pursues its ends by directly mandating compliance with legal norms through its own criminal or administrative interventions or whether it decentralizes the power to initiate such enforcement to private parties by affording them access to judicial power. In either case, the content of legal norms will express a public vision of desirable social relationships" (*id*, pp. 324-325). On the other hand, reducing public law to a law of

(*singulorum utilitas*) is the one that individuals may pursue for their own advantage. The *res publica* involves the general public utility (*utilitatis communione*), which brings the people together in a society bound by common objectives (the public good, the general welfare) as well as by legal bonds (the Constitution). The conceptualization of the *res publica* as distinct from private interests is one of the greatest legacies of Roman civilization. It is well articulated in the opening statement to the great compilation of Roman laws that form the Digest elaborated by order of Emperor Justinian in 530-533 B.C. The Digest begins with the following definition of law:

> The law obtains its name from justice; for (as Celsus elegantly says) law is the art of knowing what is good and just.
>
> (1) Anyone may properly call us the priest of this art, for we cultivate justice and profess to know what is good and equitable, dividing right from wrong, and distinguishing what is lawful from what is unlawful; desiring to make men good through fear of punishment, but also by the encouragement of reward; aiming (if I am not mistaken) at a true, and not a pretended philosophy.
>
> (2) Of this subject there are two divisions, public and private law. Public law is that which has reference to the administration of the Roman commonwealth; private law is that which concerns the interests of individuals; for there are some things which are useful to the public, and others which are of benefit to private persons. Public law has reference to sacred ceremonies, and to the duties of priests and magistrates. Private law is threefold in its nature, for it is derived either from natural precepts, from those of nations, from those of the Civil Law.[12]

---

subordination is somewhat inaccurate insofar as there are many public law situations in which there is not the slightest trace of coercion: for instance, no one is obliged to take advantage of a fiscal incentive, no one is obliged to run for a public office and, in most countries, no one is obliged to go to the polls (voting is entirely voluntary). Moreover, in those countries such as France where public law is distinct and separated from private law by separate courts, private law courts may adjudicate many situations in which public authorities are parties to the case, for example, when a public authority enters into a private law contract with a private business (as in a sales contract).

[12] Original text:

> *Hujus studii duae sunt positiones, publicum et privatum. Publicum jus est quod ad statum rei Romanae spectat, privatum quod ad singulorum utilatem: sunt enim quaedam publice utilia, quaedam privatim. Publicum jus in sacris, in sacerdotibus, in magistratibus constitit. Privatum jus tripartum est: collectum etenim est ex naturalibus praeceptis aut gentium aut civilibus* (D, I, I, 2).

The celebrated paragraph on the distinction between public and private law is a quotation drawn from the *Institutes* of Ulpianus written three centuries before. Ulpianus held the highest imperial office, the position of praetorian prefect (the emperor's principal legal officer). In 212 CE, the Emperor Antoninus Caracalla enacted an edict that turned most of the residents of his empire into Roman citizens. Known as the *Constitutio Antoniniana*, the edict was probably adopted for fiscal reasons (*i.e.*, to apply the inheritance tax levied on the estates of citizens to more people), and it was, of course, of a public nature. Apparently moved by the desire to reassure these new citizens to whom the new public law now applied, Ulpianus elucidated the distinction between public law and private law. Perhaps his goal was to convince these new taxpayers that civil law—the law that concerned their interests as private individuals—was distinct from public law.[13] The civil law, henceforth applicable to them as Roman citizens, could not be modified by the Emperor at will; it would therefore protect them against imperial interference. The idea that private law is a shield against governmental powers became foundational for modern freedoms. The ''barbarians'' who overthrew the Roman Empire had no concept of the ''public thing''; they knew nothing but the private spoils of war lords. With them, public law fell into oblivion until the beginning of the Middle Ages, when it was born again through the institution of monarchy.

B. THE GOVERNMENT OF THE *RES PUBLICA*

Presentation. Public law is based on the abstract idea that the public thing cannot be treated like a private thing. Concretely, what does that mean? What consequences are to be drawn from this principle? How special is—or should be—the treatment of the public thing? For a long time, the treatment of the public thing was very special indeed, because it was in the orbit of religion. Modern public law came into being when the *res publica* freed itself from the control of priests and pontiffs.

An English translation of the Digest by S. P. Scott (1932) is available at http://www.constitution.org/sps/sps02.htm Another English translation by Alan Watson is available in Th. Mommsen, P. Krueger, and A. Watson (Eds.), *The Digest of Justinian* [5 volumes] University of Pennsylvania Press, 1985, vol. 1, p. 1. For the purpose of defining public law, the key words are ''*quod ad statum rei Romanae spectat.*'' S. P. Scott suggests ''the administration of the Roman government'' and A. Watson, ''the establishment of the Roman commonwealth.'' Watson's translation is more in line with what constitutes the core element of public law in Roman law (*i.e.*, the *res publica).*

[13] P. Stein, *Roman Law in European History*, Cambridge University Press, 1999, p. 21.

1. The Ancient World

Supremacy of religion. Originally, the public thing was governed by religion, not by law. In ancient times, the rules regulating common life in the city-state were inspired by religious commands and precepts. This is evidenced by the Digest, which defines public law (*jus publicum*) as the law relating to the Roman public things (*statum rei Romanae*): ''Public law has reference to sacred ceremonies, and to the duties of priests and magistrates.''[14]

The definition of public law by the Digest is a perfect illustration of what public law could mean for the Ancients. The basic tenet of the ancient world was that the public thing was under the purview of religion and of religious officers. Religion and the public thing were two sides of the same coin. Each city worshiped its god and each god governed his city. The same code of rules applied to the relations between men and their duties toward the city's gods. Religion governed the city-state, particularly, in determining its rulers through drawing lots or by divination; in return, the State intervened in religious affairs by directing individual consciences and punishing any departure from the rites and the cults of the city.[15] As Benjamin Constant said of the democracy of the Ancients: ''Nothing was left to individual independence, neither as a matter of opinions nor as a matter of undertakings nor—still less—as a matter of religion. The free choice of our beliefs which we hold to be one of our most precious rights would have been regarded by the ancients as a felony and a sacrilege.''[16] If it is appropriate to refer to the concept of ''State'' in that period, the State was in religion, and the religion was in the State. In practice, the common good of the city was defined by prophesies and oracles. Public law, as we now understand it, did not exist; or, to oversimplify, religion held what later became law's place.[17] The substance of public law was therefore outside the law.

[14] See *supra* note 12.

[15] N. D. Fustel de Coulanges, *La cité antique*, Paris, Durand, 1864, pp. 517-518.

[16] B. Constant, ''De la liberté des anciens comparée à celle des modernes, Discours prononcé à l'Athénée royale de Paris en 1819,'' in *Écrits politiques*, Paris, Gallimard, Folio Essais, 1997, p. 594.

[17] In Roman law, criminal law is a matter of private law. Punishment of the crimes is made in the interest of the victims. See P.-F. Girard, *Manuel élémentaire de droit romain*, Rousseau, 1918, new edition Dalloz, 2002, p. 4; W. Kunkel, *An Introduction to Roman Legal and Constitutional History*, 2nd ed., Oxford Clarendon Press, 1972, pp. 27-29. Rules of criminal law are a rationalization of private vengeance. Their aim is to control and limit the disastrous consequences of the vendetta system. Crimes against the public good amount to crimes against the gods; they belong not to criminal law, but rather to religion.

Genuine law was "private law" which was not designated as such, but simply by the word "law."

2. The Medieval World

The Christian doctrine. Christianity turned the ancient vision of a fusion between religion and public good upside down. In teaching that his realm was not part of this world, and in instructing his disciples to give to Caesar what belongs to Caesar and to God what belongs to God, Jesus severed religion from government. As the French historian Fustel de Coulanges pointed out in his classic study on the city-state, the Christian religion was the first one that did not claim that the law depended on it, the first concerned with duties rather than rights and interests, and the first that did not attempt to regulate property, estates and wills, torts, or procedure.[18] Christianity as taught by the Catholic Church paid no attention to property law—in other words, the core private law. It only regulated some aspects of private law, in particular family law, because of the important functions of the Church in matters of civil status, birth, and marriage registration. The concern of the Catholic Church for public law followed a completely different (or much more comprehensive) path.

The influence of the Catholic Church. The Christian religion, as institutionalized in the Catholic Church, paid very close interest to the "public thing" and the government of men. In France, it was the Church that endowed the French monarchs with sacred status through the ceremony of consecration. Consecration turned the royal function into a duty to serve rather than a right to rule. The Church completely transformed not only the monarch's status, but also the function of political power by redefining the role of government. Cicero had underlined the need for government to preserve the public good in time and space; the Church went even further. "Any people," Cicero wrote, "that is to say, any gathering of a multitude under the conditions I previously explained, in short, any public thing, and by this, I mean, as I said before, the thing of the people, needs in order to persist and last over time to be ruled by an intelligent authority."[19] This intelligent authority is political power in action (*i.e.*, the government).

The new idea the Church brought to government was that of the common good. A ruler must govern, the Church said, not for his own private advantage, but for the common advantage of the whole. It seems that the notion of common good was introduced, first, to limit recourse to war in the barbaric, violent, and

[18] Fustel de Coulanges, *supra* note 15, at pp. 517-522.

[19] Cicero, *supra* note 9, at pp. 12-13.

merciless world of the high Middle Ages. Later, it came to encompass the totality of powers and rights exercised by the political authority. In the end, it completely transformed the function of government.

The invention of modern government. By investing the medieval kings with a general duty to rule over their estates and people for the common good, the Church changed the nature of government. Striving for the common good cannot be undertaken in the same ways as maintaining law and order; other means than courts of law are called for. More specifically, securing the common good calls for administrative structures such that the judicial State, the original form of the royal State, is supplemented by an administrative State.

With the transformation of a judicial State into an administrative State, we are at the heart of the radical novelty that the Church introduced in the bringing into being of the idea of the common good. Michel Foucault called it ''governmentality,''[20] a neologism he coined to convey the idea that, during the sixteenth and seventeenth centuries, political power underwent dramatic changes as a new doctrine emerged that political power was no longer in charge of the *res publica* only, but also in charge of ''men,'' or rather, in charge of ''souls''—to use the language of Saint Thomas Aquinas, the initiator of the new theory.[21] In teaching that government means leading the governed towards the end they are made for, the Church reinvented government and the practice of governing; it created governmental power, a kind of collective soul.

The medieval *regimen animarum*, the ''government of souls,'' this ''art of arts'' (*ars artium*) as the Church Fathers called it, laid down the basis for the structure and proper working of the mechanism that, once secularized, turned into modern government.[22] During the Middle Ages, the management of the *res publica* took a new turn; it became a mission, a duty, akin to service by a religious minister. Traces of the change can still be found today in French public law, with the so-called ''missions of public service'' (*missions de service*

---

[20] M. Foucault, ''La 'gouvernementalité','' *Dits et écrits II, 1976-1988*, Paris, Gallimard, Quarto, 2001, p. 635. See also M. Foucault, ''Governmentality,'' in G. Burchell, C. Gordon, and P. Miller (Eds.), *The Foucault Effect: Studies in Governmentality*, Chicago, University of Chicago Press, 1991, p. 87.

[21] On the Thomism doctrine, Saint Thomas Aquinas, *On the Governance of Rulers* (De Regimine Principium), revised ed., translated from Latin by G. Phelan, Institute of Medieval Studies, Sheed & Ward, London & New York, 1938. Adde M.-P. Deswarte, ''Intérêt général, bien commun,'' *RDP*, 1988, p. 1289.

[22] On the coming into being of the modern government, M. Senellart, *Les arts de gouverner, Du* regimen médiéval *au concept de gouvernement*, Paris, Seuil, Collection Des Travaux, 1995, pp. 22-31; ''Gouvernement,'' *DCJ*, p. 768 and ''Gouvernement,'' *DPP*, p. 293.

public), "burdens of general interest" (*charges d'intérêt général*), or "duties of solidarity" (*devoirs de solidarité*)—all obligations imposed on public authorities.[23] So long as the Church was sufficiently respected and powerful to influence kings in their exercise of power—and, thus, to render them subject to the law (for a long time imagined to be the word of God)—public law could not emancipate itself. It remained under the purview of religious officers.

3. The Modern World

Appearance of the notion of interest. In the sixteenth century, the content of the *res publica* took yet another new course. The influence of the Church was by then on the wane; ethics of charity, love for one's neighbor, and self-sacrifice were progressively abandoned. Another value—interest—won the day. In 1515, Machiavelli set the tone in *The Prince*: "Love is lasting by virtue of a link of recognition too weak for human perversity and prone to break apart at the slightest call of personal interest."[24] By stressing the shift in values that eventually brought an end to medieval Christianity, the Florentine laid the foundations for the autonomy of politics (*i.e.*, the liberation of politics from religion). He demonstrated that, in order to hold onto power, and govern, the *seigneury* (as medieval parlance put it) must perpetuate itself, maintain itself in state—eventually becoming a "State," stable and permanent. To accomplish this, the prince had to free himself from the Church's commands. Rather than work at making himself loved, he had to become feared. In other words, he had to behave in conformity with rules and standards of virtue other than those directed by the Church. Modern politics came of age, and public law accompanied it.

Starting with the Renaissance, the management of the *res publica* was organized according to political and moral standards different from those implied by the notion of common good. Due to the triumph of nominalism, "common good" soon became just a word without substance. The old notion of common good waned with the rise of individualism. Common sense limited the former "common good" to a "public good," necessarily implying a "private good"—and the old notion was diluted even further with the shift from the "public good" to the "public interest." With the notion of "public interest," public law definitively entered the secular age.

---

[23] G.-J. Guglielmi and G. Koubi are right in pointing to the "links between religious concepts and the coming into being of key notions of French administrative law," *Droit du service public*, Paris, Montchrestien, 2000, p. 18.

[24] Machiavelli, *The Prince*, Chapter XVII: Cruelty and Clemency, available at http://www.constitution.org/mac/prince00.htm.

Since the ''public thing'' is today equated with the public interest, the first step in the study of public law is to define the criteria by which this public interest is identified as distinct from the private interest. The problem goes further than the study of public law strictly speaking; it touches upon political philosophy and jurisprudence. But it is impossible to have a clear idea of the major legal systems of the world, to understand where they come from and where they are going, without analyzing the general philosophy of the public interest on which they are built. In brief, it may be said that since the fall of communism,[25] two major philosophical trends pervade the discourse on the

---

[25] Communism was a unitary theory that realized a complete fusion between public and private interest in line with the ideal of the ancient republic of the city-state and the ideas of Plato [see V. Held, *The Public Interest and Individual Interests*, New York, Basic Books, 1969, pp. 135-162]. The communist society like the ancient democracy made no distinction between the private good and the public good (good amounting in this case to happiness), the good of everyone being the condition for the good of all. No distinction was made between the public and the private; there was no public interest per se; there was one common good only under which all society's interests were subsumed. In the middle of the nineteenth century, Marxism reactivated the ancient conception of the public good as it was understood and practiced in the ancient city-state. Hence, its failure; the doctrine it professed was no longer in harmony with the mores and social evolution.

The unitary conception of the public good has its foundations in a very tight social unity. In these societies, what turns out to be in the interest of the community is necessarily in the individual interest of its members too. The greatest good of the ancient society (as well as that of the communist society) is that no one feels a need to cultivate an individual interest contrary to the interest of everyone, with the result that the question of the public good as an autonomous concept is irrelevant since the greatest happiness is made of a complete fusion between the public good and the private interest of each member of the community. In the societies where public interest is subordinated to common interest, the individual interest is sacrificed to the collective interest. The collapse of European communist societies at the end of the twentieth century demonstrated the inadequacy of a unitary conception of the public good in the modern age. The official survival of communism in China in the twenty-first century does not run contrary to this. From communism, China actually kept the authoritarian structure of political power that enable the ruling class to stay in power and whose origins go back to the Marxist-Leninist theories relying on the one party's dictatorship as a token for unity of the State power. This being said, China no longer entertains a unitary conception of the public good since private property, hence private interest, is officially recognized. From the unitary conception of the public interest, which is nowadays much asleep, it appears that modern public law cannot be the law of the common interest, a law based upon the common good. Today, the word ''common good'' when still in use (a rare occurrence) is a synonym for ''public good.'' Public law in the modern age is inconceivable without a distinction between the private and the public.

public interest today: liberalism and republicanism.[26]

Liberalism. Authors who support liberalism regard the public interest as the total aggregation of private interests. Liberal theory is characterized by the belief that the public interest can never be different from the sum of private interests; the public good is identified with the maximum aggregation of individual preferences. It is inseparable from the satisfaction of all individual interests. The liberal theory of the public interest aims at ensuring the greatest protection to individual interests; it therefore gives priority to liberty and considers that "if someone has a right to something, then it is wrong for the government to deny it to him even though it would be in the general interest to do so."[27]

Liberalism claims, in substance, that a measure meets the requirements of the public interest if it satisfies all private interests. Under an economic analysis of the law, in order to qualify as a measure of public interest, a law or a regulation must meet the criterion of the so-called Pareto efficiency or Pareto optimum. A measure is said to meet this test if it makes someone better off without making someone else worse off, or, to put it differently, if it improves someone's situation without injuring anyone else. Inasmuch as, in reality, this test can be met only in exceptional circumstances, liberalism is likely to consider measures of alleged public interest—in other words, the laws—with a skeptical, if not hostile, eye. Liberals tend to doubt that laws can be made so as to satisfy the criteria of a true public interest. Thus, they eventually come to associate less law with the citizens' well being. Much inspired by the economic theories of law, today's liberalism opposes governmental power on the ground that it is useless except to ensure public peace. They defend minimalist approaches to legislation within the general framework of an economic theory of law.

Republicanism. For those who defend republicanism, the public interest is not reducible to an aggregation of private interests. Instead, the public interest is the aggregation of the private interests that members of the society share in common or, to be more precise, that members of a society decide to regard as common in the social contract that forms the republican compact.

In this sense, the republican theory of the public interest is the opposite of the liberal theory. It does not question for a moment the existence of a public

---

[26] Both trends are still subject to intensive debate in the United States. See M. J. Horowitz, "Republicanism and Liberalism in American Constitutional Thought," 29 *Wm. & Mary L. Rev.* 57 (1987-1988)

[27] R. Dworkin, *Taking Rights Seriously*, Harvard University Press, 1977, p. 269 and the comments by F. Wieacker, "Foundations of European Legal Culture" [Translated and annotated by E. Bodenheimer], 38 *AJCL* 1, 22, note 67 (1990).

interest in itself; it believes in the existence of a public thing, a *res publica*, autonomous and independent from private things. It defends the idea of a public interest as distinct from the total aggregation of private interests. It aims at ensuring the greatest protection for common interests, even, if necessary, against private interests, because it operates on the premise laid down by Jean-Jacques Rousseau: ''The common element in these different interests is what forms the social tie; and, were there no point of agreement between them all, no society could exist.''[28] The public interest is the sum of the interests held in common by society; it means ''common security, common liberty,'' or, as Sieyès put it in one word, ''the *res publica* (*chose publique*).''[29]

The republican approach to the public interest is at the heart of the French republican model. Its founding idea is simple and can be enunciated as follows: Any gathering of people that forms a nation necessarily forms an association whose object is a ''public thing.'' There exists therefore a public interest, separate from private interests and forming a reality *sui generis*. Under this model, the public interest, or the *res publica*, becomes the State.

The State is made not by the aggregation of all private interests, but by the aggregation of those interests that men have decided to put in common by an act of free will. The republican theory thus makes a sharp distinction between the civil society and the State. Regarded as a fundamental guarantee of individual freedom, this distinction leads republican authors to defend the autonomy of public law. Their defense is based on their belief that the State (*i.e.*, the *res publica*) cannot be regulated by the same rules that regulate civil society, each entity being driven by different goals.

Republicanism believes in the public good and seeks to attain it. For a republican, the measure of public interest is that it satisfies the interests put in common in the social contract. In terms of economic analysis, a measure of public interest, for the republicans, is the Kaldor-Hicks concept of wealth maximization. Under that approach, a measure is said to be efficient if, and only if, those who benefit from the policy benefit sufficiently so as to compensate those who lose. The winners need not in fact compensate the losers, but it must be possible. This condition, which effectively transforms the public interest into

---

[28] J.-J. Rousseau, *The Social Contract*, Book II, Chapter 1 [Translated by G. D. H. Cole], available at http://www.constitution.org/jr/socon.htm. Of course, these common interests may vary from State to State. All States will include in it, at the minimum, security and defense, a monetary system, justice for all; only a few will add to that social protection against sickness, old age, unemployment, or still, a free and secular system of education.

[29] Sieyès, *supra* note 10, at p. 85. See Section A.

the general interest—"general" because it satisfies both public and private interests—may actually be easily realized in practice. Capitalizing on the optimistic prospects opened by this opportunity, republican authors attach much value to sovereignty as a principle of political action, and they give preference to the statute as an instrument for the public good. They often, but not always, defend maximal approaches to legislation in pursuance of a political theory of the statute.

C. PUBLIC LAW AND THE STATE

The coming into being of the State. Modern law is not severable from the State insofar as it came into being with it, in the aftermath of the Protestant reformation and its consequences across Europe. The invention of the State completely changed the law, because it revolutionized the exercise of both public and private power. The State united in itself all the dispersed powers of feudal society; everywhere, it meant a concentration of power. In doing so, the State freed men from oppression by private powers, by subjecting all private powers to its oversight. This marked tremendous progress for freedom.[30] By the

---

[30] The progress realized by the emergence of the State for the affirmation of modern liberty was luminously explained by E.-W. Böckenförde. Commenting upon the consequences of the emergence of the State in the sixteenth century and the gradual evolution toward a separation between the State and the civil society, the great German legal scholar explains:

> The numerous intermediary powers and the statutory orders of the old society are piece by piece torn down, progressively eroded and deprived of the political character. Step by step, individuals are freed from the former political allegiances that knitted them to the old social structures of life and domination (landlords, villages, parishes, and especially monasteries). Alone remains—and, thus, acquires a special status—the relation of domination between the monarch (territorial prince) and the subject: that relation becomes direct and, at the same time that political theory endeavours to differentiate between the State's prerogative and the King's prerogative, transforms itself into an immediate relation between the State and the subject. The principle that tries to come to life can be enunciated as follows: the power of domination must no longer be exercised by certain individuals over some others, it must no longer be exercised by an order (the nobility) over another (the commons), it must be exercised by the holder of the State power only in an all-encompassing and equal manner over everyone; for the rest, the individual is free, that is to say, free from all power, but that of the State.

E.-W. Böckenförde, *Le droit, l'État et la constitution démocratique*, [Translated by O. Jouanjan], Bruylant / LGDJ, 2000, p. 179.

same token, in concentrating all powers, the State made it possible to conceive of the public good as being outside religion and the Church of Rome.[31]

As soon as the Church lost its former legitimacy to define the public good, to distinguish between good and bad, truth and error, justice and injustice, temporal powers—princes and kings—stepped into its shoes. They spoke and acted as the Church at the peak of its glory, when it sent thousands of faithful believers to conquer the Holy Land or threw kings and princes into anguish by the threat of excommunication. Now monarchs dressed in the same rich clothes and surrounded themselves with the same magnificence; they invested themselves with the same power the Church once had over the minds of the people. They did so through a concept that the Church had largely invented and which, once secularized, revolutionized public law—the concept of sovereignty. From sovereignty, monarchs drew a power identical to that of the Church before its collapse, when it ruled over souls by virtue of its infallibility. The true character of sovereignty is, indeed, to be infallible, because it has the power of the last word.

With sovereignty regarded as the source of all power on earth, kings and princes even surpassed the Church in the power of domination they exercised over men. They added to their dominion a particular power that the Church never considered its own, insofar as it had no place in the Church's spiritual realm. That power is the right to resort to armed force and physical constraint. Kings, who possessed that right in their feudal prerogatives from time immemorial, drew it into the concept of sovereignty, asserting that the power to resort to force fell within their exclusive jurisdiction. Armed force increased the reach of sovereign power to a great extent. This made it possible, during the century from Luther's preachings to the Peace of Westphalia (1648), for the sovereign State to become the compelling framework for thinking about and undertaking the public good.

The capture of the "public thing" by the State forced public law to develop first as an exclusively domestic branch of law. There is little doubt today that domestic public law is the most important and complete branch of public law. However, the encompassment of all things that are of public interest within the sole sovereign State has long proved insufficient, making it possible for an

[31] Both the State and the Church are forms of organizing social life as underlined by M. Gauchet, "Primitive Religion and the Origins of the State," in M. Lilla (Ed.), *New French Thought, Political Philosophy*, Princeton University Press, 1994, p. 116: "Since prehistoric times, man has striven for structured social organizations. The State is only one manifestation of this structure, just as religion is another."

external or international public law to develop alongside and often above domestic public law.

Domestic public law. Every State has a public law, that is, once again, as we understand that term in the present book, the collection of rules that relate to the conceptualization and the management of the *res publica*. Public law contains the same disciplines; what varies, however, from State to State is the density and the thickness of these disciplines.

The fundamental disciplines of public law can be identified first by looking at the very object of the public thing (*i.e.*, the functions of the State). As a starting point of analysis, we may look at Adam Smith's groundbreaking work, *An Inquiry into the Nature and the Causes of the Wealth of Nations* (1776) in which he postulates "the system of natural liberty."[32] Since 1789, such a system—the system in which men are naturally free—is also the basis of French law, as stated in article 1 of the Declaration of the Rights of Man and the Citizen.[33] For the great English economist:

> According to the system of natural liberty, the sovereign has only three duties to attend to; three duties of great importance, indeed, but plain and intelligible to common understandings: first, the duty of protecting the society from the violence and invasion of other independent societies; secondly, the duty of protecting, as far as possible, every member of the society from the injustice or oppression of every other member of it, or the duty of establishing an exact administration of justice; and, thirdly, the duty of erecting and maintaining certain publick [sic] works and certain publick [sic] institutions, which it can never be for the interest of any individual, or small number of individuals, to erect and maintain; because the profit could never repay the expence [sic] to any individual or small number of individuals, though it may frequently do much more than repay it to a great society.[34]

Adam Smith's enumeration provides a clear reader's guide for outlining the major disciplines of public law.

---

[32] A. Smith, *An Inquiry into the Nature and the Causes of the Wealth of Nations*, IV, ix, Oxford University Press 1976, reprint Liberty Classics, Indianapolis, 1979, vol. II, p. 687.

[33] Article 1 of the Declaration of the Rights of Man and of Citizen of 26 August 1789: "Men are born and remain *free* and equal in rights" (emphasis added).

[34] Smith, *supra* note 32, at pp. 687-688.

From the first duty derives the necessity of a government endowed with the means (army, police) of protecting society, which implies a constitutional law and a financial law (taxes and budget). From the second duty derives the need for a system of law enforcement, that is, an administration and a system of law courts, both of which call for rules to ensure their regular functioning (rules of procedure, administrative law). Finally, from the third duty derives the necessity for the State to provide that which the market does not provide: in other words, the *res publica* must respond to the market's failures.

The foundational four disciplines of domestic public law are constitutional law, financial law, administrative law, and rules of procedure; they are the basis for the foundation of the *res publica*. They may be found in every country. On these common bases, a substantive public law, the content of which may be very diverse, developed. At a minimum, this substantive public law always includes the laws that punish felonies against the security of the State in attacks against the ''public thing,'' that is, the pact of justice and the common interests upon which the society is founded. Often, special jurisdictions are created to take cognizance of and adjudicate these felonies in contradistinction to the ordinary courts that are in charge of adjudicating all criminal cases. For instance, in the early 1960s, special tribunals were created in France to adjudicate the terrorists attacks linked to the war in Algeria; and recently, in the United States, military tribunals were established to adjudicate the cases of those suspected of involvement in the terrorist crimes of September 11, 2001. Such derogations to the private nature of criminal law[35] are to be explained by the fact that crimes against the *res publica* are crimes against public, not private, interests and may present peculiarities that make them unfit to be adjudicated by ordinary courts. In France, the fear in the early 1960s was that members of juries sitting in ordinary criminal courts could be subjected to blackmail or retaliation by the accomplices of those who were tried for terrorism. Substantive public law today also includes those laws that, due to the expansion of the objects regarded in the twentieth century as relevant to the public good, are considered to constitute the public law of the welfare State (educational law, health law, retirement and

[35] As undertsood in French legal tradition, criminal law pertains to private law because crimes against goods or persons usually involve private interests only; they are therefore adjudicated by ordinary courts. It is worth noting that the special tribunals that existed during the war in Algeria no longer exist. Terrorist crimes are nowadays adjudicated by ordinary judges, sitting however in special formation, with no juries; laymen juries are not available in cases of persons charged with terrorist activities.

pension law). The diversity of these rules is so great that one may speak of "public law systems."[36]

International public law. The end of the Middle Ages marked the decline, soon followed by the extinction, of the idea of a public good for the City of Men, akin to that of the City of God that the Church relentlessly tried to promote as a model to be followed by feudal lords. The common good became conceivable only within the framework of the State. In order to regulate the relations between the new sovereigns, a kind of code of conduct between them took shape beyond the State's borders. This code of conduct was first called the law between "*gentes*" (*law of nations*) in continuation of medieval usages, the "*gentes*" being in this case the Roman *gentes* (*i.e.*, families). For a long time, the law of nations was a law between families, regulating relations between Houses, that is, the dynasties that ruled over Europe. The law between these monarchies was originally freighted with personal feelings, such as good faith, respect for the given word, and the sworn faith. It was only in the eighteenth century that these personal elements faded away, as the State as an abstract entity made its way in the community of nations, thanks in particular to the writings of Vattel.[37] Only in the nineteenth century did the new expression "international law," coined by Bentham, at last impose itself as the official terminology.

This international law (often supplemented by the adjective "public" to underline the fact that it applies to States only, not to private persons) regulates impersonal relations between States. It is more a code of conduct than a true law, inasmuch as each State is a judge in its own cause. Having no purposes other than the well-being of its subjects, public international law turned the ancient public thing common to all nations—the soul of Christian community—into a multitude of small private things particular to each State. Having no cherished object, other than the survival of the State, each with no ambition other than its own welfare, its conservation and, if possible, the aggrandizement of its wealth—formerly at the expense of other people (colonization), today at the expense of the common good of all nations with environmental torts and pollution—the former "classical" public international law, which reached its golden age in the nineteenth century, was a law without a public thing. It became a law whose unique object is the conservation of these small national

---

[36] See C. Larsen, "The Future of Comparative Law: Public Legal Systems," 21 *Hastings Int'l & Comp. L. Rev.* 847 (1998).

[37] See E. Jouannet, *Emer de Vattel et l'émergence doctrinale du droit international classique*, Paris, Pedone, 1998.

societies, private and closed, represented by nation-states within the large inter-State society.

One of the greatest changes in the twentieth century was the renaissance of the "public thing" outside the framework of the State. There is little doubt that the international public thing is not as rich and complete as the internal public thing, but it is not an empty word; it is a reality made of patrimonial resources (the common heritage of mankind that comprises the sea-bed beyond the limits of national jurisdiction, outer space and celestial bodies, Antarctica, and common goods such as the environment and resources of the high seas) and spiritual values (peace, nonuse of force, human rights, democracy, human dignity). Both patrimonial and spiritual values are protected by actors (intergovernmental and nongovernmental organizations), rules (*jus cogens*), legal techniques (unilateral acts of international organizations), concepts (crimes against humanity), and institutions (international courts) that do not belong to classical international law. These developments introduced "elements henceforth fundamental in the international legal order."[38] For a large number of international scholars, these elements are so fundamental that classical international law is already left behind. Instead of giving preference to the State in the exposition of international law, these scholars emphasize the solidarities between people and go as far as giving to international law, which they view as a law between the people of the United Nations another name, to contradistinguish it from classical international law. Thus, they often refer to "world law" or "the law of peace."[39]

When it seeks to put the emphasis on the solidarities between people rather than on the States, the French language refers to "international public law." This terminology was used for the first time by Léon Duguit,[40] who did not believe in the superiority of the State over individuals and who put the individual first, before the State. The terms "public international law" and "international public law" cannot be interchanged. They stand for two different ways of thinking about international law. As opposed to the term "public

[38] P.-M. Dupuy, *Droit international public*, Précis Dalloz, 6th ed., 2002, § 520, p. 532. French legal scholars are deeply divided over the importance and the meaning of these developments. See the analysis of these divisions made by A. Carty, "Conservative and Progressive Visions in French International Legal Doctrine," 16 *EJIL* 525-27 (2005).

[39] For instance, see the eight-volume encyclopaedia directed by the former Secretary-General of the United Nations, Javier Perez de Cuellar, continued, expanded, and updated by Y. S. Choue, *World Encyclopedia of Peace*, 2nd ed., Oceana Publications, Dobbs Ferry, N.Y., 1999.

[40] L. Duguit, *Traité de droit constitutionnel*, vol. I, 1927, § 67, pp. 713-733.

international law'' which ignores it and considers it as a chimera, the term ''international public law'' implies the existence of a ''public thing'' above the State. The expression ''international public law'' was enshrined in French law by the Preamble to the Constitution of 1946 (14th paragraph) that provides: ''The French Republic, faithful to its traditions, abides by the rules of international public law. It will not undertake wars of conquest and will never use its arms against the freedom of any people.'' The phrase ''faithful to its traditions'' stands as a reminder that France, because of the Revolution of 1789 and, in particular, the revolutionary concept of national sovereignty, which rules out the legitimacy of most classical international principles defining the foundations of territorial jurisdiction (occupation, right of conquest, annexation), introduced new ideas to international law and brought about a new conception of relations between people.[41]

From public international law to international public law: The European case. The transition from public international law to international public law is a slow-moving process that usually advances in a piecemeal fashion and with uncertain results. It has developed unevenly, sometimes prey to severe set-backs, as exemplified by the sad destiny of collective security at the universal level, today guaranteed only partially at a lower level with regional military alliances such as the North Atlantic Treaty Organization (NATO). However, it would be misleading to suppose from its imperfect realization at the world level that it can never be achieved. An instructive example in this respect is the evolution of public international law between European States in the second half of the twentieth century.

In 1950, the law that regulated relations between European States was a classical public international law in its purest form. Today, that law between European States is, if not dead, at least deeply asleep. In less than half a century, it has been replaced another law, community law, which is neither domestic State law nor public international law, although it is public law. The truth of the matter is that, to the extent that community law is public in nature, this is not because community law is State law (the European Union (EU) is not a State), but rather because community law is the law of a 'public thing'; it is the law of European ''public thing,'' the material and spiritual heritage of Europe. The European public thing is what makes ''the specificity of the Union'' as Jean-Paul Jacqué calls it;[42] it encompasses objectives (both economic and

---

[41] On the contribution of the French revolution to international law, see E. Zoller, *Droit des relations extérieures*, Coll. Droit Fondamental, PUF, 1992, § 256.

[42] J.-P. Jacqué, *Droit institutionnel de l'Union européenne*, 3rd ed., Dalloz, 2004, §§ 54-138, pp. 44-82.

political) and values (a community as such governed by the rule of law, respect for fundamental rights, democratic principles, social justice, and cultural pluralism) that makes it similar to a national "public thing," although with less intensity.

The European integration process stands as a reminder that public law cannot be assimilated to State law. Lawyers realized this in the eighteenth century, when they started thinking about the possibility of a public law at the universal level, outside national borders. A good example of this way of thinking is to be found in the distinction between general public law and special public law made by the author of the entry "*Droit public*" (Public Law) in the great Encyclopedia by Diderot and d'Alembert, a distinction that is very close indeed to the current distinction between international public law and internal public law.[43] Public law is not the law of a State, nor can it be produced by and through the State only; public law is the law of the public thing, and the public thing is the result of solidarities between people; it begins to take shape when these solidarities are strong enough to give birth to a "thing" that men want to share, protect, and administer in common and that, because of this common management, becomes "public."

There is no doubt that this public thing, which then turns into a *res publica*, so to speak, may be placed under the protection of a State and may institutionalize itself in a sovereign State with sovereign power, as was the rule in Europe in the sixteenth century; but it may also take another institutional form than the State model, as the EU example amply demonstrates.

---

[43] The entry "*Droit public*" (Public Law) was written by Boucher d'Argis, a lawyer to the Parliament (Court of Law) of Bordeaux, whose name has not left its mark in history. It begins as follows:

> Public law is that which is established for the common utility of people considered as body politics, in contradistinction to private law which exists for the private utility of people regarded as sole individuals, without consideration for other individuals. Public law is either general or particular. General public law regulates the foundations of civil society, which is common to most States, and the common interests that States have inter se. Particular public law to each State is . . . to establish and maintain the general police necessary to the public peace and tranquillity of the State, to provide what is the most advantageous for all members of the State whether collectively, or separately, whether for the well-being of the souls, or of the body and wealth.

M. Diderot & M. d'Alembert (Eds.), *Encyclopédie ou dictionnaire raisonné des sciences, des arts et des métiers*, Book V [Discussion—Esquinancie], 1755, p. 134, available at http://gallicabnf.fr.ark:/12148/bpt6k50537q9.

Conclusion and Outline. The foregoing developments have demonstrated that public law, at least as it is understood in French law, cannot be assimilated to the theory of the State. This finding runs counter to the nineteenth-century German scholarship articulating the so-called general theory of the State. Public law today is in a state of flux because it is no longer possible to conceive the public thing entirely within the sole sovereign State, as was the case in the sixteenth century. In order to think clearly about public law, one must shift gears and begin with its object, the *res publica*, or public thing—not with its subject, the State. The State may remain a privileged framework for bringing the public thing into being, but it is no longer the only one.

If the State plays such a crucial role in the bringing into being of the public thing, it is because it has a tremendous advantage over rival institutions. The State is the only subject of law considered to be legitimately vested with the ''monopoly of physical coercion,'' as Max Weber demonstrated.[44] In this sense, the State is the sole institution thus far through which the problem of violence has been addressed. From this point of view, there is little doubt that public law as the law of a public thing cannot begin to take shape before the problem of violence is solved. This is why international public law (as opposed to public international law) began to take form—at least as an idea—once war was no longer considered a normal mode of dispute settlement between States. The present work does not address international public law, nor does it address European public law; neither can be consolidated, except by following the developments that marked the progress of domestic public law. It is this progress that is the subject of the present work.

Domestic public law went through an evolution ordered by history, so to speak. It came into being in Europe in the continental monarchies where it developed within the matrix of sovereignty (Book I). It came of age, first in America, then in France, with the two revolutions that put an end to the monarchical age and opened the republican age (Book II). It still continues to evolve today, along two completely distinct republican paths in the United States and in France, each country having chosen its own way to realize the public good in modern society. In order to understand public law—to know where it comes from and where it is going—one must pay attention to history and comparative studies.

---

[44] M. Weber, ''Le métier et la vocation d'homme politique,'' (1919), in *Le savant et le politique*, Plon (1959), Collection 10/18, no. 134, p. 101.

BOOK I
THE MONARCHICAL AGE

Sovereignty. The monarchical age is the founding era of modern public law. A European age par excellence, it began in the sixteenth century with the emergence of the modern State. It reached its apex on the continent during the seventeenth and eighteenth centuries thanks to the fruition of a concept that revolutionized both the sources of law and the exercise of political power—the concept of sovereignty.

Sovereignty completely changed the way of thinking about the *res publica* in that its first and most important consequence was to put in the hands of one single organ, the monarch, exclusive responsibility for bringing into being the common good. Before the development of the idea of sovereignty, the common good was a common concern; everyone in society had the duty and the responsibility of contributing to its realization. The nobles, the clerics, and the people all had to work for the common good. Starting in the sixteenth century, this common good became the exclusive responsibility of the sovereign. In fact, it ceased to exist as the common good, for it is at that time that the common good was divided into two distinct categories: the public good and those goods that were henceforth necessarily private. At the social and political level, sovereignty established a division between the State and the civil society, and it paved the way at the juridical level for a division between public law and private law, the former entrusted with the realization of the public good and the latter in charge of private goods.[1]

[1] Sovereignty imposed a new style of power, the power of the centralized monarchical State of the seventeenth and eighteenth century where a clear-cut distinction prevails between the sphere of the government and the sphere of private life. Public and private tend to become two very distinct spheres. The prince and his court dissociate themselves from the vast mass of subjects by emphasizing differences of ranks (titles, ceremonials, etiquette) and building a complex and sophisticated chain of command. From a general standpoint, the State became depersonalized and turned itself into "a machine." This metamorphosis of personal power into a State apparatus domination is the most important change at the beginning of modern times according to Michael Stolleis, *Geschichte des*

Sovereignty may be defined as a supreme and absolute power that requires unconditional obedience. It rests upon the belief that there exists—rather, that there *must* exist—and that there has always existed in any polity from time immemorial, a final and absolute authority. Sovereignty implies a kind of omega point that everything comes from, and goes to; it is a power of last resort on which everybody and everything depends. Sovereignty is a mental image of power; it is a manner of distinguishing a power among the many powers in society, of investing it with special status, and of entrusting it with exclusive responsibility for the common good. Although this idea became institutionalized in the sovereign State, it is worth knowing that men have not always thought like this.

Power before sovereignty. In the Middle Ages, the idea of a final and absolute power over society did not exist. To be more precise, a power of this kind did not belong to the terrestrial, but rather to the celestial world; it belonged to the divine order. Only God could be conceived as vested with such a complete power over men and things. Human power, the power of man over his fellow men, was far from possessing such completeness; it was a mix of several powers. There was not one power, but several. Each terrestrial authority had fragments of power only, all meagerly counted and weighed, depending on the functions to be performed. There is no point, therefore, when studying the Middle Ages, in pondering where at that time the supreme and final authority of the State lay.[2] The question is an anachronism that makes no sense.

In France as in England, the king did not possess power in general, but several powers, rather a collection of powers that were called "droits régaliens" (*jura regalia*) in France, and prerogatives in England. *Jura regalia* and prerogatives were rights attached and linked to the power of the king; they were feudal privileges exclusively attached to the royal person.[3] Lawyers enumerated them by dozens in long lists that exemplified the consistence of royal authority. In the beginning of the sixteenth century, Chasseneux, a French jurist, had counted up to 208 of them. Similar accounting in England would have reached

---

öffentlichen Rechts in Deutschland, Erster Band: Reichspublizistik und Policeywissenschaft, 1600-1800, Verlag C. H. Beck München, 1988, p. 70.

2 F. Maitland, *The Constitutional History of England* (1908), Cambridge University Press, reediting 1946, p. 297.

3 See J. Barbey, "Droits régaliens," *DAR*, p. 445, and C. Combe, "Prérogative," *DCC*, p. 1187. In the *Commentaries on the Laws of England*, I, 239, Blackstone says: " [T]he word prerogative [. . .] signifies, in its etymology (from *prae* and *rogo*) something that is required or demanded before, or in preference to, all others"; see also O. Hood Philipps & P. Jackson, *Constitutional and Administrative Law*, 8th ed. [P. Jackson & P. Leopold], London, Sweet & Maxwell, 2001, § 15-003, no. 14, p. 305.

similar results. These *jura regalia*, or prerogatives, included, among many others, the power to give justice, the power of dispensation from the observance of the laws, the power for the common good of the realm to make new laws (but only in exceptional circumstances), the power of pardon, the power to designate the officers of the realm, the power to coin money, the power to raise taxes, the power to wage war for the defense of the realm, the power to order respect for the rights established by nature and time.[4] The Middle Ages had a Lilliputian vision of power that was subsequently engulfed by the theory of sovereignty, the major innovation of which was to combine the multiplicity of medieval powers into one power, and one only—the power to make the law.

Legislative power, first power of the State. The theory of sovereignty that propelled the power to make law as the first power in the State was expounded by the French Jean Bodin (1530-1596). In the *Six Books of the Commonwealth* (1576), Jean Bodin turned the medieval approach to power and law upside down by subsuming all powers of the king under the power to make law. His celebrated definition of sovereignty reads as follows: ''The first attribute of the sovereign prince [. . .] is the power to make law binding on all his subjects in general and on each in particular.''[5]

Before Jean Bodin, no jurist would have ever thought of making the power to make law the first attribute of the sovereign prince. At that time, legislative power came far behind the power to dispense justice. How can we explain the need that arose in the middle of the sixteenth century to turn this power into the first power of the prince? There is no easy answer to this question. True, in the Age of Exploration, society was evolving rapidly and visibly under everyone's eyes. It was important for the sovereign to be able to respond to the needs of the time with appropriate legislation. In the first place, there was a pressing need for regulation of increasingly competitive societies, treading into capitalistic adventures and eager to embark on the conquest for new territory. There was, however, another need, even more pressing, namely, the need for a single voice to rise above the sound and the fury of the religious wars, to make the voice of civil peace heard once again. In short, a need to enforce obedience was felt. At the time of Bodin, the best means to enforce obedience was well known. It had been discovered by the Church at the beginning of the twelfth century when, following the Gregorian reform, it reorganized the exercise of power in its own body. It did so by turning the statute (*loi*)—extracted from the maze of decrees

[4] See F. Saint-Bonnet, ''Loi,'' *DCC*, p. 959.

[5] J. Bodin, *The Six Books of the Commonwealth* [Translated by M. J. Tooley], Barnes & Noble 1967, Book I, chap. X, available at http://www.constitution.org/bodin/bodin.htm.

and rules—into "the most important tool of power, first, of papal power which, by using it, succeeded in making itself obeyed by the whole Christian community; secondly, of bishops' power which, alone or with others, tried to make itself be heard in the synods."[6]

Mutatis mutandis, it is with the same device (*i.e.*, the statute (*loi*)), that a few centuries later, kings and princes in Europe put a halt to religious wars. For the king to impose law on all his subjects was also to impose religious law. This evolution took place, first, in England with the Act of Supremacy (1543), a statute by Parliament that Henry VIII, furious at having failed to obtain from the Pope what he wanted, succeeded in forcing through the Lords and the Commons. The Act of Supremacy declared that "His Majesty is the supreme head of the Church," a formula that effectively gave him the power to say what the religion was. Shortly thereafter, in Germany, the peace of Augsburg (1555) established the principle that eventually became the foundation of the new European public order, *cujus regio ejus religio* (*i.e.*, the principle according to which freedom of religion is the right of the prince). It is up to him to choose the religion he sees as fit for his realm. And later, in France, Henry IV ordained public peace to his subjects by enacting the very first statute of religious tolerance, the Edict of Nantes (1598). Nothing did more to imprint in the minds of their subjects the idea of the inherent superiority of these monarchs than these statutes by which the sovereign established, and possibly modified at will, the religion of their State.[7]

Divergent paths in Europe and in England. The theory of sovereignty was accepted by all European monarchies. But it was not conceived everywhere in the same manner and, as a result, its consequences were diverse, depending on the States. True, in all European States, sovereignty gave birth to what is to be regarded as the instrument of public law par excellence, the statute, and it transformed legislative power into the first power of the state. A sharp divide, however, rapidly opened between the continental European States and England. On the continent, in France and in Germany, sovereignty, just as it was in the Early Middle Ages, remained lodged in a physical body, that of the prince or the

[6] G. Le Bras, "Les origines canoniques du droit administratif," in *L'évolution du droit public. Études offertes à Achille Mestre*, Sirey, 1956, p. 395, in particular p. 404; A. Padoa-Schioppa, "Hierarchy and Jurisdiction in Medieval Canon Law," in A. Padoa-Schioppa (Ed.), *Legislation and Justice*, European Science Foundation, Clarendon Press, 1997, p. 1, particularly p. 12.

[7] See the remarks by F. Maitland on Henry VIII exercising the power of statute-making on religious matters in Parliament, *The Constitutional History of England*, *supra* note 2, at p. 254.

king, who exercised an absolute power and took over the common good of their subjects. In England, the monarch was unable to take over anything; sovereignty abandoned him, so to speak, and went on to lodge itself in a body politic, the body of the ''King in Parliament,'' in accordance with a historical process that has remained germane to England. One may construe this evolution as the evidence of an English ''exceptionalism'' that gave to all the legal systems born of the British model (*i.e.*, the common law systems), a particular twist that has led them down a quite different path in public law from that pursued on the continent.

Part A
The Continental Monarchies

The invention of the State. Today, the public law of the European continental monarchies is of historical interest only; it has been buried by the democratic revolutions that, at the end of the eighteenth century, replaced the sovereignty of one person with the sovereignty of the people. However, it still merits study because it produced the State, an institution distinct and separate from civil society—an abstract entity vested since the eighteenth century with the responsibility for bringing happiness to its people under the legal concept of police power. This well-intentioned will to bring about happiness was at the origin of a spectacular development of public law all over Central Europe.

Although all European monarchies in one way or another contributed to the development of the State, they did not create the same kind of State everywhere. Two types of monarchies should be distinguished: the French monarchy, which progressively unfolded into the absolute monarchy, the foundational basis of the Royal-State (freed from the constraints of the common law); and the German monarchies or principalities, imbued with imperial Roman law, which developed all over Central Europe and even beyond (up to Russia), the model of the Prince-State. It was the Prince-State that eventually engulfed the whole common law.

Chapter 1
The French Legacy

The double legacy of the old regime. Two institutions survived the collapse of the French monarchy in 1789: the State and the *loi* (statute). The State as an institution is a very meaningful notion in French legal culture; it occupies a place without any equivalent in foreign legal systems. The State, in France, is the community of the permanent interests of the nation, not the instrument of domination or coercion that it may represent elsewhere, in other legal systems; the State is the *res publica*, the Republic, and it is surrounded today with the same respect, even the same devotion, that formerly surrounded the royal institution. The cognate notions that revolve around it, such as "general interest," "public interest," or "public utility," resonate in the whole French legal system as constant reminders of its structuring principle and pervading spirit—the compelling submission of private interests to the "public thing." When these concepts affect a private legal situation in a regular and justified manner, when, in other terms, the Republic speaks by its laws, private interests must yield, just as they did in the past when the king spoke by his. The French monarchy has engraved the "public thing" and its legal institution, the State, in the "habits of the heart"[1] of the French nation.

The word "State" came into being in the sixteenth century, but the idea behind it is much older. From the beginning, the French realm possessed interests of its own that needed to be defended. As F. Olivier-Martin put it in his great classic on French absolutism: "The totality of these interests form, in line with Roman terminology, the public thing, the *res publica*, which is distinct

[1] As A. de Tocqueville put it in *Democracy in America*, [Translated by H. C. Mansfield & D. Winthrop], University of Chicago Press, 2000, I, II, ix, p. 275: "I understand here the expression *mœurs* in the sense the Ancients attached to the word *mores*; not only do I apply it to mores properly so-called, which one could call habits of the heart, but to the different notions that men possess, to the various opinions that are current in their midst, and to the sum of ideas of which the habits of the minds are formed" (emphasis in original).

from the private interests of its members, whether individuals or subordinated communities. It is this public thing that will eventually be called the State, with a capital S.''[2] And, if one clear thread runs throughout the whole history of French public law, it is this: the State is not, does not, and cannot belong to the King. The distinction between the ''public thing'' and the king, considered as an earthly or physical body, is engraved in the institution of the Royal-State (Section A), which forms the keystone of the French monarchy. The king governs this public thing received from God, the State, in an absolute manner, not arbitrarily, according to his whims or humors; the laws of the king follow special procedures and obey precise rules (Section B).

A. THE ROYAL-STATE

1. The Theory

The renaissance of the public thing. With the downfall of the Roman Empire, the concept of the public thing completely disappeared, and the Merovingian kings ruled the country without the slightest idea of the State. At the beginning, the king of the Franks exercised power in his own interest, because he was the most powerful. The realm was his property; he was *dominus*, in the sense of owner of persons and goods that happened to be part of it. He was senior, in the sense that he exercised a personal power. The Merovingian monarchy was domineering (the king was a boss who required obedience and gave protection) and patrimonial (the realm was the property of the king who occupied it with arms and by right of conquest).[3] When the first Carolingians were consecrated, royal power changed completely. The sovereign power exercised by the king was given by God himself. The king became an officer of his realm; he was no longer a proprietor, but rather a depository. All ecclesiastical authorities, from Hincmar of Reims to Yves of Chartres, unanimously declared that power is a function entrusted to the king for the governance of the public thing, ''*ad dispensacionem rei publicae.*''[4] This meant a return to the Roman notion of public thing and the affirmation of its sharp distinction from the person of the king; in short, it is the birth certificate for the State.

The consecration of the king. The consecration of the Carolingians was followed and deepened by the first Capetian, Hugues Capet, who himself was

[2] F. Olivier-Martin, *L'absolutisme français* followed by *Les Parlements contre l'absolutisme traditionnel au XVIIIe siècle*, LGDJ, Reprint 1997, pp. 35-36.

[3] J. Ellul, *Histoire des institutions, Le moyen âge*, PUF, Quadrige, 1999, p. 58.

[4] Olivier-Martin, *supra* note 2, p. 37.

elected and who used it to confirm the election of his son, Robert, by the highest dignitaries of the realm. The practice of election and consecration of the heir was followed reign after reign until the end of the twelfth century. Henceforth, heredity sufficed, but the consecration was always kept and rigorously observed by the Capetians—save for Louis XVIII—until 1825.

The consecration was a decisive element in the formation of the French conception of the State.[5] All medieval kings had themselves crowned; the king of France was not crowned, but rather, consecrated. The consecration was not strictly speaking a sacrament, but it came very close to it; common wisdom considered it "a mystery." With the ceremony of the consecration, the king entered a world that was no longer that of the common mortals, but rather of divinity. The king took an oath to the Church and to the realm; he swore to maintain his people in peace and to always act in equity. As God's mediator, the king promised not to abuse power and to fulfill the duties of his trust for the common good of the realm. His words were surrounded by an array of symbolic gestures. Undressed, except for a shirt in which several openings were made for the anointments, he was anointed by God, with the oil of Saint Ampoule mixed with balm of holy chrism, on the forehead, chest, arms, and hands. The anointment was administered in the name and power of the holy Trinity, which was believed to make it more effective. Then the insignia of the royal function were delivered; in the right hand, the scepter, symbol of the power coming down vertically from God himself; in the left hand, the hand of justice by which the king "protected the good men and frightened the bad men." The consecration created a special relationship between God and the king.

The status of the king. The king of France was a sacred person. Sovereignty in France has not been created by force or by conquest. Rather—and this is a key factor—it was given by God to the king, for special purposes and on special conditions; sovereignty is a "function," a "trust," a "duty," in the French legal tradition, well before being a "power," as it might have been in other countries. The king held his power from God; he was sovereign not inherently, but by the grace of God. He was the only one in his realm, and even among the princes of Europe, to be able to present himself as lord "by the grace of God." As Jean Barbey said, the consecration "brings about remarkable consequences, both legal and religious [. . .] that over determine the French royalty."[6]

---

[5] J. Barbey, "Le sacre," in S. Rials (Ed.), *Le miracle capétien*, Paris, Librairie académique Perrin, 1987, p. 79.

[6] *Id.* at p. 83.

Later, the monarchy by divine right proclaimed by the General Estates in 1614 would make these characteristics even stronger. As he received his power from God alone, the king was the representative of God on earth. Bossuet has pictured this attribute very vividly: "The whole State is in himself, the whole will of the people is contained in his own will. As in God who unites all perfection and virtue, all the power of the particulars is united in the person of the prince."[7]

The king and the public good. The king was to be highly conscious of the importance of his mission. As early as the twelfth century, when legislating, he made laws "for the common profit" of his realm and his people, according to the formula then used in conjunction with another, more widely used although often with different nuances: "common good." The king intends to rule for "the profit and good state of his people," or for "the pleasure and common profit of our people." In the eighteenth century, the term "common good" is exceptional; but it is replaced by other notions such as "good of the people," "good of the public thing," or "public good." These terms are to be found in the ordinances and laws of the king, and in his letters and speeches. In the fourteenth century, the national tragedy of the Hundred Years War brought out the importance of these formulas. This long and serious conflict marked a transformation, at the end of which it became obvious that the prince could no longer live from "his own" (*i.e.*, from the resources of his domain). Recourse to taxation, the techniques of which were already well known, would take a very different course of action. Taxes could no longer be extraordinary, as they had been in the High Middle Ages; they had to become permanent. The army, which thus far had been composed of the barons and the vassals, in times of great peril and always for temporary and limited missions, followed taxation and became permanent as well. The judicial State turned into the financial State,[8] and taxation became the means to contribute to the public good.

According to the exhaustive explanations of F. Olivier-Martin, all kings of France affirmed their concern for governing in favor of the public thing of the realm.[9] From the sixteenth century on, however, they became inclined to bring it closer to their person. In the royal letters of François I, there are constant references to "We and the public thing." Occasionally, the word "public thing" yielded to other terms, different in the image employed, but similar in

[7] See Olivier-Martin, *supra* note 2, at p. 52, and *Politique tirée de l'écriture sainte*, also quoted by M. Cottret, "Absolutisme," *DAR*, p. 8.

[8] P. Chaunu, "L'Etat de finance," in F. Braudel & E. Labrousse (Eds.), *Histoire économique et sociale de la France, I/1450-1660),* PUF, 1993, pp. 129-191.

[9] See Olivier-Martin, *supra* note 2, at pp. 36-55.

meaning. In the sixteenth century, the word "crown" was current. The king himself drew between his person and his crown a line whose trace appears in the new formula of the consecration: "I shall maintain the sovereignties, the rights and the nobilities of the crown of France, and shall not transfer, or alienate them."

The king and the State. Under Henri III (1574-1589), a crucial step toward abstraction was made, with the appearance of the word "State." The king, "a born orator, both seducing and moving," conjured the assembly of the General Estates of Blois in 1576, in the midst of the wars of religion, to "put this realm at peace and to cure the ills affecting the body of the State," and he urged them to conclude a good peace, "for the sake of this State." Henri IV followed in the footsteps of Henri III, constantly calling on "this State . . . this beautiful State." When the relatives of Maréchal de Biron, a childhood friend who betrayed him, begged him to forgive him and to give his pardon, Henri IV answered: "If this was only a matter of personal interest, I would give him pardon in the same manner that I forgive him from my heart, but this a matter for my State as to which I am much obliged." Under Louis XIII and Richelieu, the word "State" replaced all the ancient formulas. On the "Day of Dupes," November 11, 1630, Louis XIII decided—against the advice of the Queen mother, the most influential Catherine de Médicis—to set aside the religious party that she manipulated, so as to keep Cardinal de Richelieu in power. He concluded with these words: "I am more obliged to the State."[10] Louis XIV does not forgo the distinction made by his predecessors between the State and the king. Without ambiguity, he holds that the prince has "no other fortune to establish than that of his State. . . . When one has the State in view, one works for oneself. The good of the former makes the glory of the latter." His most famous words are those he uttered on his deathbed, with his officers surrounding him: "I am passing away, but the State stays after me."

In the eighteenth century, the word "nation" becomes common, along with that of "State." The term had been used by François I when, imprisoned by the German Emperor Charles V in Madrid, he explained in a letter to the French nobles and sovereign *Parlements* (or courts) that, "for his honor and that of the nation," he preferred a "fair jail" to a shameful evasion. At the beginning of the seventeenth century, the Edict on the legitimated princes provided that, in case of no heir from the legitimate royal lineage, it would be up to "the Nation itself," or to "the State alone," to pick a new king. These texts demonstrate that

---

[10] See Samuel P. Huntington, "Political Modernization: America vs. Europe," 18 *World Politics*, 378, 386 (1965-1966).

all the French kings have always made a clear distinction between their own person and the public thing (commonwealth). This permanent community of interests has been designated by various terms: realm, public thing, crown, State, or nation. The king has always said that he was in charge of it, that he represented it, fully and completely in his own right, and that he was in close union with it. According to F. Olivier-Martin, there was between the king and the public thing, or the State, or the nation, "both a distinction and a union at the same time," just as in a "marriage," he adds subtlety.

2. The Practice

From the servant of God to the servant of the State. The exceptional relation existing between the French king and his people was made possible only through the medium of the consecration. From an historical standpoint, the consecration transformed the physical body of the king into a body politic, in which the king, the public thing (that is, the State) and the nation were joined into one. This is the reason why Louis XIV may once have said: "*L'État, c'est moi*" ("The State, it is I"). According to historians, this is a legend, at best a jest.[11] They argue that the ceremony and oaths of the consecration—the promise to do justice to the poor as well as to the wealthy, to keep his people safe from his enemies and adversaries, to maintain the customary status of the ecclesiastical orders of his realm, and to respect the rights and privileges of everyone—demonstrate the improbability that Louis XIV ever said such a thing. The public law of the old regime, they insist, did not confuse the king with the public thing.

In theory, the historians are right: the king and the public thing were perfectly distinguishable. The king was a depository of the public thing; he had the custody of it, and he was expected to administer it for the common good of the realm only. In practice, however, the line between the physical body of the king and the body politic of the public thing became very hard to draw. It eventually became completely blurred and impossible to conceptualize, in particular with the rise of absolutism. At the beginning, in the Middle Ages, the separation between the king and the State derived from the quasi-religious conception of royal functions. The king is, then, regarded as entrusted with a special function and in charge of specific duties; he possesses rights only in

[11] For an explanation, see Olivier-Martin, *supra* note 2, at pp. 45-49. Note however that Tocqueville, *supra* note 1, at p. 83, wrote: "'*L'État, c'est moi*', [Louis XIV] said; and he was right."

order to fulfill his obligations.[12] This is the religious conception of royalty that expresses itself in the consecration. But, later on, when the consecration ceased to be the ceremony that actually empowered the king with political authority, when the king became proclaimed king just after the death of his predecessor (in line with the famous phrase "The king is dead! Long live the king!")—in other words, when the consecration is no longer constitutive, but only declarative of the sacred character of royal power—the king ceases to be a servant of God and turns into a servant of the State, and the State becomes a reality per se.

The intimate relation between the king and the nation. The historian Kantorowicz explained very well the consequences of the quasi-fusion that existed between the king and the nation. In his work *The King's Two Bodies*, he says: "France [. . .], though fully aware of the different manifestations of individual king and immortal Dignity, eventually interpreted the absolute rulership in such a fashion that the distinctions between personal and supra-personal aspects were blurred or even eliminated."[13] A decisive step was taken in the seventeenth century, when Bossuet not only asserted that the King was inherently sacred in his person ["As in God, his body holds all perfection and virtue"], but also, just as Hobbes had already argued, insisted on the fact that social order and political unity depended entirely on his existence and came out of his will alone, so that the king became the only source of a genuine public voice ["All the State is in him, his own will contains the will of all people"].[14]

Under absolute monarchy, there was no means, no institution by which a distinction between the State, the nation, and the king could have taken shape. An actual separation between the King as a physical body and the King as body politic was out of reach; the distinction was an idea, not a fact; it existed in the mind, not in reality. As opposed to the English monarchy which very early began to work at a true separation between the king as a physical body and the "King in Parliament" as a body politic, French monarchy has faithfully kept the tradition of a fusion between the king and the nation. There has never been in France, the king, on the one side, and the nation, on the other; the king embodies the nation; he is the nation. When after 1615 the General Estates no longer convened, the nation lost all institutional existence, so to speak, except through the royal person.

---

[12] Ellul, *supra* note 3, at p. 276.

[13] E. H. Kantorowicz, *The King's Two Bodies, A Study in Medieval Political Theology*, Princeton University Press, 1981, p. 446.

[14] See the analysis made by K. M. Baker, "Souveraineté," *DCRF* (Idées), p. 483, especially p. 486.

The people disappeared as if absorbed by and melted into the King. The trend was accentuated when the legists of the court further argued that the oaths taken at the consecration are made to God, not to the people. And, indeed, the king promised nothing to his people; he pledged himself and is accountable to God only. There is no covenant between the king and his people; the relation between the king and his people is not contractual, but statutory. The king unites in his body the three orders of the realm, and, therefore, the multitude of individual interests existing in the realm. In theory, none of them may be forgotten or ignored since all are represented in the royal person; the king encompasses in his royal person the united power of the many individual people.[15]

The quasi-physical fusion that existed between the king and the nation was institutionalized in a mystic phenomenon by which the king made one body with the nation, which in turn made one body with the king, both being forever united in the State. This is the reason why power, as it is still conceived in France, is regarded as a sovereign power, complete in itself, at the service of the nation, working for the benefit of all. This is far from the concept of power in England or the United States as a power separate from the people, which must be limited to protect the people. In the famous audience of Flagellation (March 3, 1776), the king, Louis XV, when rejecting the claims of the *Parlements* (which claimed to be ''sovereign'' courts of law established in the provinces) to stand as representatives of the people, recalled that he was the supreme guardian of public order and contemptuously concluded: ''My people make one with me and [. . .] the rights and interests of the nation that some dare to think as being separate from the person of the monarch are necessarily united in my hands and rest in my hands only.''[16] On such premises, it was impossible to ever dispute the conformity of royal will to the public good. In laying down an automatic equation between the ideas of the prince and the general interest of the nation, the scholars of the old regime went beyond any rational and demonstrable propositions. They operated on a postulate that they called ''the mystery of the monarchy.'' The royal monarchy demanded from the nation complete obedience, hence, this particular feature of French political culture, as noted by François Furet, ''an adoration of the French for absolute power.''[17]

From the Royal-State to the Nation-State. There is little doubt that the intimate relation existing between the king and the nation was a fountain head

[15] See M. Cottret, ''Absolutisme,'' *DAR*, p. 8.

[16] On the logic of absolutism, see the analysis of P. Brunet, *Vouloir pour la nation, Le concept de représentation dans la théorie de l'État*, Bruylant / LGDJ, 2004, p. 73.

[17] F. Furet, *La Révolution en débat*, Gallimard, Folio, 1999, p. 55.

for the force of the French monarchy and its decisive contribution to national unity. As early as the sixteenth century, the king's lawyers proudly proclaimed that the French kingdom was "All-in-one," a formula that presaged the absolutist theory of the State, well before it was put into writing by Thomas Hobbes, the English philosopher. Against these absolutist theories, La Boétie wrote an essay, *Discourse on Voluntary Servitude* (1574). A few centuries in advance of his time, this friend of Montaigne convincingly explained how the intimate relation between the king and the nation had made servitude a voluntary bound. His visionary book was aptly dubbed the "Against one."[18]

The intimate relation existing between the king and the nation was abolished by article 3 of the Declaration of the Rights of Man and the Citizen (1789): "The principle of all sovereignty remains in essence in the Nation. No public body, no individual can exercise authority that does not expressly derive from the Nation." This text forbids a public body (a legislative assembly) or an individual (a head of State) to claim to personify the nation; they may only represent it. However, even in the Republic, the nation remained what it had been under the monarchy, when it made one body with that of the king. Like the physical body of the king, it is indivisible; it is "All-in-one." Without the French monarchy, without the extraordinary unity that it built around itself, sovereignty would not be what it is today in French public law—a "national" sovereignty.[19]

B. THE LAWS *(LOIS)* OF THE KING

1. Legislative Practice

Medieval public law. In the Middle Ages, public law had little depth, being essentially made of "the fundamental laws of the realm" that applied to the status of the crown and the royal domain. As to the rest, the king was in the first place a dispenser of justice and only occasionally a lawgiver. Legislative power or, more accurately, what occupied its place, that is, the regulatory power necessary to the public order, was principally seigniorial. The king legislated only on special occasions and on very narrow topics. When, circa 1280, Philippe de Beaumanoir makes a listing of the circumstances under which the king may legislate, he draws a line between peacetime, when the king, by tradition the

---

[18] E. de La Boétie, *Le discours de la servitude volontaire*, Paris, Payot et Rivages, 2002. See also R. Descimon & A. Guery, "Justifications: la 'monarchie royale'," (1989) in A. Burguière & J. Revel, *Histoire de la France: La longue durée de l'État* (Jacques Le Goff (Ed.)), Seuil, 2000, p. 253.

[19] See the first paragraph in Chapter 7.

custodian of customs, may not legislate (law being made of customs and traditions), and wartime when, in exceptional circumstances, the king may legislate, displacing old customs and adopting new provisions imposed by necessity. The seigneurs have the same power, on the express condition, however, that they respect the rights of the king. In any case, the new law is legitimate only if it complies with certain formal conditions (the king must deliberate in his council) and substantive requirements (the new law is justified only if it aims at the "common profit").

Common belief, at that time, was that law does not change and, indeed, must not change. The best evidence of this belief is to be found in the king's oath during consecration. The essence of the oath is that the king is expected to maintain the rights of everyone—the Church "in her good freedoms and franchises," and the nobles, the plowmen and the merchants "in their good laws and old customs." Common belief held that there is no true law except that which is rooted in the past and anchored in immemorial usages and traditions. The public good consists in maintaining what is in existence. Nothing is more foreign to medieval thought than the contemporary voluntarism in law, made clear in the modern legal language that constantly refers to "normative production" or "legislative production." In the Middle Ages, law is not "made," but "given," by traditions, usages, and customs and, ultimately, by God. In the Middle Ages, therefore, law and power were held to be two very separate concepts, the former being above the latter. There was little change over the medieval era. But everything changes with the Renaissance, the Age of Exploration, and the development of the market economy.

The coming into being of modern public law. In the sixteenth century, ideas changed. The royal functions loomed larger; they were no longer limited to defending the realm, maintaining the status quo, and dispensing justice only. New needs surfaced, and a new instrument comes into being to carry them out, the ordinance, a category among the many laws of the king. The laws and ordinances of the king increasingly appear to be instruments for enacting the public good. As early as 1481, the king instructed the local officials that he may make laws and ordinances for the justice and police of the realm.[20] A new domain for modern public law emerges, police power.

In the seventeenth and eighteenth centuries, the term "police" is very broadly understood; the scope of police power includes not only public peace, but, more comprehensively, everything that may serve "the general and

[20] J. P. Dawson, "The Codification of the French Customs," 38 *Mich. L. Rev.* 765, 771, note 15 (1940).

common good of society.'' According to Nicolas Delamare, author of a 1705 treatise on police power that remains a classic in the field, police power encompasses ''religion, discipline, the mores, health, supplies, public peace and security, roads, liberal arts and sciences, commerce, factories and mechanical arts, domestic servitudes, unskilled workers and the poor.''[21] Expanding on Bodin's ideas on the duties of the sovereign in the ''well-ordered Commonwealth,'' Delamare says of police power that ''its unique purpose is to lead man to the utmost felicity he may enjoy in his life''; he explains in further writings: ''Police power includes the universality of the policies necessary to bring about the public good, of the choice and use of the means most fitted to make it real, to develop it and to make it more perfect. It is, so to speak, the science of government over men, to give them some good and to make them become as much as possible what they must be for the general interest of the society.''[22] The Encyclopedia by Diderot and d'Alembert defined police power as ''an art of delivering a convenient and quiet life.''[23] After justice, police power becomes the next domain in which modern public law will grow; it delineates its own *raison d'être* and its boundaries.

As public law grows in importance, the private law-public law distinction takes shape. In the seventeenth century, Jean Domat undertakes a systematic and very Cartesian classification of the law in his great treatise *Les lois civiles dans leur ordre naturel* (1689). Domat, dubbed by Boileau ''the restorer of reason in jurisprudence,'' orders the law of the nation (which he calls national law), like a French garden, by dividing it into two parts: public law, which deals with public peace and government, and private law, which addresses civil law.

Scope of ordinances. The ordinances have a less broad scope than the modern *lois* (statutes). As a rule, they are said to be ''of public law'' and, as such, address mostly matters of justice. The ordinances in matters of criminal justice are numerous.[24] Then, there are the ordinances relating to the policing of

---

[21] N. Delamare, *Traité de la police*, Paris, J. & P. Cot, 1705, Book I, p. 1. On the history of the police power, see É. Picard, *La notion de police administrative*, Paris, LGDJ, 1984, vol. I, p. 54.

[22] Delamare, *supra* note 21, at p. 4. See also M. Rueff, ''The Well-Ordered Police State and the Development of Modernity in Seventeenth- and Eighteenth-Century Europe: An Attempt at a Comparative Approach,'' 80 *American Historical Review* 1221, 1235, note 48 (1975).

[23] Boucher d'Argis, ''Police,'' in M. Diderot & M. d'Alembert, *Encyclopédie raisonnée des arts et des métiers*, Paris, 1751-1780, Vol. XII, p. 905.

[24] As examples of these ordinances, reference must be made to the Ordinance of Villers-Cotterêts (1539) which imports a profound reformation of justice, reorganizes the jurisdiction of the courts (in limiting the jurisdiction of ecclesiastical courts), modifies the

the realm, a term that encompasses public peace; moral order[25] ; the economy, in particular in the domain of commerce and transportation;[26] and lastly the ordinances pertaining to policing the colonies.[27] In the seventeenth and eighteenth centuries, they grow in scope to include social concerns (civil status, hospitals, and poverty) together with economic regulation (factories, public works). All these ordinances were elaborated with great care, after inquiries and consultations. An already well-staffed civil service called for the opinions of the parties most interested. It sent questionnaires to the *parlements* in the provinces on matters within their competence. It drafted bills that were examined first by the *Parlement* of Paris and then by the king's council. The *loi* (ordinance) never came into force without being reviewed by the *parlements* in the provinces before its registration in the books.[28] At this point, the sovereign provincial courts of law could address ''remonstrances'' to the king, who was thereby invited to modify his bill. This procedure gave rise to all kinds of abuses, which eventually made every reform impossible to carry out and precipitated the Revolution. If these procedures are still relevant today, it is because of their contribution to the ''culture of prevention''[29] that still characterizes the French law-making process. The idea is to write *lois* (statutes) perfect in their language,

---

criminal procedure (in reinforcing the secret of the inquisitorial procedure), and introduces many changes in civil procedure and judicial formalities. Forbidding recourse to Latin as a legal and judicial language, it prescribes that all courts' opinions, judgments, procedural documents, contracts, wills, and other legal pieces be written henceforth in ''the French mother tongue and not otherwise.'' The idea is to extirpate Latin, not vernacular dialects. In the same manner, the great ordinances of Louis XIV dealing with the procedure (Civil Ordinance of 1667 and Criminal Ordinance of 1670) fall also in the domain of justice.

[25] This is the case for the numerous edicts of the king dealing with the policing of religious practices and the affairs of the Church, with the Edict of Nantes (1598), which recognized the Protestant religion and granted freedom of religion to the Protestants in the French realm, and the Edict of Fontainebleau (1685) withdrawing the former.

[26] Such is the case with the Ordinance on Trade (1673) and the Ordinance on the Marine (1681).

[27] This is the case of the Ordinance on the Colonies (1685), known as the ''Black Code,'' which acknowledged the practice of slavery as a mere fact, a practice from purely private origin developed by private merchants under the pressure for bigger profits in their trade with the continent, and which endeavoured to subject it to elementary rules of humanity. Slavery is not a public law institution, but a private law one, rooted in the right of property and developed by Roman law, a law of servitude, into a whole array of diverse rules from acquisition to manumission (*i.e.*, the freeing of a slave).

[28] For more details on these procedures, see Olivier-Martin, *supra* note 2, at p. 419; from the same author, F. Olivier-Martin, *Les Lois du Roi*, Reprint, LGDJ, 1997, p. 290.

[29] On the culture of prevention, see N. Questiaux, ''Administration and the Rule of Law: The Preventive Role of the French Conseil d'Etat,'' 1995 *Public Law* 247, 251.

beyond reproach in their substance, in which the legislative enactment as a work of human beings is in agreement with the law and equity as a work of God. Despite the triumph of positivism in the nineteenth century, these idealistic objectives have remained the major characteristics of the French law-making process.

Until the eighteenth century, the ordinances said to be of "private law," that is, directly affecting private law matters, remained very rare.[30] The idea remained that private law was governed by customs. However, under the concept of public order, some royal ordinances indirectly modified some private law rules in the domain of the law of persons and family law. More often than not, they did away with unreasonable customs or they imposed emergency measures required by the circumstances. The *loi* in the form of ordinances started really to affect private law at the end of the eighteenth century, when the great Ordinances of the Chancellor d'Aguesseau brought about deep reforms in the law of gifts and estates, wills, and forgeries. These ordinances were a forerunner to the codifications of Napoleon. Except for them, the French monarchy did not intrude in the sphere of private life.

2. Legal Regime

The loi *as an act of sovereignty.* In turning "the power to give and break the law" into the first attribute of sovereignty, Jean Bodin imposed a new idea: law is a human work. He is the founder of the modern approach to law, which contemplates law as a product of power or, in more precise terms, as the product of the will that holds supreme power. Moreover, his emphasis on the absolute character of sovereignty supports the so-called "power of the State,"[31] the basis of modern legislation, which regards the *loi* (statute) as the expression of a sovereign word bound by the customs, rights, and privileges on the sole condition of his good will.

A brilliant lawyer of the Renaissance, Bodin (1529-1596) was aware that one effectively destroys something if one finds a replacement for it. His genius was to replace the two pillars of medieval public law with the two (new) pillars of modern public law. Instead of the act of a plurality, the formation of which involved several participants, Bodin made the law of the king a unilateral act.

---

[30] An exception is the Ordinance of Blois (1579) on marriage that, in line with the instructions by the Council of Trent, required that the consent of the spouses be received by a priest.

[31] This theory is fully expounded by O. Beaud, *La puissance de l'État*, Coll. Léviathan, PUF, 1994, in particular in Title I of Part I: "La loy ou la domination du souverain sur les sujets étatiques," pp. 53-130.

Instead of the conservative act, par excellence, always respecting vested rights, franchises, and privileges of the subjects, Bodin turned the modern *loi* (statute) into an abrogative act that may always withdraw what it had previously granted.

a. The Loi as a Unilateral Act

The initial theory. Jean Bodin made "the power to make law binding on all his subjects in general and on each in particular" a power that the sovereign must exercise alone, in full independence, "without the consent of any superior, equal, or inferior being necessary," because, he goes on, "if the prince can only make law with the consent of a superior, he is a subject; if of an equal he shares his sovereignty; if of an inferior, whether a council of magnates or the people, it is not he who is the sovereign."[32] These ideas were in complete contradiction with those of the Middle Ages, when nobody would have envisioned a king legislating without being surrounded by the councils of the various estates in the realm. They may be explained by the intractable and endless conflicts of the wars of religion and the need to find, in the wake of the solution already found by the English king and pursued by the German princes, a decision-making process that would place in the hands of one authority, and only one, that of the king, the unshared, unique, and absolute power to establish religious law. In affirming the need for an unshared power, Bodin writes against the Huguenots and their doctrine of divided sovereignty. Also called shared sovereignty, this idea was usually linked to a theory of legal limits to monarchical authority under the form of a right of resistance to oppression by a tyrant—ideas that were to be found in the essay "Against One" by La Boétie. As Bodin conceives it, sovereignty is a power that cannot be shared; it is indivisible.

Practical consequences. Beginning in the sixteenth century, everywhere in Europe, one organ, and only one, rose in each State and affirmed itself as the exclusive holder of legislative power, under which all other powers were subsumed. The nature of this organ varied depending on the State. In France, it was the king. The *lois* (statutes) of the king are the expression of one will only; all attempts to give to the king a "companion" in his legislative majesty failed. Some argued that the tradition was well established, pointing to a vote taken by the General Estates during the sixteenth century that gave the king the power to govern alone and, in addition, the power to raise a permanent tax, the *taille.*[33] It

---

[32] J. Bodin, *The Six Books of the Commonwealth* [Abridged and translated by M. J. Tooley], Barnes and Noble, 1967, Book I, chap. X, available at http://www.constitution.org/bodin/bodin.htm.

[33] See Channu, *supra* note 8, at pp. 146-147. It must be said that the estates' consent will later be overlooked by Sir John Fortescue in his terrible and very critical picture of

must be recalled that the consent of the estates was given under the pressure of tragic circumstances, the Hundred Years War.

Under the monarchy by divine right, however, no national tragedy ever forced the legists of the French king to uphold in triumph the old formulas of imperial Roman law *Quod principi placuit legis vigorem habet* (what pleases the prince acquires the force of law) or *Sic jubeo, sic volo* (As I want, so I ordain). These are the formulas that will enable Louis XV, during the memorable meeting of the Flagellation of March 3, 1766, to assert: ''To me alone does the law making power belong, without dependence, or sharing.'' Bodin's theory of absolute and nonseverable sovereignty was adopted by all States on the European continent and led to the centralization of sovereign power into a single organ in the State. European thought adopts without nuances the theory of indivisible sovereignty, well summarized in the almost hypnotic formula by Cardin Le Bret, a contemporary of Richelieu: ''Sovereignty is no more divisible than the point in geometry.''[34]

With a few exceptions (England and the Low Countries), most European states evolved toward government by one. This was a transformation. At the beginning of the sixteenth century, ''every country of western Christendom, from Portugal to Finland, and from Ireland to Hungary, had its assemblies of estates. By the end of the century most of these assemblies had been eliminated or greatly reduced in power.''[35] Absolutism introduced a new style of government, the government by one. The government by several, by all of those who made the Curia Regis, no longer existed. True, absolute monarchs governed surrounded by counselors and councils, thus forming the *polysynodie* (government by councils) that characterizes the French government of the old regime in the eighteenth century. However, all these councils staffed with courtiers[36] do not alter the fact that, in the end, the monarch can decide in a sovereign manner, alone in majesty, that is, without the consent of anyone, whatever the legislative, executive, or judicial nature of their powers. Power is not shared—or, to put use

the French monarchy in 1468-1471, when he will portray the miserable French who lived not only in misery, but also in servitude, since they were subject to a tax that they had not freely consented to.

[34] Cardin Le Bret, *De la souveraineté du roy* (1632), I, IX, quoted by É. Maulin, ''Souveraineté,'' *DCC*, p. 1435, and by M. Cottret, ''Absolutisme,'' *DAR*, p. 8.

[35] Huntington, *supra* note 10, at 386.

[36] The career of courtier comes into being with absolutism. A courtier, of course, has no representative character; he represents himself only.

to the terms that were to become famous after Montesquieu's analysis of the English Constitution, powers are not "separated."[37]

b. The Loi as an Abrogative Act

The maxim Princeps legibus solutus est. In the Middle Ages, the king was under the law and bound to respect it. This was, indeed, the condition of conformity of the law with the common good. The theoreticians of absolute monarchy introduced new ideas. No idea of Jean Bodin[38] was more striking than that which claimed sovereignty must be absolute. Sovereignty is the power "to make law"; but he insisted that it must also be the power "to unmake it," since the ruler, like the pilot of a ship, must be able to steer where he sees fit. After Jean Bodin, it was acknowledged, in complete contradiction with medieval ideas, that the king is not bound by human laws, that he may break the customs, that he may change or abrogate them by legislative enactments, and make new laws. The true sovereign is one who is not bound by the laws enacted by his predecessor or the rights he may have granted. Sovereign power is absolute (*solutus legibus*), that is, not bound by human laws in application of the Roman maxim *(princeps solutus legibus est)*. Sovereignty is a supreme power because of its abrogative character, because of its capacity to destroy what exists. The true sovereign is the one who may abrogate and derogate from the law.

At the time of Jean Bodin, the maxim *princeps legibus solutus est* was well known.[39] It had been used during the thirteenth century by the French jurists who had recourse to Roman law in order to solve a legal difficulty regarding the devolution of the crown. In order to avoid the partition of the realm, they successfully argued that the realm was not a private property that could be divided up at will and that its devolution must obey specific rules. This was the birth of public law as a law derogatory from the common law, with the consequence that this derogatory character required the establishment of a hierarchy between the laws. For if the king is not bound by his own laws, then he may absolve himself from the laws relating to his status—hence, the necessity to make a distinction between laws that are binding on the king (the fundamental laws of the realm) and the laws that are not (the ordinary laws).

---

[37] Montesquieu, *The Spirit of Laws,* [Translated by Th. Nugent, 1752, revised by J. V. Prichard], 1748, Book XI, chap. 6, available at http://www.constitution.org/cm/sol.htm.

[38] See *supra* note 32.

[39] The study of reference remains A. Esmein, "La maxime *Princeps legibus solutus est* dans l'ancien droit public français," in P. Vinogradoff (Ed.), *Essays in Legal History Read Before The International Congress of Historical Studies Held in London in 1913*, Oxford University Press, 1913, p. 201.

With "the idea of a royal constitution unattainable by its own beneficiaries,"[40] legal thought took the first steps towards constitutional law.

This being said, in Roman law, the Emperor was not in reality freed from the laws; he was, on the contrary, bound by them but with the possibility that he might occasionally obtain a dispensation from the legal rules. Then, it was allowed that he could grant dispensations to the subjects. As he could, exceptionally, grant dispensations also to himself, it was further admitted that the dispensations for himself were self-evident. For greater simplicity, it was later admitted that he was inherently free from the laws he could grant dispensations from. But, and this is a decisive point, this ability applied only to private law and, according to Esmein, who quotes Mommsen on this point, to the laws of police. By contrast, the emperor was bound by public laws and, in particular, by criminal laws, although, in accordance with general principles, it was admitted that he could not be prosecuted. In France, the maxim *princeps legibus solutus est* was applied to all laws, both public and private, although with more liberty for the former than the latter.

Application to public laws. The legists of the old regime considered that the king was not bound by public laws and that he could free himself from them, as he wished. The king made laws and dispensed justice, without being bound by prior laws. When the king intervened in person to decide an administrative matter or to adjudicate a case, he could do so without taking into account the former laws that his officers, by contrast, were obliged to respect. The royal privilege was all the more remarkable when the king dispensed justice himself to his subjects, as he was entitled to do from time immemorial. When adjudicating on the merits of a particular case, the council of the king could decide only by reference to fairness (*équité*); the council of the king was regarded as the king himself, who was held to be always virtually present at its meetings. Older authors pointed to the fact that in his coronation oath, the king promised to dispense justice in fairness. This could have been worse, as Esmein put it, although recourse to fairness could bring about serious abuses. The principle unfortunately brought about much graver dangers.

Criminal law: When he adjudicated a case in person, the king could inflict the most serious punishments *ex post facto* and without trial. Logically, there was no reason he could not have done so sitting as a judge. However, in the private hearings that the French kings held for a long time, they usually decided civil cases only, most of them of minor importance.

---

[40] S. Rials, "La dévolution de la Couronne," in Rials (Ed.), *supra* note 5, at p. 93.

On the other hand, the Council of the king put a very early end to its role in judging criminal cases. In these matters, the most well-known application of the maxim *princeps legibus* was the practice of ''*lettres de cachet,*'' warrants that could carry any kind of order by the monarch, usually for the imprisonment without trial of a specified person. French kings occasionally put to death persons whom they judged themselves to be guilty of certain crimes. Earlier commentators called such behaviors royal ''fiats.'' They insisted that legally the king was authorized to act only by and with legal means (*i.e.*, with due process of law).

General public law: At a more general level, the maxim *princeps legibus* is at the root of the principle according to which public law is withdrawn from the purview of ordinary judges, a principle destined for a great future. All new legislation passed in the form of ordinances in matters of public law was withdrawn from ordinary courts. These ordinances dealt with the administration of justice, the public peace, and policing the realm, which included the material and moral order, the general administration, and all economic regulation usually based on old customs: monitoring of professions, distribution of vital supplies, regulation of markets.

One of the most important texts in this domain was the edict of Saint-Germain of 1641, which forbade the *Parlement* of Paris to consider cases dealing with the affairs of the State or the administration in very stringent terms:

> [W]e have declared that our said *Parlement* of Paris and our other courts of law were established to do justice to our subjects only; we prohibit them by most express inhibitions not only to take cognizance of any case similar to those mentioned above, but also in more general terms of any case dealing with the State, the administration or the government which we reserve solely to our person . . . except if we happened to give them the power to do so by special command and letters patent . . . [W]e henceforth declare null and void any opinion or judgment which could be made in the future in contradiction with the present declaration as having been made by persons without power to intermeddle in the government of our realm.[41]

The remarkable part of the edict of Saint Germain is its systematic and sweeping scope. How can it be explained that the king withdrew from the courts authority over all cases dealing with the affairs of the State, the administration, and the

[41] See E. Laferrière, *Traité de la juridiction administrative et des recours contentieux*, vol. I (1887), LGDJ, Reprint 1989, p. 127; see also G. Bigot, *Introduction historique au droit administratif français*, Coll. Droit fondamental, PUF, 2002, p. 22.

government? What made them so unfit to adjudicate such cases? True, as Laferrière noted at the end of the nineteenth century, "As early as we go back in our history . . . we cannot find times when the courts in charge of enforcing civil and criminal laws were also in charge of deciding the difficulties in matter of public management."[42] True, as he observes with much precision, some special courts for eminent domain, taxation, and public accounting had been established as early as the fourteenth century. However, the creation of special courts such as the King's Council that appeared later in the seventeenth century cannot be explained solely by the technical nature of the cases to be decided, as may be so with cases dealing with public accounting; there was nothing particularly technical to consider in cases dealing with the exercise of police power. Other factors came into play.

The burden of the venality of offices. In *The Old Regime and the Revolution*, Tocqueville has argued that the willingness of the king to withdraw all cases dealing with the State and the general administration of the realm from the cognizance of the courts of law can be explained by the venality of the offices, the scourge of the old regime.[43] The vast majority of officers of the State, whether employed in the service of justice, finances, or economic affairs, were the holders and owners of hereditary offices. As owners of their offices, judges were untouchable and could not be removed for cause. As nothing could be done against them, they were denied the power to adjudicate important cases and special courts were created to decide such cases. Tocqueville astutely noted:

---

[42] E. Laferrière, *supra* note 41, at p. 109.

[43] A. de Tocqueville, *The Old Regime and the Revolution* [Translated by Alan S. Kahan], vol. I, University of Chicago Press, 1998. Venality of offices goes back to Louis XI; on October 21, 1467, he gave the first impulse (J.-P. Royer, *Histoire de la justice*, Coll. Droit fondamental, PUF, p. 114) with the ordinance for "the immovability of law officers and others" whose major consequence was to stabilize the offices. François I, however, is usually regarded as the king who gave venality of offices its biggest boost. In theory, the price for the office was a loan paid to the Treasury and always reimbursable. As a matter of fact, the Treasury was always unable to reimburse the price of their offices to the officers. Under Henry IV, the royal Declaration of December 12, 1604, established the system of the "Paulette." According to the scheme invented by the cunning financial manager Charles Paulet, an annual taxation was established; each year, the holder of the office was obliged to pay a tax equal to the sixtieth part of the total price of the charge. The system was advantageous both for the officer, who was relieved from paying in cash the former high price of the office, and for the Treasury, which henceforth avoided the disruption of unpredictable sales and benefited from a regular source of revenue. Well aware of the dangers of this system, Richelieu tried in vain to do away with it. Louis XIV is supposed to have said resignedly one day: "The most enticing prerogative of the French kings is to create new offices; as soon as he creates one, God creates a fool to buy it."

> There was no country in Europe where the ordinary courts were less subordinate to the government than in France; but there was also no country where extraordinary tribunals were more common. These two things were more related than one might think. Since the King had barely any influence over the judges' fate, since he could neither fire them, nor change their residence, nor as even promote them; since in a word he controlled them neither through ambition nor fear, he soon felt troubled by their independence. This led him, more than anywhere else, to limit their jurisdiction over matters which directly affected his power, and to create alongside the ordinary courts, for his own special use, a more dependent kind of tribunal, which gave his subjects the appearance of justice without making him fear its reality.[44]

Progressively, the idea, still alive in French law, developed that any case dealing with the government or the administration must, in principle, escape ordinary courts and hence the ordinary law.

Application to private laws. The king was freed from complying with private laws so far as his personal status was concerned. The rules on the succession to the throne are the first case in point. Together with heredity, the right of primogeniture held sway in order to avoid the partition of the realm, and it soon became a matter of law. On a more general level, if the king performed an act that any individual could accomplish, such as writing his will, making a gift or entering into a contract, he could do so legally without taking into account the laws and customs, setting them aside or even discarding them.[45]

So far as the personal status of his subjects was concerned, the position of the king *vis-à-vis* private laws was completely different. The king did not often avail himself of his power to derogate from them. His freedom of action was "impeded by a true thicket of privileges," so to speak.[46] Contrary to official appearances and the proud assertions of the king's legists, who were quite vocal in affirming in Latin maxims the sovereignty of the law [*sic jubeo, sic volo,* "as the king wishes, so the law does too"], the *loi* (statute) was not in fact wholly sovereign. Opposing it, there was the law (*droit*), or better the laws protecting the rights (*droits*)—all rights that were protected by the customs of provinces, by the franchises of cities and corporations, by the privileges of the nobility and

---

[44] Tocqueville, *supra* note 43, at p. 132.

[45] Examples of such private acts are the will of Philippe de Valois, or the contract of marriage between Louis XIII and the Infant Anne.

[46] See J.-L. Harouel, "La monarchie absolue," in Rials (Ed.), *supra* note 5, at p. 101, especially p. 105.

the clergy, all rights made of private interests, particular and communitarian, that were protected by the *Parlements* (ordinary courts of law), and that all kings when acceding to the throne solemnly swore to respect and maintain. Before the Revolution, the *loi* (statute) could override these private interests only with great difficulty. It ran up against privileges (*i.e.*, vested and private rights). These rights were effectively protected by the *Parlements*, that is, the courts of law, which were regarded as official custodians of the estates and orders of society, corporations, families, and individuals.[47]

An extraordinary discrepancy between the theory of sovereignty and the reality of legislation marked the old regime. In theory, the *loi* (statute) was sovereign; it was held to stand for the will of the prince and it sufficed that it appeared for everything else to vanish before it. In practice, it was a completely different story. No one better explained the inconsistency than Portalis. Expounding before the *Conseil d'État* on 4 Ventôse Year XI (1803), he explained the motives for a preliminary title to the Civil Code dealing with the publication, effects, and application of statutes in general:

> Under the old regime, the *loi* (statute) was the will of the prince. This will was sent to the sovereign courts of law in charge of reviewing and registering it. The statute was not enforceable in a jurisdiction without having been formerly reviewed and registered [. . .] A statute could be refused by a sovereign court, but accepted by another; it could be diversely construed by the various courts. The pace of the legislation was stumbling, shy and uncertain. Among such confusion and conflicts between different wills, there could be no unity, no certainty, and no majesty in the operations of the lawmakers. One never knew whether the State was led by the general will, or by the anarchy of particular wills. All this was the consequence of the then constitution. France, before the Revolution, was less a single nation than a collection of diverse nations, successively reunited or conquered, distinct by the climate, the soil, the privileges, the customs, by civil law and political law. The prince ruled over these diverse nations under the different titles of duke, king or count: he promised to maintain each country in its old customs and privileges. It can easily be felt that, in such a situation, it was a prodigy when the same statute could fit all parts of

[47] See P. Legendre, *Histoire de l'administration de 1750 à nos jours*, PUF, Thémis, 1968, p. 473.

the empire. Some measure of uniformity in the legislation was out of reach.[48]

As each province of France was a particular state within the State, the statute of the king had to be naturalized (in a formal acceptance followed by a regular promulgation) in order to be locally enforceable. In each province, the *Parlements* (there were thirteen of them, each being a ''sovereign'' court of law and supreme within its jurisdictional territory) had the right, upon registration of royal legislation, to address remonstrances to the king whenever his laws were likely to abridge privileges, to withdraw franchises, or to abrogate vested rights—in other words, whenever the statutes of the king affected the rights and privileges of the subjects of his Majesty. To that extent, the French realm actually was a country of freedom where the private rights of men were protected. The absolute monarchy by divine right was no despotic State.

The legacy of absolute sovereignty. Jean Bodin's book found tremendous success. It went through at least fourteen editions before 1629. In Bodin's views, absolute sovereignty did not mean unlimited sovereignty. As he saw it, sovereignty was designed to be exercised within the sphere of human laws only, leaving untouched the laws of God[49] and nature[50] which the king was bound to

---

[48] Exposé des motifs du titre préliminaire du code civil, de la publication, des effets et de l'application des lois en général par le conseiller d'État Portalis, Séance du 4 ventôse an IX, in *Discours préliminaire du premier projet de Code civil*, Paris, Éditions Confluences, Voix de la cité, Reprint 1999, pp. 63-64.

[49] In the system of Bodin, the sovereign is not at the top of the legal order. Above all earthly sovereigns, there is God. No matter how high a human authority may be, it is always supposed to act in a world governed by rules deriving from the divine scriptures or from the nature of things. These rules usually, but not always, termed *droit* (law) or *jus* are not vis-à-vis the sovereign in a position identical to statutes (*lex* or *loi*). The sovereign has complete control over the *loi*, not over the *droit*. As he was writing in the sixteenth century, Bodin could not treat the laws of God and nature as they are treated today, that is, as merely moral obligations. Like most of his contemporaries, he firmly believed that the sovereign was directly accountable to God. He was steadfast in his expectation of divine retribution for acts that violated principles of natural law. Political sovereignty, as he termed it, operated within a world governed by God.

[50] At the time of Bodin, the notion of natural law was relatively well-developed. The basic principles were to be found in Roman law; several judicial precedents had brought additional concrete guarantees. As a jurist, Bodin was familiar with these developments. He used the concept of natural law to lay down two limits to the power of the king. In the first place, like a private person, the sovereign is as tightly bound by his promise and even by the promises made by his predecessor. This limitation on the action of the sovereign is based on the idea (of religious origin) that keeping the faith and carrying out the obligations of contracts are essential to the public peace. In the second place, every one is entitled to receive his fair share (*id quod justum est*); from this premise, Bodin built such

comply with. Bodin acknowledged: ''As God only is almighty, human power can never be truly absolute.'' The principle was never forgotten and, later, in the seventeenth century, Bossuet, in often harrowing sermons, reminded the king of the consequences of these limitations on his governance.[51]

Bossuet, however, always reasoned within the framework of absolutism, that is, within a system where limitations to power, if any, originate in the king's self-restraint, not in the external limits that may be imposed on his power, whether these limits come from the provinces or from the natural law. The essence of absolutism lies in the single fact that it cannot be limited and remain absolute at the same time. Absolute power may never be heterolimited; it may at most be autolimited, with the result that, in order to fully understand it, it must be laid onto a political theology and assimilated to divine authority. In Bossuet's system, the providential prince is God himself. The growing secularization of societies and the coming into being of scientific thought turned the laws of God and nature into meaningless princ iples. Both did away with the ethical and moral authority that, during the seventeenth century, limited the State in the exercise of its sovereign power.

Whatever its theological underpinnings, the theory of absolute sovereignty turned the traditional functions of the State completely upside down by ousting the power to dispense justice as the first power of royal prerogatives, replacing it with the power to legislate. Beginning with the sixteenth century, the *loi*, in the form of the ordinance, became beyond France, throughout continental Europe, the rational instrument of public order and brought about a new style of governance, with a new approach to the *res publica*.

---

a large defence of property rights that it required prior consent by landlords before taxation unless the pressing needs of the time were such that a waiting period would put the state into jeopardy. With Bodin, the right of property is protected by natural law. The difficulty was in the real and practical application of such principles. Bodin intimated that the General Estates and the provincial estates, sole representative bodies at the time, could play a role in consenting to taxation. However, these assemblies had no separate existence from the royal person so that their possible interposition to the royal will, in particular under the form of a right of veto, was in theory hypothetical and in practice impossible.

[51] Bossuet, *Politique tirée des propres paroles de l'Écriture sainte*, Paris, Pierre Cot, 1760, Book V, Article 5, Prop. 1, p. 237, available at http://gallica.bnf.fr/ark:/12148/bpt6k103256m.

Chapter 2
The German Legacy

Public law as a science. In France, a theory of public law developed at the end of the nineteenth century, and even then, only in part, since its theorization dealt solely with administrative law. In contrast, public law in Germany was built systematically, like a scientific discipline devoted to a branch of law distinct and separate from private law, as early as the sixteenth century. This rapid development was initiated by an author today forgotten, Nicolas Vigelius (1529-1600), a law professor at the University of Marburg, who published in 1561 a 470-page treatise under the title *Methodus universi iuris civilis absolutissima* (The Most Perfect Method of the Entire Civil Law). This work appears to be where the concept "public law" (*jus publicum*) as an autonomous branch of law was introduced for the first time into the European legal vocabulary. Vigelius was looking for a method to reorganize the entire legal system (known at that time as "civil law"—hence the title of his book), which had been destabilized by the Reformation, the crisis of the Roman Catholic Church, and the disappearance of ecclesiastical courts. Looking for a new classification for the kinds (*genera*) of law, he took up the distinction made in Roman law and proposed a division between public law and private law. To be sure, his reference to a classification formerly made by Ulpianus was not original. The novelty, if any, was in the huge scope attributed to public law, which he identified as coming into play "wherever a public interest is present" and therefore included under the new branch of law "legislation, magistracy, judgments, both secular and ecclesiastical, as well as criminal law and criminal and civil procedure, together with the affairs of the Empire including taxation, municipalities, public duties, and honors."[1]

Public law was born; it grew and developed continuously throughout the principalities of the Empire. In the eighteenth century, two states, Prussia and

[1] On Vigelius's ideas, see H. J. Berman & C. J. Reid, "Roman Law in Europe and the *Jus Commune*: An Historical Overview with Emphasis on the New Legal Science of the Sixteenth Century," 20 *Syracuse J. Int'l L. & Comm.* 1, 23-26 (1994).

Austria, played a decisive role in the deepening of the new discipline, which soon turned into a true science—the science of the State. In all countries with Germanic cultures, public law became a scholarly discipline that rested on the same pedagogical traditions, a feeling shared by professors and students of belonging to the same corporation and sharing common problems.[2]

Public law as a general theory of the State. The second major difference between the French and German traditions of public law is related to the very conception of the field. As opposed to French legal thought, which always thought of public law in reference to its object from the *res publica* of the first Capetian dynasty to the general interest of the twentieth century, German legal thought has always thought of public law in reference to its subject, the State, which was, in the first place, the State personified by the prince. A decisive factor in the historical formation of public law is that public law in Germany has developed on the basis of the Prince-State. The divergent routes taken by both countries resulted in a German doctrine of public law so preoccupied with the idea of the State that it endeavored to detach it from the physical body of the prince, so as to create a pure legal concept under which the whole legal order could fall, rearranged and put into place in a so-called general theory of the State.[3] German legal science went so far in construing an abstract concept of State that it eventually identified public law with the State and rejected the possible existence of public law outside the framework of a State, or at least under its tight control.[4] Unsurprisingly, long and well-established German legal

---

[2] On the development of public law as a science in German universities, see M. Stolleis, *Geschichte des öffentlichen Rechts*: München-Erster Band: *Reichspublizistik und Policeywissenschaft, 1600-1800,* Verlag, C.H. Beck, 1988, p. 48.

[3] For a French analysis of the general theory of the State, see the developments by O. Beaud, ''Préface, Carl Schmitt ou le juriste engagé,'' Introduction to the work by C. Schmitt, *Théorie de la Constitution*, PUF, Coll. Léviathan, 1993, pp. 59-75.

[4] The absorption of public law by the State had drastic consequences on international public law. One of the most important was to oust international public law from the field of general public law, since public law can be internal only. When public law is envisioned and theorized as the law of a state, all law that does not fit into it is reputed to be out of it and, even more, of a different essence. There is no surprise in the fact that Germany became the birthplace of dualism that postulates international law as completely distinct from domestic law and that regards international public law (as defined above [Introduction, Section C] as the law of an international *res publica* or international public good) as being an oxymoron, a pipe dream or, at best, part of a distant future. German legal thinking of the nineteenth century is the fountain head of the so-often made distinction between, on the one hand, public law defined as a law of domination between unequal subjects (the State and its subjects) and, on the other, international law viewed as a law of coordination among equal subjects of law (the sovereign States). In identifying public law with the law of a State, German scholarship had no other option than to erect a

tradition used to make it impossible to reflect on public law without starting with a ''general theory of the State,'' understood as the study of the State envisioned as both a social and a legal phenomenon.[5]

After World War II, German public law took a completely different turn with the adoption of the Fundamental Law (*Grundgesetz*) of May 23, 1949. Nowadays, it is no longer possible for German legal scholars to elevate the idea of the State to the rank of an object for legal analysis and attribute to it normative power. The new bases of the German legal order (fundamental rights and popular sovereignty) no longer allow it. Moreover, they even preclude thinking of the State as a reality per se; the former ''general'' theory of the State has become obsolete. With fundamental rights as the basis of the legal system, legal scholars can no longer build the legal system upon the State. The State is no longer a reality per se. The result takes two main forms. Either the general theory of the State absorbs itself into a ''legal'' theory of the State,[6] or it reconstructs itself on foundations (popular sovereignty) and with materials (fundamental rights) so different from those of the former theory that it is no longer the same theory.[7] The legal theory of the State consists in thinking of the State as a pyramid of norms set up in the neutral and smooth world of legal

---

wall of separation between relations of subordination in internal law and relations of coordination in the international legal order. This conception, which had tremendous success and to which many scholars are still very faithful, has become much dated; it is powerless to explain current international regimes, which are far from a law of coordination, such as the law of collective security under Chapter VII of the U.N. Charter or the law of nuclear nonproliferation of the Treaty on Nonproliferation of Nuclear Weapons (1968), in which some States, often said to be ''particularly interested,'' are actually more equal than others and exercise a domination over other States, quietly and without publicity, diplomatic practice giving the illusion than all actors interact under a law of coordination.

[5] Notwithstanding the famous *Contribution à la théorie générale de l'État* by R. Carré de Malberg, 2 volumes, 1920, reprint CNRS 1962, and volume II of *Traité de science politique* by G. Burdeau, entirely devoted to the State, LGDJ, 1968, French legal scholarship has not much invested in the general theory of the State. For an explanation and a criticism of this lack of interest, see O. Beaud, ''La théorie générale de l'État (*Allgemeine Staatslehre*) en France, Quelques notations sur un dialogue contrarié,'' in O. Beaud & E. Volkmar Heyen (Dirs.), *Eine deutsch-französische Rechtswissenschaft? / Une science juridique franco-allemande?* Nomos Verl.-Ges., 1999, p. 83.

[6] The evolution is well explained by O. Lepsius, ''Faut-il au droit constitutionnel une théorie de l'État? Point de vue allemand: de la théorie de l'État à la théorie des formes de domination,'' *RUDH*, vol. 15, no. 3-6, October 30, 2003, p. 86.

[7] This development is remarkably well analyzed by C. Grewe, ''L'État de droit sous l'empire de la Loi fondamentale,'' in O. Jouanjan [Dir.], *Figures de l'État de droit*, Presses Universitaires de Strasbourg, 2001, pp. 385-393.

formalism propounded, for example, by the normative school of Hans Kelsen. In contemporary German legal scholarship, the State is assimilated to the law, more specifically, to its own law, always within and under the Constitution.[8]

Nowadays, the Prince-State, which eventually turned into the idea of the "God-made State," is a historical phenomenon only. The study of its basic tenets, however, remains necessary for understanding what the cradle of European public law was. The Prince-State (Section A) actually was the ancestor of the modern State, the powerful agent of economic and social transformations, under the form of an institution peculiar to the European continent, the well-ordered Police-State (Section B).

A. THE PRINCE-STATE

Difference from the Royal-State. Beginning with the Renaissance, the sovereign State in most polities of the Holy German Empire developed under the form of the Prince-State (*Furstenstaat*).[9] By contrast to the Royal-State based upon a complete fusion between the monarch and his people, the Prince-State built itself upon a sharp, clear-cut, and rigid distinction between the prince and his people. The Prince-State is the prince made a State, so to speak; it is the personified State.[10] However, the prince is not the king. The German conception of the monarchical State is that of the Person-State; it regards the State as a person, a person that was, in the first place, a physical person and that much later, in the nineteenth century, has been turned into a legal person, or a juridical person; whereas the State in the French tradition is a thing that has been entrusted to a person, the sovereign.[11]

---

[8] See Zippelius & Würtenberger, *Deutsches Staatsrecht*, 31. Auflage, Verlag C. H. Beck, München, 2005, p. 12.

[9] See H. Möller, *Furstenstaat oder Bürgernation? Deutschland 1763-1815*, 4th ed., Berlin, Verlag Gruppe Random House, Bertelsmann, 1998.

[10] See E. H. Kantorowicz, *The King's Two Bodies, A Study in Medieval Political Theology*, Princeton University Press, 1981, p. 446.

[11] The German conception of the Person-State still entails today two important differences between the French and German approaches to public law. The first one is that, from a historical standpoint, the conception of the Person-State made the idea of a contract between the prince and the people possible, whereas the same idea of a contract between the French king and the people was ruled out by the theory of the divine right of the king, the king being under obligation only to God. The second consequence is that, when the State is regarded as being a person and, in particular, a juridical person, it is possible for a citizen to have rights against it, "subjective rights" as German scholars put it, and therefore to enjoy better protection for them. By contrast, the French conception of the Nation-State, which regards the State as an institutionalization of the nation, makes it impossible for the citizen, a member of the nation, to have rights against the nation, or

1. Foundations

a. The Doctrine of Luther

Lutheranism as the basis of continental public law. The Prince-State cannot be understood without reference to the ideas of Martin Luther. Luther by himself did not create, of course, the Prince-State that emerged from the turmoil of the Reformation that radically transformed the principalities of the Holy German Empire. But it is impossible to understand what the Prince-State meant for the development of public law, and how far beyond Germany it left its mark on fundamental notions of contemporary public law, without an inquiry into Luther's ideas.

In 1517, Martin Luther, professor of theology and jurist by education, published his famous theses against the business of indulgences. It was a revolt against the state of the Catholic Church at the beginning of the sixteenth century. His ideas destabilized the Church, wrought havoc in the Holy German Empire, and laid the foundations of modern public law, from at least a triple perspective.

Affirmation of a private space distinct from a public space. In the Middle Ages, the spiritual quest of man was in the first place the salvation of his soul. The "true" life of the Christian was the everlasting life, not daily life on this earth. The Church taught that man could, to a certain extent, contribute to his own salvation; he could by the grace of God and with the help of the Church

---

against the State, as this would imply that the citizen may have rights against himself (or herself).

The differences between the French and the German conceptions of the State had important consequences for administrative law and procedure, in particular regarding the position of the citizen *vis-à-vis* the administration. Judicial review of administrative acts in French law (*recours pour excès de pouvoir*) is an objective adjudication; the plaintiff is suing an act, not a person; standing therefore need not be based on a right, strictly speaking; a mere interest suffices: scholars refer to it as the "model of objective legality." By contrast, judicial review of administrative action in German law operates on different premises; the plaintiff is suing the administration and he (or she) must base his cause of action on a right, a legal right, which has been violated. As the starting points diverge, so do the judicial processes. The French model invites the judge to decide whether the administration followed a regular decision-making process; the German model invites the judge to decide whether a right has been violated. For a general survey of theses differences, see R. Denoix de Saint Marc, "Allocution d'ouverture," *R.A,* 2001, Deuxième centenaire du Conseil d'État, p. 535, and M. Fromont, "Regards d'un juriste français sur la juridiction administrative allemande," *R.A,* 2001, Deuxième centenaire du Conseil d'État, p. 560; see also N. Foulquier, *Les droits publics subjectifs des administrés. Émergence d'un concept en droit administratif français du XIXe au XXe siècle*, Paris, Dalloz, 2003.

accomplish good deeds, which accrued rewards that, in turn, enabled him to be saved. Luther revolutionized medieval thinking in asserting that, to earn salvation in the beyond, the Christian does not need intercession of the Church. Salvation, he said, is a private matter that results exclusively from a direct and immediate relationship between man and God. Whereas in the Middle Ages the Church had delineated a temporal world separate from a spiritual one, Protestantism as initiated by Luther and developed by Calvin drew a line between two worlds meant to coexist next to each other but as separate domains: the private sphere, which the individual possesses as his own, which belongs to him only, and in which he enjoys the right of free examination—a womb for all modern rights; and the public sphere, the sphere of the State, and submission to its power, where public affairs are debated and decided by common consent. In the sixteenth century, privacy and the rights attached to it started to detach themselves from public life.

Broader responsibilities for political power. From Luther's predications, all the countries that had been won over to Reformation rapidly concluded that the Church, with its institutions and structures, had not much good to offer and was in fact doing more harm than good. From the beginning, the author of the ninety-five theses requested abolition of the ecclesiastical courts. The Church, said Luther, is not a law-making institution; the Church is the invisible community of the faithful, of all those who believe in God, inside of which all are priests, and in which everyone participates, but always in a private and personal relation with God. Each one must read and react individually to the Bible; the institutional Church is not needed. It is up to the secular political authority, to the prince and his counselors, to the magistrates of the cities, to endorse the legal responsibilities that used to be in the jurisdiction of the Roman Catholic Church. With these revolutionary ideas, Luther drew a line between two worlds, that of the invisible church, which unites the community of the faithful, which belongs to the realm of grace and faith, and which is governed by the scriptures; and the earthly and temporal world, to which belongs the visible institutional Church, itself governed by law and solely within the jurisdiction of the prince. Once the Catholic Church was ousted from the world of law, its former responsibilities had to be followed up and pursued, and the Prince-State naturally stepped into its shoes. Luther's doctrine tends to make the prince the master of both the bodies and the souls of his subjects.

Submission and absolute obedience to authority. The direct relation between man and God of the Lutheran doctrine completely transformed the conditions of salvation formerly earned by, and with the intercession of, the Church. For the good Christian, in Luther's view, obedience to God requires, in the first place, fulfilling his duty to be what he was meant to be, to be what

God's will intended him to be. The good Christian must be happy and satisfy himself with his condition, and he must not try to change it by getting richer or moving up in the social hierarchy; however, when one is rich and powerful, one must, all the more, fulfill the duties of one's charge, one's state of being, one's "*Stand.*" As Joseph Rovan explains,[12] those who have received a mission from God to fight against the Devil, have a particular *Stand*, a station, which constitutes their *Beruf*, or their calling or profession, which is also under Luther's views their *Berufung*, or their vocation. The *Beruf* of the mighty is to be the *Obrigkeit* (from *oben*, above), that is, the power imposed by God.

Luther's ideas played an important role in the merciless repression of the peasants' revolt (1524-1525) by the princes of the Empire. Emboldened by the wind of reforms that blew all over Germany, the peasants asked for the abolition of feudal fees and *corvées* (taxation in kind—which amounted to forced labor—such as paving roads, repairing streets, cleaning ditches, etc.), together with a return to the old customary law (which had been replaced by Roman law in the fifteenth century) and to a system of justice administered by elected judges. Luther took sides with the princes and called the peasants "criminal and wild hordes of looters."[13] He invited the princes to fully and completely exercise their powers in order to tame the revolt; he exhorted them to plunder, put on the wheel, hang, and cut throats. Having destroyed the Catholic Church and stripped its clergy of all legitimacy, Luther had no other option than to transfer the power of moral and spiritual guidance to the temporal authority and, thereby, to invest the princes with a complete power over men and things. All temporal power, however perverse, is willed by God, so obedience is always due, in Luther's doctrine. There is no longer a right of resistance against unjust or unfair power. The good Christian must suffer or flee by emigration. In affirming a principle of absolute obedience to the State, Luther established an ideology of subservience to political authority. His exaltation of the secular authority of the princes destroyed the authority of the Church and its law.[14] Of Luther's ideas, Michel Villey said: "The fairness of the law is no longer a condition of its validity. I mean, at the minimum, the fairness of its *substance*; what henceforth matters, as German legal thought would say, is its *formal* fairness, that is to say, its being issued by the regular authority according to the regular procedure. Law must be obeyed because it is a command of the

---

[12] J. Rovan, *Histoire de l'Allemagne: des origines à nos jours* (1994), Paris, Seuil, Coll. Points Histoire, 1999, p. 258.

[13] M. Villey, *La formation de la pensée juridique moderne*, Paris, PUF, Coll. Léviathan, reprint 2003, p. 298.

[14] See L. Pfister, "Réforme (La) et le droit," *DAR*, p. 1311.

Prince.''[15] Luther is a forerunner of positivism, which holds all law legitimate from the moment it is laid down by the State.

b. Roman Law

A dual contribution. The Prince-State would never have gained its legendary strength if, in addition to that of Protestantism, it had not received a decisive contribution from Roman law. German public law from its origins had been fed *ad nauseam* by Roman law, which brought to it two main characteristics: the idea of the division of law between private and public law, and an imperial conception of power.

Reception of Roman law. Beginning with the twelfth century and the first lectures delivered on the ''*Corpus juris civilis,*'' Roman law never ceased to irrigate continental legal scholarship. Accepted very early in Italy as the subsidiary law in force in case of a conflict between local customs and laws, Roman law was well known in Germany at the end of the Middle Ages. Because of lectures given at the University of Bologna that attracted many law students, it had become the major and almost exclusive source of study for German lawyers, without however being formally part of the law in force.[16] At the end of the Middle Ages, the German courts adopted Roman law in its totality. The reasons for this adoption, which was formally recognized by a decree of the Imperial Court of Law (*Reichskammergericht*) in 1495, remain a mystery. German historians attribute it to two causes:

(1) an attraction to the languages and literature of antiquity that characterized the spirit of the times; and

(2) the idea of an historical continuity between the Roman Empire and the Holy German Empire, with the latter being the successor to the former, even in legal matters.

However, other factors also came also into play, such as the absence of legal unity in the Empire, of written law, and (because of the fragmented nature of the legal system) of professional jurists who could stand in defense of the customs and local usages. A further factor was the necessity of educating and raising a

[15] Villey, *supra* note 13, at p. 298 (emphasis in original).

[16] Beginning in the thirteenth century, France too received Roman law, but it never succeeded in completely setting aside the customs and local usages of feudal law that survived for a very long time.

class of skilled civil servants with a solid legal background in order to replace the former administrators drawn from the nobility who were not jurists.[17]

Consequences. The adoption of Roman law in Germany had important consequences, from both a social and political standpoint.

On the social plane, the condition of the peasantry got worse. In his book *The Old Regime and the Revolution*, Tocqueville noted:

> I have reason to believe that, through the jurists' work, many conditions of old German society became worse, notably that of the peasants; many of those who had up to then managed to keep all or part of their freedom or their property lost them then by pedantic analogies to the situation of Roman slaves or hereditary lessors.[18]

At the political level, the new elites had extensive recourse to Roman law in order to acquire complete and absolute sovereignty over their subjects and to bring within their power several large German towns. Again, as per Tocqueville, it must be recognized that the extraordinary success of Roman law throughout Europe can be explained by the fact that it accelerated the drive of the new princes, newly enriched by the confiscation of the goods and properties belonging to the Catholic Church, towards absolute power. As Tocqueville notes, "this came from the fact that, at the same time, the absolute powers of rulers was solidly establishing itself everywhere, on the ruins of the old liberties of Europe, and thus that Roman law, a law of servitude, agreed wonderfully with their perspectives." He adds:

> Roman law, which everywhere improved civil society, everywhere tended to degrade political society, because it had chiefly been the work of a very civilized and subordinated people. The kings therefore enthusiastically adopted it, and established it everywhere where they were the masters. The interpreters of this law became their ministers or their chief agents throughout Europe. At need, the jurists furnished them legal support against the law itself. Thus they have often done since. Alongside a ruler who is violating the law, it is very rare not to see a lawyer appear who assures you that nothing could more legitimate, and who proves academically that the violation was just and that the oppressed were in the wrong.[19]

---

[17] See J.-R. Gordley & A. T. von Mehren, *The Civil Law System*, 2nd ed., Boston, Little Brown, 1977, p. 11.

[18] A. de Tocqueville, *The Old Regime and the Revolution*, [Translated by Alan S. Kahan], University of Chicago Press, 2 vols., 1998, p. 257.

[19] *Id.*, p. 258.

2. Characteristics

Rise of a princely legal system. The Prince Electors of the Palatinate, Saxe, Brandenburg, the landgrave of Hesse, and more, together with the municipal councils of many free towns, embraced the Lutheran faith. They took advantage of their conversion to allocate to themselves properties belonging to the Church that were enclaves in their own territories. These confiscations, known under the name of "secularizations" (the ecclesiastical properties were diverted from their former spiritual destination and reassigned to secular purposes), were used to finance the development of a civil service and the creation of a standing army. With the annexation of new territories, princes and towns gained in prestige and wealth. They invaded social and religious space and filled the void left by the Church. In the universities, the curriculum on Church and canon law was replaced with secular law. A legal system made by princes developed and became the privileged means by which the princes asserted their sovereignty over their subjects.

The new law called for new governance, which in turn called for new elites. A new class of administrators appeared and staffed the princes' courts. Most of them were civil servants; a great many were lawyers. Educated in universities, endowed with broad Roman law training, well aware of the new thought on natural law, these agents were the first staff of a permanent civil service in the State.[20] They propagated ideas and beliefs that, in the long run, profoundly changed European societies; in particular, they spread the idea that societies are governed by laws that may be drawn by the human mind from reason and conscience. They taught that government must aim at discovering the best laws, those that will conduce to the happiness of society.

The new theologians who entered the service of the princes in the sixteenth century believed that law must be inspired by principles that the human mind can find through reason and conscience. In particular, they offered a new theory of natural law, which in their opinion had its origin in the essential nature of man. God, they said, has implanted in all persons certain elements of knowledge, including both logical and moral concepts. These inborn concepts are facts of human nature that form the premises, not the objects, of rational inquiry. They are beyond the power of human reason to prove or disprove.[21]

---

[20] See C. J. Friedrich, "The Continental Tradition of Training Administrators in Law and Jurisprudence," 11 *Journal of Modern History* 129 (1939).

[21] On the role of the Protestant theologians in the formation of modern public law, see H. J. Berman & J. Witte, "The Transformation of Western Legal Philosophy in Lutheran Germany," 62 *South. Calif. L. Rev.* 1573, 1617 (1989).

Thus, it is no longer possible to validate legal propositions by demonstrating that they come from authoritative texts. The validity of legal rules must be demonstrated by reference to their conformity with principles of conscience recognized to be just by human reason. These new jurists felt a need to define a method that could enable them to show the legitimacy of their law; to this end, they had extensive recourse to Roman law and principles of natural law. Public law affirmed itself as a law of reason, a law of abstract principles, a collection of rules elaborated by the bureaucracy.

External sovereignty and the dawning of the law of nations. Vis-à-vis the Emperor, the conquest of sovereignty by principalities was progressive. Princes claimed, in the first place, external sovereignty in the conduct of war and diplomacy. They obtained large portions of it in 1648 at the peace of Westphalia. Treaties then concluded enabled them to carry out an autonomous diplomacy that eventually precipitated the dissolution of the Holy Roman Empire. Former feudal and hierarchical relations between members were replaced by diplomatic and quasi-international relations. Sovereignties being deemed equal, each prince became fully sovereign and judge of his own cause. As conflicts between them could no longer be decided by the high court of the Empire, a new law emerged in order to avoid annihilation between belligerents. New rules of law came into being for peacetime (law of treaty and diplomatic relations) and wartime (with a distinction between *jus ad bellum*—law on the right to wage war, with the problem of the just war—and *jus in bello*—law applicable in the conduct of hostilities). States sought to protect themselves in a society of equals. A first outline for a modern law of nations, which would later turn into international public law, began to take shape.

Internal sovereignty and the rise of ordinances. The princes also claimed complete internal sovereignty, with its two components: juridical and legislative sovereignty.

In demanding complete juridical sovereignty from the Emperor, in particular, exclusive jurisdiction to adjudicate cases, the prince argued that he was a "judge"; both justice and preservation of the public peace were his political aims and the condition of his legitimacy. His legists exhumed the powers of the Roman praetor, the highest Roman dignitary after the consuls. The praetor, they said, had two powers, *imperium* and *jurisdictio*. The *imperium* is the power to bring the accused before the court and to enforce the decision; the *jurisdictio* is the power to say what the law is. The German princes requested both powers, the *imperium mixtum*.

The sovereignty of the prince was also, and in particular, illustrated by his power of command, the power to legislate. Only with the successful claim by the princes of the power to legislate did the real *jus publicum*, modern public law, come into being. In the second half of the sixteenth century, the power to legislate came to public notice in the form of ordinances. These ordinances were more ambitious in their scope than those of the French monarchy. Drafted by theologians educated in law, including Luther himself and Philip Melanchton, they regulated all subject matters that used to be within the jurisdiction of Roman Catholic Church: marriage, family law, social behavior and redress for moral torts, school curricula, children's education, and assistance for the needy (widows, orphans, ill people, vagrants). Progressively, in the seventeenth century, the ordinances extended their reach to all domains of economic and social life of the State.

To characterize this shift in the responsibilities of power, a new word is coined: ''*policey*,''[22] a term that has a broader meaning and scope than mere public peace. The type of State that developed in Germany beginning in the sixteenth century and reaching its apex in the eighteenth went far beyond maintaining public peace and order. With the exception of criminal law and private law, secret affairs of the State, war, and ecclesiastical matters, all domestic policies of the German States in the seventeenth and eighteenth centuries belonged to the ''*policey*.'' As the term was understood at that time, the police (*policey*) was supposed, as Vattel put it, to ''preserve every thing in order.''[23] Throughout most of continental Europe, the ordinances were the legal instruments of the ''police'' or, to use more modern language, of the public policy of order. They were made to preserve order in all its possible forms, that is, in the first place, public order as public peace, and in the second place (the enumeration being not all-inclusive), economic, social, religious, and professional order. As it transformed into a true science of the State during the eighteenth century, police power eventually came to encompass everything that could contribute to enactment of the ''well-ordered police State.''

B. THE WELL-ORDERED POLICE-STATE

1. Origins and Ideological Foundations

The search for felicity. In the eighteenth century, political power in Germany began an evolution that eventually resulted in the creation of a State

[22] See Stolleis, *supra* note 2, at p. 334.

[23] E. de Vattel, *Le droit des gens ou Principes de la loi naturelle* [Translated by Joseph Chitty], 1883, Book I, chap. XIII, § 174.

model, the well-ordered Police-State,[24] the birthplace of modern public law, which conquered all Central Europe. Order and police are its two main pillars.

The ''well-ordered'' State was the ultimate goal of Jean Bodin. The expression ''Well-Ordered Commonwealth'' (*République bien ordonnée*) has pride of place in his work (*i.e.*, it is the title of the first chapter of the first book of *The Six Books of the Commonwealth*, which is entirely devoted to the definition of this new kind of State). A well-ordered Commonwealth, according to Bodin, is ''the rightly ordered government of a number of families, and of those things which are their common concern, by a sovereign power.'' In order to attain the state of perfection that is ''the rightly ordered government,'' where law that proceeds from the sovereign conforms to equity that proceeds from God, Bodin starts with the premise that ''the final end must be understood as the starting point of any subject.''[25] ''The final end''—these are the decisive words, for it is from the ''final end'' of the State that everything flows.

The ''final end'' of government for the Ancients was happiness. For Aristotle, a republic is ''a society of men gathered together for the good and happy life.'' Bodin is not satisfied with this definition and the term ''happy.'' In his opinion, this is not enough, for this does not keep the republic from being ''given over to every wickedness and abandoned to vicious habits.'' What Bodin is interested in is not happiness, but felicity. The difference between the two concepts is that felicity implies virtue, not the virtue of the Ancients, which is understood as courage or moral strength, but the virtue of Christians, which commands self-abnegation. In order to come as close as possible to the ''rightly ordered government,'' ''we must aim higher'' and attain ''the true felicity,'' that is, a situation where ''the conditions of [. . .] felicity are one and the same for the commonwealth and the individual.'' Clearly, the ''rightly ordered government'' is related to the late and obviously lamented model of the religious community of medieval Christianity, which was swept away by the Reformation, and which Bodin's theory endeavors to bring back to life. Later, Hobbes will follow in the footsteps of Bodin. In the blueprint that he outlines for a ''Christian Commonwealth'' at the end of *Leviathan*, he, too, considers ''it to be granted that the civil government be ordained as a means to bring us to a

---

[24] The historian Marc Raeff combined the two terms in his book *The Well-Ordered Police State, Social and Institutional Change through Law in the Germanies and Russia (1600-1800)*, Yale University Press, 1983.

[25] J. Bodin, *The Six Books of the Commonwealth*, [Abridged and translated by M. J. Tooley], Barnes & Noble, New York, 1967, Book I, chap. 1, available at http://www.constitution.org/bodin/bodin.htm.

spiritual felicity."[26] As these authors describe it, the ideal of the modern State is a secularized Church, so to speak. Their model of the well-ordered State that leaves nothing to chance and undertakes to regulate everything, where liberty is checked, has developed nowhere so well as in Germany and all continental Europe.

Felicity and public good. The model of the well-ordered State blossomed in the Holy Roman Empire because of the huge void left after the collapse of the structures and institutions by which the Catholic Church had organized and regulated medieval society. It was less successful in France because, on the one hand, far from collapsing onto itself, the French Church with its clergy, its properties, and its institutions that structured French society grew stronger with the principles of Gallicanism,[27] and, on the other hand, the freedom of action of the king was much narrower than that of German princes, limited as it was by the franchises, freedoms, and countless privileges of the subjects that the king swore to maintain and defend in his consecration's oath. The well-ordered police State did develop in part in France, without, however, ever reaching the strength, vigor, and force of intrusiveness that it reached in Central Europe. The well-ordered Police-State in France, if any, was manifest primarily in the system of political economy undertaken by Colbert.

Whether triumphal (as in Germany, Austria, or Russia),[28] or more modest because it was limited and constrained (as in France), one thing is sure, the well-ordered Police-State is a Police-State, and police is the means by which the State leads its people not only to happiness but even to felicity (*Glückseligkeit*). It is not enough for a subject of the prince to be happy alone; he may be happy only on the condition that everybody else is too. The prince makes sure that his subjects are happy individually and collectively. The concept of public interest is neither liberal nor republican; it is unitary. The theme of the common good remains very pervasive. The idea is to attain the good, at all cost, and to reach a situation where private and public interest would be, if possible, united; individual liberty is stifled. The Police-State tends toward taking charge of the entire society. In order to help it in this huge undertaking, a new scientific

---

[26] T. Hobbes, *Leviathan*, Part III, chap. 42, Penguin Classics, 1985, p. 601.

[27] Gallicanism is made of the principles and practice of the Gallican party, a school of French Roman Catholics of which Bossuet was the leader, which maintained the right of the French church to be in certain important matters self-governing and free from papal control.

[28] On the Police-State spreading out all over Europe, see J. Van Horn Melton, "Absolutism and 'Modernity' in Early Modern Central Europe," 8 *German Studies Review* 383 (1985).

discipline, comprising the so-called cameral sciences, emerges. Cameral sciences are a true science of the State;[29] they are the ancestor to modern administrative sciences and public management of the twentieth century.[30]

Cameral sciences. Cameral sciences are often presented as the German expression of mercantilism (the *Kamera* used to be the place where the public treasury was kept). These sciences were indeed concerned first with the good management of the State's finances.[31] However, they went beyond the merely economic.[32] Cameral sciences began to be taught at the university in the eighteenth century; the first chair was established in Halle in 1727. They were made of three disciplines: (1) economy, which, once distinguished from its domestic component, encompassed the whole society and included in its object all the territorial resources and productive activities aimed at ensuring general prosperity, with the result that it eventually led to political economy; (2) the police, strictly speaking, being itself divided into eight subdisciplines, that is, eight domains freely open to the legislative activity of the State—population, schools and universities, religious practices, labor, health, land use, security, assistance to the poor; (3) the cameralistics, the disciplines dealing with internal revenue and its optimum use in order to increase the strength of the State and the well-being of the subjects, a forerunner of the modern science of public finances.[33]

2. Developments

The ordinances of the Police-State. As the legal instrument of the Prince-State, the Police-State has not remained static but has evolved over time, as the felicity supposed to be distributed among the Subjects has been defined differently over time. Initially, the ordinances of the Police-State sought to put an end to the religious crisis born of the Reformation, and it is indeed in religious matters that they were most plentiful. Secular authorities sought to fill

---

[29] See K. Tribe, "Cameralism and the Science of Government," 56 *Journal of Modern History* 263 (1984)

[30] See J. Chevallier, *Science administrative*, 3rd ed., Paris, PUF, Collection Thémis Science politique, 2002, pp. 10-13.

[31] See Georget, "Les caméralistes allemands: du principe de réalité à la théorie codifiée," avalaible at http://www.lameta.univ-montp1.fr/PEA/ pages_composantes/ Communications/georget.pdf.

[32] On cameral sciences, see the study available at http://accfinweb.account.strath.ac.uk/ df/b2.html.

[33] See P. Napoli, *Naissance de la police moderne: Pouvoir, normes, société*, Paris, La Découverte, 2003, pp. 257-266.

the void left by the rejection of the former ecclesiastical authorities. In Protestant countries, princes legislated by ordinances to establish and organize the new Protestant churches, while, in the countries that remained faithful to Catholicism, they endeavored to put an end to the disaffection of the faithful and legislated to oblige them to attend the traditional religious services. One of the first police ordinances enacted in the Empire was a series of regulatory provisions on Sabbath observance and attendance at mass and church services, with a prohibition of superstitious beliefs and practices. After the dramatic demographic consequences of the Thirty Years War, which bled the country dry (the population dropped from seventeen to five millions inhabitants), all German States undertook policies aimed at renewing and maintaining a healthy population. Under the influence of natural law theories (Wolff), felicity tends to be equated with wealth. This transformation in political theory led to the State assuming responsibility for a new discipline—one destined to a great future—political economy.[34]

In the seventeenth century, public law is in full expansion. The prince devotes himself to ensuring that his subjects are in good health, well fed, and that agriculture produces enough surpluses to be exported in order to increase the country's wealth. Everyone's work is essential to everybody's prosperity, and the State ensures that everyone is efficacious (*i.e.*, contributing appropriately to collective welfare). Gradually, the ordinances enter the social domain. In particular, the regulation of agricultural property (the prohibition against farmers leaving their lands) and family matters (the regulation of conjugal life, filial relations, and wills and estates—sometimes to avoid a loss of wealth, sometimes to punish intemperance or idleness) are new areas of regulation. The ordinances enter the economic domain too (commerce, industries, agriculture, fiscal matters); they invade health and public hygiene (medical ordinances to avoid epidemics, town-planning and city ordinances to limit the number of insalubrious buildings and to oblige inhabitants to protect themselves against fire, and numerous regulations for the organization and the discipline of each profession); they even apply to education (regulations for mandatory school attendance) and culture.

There is no domain of civil society in which the prince may not interest himself. Everything is open to regulation by ordinance. Everyone is under the benevolent protection of the prince; his solicitude is constant. His projects for his people are often grandiose, always impressive. At the end of the eighteenth

[34] On these developments, see C. Larrère, *L'invention de l'économie au XVIIIe siècle*, PUF, Coll. Léviathan, 1992.

century, in 1794, a Prussian general code (*Allgemeines Landrecht für preussischen Staaten*) is published. The document is unprecedented; no distinction is made between private and public law; the code legislates on everything.[35] Tocqueville aptly summarizes its sprawling content: ''This law code is a real constitution, in the sense that was then attributed to that word; its purpose was not only to regulate relations among citizens but between citizens and the State: it is simultaneously a civil code, a criminal code, and a political constitution.''[36] With this document, not only does the police power enter into the law; the entire law falls under its control. Law becomes engulfed by statutes (ordinances), or, in other words, private law henceforth survives subsumed under public law. The codification of Frederic II is a forerunner of the French and German codifications of the nineteenth century, by which the State becomes the sole source of law.

The governmental structure: despotism. The government of the Police-State boils down to government by one: the entire sovereignty is in the person of the prince. Bound by no fundamental law, the prince unites in his person all powers, legislative, executive, and judicial. All provincial estates, all intermediate bodies are suppressed; nothing may stand between the prince and his subjects, not even his ministers. The justification for such a concentration of powers into one man's hands lies in the belief that he is the only one able to discern the general interest and to strive for the public good. This prejudice will later become the backbone of the so-called monarchical principle; it comes directly from Luther's ideas and from the Reformation.

In the sixteenth century, a new figure emerged in Germany, that of the *landesvater*, the sovereign as the father of his subjects (his ''children,'' as he occasionally may say), who is in charge of the common good for his State and his administration and who has no other goal than to make his people happy. This State model will reach its pinnacle with despotism, dubbed by those who benefited from it (such as Voltaire), ''enlightened despotism.''[37] The personal component of this form of government was considerably accentuated by Frederic II, who deprived his ministers of any legitimacy to govern alongside him. A minister, he said, ''will fill the public offices with his own creatures and

---

[35] See G. Birstch, ''Reform Absolutism and the Codification of the Law, The Genesis and Nature of the Prussian General Code (1794),'' in J. Brenner & E. Hellmuth (Eds.), *Rethinking Leviathan, The Eighteenth Century State in Britain and Germany*, Oxford University Press, 1999, p. 343.

[36] A. de Tocqueville, *supra* note 18, at p. 261.

[37] Enlightened despotism and the mechanics of the Police-State are well explained by F. Bluche, *Le despotisme éclairé* (1969), Hachette, Pluriel, 2000, p. 35.

try to gain power by the number of people attached to his own person; [. . .] the State does not belong to the ministers.'' The prince therefore must govern by himself. There is no other way to ensure the public interest and the well-being of the commonwealth.

As sovereigns who aspired to appear ''modern,'' Frederic II of Prussia and Joseph II of Austria introduced the theory of the social contract in the government of the Police-State, but they completely distorted its meaning. According to them, the contract between society and the monarch is permanent; both of them took pains to explain how such a contract could endure even if power fell into the hands of an incompetent or irresponsible monarch and how the subjects could be protected against the mistakes made by their prince.[38] Their theory was that the people consented once and forever that all powers should be entrusted to the monarch, including juridical power of last resort, with the consequence that every decision made by the prince under his police powers is withdrawn from any review by courts. The only domain left to the jurisdiction of the courts deals with the *fiscus*, which concerns the property of the Prince-State (*i.e.*, eminent domain). Public domain is supposed to belong to a private person distinct from the State, who is called the *fiscus*. As a result, property relations between the prince and his subjects are regarded as private law matters and may be reviewed by courts—on the condition, however, that property be directly affected.[39]

From a general viewpoint, the subjects of the prince in a myriad of domains are entirely under his will and the regulations he sees fit to adopt without any possibility of judicial review. The prince always justifies his actions by claiming it is his right—or rather, his duty—to protect his subjects from the dangers that threaten their security, well-being, and happiness. No economic or social domain is free from his exacting and bureaucratic rules.

---

[38] The contradictions of the Police-State are well explained by E. Weis, ''Enlightenment and Absolutism in the Holy Roman Empire: Thoughts on Enlightened Absolutism in Germany,'' 58 *Journal of Modern History* (1986), Supplement: Politics and Society in the Holy Roman Empire, 1500-1806, S181-S197, particularly SS192-S193.

[39] This theory has left traces in contemporary German administrative law, particularly in how the distribution of competences is organized between administrative and civil tribunals. See M. Fromont & A. Rieg, *Introduction au droit allemand*, vol. I: Les fondements, Paris, Editions Cujas, 1977 p. 19.

C. FROM THE STATE AS A PHYSICAL PERSON TO THE STATE AS A JURIDICAL PERSON

1. The Building of the *Rechtsstaat*

The crisis of the Police-State. At the end of the eighteenth century, the model of the Police-State goes through a critical phase. Not everyone is made happy by this overwhelming will to make everybody happy. The liberals require civil liberty, *libertas civilis*, which they find in natural law; they request a declaration of rights, in a first attempt to carve out a space that is free from the control of the *polizei*, which wants to regulate all the spaces of private life.

The criticism of the Police-State begins in the eighteenth century with the philosophical works of Immanuel Kant.[40] The Kantian interpretation of the relationship between the State and civil society is in complete opposition to the principles of enlightened despotism, which claims to make people happy at all costs. Happiness for Kant is an individual matter: The State must not meddle with what citizens ought to do; the role of the State is to guarantee a sphere of liberty within which everyone may pursue his own chosen ends, chosen to further his own happiness. The ultimate goal of the State is "neither the citizen's well being, nor his happiness," but "the agreement between the constitution and the principles of law."[41] Defense of and respect for the inalienable rights of man are the foundations and the ends of a legitimate political order. In the wake of Kantian ideas, W. von Humboldt develops the theme of a State whose unique function is to ensure protection for human rights.[42]

The coming into being of the Rechtsstaat. In 1798, a pamphlet authored by a certain Placidus (*alias* Wilhelm Petersen) and published in Strasburg contained a chapter entirely devoted to the liberal criticism of the *Polizeistaat*. In one of these semantic twists possible only in the German language, the book contrasts the students of the law made by the State (*Staats-Rechts-Lehrer*) with those of the State made by the law (*Rechts-Staats-Lehrer*).[43] This publication marks the first time the word *Rechtsstaat* occurs; the new term makes sense only in

---

[40] On the legacy of Kant for the *Rechtsstaat*, see J. Hummel, *Le constitutionnalisme allemand (1815-1918): le modèle allemand de la monarchie limitée*, Paris, PUF, Léviathan, 2002, p. 114.

[41] *Métaphysique des mœurs, Première partie: Doctrine du droit*, quoted by J. Hummel, *id.* at p. 115.

[42] See Wilhem von Humboldt, *The Limits of State Action* (1852) (ed. J. W. Burton), Liberty Fund, Indianapolis, 1993.

[43] See L. Heuschling, *État de droit, Rechtsstaat, Rule of Law*, Paris, Dalloz, 2002, p. 37.

contrast with its opposite. The law made by the State (*Staatsrecht*) is, of course, public law—the *jus publicum*, the law of ordinances—which limits, at discretion, the Law (with a capital L)—the law of private persons, the law of liberty and of property, in a nutshell, natural law, that is, the law of the rights of man. The *Rechtsstaat* is, therefore, a State that puts the rights of man before the law (statute) or, in other words, that makes the validity of the law (statute) dependent on its conformity with the law (rights). It is the opposite of the *Polizeistaat* in which, by contrast, the statute (under the princely form of ordinances) not only precedes the law (rights) but also negates it by determining its domain and its substance.

The constitutional expression of the Rechtsstaat. The logical end result of the new liberal ideas should have been the abolition of the Police-State, the transfer of sovereignty from the prince to the people, and the establishment of a representative democratic State.[44] This, however, does not happen, or happens only partially. The problem is that although the German nation has been in existence for centuries, it cannot affirm its sovereignty; it cannot find its political institutionalization. The idea of national representation fails to become a political reality under the form of a Reichstag that would represent the many historical estates of the German nation. Sovereignty remains prisoner of the secular form of the Prince-State, which survives, and in the legal form of the Police-State, which the liberals are at pains to overthrow. The *Rechtsstaat* does not succeed in affirming itself in its plenitude at the constitutional level. At best, the new ideas oblige the princes to make concessions and accept some limitations to their absolute power.

Between 1806 and 1850, absolute monarchy is progressively replaced by constitutional monarchy.[45] The German model of limited monarchy lasted until 1918. It is a bridge between an impossible national sovereignty and an outdated monarchical sovereignty—a two-headed eagle, so to speak. Prussia represents its most fully realized example. It is a dualist political regime in which two powers, the king and the Parliament (*Landtag*), coexist. These two powers are

---

[44] As Olivier Jouanjan explains, the very first problem in the Kantian doctrine is that of the "constitutional form" and this form can only be that of representation, insofar as only a representative system of government makes it possible to distinguish between the abstract entity of the State and the actual human being in charge of power, so that "*Rechtsstaat*" is synonymous with "representative State," "free State," "State of reason"; see his article "État de droit, forme de gouvernement et représentation," in O. Jouanjan (Ed.), *Études de droit théorique et pratique*, Presses Universitaires de Strasbourg, 1998, pp. 279-301.

[45] See Fromont & Rieg, *supra* note 39, at p. 28.

not on an equal footing, and the monarchical principle remains very strong. The king accepts limitations on his legislative power only as far as the so-called "legal" rules are concerned. Here lies the victory of the basic tenet of the *Rechtsstaat*, namely, that the State's interferences with liberty and property are legal (and legitimate) only if undertaken in pursuance of a law in the making of which citizens participate by electing representatives to Parliament. Invasions of liberty and property rights fall within a so-called "reserve of legislative power," including especially budgetary matters. The victory is modest. The *Rechtsstaat* protects the citizen with respect to his personal interests only. The prince keeps a "reserve of executive power" (*Vorbehalt*) that includes foreign affairs (war and diplomacy). His power is absolute over all political and State affairs, direction of the administrative departments and control of the civil service, organization and command of the army and defense of the State in times of emergency. He has the constitutional power to enact as ordinances all decisions that do not concern his subjects directly or that the Constitution does not forbid him to make. The prince holds onto supreme authority. True, the legislative assembly has some real powers, especially in budgetary and fiscal matters; but it cannot impose its will on the king. From a constitutional standpoint, the victory of the *Rechtsstaat* is a half-victory.

The administrative expression of the Rechtsstaat. As the *Rechtsstaat* fails to grow in the field of constitutional law, its basic ideas are sown instead in the field of administrative law, and it will come to full bloom there, especially with respect to the relations between the administration and the citizens. Here, in this precise domain, is where all efforts to cast off the Police-State have concentrated. They are crowned victorious when Prussia establishes the bourgeois Law State (*bürgerlicher Rechtsstaat*), which will reign supreme for almost half a century (1871-1918). Although it does not eliminate the monarchical principle, the backbone of the Police-State,[46] the bourgeois Law-State is a moderate Police-State that respects civil rights and accepts judicial review. It forms the half-liberal, half-authoritarian version of the bourgeois Law-State, as theorized by R. von Mohl.

Not going as far as Kant, who required only judicial enforcement of the laws by the State, Mohl believes that effective protection of rights may also require administrative enforcement. The ideology of the Police-State remains very much alive in his theory. In his opinion, judicial power is not enough; an administration endowed with police power is also required. However, this police

---

[46] See Ph. Lauvaux, "Le principe monarchique en Allemagne," in O. Beaud & P. Wachsmann (Eds.), *La science juridique française et la science juridique allemande*, Strasbourg, Presses Universitaires de Strasbourg, 1997, p. 65.

power is now reviewed by a judge, but not an ordinary judge. German States established administrative courts distinct from ordinary courts and endowed them with the authority to decide cases between the administration and citizens. These administrative courts were granted the power to set aside any regulations contrary to the laws. This power was a decisive turning point in the evolution of German public law. It represents a first step, followed by many more: a link is henceforth established between the police and the law; and the State is henceforth under the rule of law.

The problem, however, is that the Law-State does not go further; it remains frozen in a purely formal interpretation that dispenses with the problem of the ends, the crucial question of the aims of the State. In the definition given, for instance, by F. J. Stahl, the Law-State is not characterized by the aims of its actions but only by the manner in which it performs them. The sole relevance of State action is the State's method. At the end of the nineteenth century, the Law-State became an empty shell of legal dogmatism that no longer had anything in common with the liberal constitutional doctrine. It was distinguished from the Police-State only because it silenced liberty while complying with its formal legal requirements. There is no longer an interest in finding the essence of the *Rechtsstaat* in a suprapositive law made of moral values but in efficient formalism. The State is said to be under law only insofar as the validity of its actions derives from their conformity to a principle of legality; the sovereignty of the State absorbs itself in the sovereignty of positive law. The *Rechtsstaat* has become, as Otto Mayer put it, the "well ordered administrative State."[47]

2. The Transformations of the State

The theory of the State as a legal person comes into being. The unfortunate petrifaction of the great theory of the Law-State into a legal doctrine of pure administrative law is the result of all kinds of factors. These boil down to a blockage at the constitutional and political level. The German people cannot get rid of the Prince-State. To be fair, they have been refused the possibility to do so; they have been forbidden even to attempt to do so, since the Final Act of the Ministerial Conference to Complete and Consolidate the Organization of the Germanic Confederation signed at Vienna (1820), article 57, which aimed at maintaining the monarchical principle throughout the Germanic Confederation.[48] The idea then prevailing was that, although the monarch may be limited

[47] On all these points, see the excellent analysis by Hummel, *supra* note 40, at pp. 123-127

[48] Clive Parry (Ed.), *Consolidated Treaty Series*, vol. 71 (1820-1821), p. 89, especially pp. 103 and 120.

in the exercise of certain powers, he must remain the sovereign in the State. The German people were doomed to conceive of themselves as a unity only through the person of a prince—hence, the proclamation of Wilhelm I as Emperor of the II Reich in the gallery of mirrors at the palace of Versailles on January 18, 1871. The German dilemma lies in a State conceived as a physical person, which Kantorowicz called the ''personified State,''[49] that is, in this identification inherited from history between sovereignty and the person of the prince.

At the end of the nineteenth century, German legal scholarship accomplishes a feat of great magnitude. It reinvents the concept of the State as a physical person by using the theory of legal personhood, and it replaces it with the former theory. The doctrine of the legal personhood of the State was not a novelty in the nineteenth century. The legal personhood of the State was well established in the law of nations. Vattel makes reference to it at the beginning of his treatise *The Law of Nations*.[50] In the relations between States, legal (or moral) personhood makes it possible to ensure continuity in the law. Treaties, for instance, do not come to an end when the sovereign passes away. By contrast, however, inside the nation, the State whose organization was shaped by the monarchical principle was no abstraction at all; it was a physical person alive and well, so to speak. The State was the prince, and the prince was the State. German legal scholarship escaped this confinement and left the Prince-State behind, by simply inverting the traditional approach. It decided to detach the State from the person of the prince and built the theory of the legal personhood of the State accordingly.[51]

The State as a legal person of public law. The legal personhood of the State was modeled after the private law institution of legal or juristic personhood as a ''system of possibilities of wills'' (C. F. Gerber), all these wills being

---

[49] Kantorowicz, *supra* note 10, at p. 446.

[50] Speaking of ''Nations'' or ''States,'' which he defines as ''bodies politic, societies of men united together for the purpose of promoting their mutual safety and advantage by the joint effort of their combined strength,'' he adds: ''Such a society has its affairs and its interests; it deliberates and takes resolutions in common; thus becoming a moral person, who possesses an understanding and a will peculiar to itself, is susceptible of obligations and rights'' in *The Law of Nations or Principles of the Law of Nature Applied to the Conduct and Affairs of Nations and Sovereigns* (1758) [Translated by Joseph Chitty (1852)], Preliminaries, §§ 1-2.

[51] For an excellent analysis of the differences of approaches between France and Germany on this question, see F. Linditch, ''La réception de la théorie allemande de la personnalité morale de l'État dans la doctrine française,'' in Beaud & Wachsmann (Eds.), *supra* note 46, at p. 179.

attributable to a person.[52] The State has legal personhood because it has a will—or better, because it has the power to want.

The personhood of public law (based on the works of Savigny) shares with the personhood of private law a common foundation in the will.[53] But the former does not have much in common with the latter. The difference lies in the content that the will may express. Whereas the private will is always that of an individual, free to choose whatever direction he likes, the will of the State is not free; it is determined by its end. That end in turn is determined by the constitution of the State, and it is a political choice par excellence. As proof of the continuous influence of this mode of thought, note that it is precisely on the end of the State that German public law made a U-turn after World War II by designating the protection of fundamental rights as the only legitimate end of the State.

The theory of the legal personhood of the State represents tremendous progress for advancing both the liberal State and the *Rechtsstaat*. Regarding the building of a liberal State and establishing a constitutional monarchy, Olivier Jouanjan accurately notes:

> To affirm the personhood of the State, and to attribute to it sovereignty [means] to downgrade the monarch to a secondary and inferior rank, a rank of ''civil servant of the people'' or, as later said, to a rank of mere ''organ'' of the State which he may no longer possess; it also means, at the same time, to reassert the value of the elected assemblies which, even with their limited competences, must henceforth exercise the sovereignty of the State, with the rank of ''civil servant of the State,'' together with the monarch.[54]

Regarding the building of the *Rechtsstaat* and the protection of individual rights against public power, the legal personhood of the State made it possible to analyze the relation between the State and the citizen as a bilateral relation between two persons. This method was used for the first time by Carl Friedrich Gerber, the first author to imagine a notion of individual public right and to use it as the groundwork for building a new science of public law that no longer goes from the State to the individual, but rather starts from an individual

---

[52] On all these points, see O. Jouanjan, ''Carl Friedrich Gerber et la constitution d'une science du droit public allemand,'' in Beaud & Wachsmann (Eds.), *supra* note 46, at p. 11, especially pp. 53-55.

[53] On this crucial filiation, see O. Jouanjan, *Une histoire de la pensée juridique en Allemagne (1800-1918)*, Paris, PUF, Collection Léviathan, 2005.

[54] *Id.* at p. 206.

endowed with rights and builds from there a public law against power. The scientific study of administrative law is pursued in the works of Bähr, for whom the totality of public law, especially administrative law, had to be thought out using the notions and concepts of private law and civil procedure. It is finalized by Otto Mayer, who demonstrates that the Law-State can materialize only if based on the premise of subjective public rights, that is, on the premise of a legal relationship governed by public law.[55] The individual can assert himself and find efficient protection against power (whether public and private) only by the rights bestowed upon him. The notion of subjective rights is as important in public law as it is in private law. It would never have come of age without the Prince-State. The theory of public subjective rights is, indeed, one of the greatest legacies of German public law in the monarchical age.

---

[55] E. Forsthoff, *Traité de droit administratif allemand* [Translated by M. Fromont], Bruxelles, Bruylant, 1969, p. 102.

Part B
The English Monarchy

A peculiar path. The English monarchy stood apart from the evolution that led the continental monarchies toward the institutionalization of the State. The State did not develop in England under either the French approach of the State understood as the *res publica* or still less under the German concept of the personified State. The English legal system therefore has no public law, either as the law of the public interest or still less as the law of the State. There is only one law. The public interest, as a rule, does not call for special laws other than those that apply to private matters. On the rare occasions that public affairs do call for a settlement different from that applicable to private affairs, the different rules or particular institutions that fit the case are always contained in the common law and administered by ordinary courts. Under such circumstances, the words "State" and "public law," in the English language, have different meanings from those in use on the continent.

The word "State" in England is legally meaningful principally in reference to the official denomination of "United Kingdom of Great Britain and Northern Ireland." It designates a subject of law in international law, that is to say, the State, the international legal person with a will of its own, formed by the union of England, Scotland, Wales, and Northern Ireland. The United Kingdom taken as such is a State for international purposes or, to put it differently, the word "State" is legally meaningful in relation to international law only. Regarding internal affairs, there is no "State" in England, but rather a "Crown."[1] The absence of the concept of "State" in England indicates that sovereignty is not, and cannot be, approached in the same manner as on the continent. This is the reason why English lawyers, and all those who have been educated in the British legal tradition, make a distinction that continental lawyers usually do not make and may even find odd; they distinguish between "internal" and "external"

[1] M. Loughlin, "The State, the Crown and the Law," in M. Sunkin & S. Payne (Eds.), *The Nature of the Crown*, 1999, Oxford University Press, pp. 33-76.

sovereignty. The major interest in this distinction is its assertion that sovereignty must be treated differently depending on where it acts. Concretely, those who govern do not have the same powers and the same discretion; their particular powers depend on whether they conduct the external or the internal relations of the country. Internally, the government is under the law and amenable to the courts; externally, it is fully sovereign and a judge in its own cause.

The term ''public law'' in England has no specific content, as opposed to ''common law.'' It does not refer to a body of rules distinct from the latter. According to the definition given by Lord Denning in *O'Reilly* v. *Mackman*, a 1982 case that stirred great concern: ''[P]ublic law regulates the affairs of subjects vis-à-vis public authorities.''[2] In other words, the term ''public law'' as understood by the highest court of England has, first and foremost, a purely procedural content; the High Court used it to draw a line between two kinds of adjudication. Does it have the revolutionary import that some lawyers attach to it? There is no easy answer. It depends on what judges see fit to do when reviewing activities of public authorities. One thing is certain: failing a better term, the word ''public law'' was resorted to in order to oblige plaintiffs (and their counsels) to distinguish between two legal remedies, the private law remedies directed against private persons and the public law remedies used against public authorities.

As on the continent, public authorities may be sued with legal remedies that are unavailable against private persons. This enables the judge to intrude deeply in public activities and to request from public actors a behavior without equivalent in private legal matters.[3] For instance, public authorities are obliged to comply with and respect the rights provided for in the European Convention of Human Rights *vis-à-vis* the citizens. Moreover, individuals may have recourse to specific legal remedies to enforce their rights against public authorities, particularly by way of judicial review. However, it is also still possible to sue them by common law remedies and to claim compensatory damages. Under such circumstances, the House of Lords, in a show of solid

---

[2] *O'Reilly* v. *Mackman* [1983] 2 AC 237, 255.

[3] There is no principle of freedom or autonomy of will in public law. In private law, an individual may act by selfishness, by personal interest, out of spite or generosity, for capricious or reasonable motives, as long as he, of course, does not break the law in using force. In public law, this principle does not exist. A public authority may act for motives of public interest only, with due consideration for the public good and the *res publica*. The will in public law is not autonomous; this is indeed the *raison d'être* of public law. This is particularly well explained by Sir William Wade, *Administrative Law*, 9th ed., Oxford University Press, 2004, p. 355. Sir William is himself referring to G. Vedel & P. Delvolvé, *Droit administratif*, 12th ed., p. 328.

common sense, decided that allowing a plaintiff to assemble against a public authority the advantages of both a common law action (compensatory damages, for instance) and judicial review (intrusive judicial inquiry into the decision-making process of the public body) would be an abuse of the right to sue, and it decided that it would be henceforth an abuse of procedure not to submit a public law case to justice by way of judicial review whenever this is possible.

In a noted comparative legal essay, J. W. F. Allison argued that in distinguishing between private and public law remedies, the House of Lords had introduced public law like a Trojan horse into English law.[4] At any rate, it recognized that administrative law adjudication should obey special rules. At the present time, the term "public law" in England, to the extent that it has a precise definition, means administrative adjudication, not administrative law. Will this adjudication give birth to a public law in the continental sense, that is, a law of the *res publica*? It is still too soon to say.

The English exception. England never experienced public law, and British scholars today are divided as to whether it should. One thing is certain; in the eighteenth century, when the kings and princes of continental Europe were occupied with making their people happy, the British rejoiced that they did not live under the rule of continental public law, derided by their lawyers as "imperial law."[5] Nothing could be more alien to the English spirit than the well-ordered Police-State then thriving on the continent. England, of course, knew the police power necessary to the public peace and security. But it was not the well-ordered, "well-fed," continental State that promulgated happiness among the people by exacting laws. England was a land of freedom. The laws of police there had a different object than on the continent; they were aimed not at producing the happiness (even less the felicity)[6] of the people, but more modestly at providing "the due regulation and domestic order of the kingdom."[7] England was regulating, not policing, the country; its laws were more concerned with the individual than the State.

---

[4] J. W. F. Allison, *A Continental Distinction in the Common Law, A Historical and Comparative Perspective on English Public Law*, Clarendon Press, Oxford, 1996, p. 72.

[5] Sir William Blackstone, *Commentaries on the Laws of England*, Introduction, Section I, p. 5.

[6] On the distinction between happiness and felicity, see Chapter 2, Section B.1.

[7] Blackstone, *supra* note 5, Book IV, chap. 13, at p. 163:

> By the public police and economy I mean the due regulation and domestic order of the kingdom: whereby the individuals of the state, like members of a well-governed family, are bound to conform their general behaviour to the rules of propriety, good neighbourhood, and good manners; and to be decent, industrious, and inoffensive in their respective stations.

Montesquieu grasped the difference better than anyone else when, as a prelude to the few pages that laid down the foundations of modern constitutional thinking (Chapter 6, Book XI of *The Spirit of Laws*),[8] he wrote: ''One nation there is also in the world that has for the direct end of its constitution political liberty. We shall presently examine the principles on which this liberty is founded; if they are sound, liberty will appear in its highest perfection.''[9] This nation was, of course, England. Free from the intrusive police power that was reigning supreme on the continent, its citizens enjoyed political liberty, that is, ''a tranquility of mind arising from the opinion each person has of its safety.''[10]

The position of England *vis-à-vis* public law has always been exceptional. This was true in the eighteenth century, and it is still true today. England never developed a public law like that of the States in continental Europe, where the word of the sovereign, the law of the State, was separated from ordinary law and immune from any review by the courts of law. English monarchs were never strong enough to make such a State prevail or, more precisely, when they were strong enough (after the Conquest), the idea of public law was not born yet, and when the idea was born (after the Reformation), they had lost the power to make it prevail. The British monarchy has been able to perpetuate itself only by forgoing absolutism (Chapter 3) and by accepting the rule of law (Chapter 4).

---

[8] Chapter 6 of Book XI is merely entitled ''The Constitution of England''; see Montesquieu, *The Spirit of Laws* [Translated by Th. Nugent, 1752, revised by J. V. Prichard], 1748, available at http://www.constitution.org/cm/sol.htm.

[9] *Id.*, Book XI, chap. 5.

[10] *Id.*, Book XI, chap. 6.

Chapter 3
The Defeat of Absolutism

The status of the monarchy. Unlike continental monarchies, the British monarchy never fell into absolutism, still less into despotism. Historical conditions never made it possible.

In the first place, English monarchs were never able to call themselves, as the French kings did, king "by the grace of God"; the conquest of 1066 forbade it. It took a very long time for the hereditary succession to the throne to become settled law. The conqueror himself could not rely upon hereditary right; he relied rather on gift or devise. He argued that Edward had given him the kingdom.[1] The kings of England were crowned; but the coronations were not consecrations. No bishop ever said that coronation ruled out the king's deposition. The ceremony created a religious bond between the king and his people, but it did not transform him into a sacred person.

In the second place, English monarchs were never able to turn the precepts of Roman law to their own advantage. As early as the thirteenth century, under the reign of Edward I (1272-1307), the ecclesiastics, the scholars learned in Roman law in the Middle Ages, ceased to sit on the bench of royal courts. English law became more and more insular, and the judges as well as the lawyers increasingly ignorant of any other law but their own. The Roman law of the late Roman Empire, which filled continental lawyers' thoughts, remained foreign to them. English law has lost a great deal in cutting itself off from Roman law. It lacks principles: Property law, for instance, is a maze of intricate rules riddled with exceptions. It has no distinct idea of the *res publica* in which it does not believe and that it does not conceive of as being able to be anything more than a mere aggregation of private interests. But the loss was outweighed by a tremendous advantage.

[1] F. W. Maitland, *The Constitutional History of England*, Cambridge University Press, Reprint, 1955, p. 97.

English law never received the late Roman law maxims that on the continent made absolutism so successful. The king of England has never been *princeps legibus solutus* (free from complying with the laws). The rule has never succeeded in becoming firmly rooted. True, the monarch possesses a certain status *vis-à-vis* the law. For instance, early in the Middle Ages, it was commonly acknowledged that the king could not be sued by virtue of the rule that the King could do no wrong. But the king was not above the law. If he happened to cause damage, the remedy consisted in the right to petition him. In the thirteenth century, Henry de Bracton (who was a judge for twenty years under Henry III) affirmed the absolute empire of the law many times. According to his famous formula, he repeated over and over that England is ''not under the King but under God and the law.''[2] The law itself makes the king: *Ipse tamen rex non debet esse sub homine sed sub Deo et sub lege, quia lex facit regem*. As far as one goes back in time, the common law tradition has put sovereignty under law; this medieval tradition has remained immutable because the common law escaped the influence of imperial Roman law.

The status of sovereignty. According to the great historian Maitland, there were in England, at the beginning of the seventeenth century, three claimants for sovereignty:

(1) the king all alone and in majesty, as the French Jean Bodin had presented him;

(2) the king in Parliament (*i.e.*, the medieval king surrounded by his counselors of the Curia Regis), deciding with the advice and consent of those who formed with him the Parliament, namely, the discrete estates of the realm (the spiritual and temporal Lords, and the representatives of the Commons); and

(3) the law that, according to medieval scholars, was in every way above the king.[3]

The struggle between the three contenders began in the early seventeenth century with an offensive of the first against the second that was arbitrated by the third and eventually decided of the Fate of the Prerogative (Section A). It came to a close at the end of the seventeenth century with the victory of the second over both the first and the third. Indeed, it was a glorious Revolution,[4]

[2] Henry de Bracton, *Bracton De legibus et consuetudinibus Angliæ* (George E. Woodbine ed.), Yale University Press 1915-1942, vol. II, p. 33.

[3] *Id.*, pp. 297-298.

[4] The term ''glorious Revolution'' is to be found in E. Burke, *Reflections on the Revolution in France* (1790), Penguin Classics 1968, p. 86.

since a single act sufficed to make it understood that sovereignty had changed hands once and for all and was henceforth in the king in Parliament; the king could no longer govern except with the Lords and the Commons. The watershed opened the way towards a consolidation of the fundamental principle of English law, Parliamentary Sovereignty (Section B).

A. THE FATE OF THE PREROGATIVE

The offensive of absolutism. When Elizabeth I died in 1603, the crown of England fell to James I, son of Mary Stuart and king of Scotland. James I was Catholic, and he was very influenced by the ideas of Jean Bodin, whose works he had read closely. While he was king of Scotland, he wrote a book *The Trew Law of Free Monarchies*, which was a rebuttal to both the Calvinist antimonarchical views and the Catholic Church's claims regarding the supremacy of the Pope. He argued in this book that power comes from God and that disobedience to the king was as much a sacrilege as disobedience to God. Indeed, as he told Parliament in 1610, "Kings are not only God's Lieutenants upon earth, and sit upon God's throne, but even by God himself they are called Gods."[5]

During the first years of his reign, he tried to put these ideas into practice. He claimed to govern the country by virtue of his inherent powers—powers belonging to the king only—and these were usually gathered under the broad term of "prerogative." But he failed. The English people did not accept the king's eccentric claims, which were in complete opposition to the already entrenched ideas of his contemporaries. The absolutist pretensions of the Stuart dynasty to govern only by prerogative ran up against well-established institutions:

(1) The ancient idea of rights as laid down in the *Magna Carta*,[6] a famous document the free men of England forced King John II to sign when he tried to send them to France to fight to regain his lost possessions. The *Magna Carta* established the fundamental law of the English Constitution that rights exist before the king, so law precedes power. To that extent, the king of England is indeed "under law."

---

[5] See G. Burness, "The Divine Right of Kings Reconsidered," 107 *English Historical Review* 827 (1992) quoted by H. J. Berman, "The Origins of Historical Jurisprudence: Coke, Selden, Hale," 103 *Yale L. J.* 1651, 1667 (1994).

[6] See C. Stephenson & F. G. Marcham, *Sources of English Constitutional History, A Selection of Documents from A.D. 600 to the Interregnum*, vol. I, New York, Harper & Row, 1972 [hereinafter *Stephenson & Marcham*, I], p. 115

(2) The representative institutions existing at that time, in particular, a Parliament, composed of the Lords Spiritual and Temporal and the Commons, representing all the estates of the people of the realm, associated with all major religious reforms under the Tudors. Both Henry VIII and Elizabeth I had taken great care in establishing the Anglican Church with the full support of Parliament. In giving to this political body the power to establish, together with the king, the religion of the State, the Tudors did much to instill into the English mind the idea of the sovereignty of Parliament—so much so that sovereignty at that time was associated with God.

(3) The tradition of the common law established by Henry II (1154-1189) and well developed in the sixteenth century. The common law courts were the king's courts. It was only through their intermediary that the king could dispense justice, in particular, that they could decide cases dealing with the property of his subjects or with punishment of violent crimes. But it was recognized that the king had a residual power to dispense justice whenever the common law courts were inadequate.

The notion of prerogative. At the time of James I, the prerogative, a generic term like *droits régaliens* in French, designated all the various powers exercised by the king. A well-known and well-established institution, it encompassed two kinds of powers: (1) inherent powers to defend the realm against foreign enemies, and (2) residual powers that the king could exercise for the common good. The prerogative was a bundle of sticks, so to speak, a bundle of rights recognized as inherent to the royal function, such as the right to defend the realm and ensure the public peace, to put into effect the missions implied by the right to wage war, to conduct diplomacy and foreign affairs, to dispense justice, and to make the laws necessary for the conservation of the kingdom. In the seventeenth century, the lawyers made distinctions among these powers depending on their ordinary or extraordinary character.

1. The Status of the Ordinary Prerogative

The judges' moment: Sir Edward Coke. The ordinary prerogative was the royal function that the king exercised in definite forms and not at his discretion. Since Henry II, the judges had held to two tenets: first, that the king had no legislative authority without Parliament and, second, that he could not judge except through the intermediary of his judges. Sir Edward Coke, one of the greatest defenders of the common law, had to remind King James I of both principles in two cases that called into question respectively his power to make law and to give justice.

a. *The Question of Prohibitions (1607)*

In 1605, Bancroft, Archbishop of Canterbury, complained to the king about the writs of prohibitions issued by common law courts against judicial decisions made by ecclesiastical judges. As he wanted the king to put an end to this practice, he argued that the king himself may decide any cases in his royal person. The judges are but the delegates of the king, he maintained; further, the king may take cases as he wishes from the determination of the judges, to determine himself. The matter was eventually referred to the Court of Common Pleas.

The opinion of Chief Justice Coke and his colleagues was to the effect that

> the King in his own person cannot adjudge any case, either criminal, as treason, felony, etc., or between party and party, concerning his inheritance, chattels, and goods, etc., but this ought to be determined and adjudged in some Court of Justice, according to the law and custom of England [. . .]; that no King after the Conquest assumed to himself to give any judgment in any cause whatsoever, which concerned the administration of justice within his realm, but these were solely determined in the Courts of Justice [. . . .]
>
> Then the king said that he thought the law was founded upon reason, and that he and others had reason as well as the judges. To which it was answered by me that true it was that God had endowed his majesty with excellent science and great endowments of nature; but his majesty was not learned in the laws of his realm of England, and causes which concern the life or inheritance or goods or fortunes of his subjects are not to be decided by natural reason, but by the artificial reason and judgment of law—which law is an act which requires long study and experience, before that a man can attain to the cognizance of it—and that the law was the golden metwand and measure to try the causes of the subjects, and which protected his majesty in safety and peace. With which the king was greatly offended, and said that then he should be under the law—which was treason to affirm, as he said. To whom I said that Bracton said *quod rex non debet esse sub homine, sed sub Deo et lege.*[7]

b. *The* Case of Proclamations *(1611)*

In the early seventeenth century, James I wanted to prohibit by ''proclamation'' (an act very similar to the ''ordinance'' of continental Europe) the

[7] *Stephenson & Marcham*, I, *supra* note 6, at pp. 437-438.

building of new houses in London, in order to check the overgrowth of the capital, and the manufacture of starch from wheat, so as to preserve wheat as a food supply. The Commons complained of an abuse of proclamations. The opinion of Chief Justice Coke and four of his colleagues was to the effect that

> the king by his proclamation cannot create any offence which was not an offence before; for then he may alter the law of the land by his proclamation in a high point. For, if he may create an offence where none is, upon that ensues fine and imprisonment. Also the law of England is divided into three parts: common law, statute law, and custom. But the king's proclamation is none of them. . . . Also it was resolved that the king hath no prerogative but that which the law of the land allows him. But the king, for prevention of offences may by proclamation admonish his subjects that they keep the laws and do not offend them, upon punishment to be inflicted by the law.[8]

Consequences. Both cases are of fundamental importance insofar as they placed the king of England as far as possible from the king of France. The English monarch was to be neither lawgiver nor lawmaker. Sir Edward Coke gave a death blow to the idea of king as fountain of justice. The king is henceforth definitely *sub Deo et lege*. Both cases are also important as forerunners to a separation of functions (first judicial, then legislative functions are drifting away from the royal function) buttressed by a separation of organs (the royal organ is increasingly limited to the executive function, while the judicial organ and the legislative organ acquire their autonomy). The realm of England is not whole in one; one organ does not concentrate all the powers.

2. The Status of the Extraordinary Prerogative

Judicial deference and Parliament's moment. As resort to the ordinary prerogative proved to be of no avail, the king of England turned to the extraordinary or absolute prerogative that the king could exert in person at his own discretion and subject to no restrictions of a formal or legal kind. Medieval lawyers applied it to the power of dispensing with laws, of granting pardon, of granting peerage, and, more generally, the power to take all measures necessary in the time of emergency.[9] Charles I attempted to govern by invoking the extraordinary prerogative only. His pretension amounted to a claim of absolute power; for the king invoked sovereignty in its highest and strongest expression,

---

[8] *Id.*, pp. 441-442.

[9] For a general study on the law of necessity, see F. Saint-Bonnet, *L'état d'exception*, Paris, PUF, Collection Léviathan, 2001.

the power to decide in exceptional circumstances.[10] The judges (who, at that time, were still very much "his" judges, as they were nominated and dismissed at his own discretion) did not dare to stop him. This may be illustrated by three cases in which the judges respectfully deferred to the king as the sole holder of sovereignty and, thus, the exclusive authority to determine the common good for the realm. Later, their inaction was reversed by Parliament.

a. Case of Impositions (Bate's Case) *(1606)*[11]

John Bate, a merchant trading with Venice and the Levant, refused to pay an extra poundage on imported currants, which James I had imposed in addition to the statutory poundage. Bate's counsel argued that the new poundage had been imposed unjustly against a statute that prohibited indirect taxation without the consent of Parliament. The decision of the Barons of the Exchequer was unanimous for the king. They decided that the king might impose what duties he pleased, if it was only for the purpose of regulating trade and not raising revenue, and that the court could not question the king's statement that the duty was in fact imposed for the regulation of trade.

b. Darnel's or the Five Knights' Case *(1627)*[12]

In 1626, letters under the privy seal were issued assessing certain individuals for contributions to a forced loan. Sir Thomas Darnel and four other knights refused to pay, and they were sent to the Fleet prison. Darnel obtained from the king's bench a writ of *habeas corpus* directed to the warden of the Fleet to show cause for his imprisonment. The reply made by the warden stated that the prisoner was detained in his custody "by special command of his

---

[10] According to the famous definition of Carl Schmitt: "Is sovereign he who decides on the exception." In a footnote, George Schwab underlines:

> In the context of Schmitt's work, a state of exception includes any kind of severe economic or political disturbance that requires the application of extraordinary measures. Whereas an exception presupposes a constitutional order that provides guidelines on how to confront crises in order to re-establish order and stability, a state of emergency need not have an existing order as a reference point because *necessitas non habet legem.*

Carl Schmitt, *Political Theology: Four Chapters on the Concept of Sovereignty* (1934) [Translated by George Schwab], MIT Press, 1985, at p. 5, note 1. Concretely speaking, the definition must be understood as implying the power of determining both when and what the situation of emergency requires.

[11] D. L. Keir & F. H. Lawson, *Cases in Constitutional Law*, 6th ed., Oxford, Clarendon Press, 1979, pp. 74-75.

[12] *Id.*, pp. 75-76.

majesty'' (*per speciale mandatum domini regis*). Similar replies were made with respect to the other four knights.

Counsel for the prisoners argued in substance that the true meaning of a writ of *habeas corpus* was to show cause and, possibly, a valid cause for imprisonment. The court did not agree. It recognized that ''the main point in law [was] whether the substance or matter of the return be good or no,'' but said that ''if no cause of the commitment be expressed, it is to be presumed to be a matter of state, which we cannot take notice of.''

c. R. v. Hampden (The Case of Ship Money) *(1637)*[13]

In 1634, Charles I, being in need of a navy for the protection of English shipping, but unwilling to call a Parliament, issued writs commanding seaport towns to furnish ships fully manned and equipped and instructing the municipal authorities to raise money from the citizens for that purpose. A year later, writs were issued again, this time to inland counties too. John Hampden, a Buckinghamshire gentleman, having been assessed to pay the tax, refused to pay. His counsel argued that the king in time of emergency did have the right to raise taxes without the consent of his subjects but that he could do it only in time of actual and real, not simply alleged, emergency. On behalf of the Crown, it was argued that the king alone was in charge of deciding what the emergency required. The judges unanimously decided that

> when the good and safety of the kingdom in general is concerned and the whole kingdom is in danger, your majesty may, by writ under the great seal of England, command all the subjects of this your kingdom at their charge to provide and furnish such number of ships, with men, munitions, and victuals, and for such time as your majesty shall think fit, for the defense and safeguard of the kingdom from such danger and peril; and that by law your majesty may compel the doing thereof in case of refusal or refractoriness. And we are also of opinion that in such case your majesty is the sole judge both of the danger and when and how the same is to be prevented and avoided.

Action by Parliament. All three previous cases were later overruled by Parliament, which put an end to the claim of the Stuarts to govern by extraordinary prerogative only.

The power to tax without the consent of Parliament and the power to imprison without cause were declared unlawful in the *Petition of Rights* (June 7,

---

[13] *Id.*, p. 77.

1628).[14] The Petition reiterated a long-established principle in force since the *Magna Carta* and the Statute *De Tallagio non Concendendo* that the king's subjects should not be taxed but by consent in Parliament.

The struggle for supremacy between the king and Parliament continued and deepened when the king claimed the power to dispense with the laws, which amounted to a claim of the right to grant privileges and make unequal laws. The Stuarts, who remained faithful to the Catholic Church, did, however, support the Anglican Church, but they did not want to enforce the laws of exclusion applicable to those who were not Anglicans, in particular the Catholics, keeping them out of all official positions. Judges endeavored to draw a line between permissible and impermissible dispensations in *Thomas* v. *Sorrell* (1674), but in *Godden* v. *Hales* (1686),[15] a case that scandalized people, they held that the power to exempt a convict from a lawfully pronounced sentence was not severable from the prerogative of the king. The struggle ended in 1689 with the adoption of the Bill of Rights by Parliament, which solemnly affirmed that the king may not exempt his subjects from the laws and the execution of the laws, and thus implied that laws cannot be unequally applied and enforced.

B. PARLIAMENTARY SOVEREIGNTY

1. Historical Construction of the Principle

The Bill of Rights (1689).[16] Charles II died in 1685. His brother, the Duke of York, who succeeded him, undertook to bring Catholicism back to the country. He suspended the anti-Catholic laws, called back the Jesuits, and nominated Catholics in the parishes, the universities, the courts, and the army; and he enacted a declaration of indulgence—all measures taken directly against the will of a large majority of the people who were strongly opposed to this policy.

From a first marriage, James II had two daughters, both of them Protestants married to Protestant princes: Mary, married to William, Prince of Orange, stadholder (chief magistrate) of Holland, and Anne, married to the heir apparent of Denmark. In 1688, James's second wife, an Italian and a Catholic, gave birth to a son. The situation then changed completely, for it meant that the successor to James II was a Catholic child. Many Tories, nervous before a perceived papist

---

[14] *Stephenson & Marcham*, I, *supra* note 6, at pp. 450-454.

[15] C. Stephenson & F. G. Marcham, *Sources of English Constitutional History, A Selection of Documents from the Interregnum to the Present*, vol. II, New York, Harper & Row, 1972 [hereinafter *Stephenson & Marcham*, II], pp. 582-583.

[16] *Id.*, pp. 599-605.

danger, allied with the Whigs to offer the throne of England to William of Orange, son-in-law of the king, in the hope that his accession would save Protestantism in the country. William, eager to use the revenue of England at a time when he was considering waging war against France, accepted. On November 5, 1688, he landed and found no resistance; on December 11, James, surprised and frightened, fled London and dropped the great seal of England into the Thames. On December 22, he left the country and took refuge at the court of his cousin, Louis XIV, king of France.

As James had dissolved the Parliament in the preceding summer, William called an assembly that was rapidly convened. The assembly met on December 26, 1688, and it advised the prince to summon a convention of the estates of the realm, which met in January 1689. Then, the Commons resolved that King James II, having subverted the Constitution of the kingdom, had abdicated, and that the throne had thereby become vacant. After some hesitation, the Lords agreed to this resolution, and it was resolved that William and Mary should be proclaimed king and queen. On February 13, the Houses waited on William and Mary and tendered them the crown, accompanied by a Declaration of Rights. The crown was accepted. The convention passed an act declaring itself to be the Parliament of England, and it adopted the Bill of Rights, which incorporated the Declaration of Rights. This succession of events marked the Glorious Revolution that established the sovereignty of Parliament.

Content. The exact title of the Bill of Rights is "An act for declaring the rights and liberties of the subjects and settling the succession of the Crown." It begins by an enumeration of James II's misdeeds regarding the Protestant religion and the rights of the subjects, and declares all of them "utterly and directly contrary to the known laws and statutes and freedom of this realm." The act then takes notice of James II's abdication and the vacancy of the throne, and turning to William and Mary, the Lords Spiritual and Temporal and Commons, being "assembled in a full and free representative of this nation" and recalling "in the first place (as their ancestors in like case have usually done) . . . their ancient rights and liberties," decide to give the crown of England to William and Mary upon an oath from both to respect them.

> Having therefore an entire confidence that his . . . Highness, the prince of Orange . . . will still preserve them from the violation of their rights which they have here asserted, and from all other attempts upon their religion, rights and liberties, the said Lords Spiritual and Temporal and Commons assembled at Westminster do resolve that William and Mary, prince and princess of Orange, be and be declared king and queen of England.

The Bill of Rights marks a turning point in the constitutional history of England. It is indeed a true revolution insofar as it is actually the Lords Spiritual and Temporal and Commons assembled who elected the monarchy, chose their monarch and installed him on the throne upon their own conditions. The following excerpts are noteworthy insofar as they, on the one hand, discard the former royal pretensions to govern by prerogative and, on the other, assert the political liberties of a government henceforth truly constitutional, that is, subject to fixed and established rules.

> The Lords Spiritual and Temporal and Commons [. . .] declare
> —That the pretended power of suspending the laws or the execution of laws by regal authority without consent of Parliament is illegal;
> —That the pretended power of dispensing with laws or the execution of laws by regal authority, as it hath been assumed and exercised of late, is illegal;
> —That the commission for erecting the late Court of Commissioners for Ecclesiastical Causes, and all other commissions and courts of like nature, are illegal and pernicious;
> —That levying money for or to the use of the Crown by pretence of prerogative, without grant of Parliament, for longer time, or in other manner than the same is or shall be granted, is illegal [. . .]
> —That election of members of Parliament ought to be free;
> —That the freedom of speech and debates or proceedings in Parliament ought not to be impeached or questioned in any court or place out of Parliament;
> —That excessive bail ought not to be required, nor excessive fines imposed, nor cruel and unusual punishments inflicted [. . .]
> And that for redress of all grievances, and for the amending, strengthening and preserving of the laws, Parliaments ought to be held frequently.

With the Glorious Revolution, the principle is definitively established in England that the king is under the law as it is administered by the courts of justice or enacted by Parliament and that there is no law of exception even when it is a matter of doing the public good, except with the consent by Parliament. The king is henceforth bound to govern with Parliament, in most domains of governmental activities.

The Act of Settlement (1700).[17] In 1700, Parliament, anxious to settle the religious question and the succession to the throne of England, resolved in the Act of Settlement that ''the [. . .] Crown and government shall [. . .] descend to and be enjoyed by such person or persons, being Protestants.'' The problem was to rule out forever the possibility that a Catholic might inherit the Crown. The Act explicitly provided that

> all and every person and persons that then were, or afterwards should be reconciled to, or should hold communion with the see or Church of Rome, or should profess the popish religion, or marry a papist, should be excluded, and are by that act made for ever incapable to inherit, possess, or enjoy the Crown and government of this Realm.

It also provided that after the death of the king's heir (Queen Anne succeeded to William in 1702), the Crown would descend to a granddaughter of James I, Princess Sophia, Electress and Duchess Dowager of Hanover, or her son. For the second time, Parliament disposed of the Crown. The Act of Settlement still deserves notice insofar as it established for the first time the principle of the independence of the judiciary: ''[J]udges commissions be made *quamdiu se bene gesserint* [*i.e.*, during good behavior''] and their salaries ascertained and established; but upon the address of both houses of Parliament it may be lawful to remove them.''

The prerogative's final fate. At the beginning of the eighteenth century, legal sovereignty was in the hands of Parliament. The Lords and the Commons demonstrated both with the Bill of Rights and the Act of Settlement that the king held his power from them and from them alone. However, some caution is called for when ascribing political meaning to these events. The king at that time was still a powerful actor. He had not lost all the powers exercised by prerogative, and some of them were far from trifling. In particular, the king had governmental power, the power to inspire and lead governmental action. Major decisions still depended on him, and he had exclusive power to nominate as his ministers persons whose loyalties were attached to his person. The policy then undertaken was still his policy, and the ministers were still his ministers. True, Parliament exercised legal sovereignty; however, political sovereignty was still in the hands of the monarch.

The decisive fact is that he lost this power progressively; it migrated, so to speak, to Parliament through a political process that lasted the entire eighteenth century, during the course of which governmental power fell into the hands of a small governmental team, legally nominated by the king, but, politically, chosen

---

[17] *Id.*, pp. 610-612.

by Parliament, to which it was responsible and by which it could be overthrown.[18] The development of responsible government together with the establishment of constitutional monarchy marked a second phase in the history of the prerogative. The principle was eventually established that the prerogative could be exercised only on the advice and consent of a cabinet of ministers responsible before Parliament. Parliament became the central institution of English public law. Its legal ascension, patiently achieved step by step from the Middle Ages, received a political endorsement.

2. Political and Social Conditions

The end result of a secular historical process. From the outset, the conqueror had to exercise his powers in a feudal environment, which was prone to subject him to limitations on his personal power. The king was able to rule only by paying respect to feudal traditions, chief among these that, in solemn circumstances, he had to govern surrounded by his vassals, who formed around him an institution very similar to the Curia Regis of the first Capetians. These meetings usually convened to decide important issues.

In the twelfth century, even before the granting of *Magna Carta*, it became established custom that, before deciding certain issues or making important decisions, the king had to put them on the agenda of a *concilium* (*i.e.*, a council made of the prelates and most important vassals of the Crown). Apparently, the king followed this course of action in order to fend off encroachments by the clergy on secular power. He sought to strengthen the authority attached to his acts by associating the most important Lords of his realm with their making. The practice soon became a principle of English law and, under Henry II, Glanville made it a theory. Besides the initial name of *concilium*, the assemblies surrounding the king were also subsequently called "Assizes" (such as the Assizes of Clarendon in 1164, during the course of which Henry II succeeded in obtaining a limitation of ecclesiastical courts' jurisdiction) or "Parliament," a name that eventually stayed with them.

In the thirteenth century, the practice gained in depth and precision. There existed henceforth two *concilium* bodies. The *Magnum Councilium*, the parliament of prelates and barons, functioned as a court of law and as a legislative advisory body. The *Commune Councilium*, which was supposed to include those who held tenures directly from the Crown, as well as prelates and barons, and had to be convened whenever the Crown wants to raise any kind of financial contribution. This assembly does not seem to have functioned properly.

---

[18] See D. Baranger, *Parlementarisme des origines*, PUF, Coll. Léviathan, 1999.

Everything changed, however, in 1254 when the knights representing the shires were summoned to parliament and sat next to the prelates and barons; it was a turning point because the shire, as Esmein put it, formed "an organic body and, to some extent, an independent collectivity which had long been used to elect representatives to fulfill various local functions."[19] In 1261 and 1265, delegates from the privileged cities and boroughs were added to these knights. The practice was repeated and, in 1295, Edward I summoned a parliament that remained a model for all future parliaments. The whole nation was represented in the estates that formed the realm: first, the archbishops and bishops with the heads of their chapters, one proctor for the clergy of each cathedral and two for the clergy of each diocese; second, every sheriff was to cause two knights of each shire, two citizens of each city and two burgesses of each borough to be elected; and, finally, seven earls and forty-one barons were summoned by name. At the end of the thirteenth century, the representative assembly of the nation ceased to be a feudal court; it transformed itself into a true parliament, and the king began to reign in Parliament.

Formation of the body politic of "King in Parliament." The decisive element is that the king regularly summoned parliaments made after the model of 1295. These made the precedents that contributed to establish the firm belief, then the customary rule, that the sovereign power in England was exercised by a body politic made up of the king surrounded by Parliament. The importance of these parliaments kept growing; originally summoned to give the king "aid and assistance," they were also called to give their consent to the statutes; moreover, they made a clever use of two of their most important rights—the right to consent to taxation (reinforced with Edward I' Confirmation of the Charters which clearly embodied the issue of parliamentary control of taxation),[20] and the right of petition, which enabled them to put forward bills.

By the end of the Middle Ages, the principle is firmly established that the king may not govern in an absolute manner. On the one hand, he is under the law, as Bracton had put it with force in the thirteenth century;[21] on the other hand, he governs "with" and "in" Parliament, so that the Roman law maxim

---

[19] A. Esmein, *Eléments de droit constitutionnel français et comparé*, 1914, Réédition 2001 Éditions Panthéon Assas, p. 76. See also W. Stubbs, *The Constitutional History of England*, vol. II, Hein Reprint, 1987, pp. 214-36, no. 202-215.

[20] See *Stephenson & Marcham*, I, *supra* note 6, at pp. 164-165. The Confirmation embodies the first article of what used to be called the Statute *De Tallagio non Concedendo* but that seems rather to have been a petition drawn up by the parliamentary opposition during the crisis of 1297.

[21] See the introductory material to this chapter.

quod principi placuit legis habet vigorem (what pleases the prince has the force of law) finds no place in England, as opposed to France where, due to the tragedy of the Hundred Years War, it became common practice. As Fortescue explains in a book written in 1496, *De Laudibus Legum Angliae*, a work that was instrumental in establishing the superiority of English monarchical institutions:

> For the King of England is not able to change the laws of his kingdom at pleasure, for he rules his people with a government not only royal but also political. If he were to rule over them with a power only royal, he would be able to change the laws of the realm, and also impose on them tallages and other burdens without consulting them; this is the sort of dominion which the civil laws indicate when they state "What pleased the prince has the force of law."[22]

The distinction between the royal government (*dominium regale*) and the royal and political government (*dominium politicum et regale*) is based on the manner power is exercised. The monarch of the royal government rules with laws at his pleasure, laws that he makes alone or in restricted council and that he imposes upon his subjects at his own will without their consent. By contrast, the monarch of the royal and political government cannot rule over his subjects with laws they did not consent to; he governs surrounded by representative institutions of the estates of his kingdom (nobility, clergy, and commons), and he cannot tax his people at will without their consent.

The "English miracle" and the excellence of the mixed government. At the end of the Middle Ages, the institution of Parliament is firmly established in England; the gap between England and the continent is about to widen. All continental monarchies at the time had similar representative institutions (representative assemblies of estates surrounded European monarchs everywhere). However, whereas on the continent, due to the Reformation, these institutions entered into a crisis that eventually ended in absolutism,[23] in England, the same institutions emerged from the crisis stronger and more fully consolidated. In complete opposition to what happened on the continent, the parliamentary institution in England came through the turmoil reinforced. The crisis triggered by the claim of the Stuarts to govern by prerogative even accentuated the institutionalization of Parliament as the central piece of the

---

[22] Sir John Fortescue, *On the Laws and Governance of England* (Shelley Lockwood Ed.), Cambridge University Press, 1997, p. 17.

[23] See H. G. Koenigsberger, "Monarchies and Parliaments in Early Modern Europe: *Dominium Regale et Dominium Politicum et Regale,*" 5 *Theory and Society* 191 (1978).

British government. The end result of all this is that, in the eighteenth century, England was regarded all over Europe as having accomplished a miracle. It had a moderate government that bore no comparison with the well-ordered Police-States of the continent; the English monarch had limited powers and governed his kingdom with due respect for the rights of his subjects. It did not take long before England was represented as having succeeded in realizing the impossible dream of ''mixed government,'' which the Ancients held to be the best possible government.

According to the Ancients, mixed government came closest to excellence because in mixing and blending the features of the three possible forms of government (democracy, aristocracy, and monarchy), it partook of the advantages of each. It has concern for the public good, the common good that is the end of democracy; it has the wisdom that pervades the aristocratic government led by the best of men; and it has the might of the monarchy. The problem was that experience had proved that this exemplary government could never be lasting or secure; sooner or later, it fell into one of the three forms of government it was made of, and it lost the advantages of the two others.

In a work that exercised an overwhelming influence on political theory at the end of the eighteenth century, Blackstone wrote: ''Happily for us of this island, the British constitution has long remained [. . .] a standing exception to the truth of this observation.'' In England, he explains, legislative power (the sovereign power par excellence since Bodin, and the most dangerous for liberty)

> is entrusted to three distinct powers, entirely independent of each other; first, the king; secondly, the lords spiritual and temporal, which is an aristocratic assembly of persons selected for their piety, their birth, their wisdom, their valor, or their property; and thirdly, the house of commons, freely chosen by the people from among themselves, which makes it a kind of democracy; as this aggregate body, actuated by different springs, and attentive to different interests, composes the British parliament, and has the supreme disposal of every thing; there can no inconvenience be attempted by either of the three branches, but will be withstood by one of the other two; each branch being armed with a negative power, sufficient to repel any innovation which it shall think inexpedient or dangerous.[24]

---

[24] W. Blackstone, *Commentaries on the Laws of England, A Facsimile of the First Edition of 1765-1769,* Chicago & London, University of Chicago Press, 1979, Vol. I, pp. 50-51, 4 volumes, available at http://www.constitution.org/tb/tb=0000.htm (edited by St. George Tucker).

The conditions of the miracle: The society in estates or orders. Blackstone proudly emphasized the perfect balance of power that existed in England, and he concluded: ''Here [. . .] is lodged the sovereignty of the British constitution; and lodged as beneficially as is possible for society. For in no other shape could we be so certain of finding the three great qualities of government [*i.e.*, wisdom, care for the public good and strength] so well and so happily united.'' In other words, the Constitution of England was the guarantor of the common good for all.

What Blackstone did not say, which will be understood much later, is that the miracle was made possible only because the political constitution of the kingdom mirrored its social constitution—a legacy of the feudal times. Only the division of the society into estates, three social classes having specific political powers, and their representation as such in the government (the Lords temporal for the nobility, the Lords spiritual for the clergy, the Commons for the bourgeoisie) made the balance of powers workable. The ''mixed government'' was the best government in the monarchical age because it was the most effective to limit sovereignty; it was possible only because it drew the resources of its existence from the inequalities and hierarchies of the social fabric.

The origins of the miracle: the theory of the king's two bodies. The path taken by England to accomplish the miracle of its moderate (or constitutional) monarchy has remained mysterious for a long time. Historiography in the twentieth century brought decisive clarifications.

A distinction universally made in the Middle Ages attributed two bodies to the king, a physical body and a political body, the first being mortal, the second immortal. The institution of the king's two bodies ensured the continuity of the State. The remarkable exception represented by the English monarchy in European history is tied to the fact that it has been the only one in which the king's two bodies succeeded in being actually separate and distinct. They became two discrete entities because they took shape in two different realities. The physical body of the king and his political body correspond to the distinction between the king and the king in Parliament. At the Reformation, the manner in which Henry VIII addresses his Parliament, ''in the time of Parliament, [. . .] we as head and you as members are conjoined and knit together into one body politic,'' bears witness that the institution has already reached maturity.[25] The ''King in Parliament'' forms a unity; it is a ''body politic.''

[25] Letter and Papers of Henry VIII, vol. xvii, pp. iv, 107 quoted by A. F. Pollard, *The Evolution of Parliament*, London; New York, Longmans, Green, 1920, p. 231.

As the historian Kantorowicz explained, England alone developed a consistent political, or legal, theory of the "King's two bodies" from factors historically given to all European nations and therefore common to all. Some of them harbored in their constitutional thought very similar ideas; but they took completely different forms. France, Kantorowicz says, although well aware of the dual expression of the immortal dignity of the monarchy and the mortal feature of the individual monarch ("The King is dead, Long live the King!"), came out with an interpretation of absolute monarchy so extreme that all distinctions between personal and suprapersonal components of the king's dignity became blurred and eventually disappeared.[26] He adds that "in Germany, where constitutional conditions were most unclear and complicated anyhow, it finally was the personified State which engulfed the romano-canonical concept of Dignity, and it was the abstract State with which a German prince had to accommodate himself."[27]

The historian underlines that it is impossible to separate the notion of the king's two bodies from the early development and pervasive influence of Parliament in English political thought and institutions. Parliament was by representation a lively body politic of the realm, a very actual and real representative element (*corpus repraesentans*) in the kingdom. Therefore, in England, the term "body politic of the kingdom" had concrete meaning and palpable content, the effect of which was to make recourse to abstract concepts (such as "State") to convey the idea of the "*res publica*" useless, since it was present and represented in Parliament. In the sixteenth century, because of the turmoil caused by Reformation, England entered a brief period when it came close to adopting the same path that carried most European nations toward absolute power. This happened when, in the year 1539, the Act 31 Henry VIII., c. 8 formally empowered the Crown to legislate by means of proclamations. This enactment was an apex in the authority reached by the Crown. Had this path been pursued, it might have led England towards the same developments as in continental Europe. But it did not take hold in English law; it did not find therein any favorable ground to grow, and the Act was repealed only ten years after its adoption, in the reign of Edward VI. The Tudor century, exemplified by the long reign of Elizabeth I, was made up of authoritarian monarchs, but they always took great care to govern "in Parliament," that is, surrounded and advised by the Lords and the Commons on every sensitive question of the time, particularly religious matters.

---

[26] See Chapter 1, Section A.2.

[27] E. H. Kantorowicz, *The King's Two Bodies, A Study in Medieval Theology*, Princeton University Press, 1981, p. 446.

3. The Theory of Albert V. Dicey

Parliamentary sovereignty comes out of age. At the end of the nineteenth century, a professor of law at Oxford, Albert V. Dicey, looking for an apt formula to capture the historical evolution of the eighteenth century that made Parliament in Westminster the heart of English political institutions proposed the expression "Parliamentary Sovereignty."[28] The term outlived its author and refers today to the very first principle of English public law.[29] According to Dicey's definition:

> The principle of Parliamentary sovereignty means neither more nor less than this, namely, that Parliament [. . .] defined [as the King, the House of Lords, and the House of Commons; these three bodies acting together] has, under the English constitution, the right to make or unmake any law whatever; and, further, that no person or body is recognized by the law of England as having a right to override or set aside the legislation of Parliament.[30]

Inherent sovereignty. As theorized by Dicey, parliamentary sovereignty is a merely legal concept. It neither derives from nor depends on underlying popular consent. Parliament in England is inherently sovereign, in its own right, not because it represents the sovereign (*i.e.*, the people). Parliament is the sovereign by itself; it is not the representative of the sovereign. It does not hold its sovereign powers from the people, but from itself, and this is precisely why, being inherently sovereign, Parliament cannot be in any legal sense a trustee for the electors. Courts are therefore powerless to relate statutes adopted by Parliament to the will of the electors and *a fortiori* to invalidate them for having betrayed an alleged duty to respect the will of the people.[31] If that duty exists, it is political, not legal.

Courts take cognizance of the will of the electors only insofar as it is laid down in a statute adopted by Parliament. To that extent, the following words by Dicey are still true: "The judges know nothing about any will of the people

---

[28] A. V. Dicey, *An Introduction to the Study of the Law of the Constitution,* with an introduction by E. C. S. Wade, 10th ed., London, The McMillan Press Ltd., 1959, p. 39, available at http://www.constitution.org/cmt/adv/law=con.htm.

[29] Today, some authors prefer the expression "Parliamentary supremacy" on the ground that "it is less likely to be confused with the notion of national sovereignty; and to avoid supporting the jurisprudential doctrine of John Austin and his successors that in every legal system, there must be a sovereign," A. W. Bradley & K. D. Ewing, *Constitutional and Administrative Law*, 13th ed., Harlow, Pearson Education, 2003, p. 53.

[30] Dicey, *supra* note 28, at pp. 39-40.

[31] *Id.*, p. 75.

except in so far as that will is expressed by an Act of Parliament, and would never suffer the validity of a statute to be questioned on the ground of its having been passed or being kept alive in opposition to the wishes of the electors.''[32] For Dicey, the sole legal right under the English constitution is to elect members of Parliament. Electors have no legal means of initiating, of sanctioning, or of repealing an act of Parliament. No court will consider for a moment the argument that a law is invalid for being opposed to the opinion of the electorate; their opinion can be legally expressed through Parliament, and through Parliament alone.[33]

As a legal concept, the word ''sovereignty'' means nothing but the legislative power of Parliament, freed from any legal constraint. If there is no answer to the question why Parliament is sovereign (except this one, purely circular: Parliament is sovereign because it is sovereign), there is an answer to the question of how Parliament became and remains sovereign. Parliament became sovereign because courts said it was sovereign. As Denis Baranger put it, ''Parliament is legally sovereign only by judicial approval.''[34] Here lies one of the most difficult points for a continental lawyer to understand when studying the English Constitution, namely, that, failing a written constitution—and thus, failing a constituent power (*pouvoir constituant*)[35] —the courts themselves wrote the Constitution of England. The upshot is that parliamentary sovereignty is the consequence, not the cause, of the rule of law, or, as Dicey himself put it, ''our constitution, in short, is a judge-made constitution, and it bears on its face all the features, good or bad, of judge-made law.''[36]

Legal sovereignty and political sovereignty. British scholars agree these days in assigning the sovereignty of Parliament a basis other than its own right to exercise sovereignty. The shift in the foundations of parliamentary sovereignty was made gradually, step by step, in line with the British legal tradition, which knows no revolution but evolution. Everything was settled on the evolution of the franchise. Before 1832, the right to vote in legislative elections was based upon ownership of property; it was bestowed on only 5 percent of the active population. The Representation of the People Act 1832 (''the Reform Act'') extended the franchise by means of property qualifications

---

[32] *Id.*, p. 74.

[33] *Id.*, p. 59.

[34] D. Baranger, ''Angleterre (Culture juridique),'' *DCJ*, p. 58.

[35] On this concept, see the introductory paragraphs of Chapter 8. In French constitutional theory, the ''constituent power'' is the author of the Constitution; it is the sovereign power par excellence.

[36] Dicey, *supra* note 28, at p. 196.

from the landed gentry and borough caucuses to the middle classes. This electoral reform triggered a series of consequences that reverberated throughout the whole century. The Commons became the predominant element in the government of the country. In 1910, however, the right to vote was still limited to 28 percent of the population. In 1918, significant changes occurred, with the decision to substitute residency for ownership as the legal basis of the right to vote and to give the vote to women. but only at the age of thirty. In 1928, thanks to the suffragettes' tenacity, the right to vote for women at the age of twenty-one paved the way for the generalization of the franchise.

The successive electoral reforms made representative democracy a bedrock principle of the constitutional government of England. They drastically changed the context of Parliamentary sovereignty and turned this legal doctrine into the vehicle that eventually led England to modern democracy. That evolution had been foreseen by Dicey. Nowadays, the legal sovereignty of Parliament is based on the fact that the composition of Parliament is decided by the electoral body in which, ultimately, political sovereignty resides. The legal sovereignty of Parliament is therefore subordinated to the political sovereignty of the nation, which finds its political expression in parliamentary government.

Parliamentary sovereignty and responsible government. The history of the conquest of sovereignty by Parliament throughout the seventeenth century demonstrates that the long struggle of Parliament against the Crown was aimed at obliging the king to take into account the wishes of his subjects in governing. Parliamentary sovereignty did not come of age in one day, like the French national sovereignty—a thunderbolt in the blue sky of an age-old public law. It grew slowly, patiently, in an evolutionary manner, which, according to Dicey, made it possible to reduce and eventually to eliminate "the existence of such a divergence, or (in other words) of a difference between the permanent wishes of the sovereign, or rather of the King who then constituted a predominant part of the sovereign power, and the permanent wishes of the nation."[37] The decisive step was taken in 1689, when Parliament placed monarchs of its own choosing on the throne of England. But the evolution kept on. Parliamentary sovereignty matured; it became more complete at the political level with the gradual coming into being of responsible government before Parliament.

The political responsibility of the king's ministers before Parliament, with the power of the latter to force the former to resign, put the final touch on the transformation of monarchical government into parliamentary government and turned the nature of the Cabinet upside down. The government became

---

[37] *Id.*, p. 83.

accountable for its policy before Parliament instead of the king. Once Parliament held over the government the threat of being overthrown, the government had no option but to govern in accordance with the wishes of Parliament. The 1832 electoral reform that enlarged the franchise accelerated the evolution. Political sovereignty passed to the people, represented in the Commons, which eventually became the final authority.

Nowadays, the Cabinet, the prime minister, and the ministers are chosen by Parliament, and no longer by the king, even if, legally speaking, it is still the king (or the queen) who appoints them. The upshot, as Dicey said, is that "the divergence between the wishes of the sovereign [. . .] and the wishes of the nation,"—a divergence that at the end of the seventeenth century could have real substance, since the ministers were the king's men—is nonexistent today, since the ministers are Parliament's men. From a political standpoint, the analysis by Walter Bagehot adds to, and confirms that by Dicey: the Cabinet illustrates "the close union, the nearly complete fusion"[38] and no longer, as in the eighteenth century, the separation of the executive and legislative powers. The fusion of executive and legislative powers is the key to understanding the secret of British institutions, namely the efficiency of its government, so much admired abroad at the end of the nineteenth century. As a connecting link between the legislative and executive powers, the Cabinet is the linchpin of the English government. It is the political engine that puts the whole system into motion and makes it possible to portray the British system of government as efficacious and efficient as a modern government. And Bagehot may rightfully conclude that the inherent coherence of the parliamentary system is monist; it is "framed on the principle of choosing a single sovereign authority, and making it good."[39]

Parliamentary sovereignty and the parliamentary system complement one another and work for the common good by putting at the helm State's men who, because of their dependence on Parliament, are naturally inclined to tailor their policies according to the preferences of the nation. The divergence that could exist formerly between the wishes of the sovereign and the wishes of the nation blur and eventually completely disappear when the system of government is truly representative. According to Dicey, when the Parliament is truly and fully representative of the people, the wishes of its representative portion can hardly in the long run differ from the wishes of the English people, or at any rate of the

---

[38] W. Bagehot, *The English Constitution*, 1867, Oxford World's Classics, Reed. 2001, p. 11.

[39] *Id.*, p. 160.

electors. He added: "that which the majority of the House of Commons command, the majority of the English people usually desire."[40]

Parliamentary sovereignty and public interest. The weak point in the theory of parliamentary sovereignty is that it does not explain how the sovereign statute to which it contributes, once adopted, is the one most fitted to the public interest. Indeed, concern for the public interest is not even part of the analysis. Dicey pays no attention at all to the question of whether the statute is good or bad; for his purposes, there is no need to ask whether the results of representative government (*i.e.*, the laws actually adopted and enacted) are good or bad. All that seems of interest to Dicey is what he regards as the key feature of true representative government, that is, its ability to produce a perfect match between the wishes of the sovereign and these of his subjects.[41]

The statute is a command, because it is the will of the sovereign. The will of the sovereign does not differ from that of the subjects or, rather, from the will of a majority of subjects. In his Commentaries, Blackstone had noted that the excellence of the British constitution was to be found in the composition of Parliament, "this aggregate body, actuated by different springs, and attentive to different interests."[42] The quality of its composition was a guarantee that its acts would always conform to the public interest. Parliamentary sovereignty favors government by opinion; the public interest in the end is what the public opinion, or at least a majority of it, wants. There is no concern, still less an obsession, with ensuring that the statute conforms to the public interest.

Parliamentary sovereignty and public good. From an historical standpoint, concern for the public good was originally contained in the royal prerogative, which eventually was absorbed by Parliament and which came under its control. In the time of the Stuarts, Sir Francis Bacon claimed that the Crown possessed under the name of the "prerogative" a reserve, so to speak, of wide and indefinite rights and powers, and that this proposition was superior to the ordinary law of the land.[43] In the same vein, Locke believed that

> Prerogative being nothing, but a Power in the hands of the Prince to provide for the publick good [*sic*], in such Cases, which depending upon unforeseen and uncertain Occurrences, certain and unalterable Laws could not safely direct, whatsoever shall be done manifestly for

---

40 Dicey, *supra* note 28, at p. 83.

41 *Id.*, pp. 83-84.

42 Blackstone, *supra* note 24, pp. 50-51.

43 See Dicey, *supra* note 28, at p. 63.

> the good of the People, and the establishing the Government upon its true Foundations, is, and always will be just Prerogative.[44]

These views did not prevail. If one lesson may be drawn from the contrasted evolution between the decline of royal authority and the rise of parliamentary power in the eighteenth century, it is this: The executive must obtain authorization from Parliament to carry out the public good. The principle of the rule of law preempts any governmental initiative to that end, no matter how well-intentioned that initiative may be. As Dicey recognized himself, "the rigidity of the law constantly hampers (and sometimes with great injury to the public) the action of the executive."[45] From a secular and rigid case law built over the years, it is plainly clear that the government cannot evade the obligation to obtain from Parliament, under statutory form, the discretionary authority to provide for the public good—an authority that is denied the Crown by the law of the land. In addition, while Parliament never faced any obstacle or limit that might have prevented its shaping and regulation of the use of the prerogative, it never itself claimed to exercise the powers attached to it.

At a more general level, the prerogative was brought under the control of the common law, and thus Parliament (the latter having the power to modify the former at will), with the result that Parliament alone may vest the government with the necessary powers to carry out its ends. Nowadays, the prerogative is viewed as belonging to the common law, with the consequence that the idea of a public good in the continental sense may barely take shape in England. The realization of the public good—this common good that was formerly contained in the prerogative—is subject to parliamentary authorization and under the control of the common law, which is principally interested in the protection of individual interests.

Limitations on the sovereign power of Parliament. The houses of Parliament extracted from royal authority just the amount of power needed to make lasting the correspondence dear to Dicey between the wishes of the subject and the wishes of the sovereign, without paying any attention to what sovereignty may imply in terms of the public good, common utility and justice for all. Parliamentary sovereignty postulates the conformity of statutes to the public good because, on the one hand, it derives from and is implied by a truly representative government, and, on the other, the public good, if it exists, "is in

---

44 J. Locke, *Two Treatises of Government, Second Treatise*, Cambridge University Press, 1988, p. 373.

45 Dicey, *supra* note 28, at p. 411.

nothing more essentially interested, than in the protection of every individual's private rights, as modeled by the municipal law.''[46]

Should this conformity not materialize, or in other words, should Parliament ignore the necessity to legislate for the protection of individual rights only, Dicey considers that representative government is a self-contained system that embodies regulatory devices aimed in the long run at inducing the government to legislate in conformity with the public good. According to Dicey, the sovereign power of Parliament is bounded or controlled by two limitations. One is an external limitation; the other is internal.[47]

The *external limit* to the real power of a sovereign is to be found in resistance to oppression or civil disobedience. This limit exists everywhere, even under the most despotic rulers, such as a Russian czar. Pointing to Louis XIV, Dicey argues that, even though the French king at the height of his power might have repealed the Edict of Nantes, he would have found it impossible to establish the supremacy of Protestantism. He also points to the French National Assembly, a majority of which in 1871 would have accepted the restoration of the monarchy, but was not prepared to restore the white flag. The French army could have acquiesced in the return of the Bourbons, but it would not have tolerated the sight of such an antirevolutionary symbol: ''the chassepots would go off of themselves.''[48] What is true of the power of an absolute monarchy is also true of the authority of a constituent assembly. Dicey here agrees with Hume, who argued that governments have no other support but public opinion.[49]

The *internal limit* to the power of a sovereign arises from the nature of sovereign power itself. Even an absolute monarch such as Louis XIV exercises his powers in accordance with his character, which is itself molded by the circumstances, the moral feelings, and the social ethics of his time. The French king might have imposed Protestantism on his subjects; but to imagine Louis XIV wishing to carry out such a reform is to imagine him to have been a being quite unlike the ''Grand Monarque.''[50] From a different perspective, Dicey, in quoting an excerpt from Leslie Stephen's *Science of Ethics*, suggests hypothetically that a legislature decided that all blue-eyed babies should be murdered. Under such a law, the preservation of blue-eyed babies would be illegal; ''but

---

[46] Blackstone, *supra* note 24, at p. 135.

[47] Dicey, *supra* note 28, at pp. 76-81.

[48] *Id.*, p. 79.

[49] *Id.*, p. 77.

[50] *Id.*, p. 80.

legislators must go mad before they could pass such a law, and subjects be idiotic before they could submit to it.''[51]

The upshot of these arguments is that parliamentary sovereignty is not to be feared. And it is even less to be feared under a representative government, which naturally works at reducing the distance that may exist between the wishes of the sovereign and the wishes of the nation. When Parliament is truly representative of the people, there cannot be a meaningful difference between internal and external limits to the exercise of sovereign power, or if there is one, it is bound to disappear.[52] The wishes of the parliamentary majority cannot in the long run diverge from the wishes of the English people or, at least, from the electors' wishes. Bills adopted by a majority in the House of Commons mirror the wishes of the majority of English people. Such is the effectuation of representative government, namely, to close any possible gap between the wishes of the sovereign and the wishes of the subjects. From the moment there is a coincidence between the two, Parliament cannot be dangerous for the liberties and, accordingly, it works constantly for the public interest.

Conclusion. Public law in England has been driven by very different forces than on the continent. Its principle of legitimacy is, in the first place, to put government under the law, not to ensure the happiness of the subjects by carrying out the public good. Of course, it is always hoped that government will act for the public good, but it is not postulated. The end of government is not to bring about happiness for all but to give to everyone the means to achieve his or her own happiness. There is no need for public law to do this. This is the reason why all countries sharing the legacy of the British heritage have no public law and no State, in the sense that these terms are understood on the European continent. However, in order to ensure that every one may achieve his or her happiness, it is absolutely crucial to put government under the rule of law.

---

51 *Id.*, p. 81.
52 *Id.*, p. 83.

Chapter 4
The Rule of Law

The spirit of the lawyer. The term ''rule of law'' was coined by Dicey in the same work in which he elaborated the theory of Parliamentary sovereignty.[1] It is not easy to translate into foreign languages such as French or German inasmuch as it does not refer to a clearly identified legal institution such as the ''hierarchy of norms'' in the French ''*État de droit*'' or the German ''*Rechtsstaat.*''[2] Rather, the rule of law is a trait of British civilization, what Tocqueville would call, a ''habit of the heart'' of the British people.

In his *Notes de voyage* (1836), on which Dicey heavily relied to explain his new terminology, Tocqueville noticed that a salient trait of the English people was ''their love of justice'' and ''the place taken by the courts of law in public opinion, next to the political wheels.'' The Frenchman who had experienced with his family the anguish of waiting in a cell during the Terror, expecting to be called at any moment before the Revolutionary Tribunal, added that ''no nation can be free'' without ''the same deep respect for the *law*, the same love for the *legality*, the same loathing for the use of *force*, [. . .] which so vividly call the attention of the foreigner in England.''[3] One year before, in 1835, he had noted the same trait as a distinctive feature of *Democracy in America*. He then called it ''the spirit of the lawyer'' (*l'esprit légiste*).[4] Those who share the same spirit and abide by the rule of law, he said, ''have drawn from their work the habits of

[1] A. V. Dicey, *An Introduction to the Study of the Law of the Constitution*, with an introduction by E. C. S. Wade, 10th ed., London, The McMillan Press Ltd., 1959, Part II 'The Rule of Law,' pp. 181-414, especially Chapter IV: 'The Rule of Law: Its Nature and General Applications,'' pp. 183-205, available at http://www.constitution.org/cmt/avd/law_con.htm.

[2] See L. Heuschling, *État de droit, Rechtsstaat, Rule of Law*, Paris, Dalloz, Nouvelle bibliothèque des thèses, 2002.

[3] A. de Tocqueville, *Voyage en Suisse*, in *Œuvres*, vol. I, Gallimard, Bibliothèque de la Pléiade, 1991, p. 619 (emphasis in original).

[4] A. de Tocqueville, *Democracy in America*, [Translated by H. C. Mansfield & D. Winthrop], University of Chicago Press, 2000, I, II, 8, p. 251.

order, a certain taste for forms, a sort of instinctive love for the regular sequence of ideas, which naturally render them strongly opposed to the revolutionary spirit and unreflective passions of democracy.''[5]

Its institutionalization in the judiciary. From Tocqueville's reflections, it appears, in the first place, that the rule of law is possible only through the agency of courts of law. This trait of British legal culture that England bequeathed to all common law countries cannot take shape unless independent courts and tribunals act as intermediaries. The rule of law means supremacy of the law as a rule of social conduct. It also means supremacy of the courts to settle the disputes that pervade and trouble social life. Behind the rule of law stands the firm belief that the judiciary is superior to the administration in protecting and guaranteeing individual rights.

It follows from this that a major difference exists between common law and civil law traditions. Unlike European continental monarchies, the British legal tradition did not develop a strong State administration. To guarantee individual liberties, it always favored a judicial over an administrative system of law enforcement. The difference was already in place in the eighteenth century. In contradistinction to the continent, England was held to be a land of freedom because daily life was regulated by courts of law rather than by the administration of the Police-State. Montesquieu well understood that if political liberty was the very object of the constitution of England, this was because courts of law in England were the true law enforcers. Only judges could guarantee the political liberty of Englishmen, that is, the ''tranquility of mind arising from the opinion each person has of his safety.''[6] The system has not fundamentally changed. In England, the public good rests first and foremost with the judges whose mission is to protect individual rights.[7] In England, the public good consists in ensuring the rule of law.

---

[5] *Id.*, at 252. Tocqueville dreamt of a similar temper for the French people and went as far as writing in his *Voyage en Suisse*, quoted above, *supra* note 3: ''The love of justice, the peaceful and legal introduction of the judge into the domain of politics, are perhaps the most standing characteristics of a free people.'' The principle of the rule of law theorized by Dicey had a deep impact on jurisprudence and political theory. It was used and expanded by Friedrich Hayek, particularly in his work *The Constitution of Liberty* (1960). In the same manner, the rule of law as the bedrock principle of political ethics and just social order was extensively used by John Rawls, in particular in *A Theory of Justice* Harvard University Press, 1971.

[6] Montesquieu, *The Spirit of Laws* [Translated by Th. Nugent, 1752, revised by J. V. Prichard], 1748, Book XI, chap. 6, available at http://www.constitution.org/cm/sol.htm.

[7] The rule of law is not the perfect mirror of the continental *Rechtsstaat*; its content is more substantive than formal. The rule of law is less interested in the hierarchy of norms than in the primacy of the individual over the State.

A. ORIGIN AND HISTORICAL EVOLUTION

Greek and Roman origins. Insofar as it implies a power under law, the rule of law has very ancient origins. The Ancients very early understood that possession by political authority of coercive powers that it may use for the best (to ensure public peace and justice for all) as well as for the worse (to establish an odious tyranny) raised fundamental problems for political and legal theory. The Greek philosophers were the first to resort to law to solve the dilemma and to explain that the most important way to limit the powers of government over the governed was to subject it to legal rules. As a guarantor of liberty, a government of laws is better than a government of men. Aristotle gave a first expression to this principle in the Politics, when he asserted that a free citizen is one who obeys laws, not men. The idea was taken up and developed by the Roman jurists, in particular Cicero, who insisted on the true duty of the magistrate, namely, that he represents the State and must respect the laws.[8]

The medieval turning point. The subordination of political power to legal rules took a very different course in the Middle Ages. When Aristotle saw freedom (and citizenship) in obedience to laws, not men, the laws in question were human laws; they were the laws of the city-state that free men freely adopted. These free men could say they were free, hence citizens, because they obeyed the law that they freely gave themselves. Under the influence of the Church, the medieval world also made the supremacy of law over power the measure of a fair government, but—and this is a crucial difference from the Ancients—the law in question is no longer a human work. The Church fathers reinvented the law; they redefined it as a collection of rules very close to, or at least, inspired by the word of God. After them, it was commonly held throughout the whole western Christian world that there was a universal law that ruled over the world, and that this law took precedence over the laws of kings and princes. In the Middle Ages, law was not equated with statute, as it is today in the civil law system; as a matter of fact, it was distinct from it. Where Greeks and Romans regarded legal rules and the city-state as correlative notions, the Christian scholars of the Middle Ages viewed them as discrete.[9]

In England, perhaps because of the Conquest, the medieval idea of a complete separation between the law and the State assumed an exceptional meaning. From the beginning, it became one of the most solid and entrenched ideas of English legal thought, and, beyond England, it has remained a basic

[8] Cicero, *De Officiis*, I, 34, 124, quoted by A. Passerin d'Entrèves, *The Notion of the State*, Oxford University Press, 1967, p. 82.

[9] *Id.*, p. 83.

tenet of the common law systems. In the thirteenth century, in his long treatise on the laws and customs of England (*De legibus et consuetudinibus Angliae*), Bracton forcefully asserts that rulers are under law: "The king ought not to be under man, but under God and law, because law makes the king."[10] "The king must give justice" was a key component of the royal function. However, the provision was always made that he must give justice according to law, the law of the land, which like God's word is ageless. The *Magna Carta* of 1215 bears witness to the importance of this principle in medieval thought: "No free man shall be seized or imprisoned, or stripped of his rights or possessions, or outlawed or exiled, or deprived of his standing in any other way, nor will we proceed with force against him, or send others to do so, except by the lawful judgment of his equals or by law of the land." The idea of a law that is supreme, above the kings and limiting their powers, was and remains the bedrock principle of the English legal system. Later, in the fifteenth century, the same idea enabled Sir John Fortescue to assert that there could be no taxation without representation.

The conflict between sovereignty and the rule of law in the seventeenth century. With the Reformation, the idea of a universal law was on the wane. On the continent, the principle of sovereignty replaced it, and the continental monarchies went down the path of absolutism. True, the Stuarts tried to follow the same path, and they invoked the divine right of kings to dispense justice by virtue of their inherent knowledge of the law and, in particular, by the means of extraordinary courts such as the Court of Star Chamber, which was not bound by the common law. Their ambitions failed when they met the resistance of judges, resistance soon taken up by Parliament. During the long conflict that, in the beginning of the seventeenth century, pitted the king and Parliament against each other, Chief Justice Coke and the lawyers who rallied behind him continually proclaimed the absolute supremacy of the common law over the king and the executive. The abolition of the detested Court of the Star Chamber, in 1640, marked their victory. From this date, it was acknowledged that the common law was to be the common law of all public and private acts, unless Parliament decided otherwise.

The rule of law did indeed vanquish sovereignty, but its triumph obliged it to reinvent itself. From the moment its oracles (*i.e.*, the judges) faltered before the king and hesitated to resist against the extraordinary prerogative precisely in the name of the common law, they had no option but to recognize that

---

[10] H. de Bracton, *On the Laws and Customs of England*, vol. II [translated Samuel E. Thorne], Cambridge, MA, Belknap Press, 1968, p. 33.

Parliament could change the common law. To put it in different terms, they had to recognize that "parliamentary legislation [could] qualify the pretensions of the common law."[11] Since then, it is acknowledged that the rule of law always means the supremacy of the law, but the law in question is made of the statutes adopted by Parliament and the case law of the courts of England, insofar as the latter is not discarded by the former.

B. CONTENT

The definition of Albert V. Dicey. According to Dicey, the rule of law has in English law three consequences that may be summarized as follows:

> When we say that the supremacy or the rule of law is a characteristic of the English constitution, we generally include under one expression at least three distinct though kindred conceptions.
>
> We mean, in the first place, that no man is punishable or can be lawfully made to suffer in body or goods except for a distinct breach of law established in the ordinary legal manner before the ordinary Courts of the land. In this sense the rule of law is contrasted with every system of government based on the exercise by persons in authority of wide, arbitrary, or discretionary powers of constraint[12] [. . .]
>
> We mean in the second place, when we speak of the 'rule of law' as a characteristic of our country, not only that with us no man is above the law, but (what is a different thing) that here every man, whatever be his rank or condition, is subject to the ordinary law of the realm and amenable to the jurisdiction of ordinary tribunals[13] [. . .]
>
> There remains yet a third and a different sense in which the 'rule of law' or the predominance of the legal spirit may be described as a special attribute of English institutions. We may say that the constitution is pervaded by the rule of law on the ground that the general principles of the constitution (as for example the right to personal liberty, or the right of public meeting) are with us the result of judicial decisions determining the rights of private persons in particular cases brought before the Courts; whereas under many foreign constitutions the security (such as it is) given to the rights of

---

[11] C. Holmes, "The Legal Instruments of Power and the State in Early Modern England," in A. Padoa-Schioffa (Ed.), *Legislation and Justice*, European Science Foundation, Clarendon Press, 1997, p. 269 s., especially p. 286.

[12] Dicey, *supra* note 1, at p. 188.

[13] *Id.*, p. 193.

> individuals results, or appears to result, from the general principles of the constitution.[14]

An analysis of the precise content of these three propositions (the principle of legality, the principle of equality before the law, and the principle of a judicial guarantee for individual rights) is called for.

Principle of legality. The rule of law means, in the first place, the absolute supremacy of ordinary law established in the ordinary legal manner before the ordinary courts. The ordinary law must be understood as the legal rules decided by the courts or adopted by Parliament as opposed to the influence of arbitrary power. The rule of law excludes the existence of arbitrariness, of prerogative, or even of wide discretionary power on the part of government. It means that a man in England may be punished, or deprived of life, liberty, or property, only for a clear breach of a law duly enacted. A man may be punished for a breach of law, but he can be punished for nothing else.

The rule of law under the form of the principle of legality was affirmed with particular force in *Entick* v. *Carrington* (1765). Two king's messengers were sued for having unlawfully broken and entered the plaintiff's house, a well-known journalist of the time, Entick, allegedly the author of seditious writings. When the messengers were sued by Entick for trespass to his house and goods, the defendants relied on a warrant issued by the Secretary of State ordering them to search for Entick and bring him with his books and papers before the Secretary for examination. The Secretary claimed that the power to issue such warrants was essential to government, "the only means of quieting clamors and sedition." Lord Camden said:

> This power, so claimed by the Secretary of State, is not supported by one single citation from any law book extant. [. . .] If it is law, it will be found in our books. If it is not to be found there, it is not law. [. . .] What would the parliament say if the judges should take upon themselves to mould an unlawful power into a convenient authority by new restrictions? That would be, not judgment, but legislation. [. . .] It is then said, that it is necessary for the ends of government to lodge such a power with a State officer; and that it is better to prevent the publication before than to punish the offender afterwards. . . . [W]ith respect to the arguments of State necessity, or a distinction that has been aimed at between State offences and others, the common law does

[14] *Id.*, pp. 195-196.

> not understand that kind of reasoning, nor do our books take notice of any such distinctions.[15]

The court held that, in the absence of a statute or a judicial precedent upholding the legality of the warrant, the practice was illegal.

The major lesson to be drawn from *Entick* is that the rule of law is an essential guarantee for the protection of individual rights. *Entick* means that a person may not be deprived of life, liberty, or property except by virtue of a rule of law duly enacted by Parliament or established by ordinary courts. The principle however is not faultless; the rule of law protects against the abuses of the executive, not against those of Parliament. Concretely, if an act of Parliament had authorized the search and seizure of seditious libels, Entick would no longer have been protected. This was true in the eighteenth century; it is still true today. Parliamentary sovereignty prevails over the common law, and in theory an act of Parliament may take away with the strike of a pen all the guarantees patiently gathered over the centuries to protect human rights.

True, English judges may resort to interpretive methods that may work as shields against this danger. In particular, they never presume an implicit will on the part of Parliament for having voluntarily departed from the common law; the departure must always be clear and explicit. Nonetheless, the principle of realism may always trump the common law, and the courts must yield to the will of the sovereign. This is the reason why there was strong feeling in the past for the rule of law; it took the form of an incorporation and entrenchment of the European Convention of Human Rights into English law under original conditions that consolidated the rule of law without infringing on Parliamentary sovereignty. This decisive step was taken with the Human Rights Act (1998).[16]

Equality before the law. The rule of law, in the second place, means legal equality (*i.e.*, the universal subjection of all classes to one law administered by the ordinary courts). Dicey put great store in the fact that the idea of legal equality in England had been pushed to its utmost limits. ''With us,'' he insisted,

> every official, from the Prime Minister down to a constable or a collector of taxes, is under the same responsibility for every act done without legal justification as any other citizen. The Reports abound

[15] C. Stephenson & F. G. Marcham, *Sources of English Constitutional History, A Selection of Documents from the Interregnum to the Present*, vol. II, New York, Harper & Row, 1972, pp. 705-710.

[16] See A. W. Bradley & K. D. Ewing, *Constitutional and Administrative Law*, 13th ed., Pearson, 2003, pp. 96-97 and p. 416.

> with cases in which officials have been brought before the Courts, and made, in their personal capacity, liable to punishment, or to the payment of damages, for acts done in their official character but in excess of their lawful authority. A colonial governor, a secretary of state, a military officer, and all subordinates, though carrying out the commands of their official superiors, are as responsible for any act which the law does not authorize as is any private and unofficial person.[17]

There are therefore, he emphasized strongly, no special courts or tribunals to take cognizance of cases involving public officials and apply to them a law derogatory from the common law as was the case in his view in France at the end of the nineteenth century with "*droit administratif.*"

Today, the kind of equality that Dicey was concerned with is no longer the one that matters the most. In the first place, regarding the inequalities that French "*droit administratif*" made possible between private individuals and officials, Dicey himself recognized in his lifetime that the latter were not immune from the rigor of the law and that his charge was unfair. More importantly, the inequalities against which the rule of law is powerless and which could not be foreseen by Dicey because the generality of the law at his time was still a reality are the inequalities deriving from legislative discriminations. Today, Parliament may resort to all sorts of fanciful classifications in economic and fiscal matters against which the rule of law offers no protection when they are arbitrary.

The protection of the courts. The rule of law carries a third meaning that, according to Dicey, is more relevant to the spirit than to the letter of English law and may be described as a special attribute of English institutions. We may say, Dicey underlines, that the Constitution is imbued with the rule of law on the ground that the general principles of the Constitution (as for example the right to personal liberty, or the right of public meeting) are with us as the result of judicial decisions determining the rights of private persons—in particular, cases brought before the English courts. On the continent, by contrast, security (such as it is) for the rights of individuals results, or appears to result, from general principles solemnly affirmed in ambitious declarations of rights, but these are not necessarily effective.

More deeply, the rule of law highlights the idea that the rights of Englishmen are the result of a slow and sedimentary law-making process, not the result of thundering declaration of rights not judicially enforceable. Dicey

---

[17] Dicey, *supra* note 1, at pp. 193-194.

proudly insisted that Englishmen never felt a need to set down in writing their rights and freedoms in hollow and empty declarations of rights as was done on the continent, because Parliament and the courts effectively protected them. This does not mean, he said, that the Constitution of England does not contain the same rights as the continental declarations; it does contain them, but as inferences that may be drawn from numerous courts cases and parliamentary statutes. Under such circumstances, the articulation between the rule of law and the individual rights is very different than on the continent. Whereas the constitutions on the continent are the product of human will and energy, made by a legislative power and grounded on the constitution-making power, the Constitution of England is a judge-made Constitution. In England, the right to individual liberty is part of the Constitution, because it is secured by the decisions of the court as these are extended or confirmed by the *Habeas Corpus* Acts. In other words, whereas rights and liberties on the continent are deductions drawn from the principles of the Constitution, the so-called principles of the Constitution in England are inductions or generalizations based on particular decisions pronounced by the courts as to the rights of given individuals.

The most important consequence of all this is that rights and liberties in England are ensured not by the guarantees that may be found in sweeping declarations of rights, but by the remedies that the common law provides to those whose rights have been illegally infringed, whether they are ordinary citizens or public officers. In other words, if rights and liberties are to be ''taken seriously'' (as a famous American philosopher has put it),[18] attention must be paid in the first place to the remedies available in case of their infringement. According to the maxim of English law, remedies precede rights; that is, there is no true right without a remedy attached to it to make it enforceable by a judge. Such is the reasoning by which public law has been actually introduced into English law, at least under a procedural form. A flaw of the common law was that it did not adequately empower the citizens against the administration and public authorities. To remedy the situation, the British did not imitate the Americans after the war, when Congress in 1946 adopted a large statute on administrative procedure that gives due process rights to citizens—in particular the right to be heard during the rule-making process. Instead, they undertook a reformation of the judicial remedies against public authorities and carved out a special role for the remedy of judicial review.

Rule of law and common law. Insofar as the common law is the foundation of the rights and liberties of Englishmen, the rule of law tends to regard it as the

[18] R. Dworkin, *Taking Rights Seriously*, Harvard University Press, 1977.

best and most efficient means against arbitrariness and abuse of power. One of Dicey's governing ideas is that the common law gives the citizen better protection than a written constitution. From an historical standpoint, it is indisputable that the common law was a solid bulwark against arbitrariness and tyranny. However, today, the common law is no longer regarded with the same eyes, and Englishmen themselves are doubtful about the absolute efficacy of the common law as the better shield for their rights and freedoms. The reason for this doubt comes from the fact that the common law is subject to whatever changes Parliament, which happened to be no longer tempered by the mixed government and the balance of powers, may see fit to introduce. The truth of the matter is that their rights and freedoms may be curtailed, modified, and even suppressed by a sovereign act of the House of Commons. The dramatic events of Northern Ireland gave rise to derogations from the common law against which the principle of the rule of law was of very limited use, to say the least. On the other hand, the common law as such does not protect economic and social rights.

In the beginning of the 1990s, public opinion in Great Britain was largely in favor of a Bill of Rights that would have inscribed the rights so that Parliament could no longer have legislated against them. Failing a clear will to bring such dramatic changes to the principle of parliamentary sovereignty, the Blair government took the middle road, with the Human Rights Act (1998). The most important characteristic of the act is to compel judges, so far as it is possible to do so, to read and give effect to primary legislation and subordinate legislation in a way that is compatible with the European Convention on Human Rights. If it turns out that this is impossible, the judge may make a declaration of incompatibility, which is forwarded to the minister who may by order make such amendments to the legislation as he considers necessary to remove the incompatibility. The crucial point is that courts still have no power to invalidate the legislation; Parliament remains sovereign. The Human Rights Act has already enabled English courts to rejuvenate the principle of the rule of law by resorting to a European text to which English lawyers made a decisive contribution.

C. SCOPE

1. Traditional Principles

Rule of law and public law. By tradition, the rule of law and public law do not fit together; their respective ends are very different. Rule of law and public law do not obey the same logic. The rule of law is aimed at protecting private, individual rights, not public, collective rights; it works for the benefit of the individual, not the community. The public thing, or the public good, is not within its compass, except insofar as the public good is regarded as a maximization of individual interests. In the common law tradition, ensuring the public good consists of ensuring the rule of law, and ensuring the rule of law consists of bringing individual interests to the highest point of satisfaction: no more, no less. English law is deeply individualistic. The traditional definition of the public good as found, for instance, in Blackstone's works bears witness to this tradition: "[T]he public good is in nothing more essentially interested, than in the protection of every individual's private rights."[19]

Common law and public law. That being said, there has always existed in the common law tradition some measure of concern for the public interest and public law values.[20] In a law as old as the common law, one can find everything, and it is true that at some point in its long history, in the Middle Ages, when there was barely a distinction between public law and private law, the common law made some room for the common good and showed some concern for the public good. However, those interested in this period of its history, to the point of digging into the "public law" institutions or concepts of the common law to find answers to the problems raised by the industrialization of the modern age, were the Americans, not the English. In the beginning of the nineteenth century, a few state judges in the United States were particularly inventive, going so far as to identify a distinction between public and private law within the common law itself.[21] At the federal level, the Supreme Court discovered the legal category of "public rights" and, later, that of "public utilities," together with its companion doctrines, such as the "business affected with a public interest" or the "prime necessity."[22] In the same vein, the Supreme Court voided the state's grant in fee to a railroad of a large section of land submerged beneath Lake Michigan in the Chicago harbor. The Court held that the people of the state, not the state itself, were the land's beneficial owners and that the state held the submerged land "in trust for the people of the state."[23]

---

[19] W. Blackstone, *Commentaries on the Laws of England, A Facsimile of the First Edition of 1765-1769,* vol. I, Chicago & London, University of Chicago Press, 1979, p. 135.

[20] See D. Oliver, "The Underlying Values of Public and Private Law," in M. Taggart (Ed.), *The Province of Administrative Law*, Oxford, Hart, 1997, p. 217.

[21] See, in particular, an opinion by the Supreme Court of Massachusetts (Shaw, J.), *Commonwealth* v. *Alger*, 61 Mass. 53, 93 (1851).

[22] See, in particular, *Munn* v. *Illinois*, 94 US 113 (1877).

[23] *Illinois Central Railroad* v. *Illinois*, 146 US 387, 452-453 (1892). See also D. R. Coquillette, "Mosses from an Old Manse: Another Look at Some Historic Property Cases About the Environment," 64 *Cornell L. Rev.* 761 (1979).

This American development may be explained by the fact that, although a country of common law that each state incorporated into its own law, the United States has always lived under a republican form of government, with the result that Americans have tended to be more concerned with the public interest than the English and that state judges (who usually are elected) have been, implicitly, driven by popular demand to explore the public components of the common law. State judges throughout the nineteenth century tried to resurrect old common law institutions, going back if necessary to the Middle Ages, and breathing new life into them so that the public interest could trump private egoisms.[24] However, at the end of the nineteenth century, the Supreme Court converted to conservative ideologies, nipping these initiatives in the bud and twisting them to make sure that they would give priority to the satisfaction of private interests.[25]

2. Recent Developments

Traditional reserve on the part of English judges. English judges were much more reserved than their American counterparts. They never followed the same "publicist" path as American state judges. The idea that public interests under the notion of public good or public interest may put limitations on the exercise of private freedoms and rights remained foreign to them, save, of course, when these limitations are decided by an act of Parliament, parliamentary sovereignty trumping the common law. Excepting those cases where Parliament commands otherwise, the control exercised by English judges over the uses of power, whether public or private, has generally been minimal.

Common law and private power. In the nineteenth century, English judges eschewed the idea that common law could work for the public interest; they construed and interpreted it as the strongest bulwark for private interests against public interest. The private law leaning of the common law in the nineteenth century is well illustrated by a water dispute between Edward Pickles and the

---

[24] See W. J. Novak, "Common Regulation: Legal Origins of State Power," 45 *Hastings L. J.* 1061 (1994).

[25] The most famous example in the turnaround of meaning in the public law values of the common law is to be found in the destiny of *Munn* v. *Illinois* quoted *supra* note 22 (1877). In that case, the Court held that the legislature had the power to regulate the rates of companies running public utilities such as ferries, railroads, tolls, canals and, as in the case at hand, grain warehouses. Soon after being decided, Munn became in the hands of an increasingly conservative Court an obstacle to the regulation of activities regarded by the Court as "strictly private"; see H. N. Scheiber, "Law and Political Institutions," *Encyclopedia of American Economic History: Studies of Principal Movements and Ideas*, (Glenn Porter (Ed.)), 3 vols., New York, Charles Scribner's Sons, 1980, vol. II, p. 487, in particular, pp. 501-502.

Mayor of Bradford in Victorian England.[26] Edward Pickles owned land adjoining a spring that the Corporation of Bradford had used for nearly forty years to supply water to the town of Bradford seven miles away. In the early 1890s, Pickles started to drain the water in an attempt apparently to force the corporation to pay a premium for his land, and he eventually fatally threatened the water supply as the corporation steadfastly refused to buy his land or his water. The House of Lords refused to qualify his absolutism with an exception for malice; it held that the common law empowered Pickles to act as he pleased and for whatever motives he chose, as long as his action did not cause a tort resulting from a legal injury,[27] and the corporation lost its case. Not so long ago, the common law protected private interests so thoroughly without the slightest consideration for the public good, that H. C. Gutteridge, commenting upon the Pickles case, could write: ''[O]ur law has not hesitated to place the seal of its approval upon a theory of the extent of individual rights which can only be described as the consecration of the spirit of unrestricted egoism.''[28] As long as no tort resulting from a legal injury was done, no limitations could be imposed on the exercise of private power. Today, the legendary selfish content of English has been mitigated to the point that it is possible to refer to public law values belonging to both the common law and public law.[29] This evolution, however, was mostly the consequence of legislative action.

Common law and public power. The English judge exercises judicial review over public power only when it is exercised by an executive or administrative authority, the public power exercised by Parliament being by definition nonreviewable, by virtue of the doctrine of parliamentary sovereignty. Public authorities as a rule may infringe on private rights only for objective motives, legally established, and they must always act for the public good. English judges verify this condition every time they review the legality of administrative or executive action. English legal scholars regard hard-look judicial review exercised over the motives for decisions made by public authorities to be at the heart of the difference between private and public law.

The difference was underlined with great force by Wade:

> The powers of public authorities are [. . .] essentially different from those of private persons. A man making his will may, subject to any

[26] See M. Taggart, *Private Property and Abuse of Rights in Victorian England: The Story of Edward Pickles and the Bradford Water Supply*, Oxford University Press, 2002.

[27] *The Mayor of Bradford* v. *Pickles*, [1895] AC 587, 601.

[28] H. C. Gutteridge, ''Abuse of Rights,'' 5 *Cambridge L. J.* 1, 22 (1933).

[29] See D. Oliver, *Common Values and the Public-Private Divide*, London, Butterworths, 1999.

> rights of his dependant, dispose of his property just as he may wish. He may act out of malice or a spirit of revenge, but in law this does not affect his exercise of his power. In the same way a private person has an absolute power to allow whom he likes to use his land, to release a debtor, or, where the law permits, to evict a tenant, regardless of his motives. This is unfettered discretion. But a public authority may do none of these things unless it acts reasonably and in good faith and upon lawful and relevant grounds of public interest. So a city council acted unlawfully when it refused unreasonably to let a local rugby football club use the city's sports ground. Nor may a local authority arbitrarily release debtors, and if it evicts tenants, even though in accordance with a contract, it must act reasonably and 'within the limits of fair dealing.' The whole concept of unfettered discretion is inappropriate to a public authority, which possesses powers solely in order that it may use them for the public good.[30]

The ultra vires *doctrine.* Although English judges have always reviewed the legality of the motives behind decisions made by public authorities, their review was usually mild. The fundamental principle is that public authorities may not overstep the limits on their actions imposed by Parliament; that is, they may not act *ultra vires*. Lord Greene, in the landmark case *Associated Provincial Pictures Houses Ltd.* v. *Wednesbury Corporation* (1948), limited the doctrine *ultra vires* to a mere review of the reasonableness of the decision. In his view, it meant that "it must be proved to be unreasonable in the sense that the court considers it to be a decision that no reasonable body could have come to it."[31] A slightly different reformulation of the reasonableness test was given in the *GCHQ* case by Lord Diplock, who preferred to use the term "irrational," which he described as applying to "a decision which is so outrageous in its defiance of logic or accepted moral standards that no sensible person who had applied his mind to the question to be decided could have arrived at it."[32] With such criteria for review, the chances that a citizen could win a case against a public authority were very slim. As a rule, public authorities were bound to be regarded as always in the right, and the citizen as always wrong. Until very recently, English judges were powerless to effectively review abuses of discretion by public authorities; the new despotism (*i.e.*, the bureaucracy), according to the famous

---

30 H. W. R. Wade & C. F. Forsyth, *Administrative Law*, 9th ed., Oxford University Press, 2004, p. 355.

31 *Associated Provincial Pictures Houses Ltd.* v. *Wednesbury Corporation* [1948] 1 KB 225, 230.

32 *Council of Civil Service Unions* v. *Minister for the Civil Service* [1985] A.C. 374.

title of a classical work, ran into no obstacle but an appearance of review. The rights of citizens were on the verge of being jeopardized. Several MPs and some enlightened judges sounded the alarm. The situation did not really change until Parliament decided to step in and to put into motion some of the reforms initially envisioned by a few visionary judges, such as Lord Diplock.

Legislative action. In the second half of the twentieth century, the British Parliament undertook two major reforms, different in substance, which dramatically changed the traditional British position *vis-à-vis* public law.

The first change, introduced in the 1970s, consisted of a sweeping reform of judicial remedies against public bodies and a comprehensive set of rules for making claims for judicial review. Prior to 1977, the procedures governing the prerogative remedies and the ordinary remedies (of declaration or injunction) were entirely separate. The purpose of the 1977 reforms was to introduce a procedure whereby the prerogative remedies and declarations and injunctions (and, in appropriate circumstances, damages) could be claimed in one claim. Shortly afterwards, in order to keep the public authorities from being swamped by abusive suits, the House of Lords in *O'Reilly* v. *Mackman* found that "now that judicial review is available to give every kind of remedy, [. . .] it should be the normal recourse in all cases of public law where a private person is challenging the conduct of a public authority or a public body, or of anyone acting in the exercise of a public duty."[33] Following this decision, the distinction between public law and private law has become fundamental.

The second change derives from the adoption of the Human Rights Act in 1988, which made the European Convention of Human Rights enforceable against all public authorities. It is difficult to imagine how the judge could effectively enforce this instrument if he still adhered to the former test of the measure's reasonableness as set out by *Wednesbury*.

The new English "public law." These reforms have brought about dramatic changes in the traditional positions of the English legal system *vis-à-vis* public law and the public interest. English judges today review the existence of the public interest more often than they used to. At the invitation of Parliament, they have developed their role in public law, especially in the domain of the relations between public authorities and the citizen. Although the foundations of English administrative law are procedural in nature, its substantive content in the years ahead should deepen and get stronger because the courts, leaving aside the dry and limited *Wednesbury* test, are more and more inclined to verify the manner in which the public interest is concretely applied in the cases coming before

[33] *O'Reilly* v. *Mackman* [1983] 2 AC 237, 256.

them.[34] The crucial point is that the judge no longer envisions his function as being exclusively limited to the protection of private interests and only partially in the protection of the public interest. English judges today measure and evaluate the public interest in the decisions of the public authorities more often and with more bite than they used to do under their traditional role of guardians of private interests.[35] The extension of the power of judicial review over formerly purely discretionary acts brought under judicial scrutiny the so-called prerogative powers of the Crown, in particular in the field of national security,[36] as well as the powers exercised by nongovernmental (or ''private'') bodies (especially regulatory bodies) such as a panel on takeovers and mergers operating in the city of London and regulating a very important part of the financial market.[37] In the same vein, English courts have developed new doctrines, such as ''natural justice,'' which compel decisionmakers, regardless of their administrative or judicial functions, to respect the right to be heard.[38] The power of judicial review today goes so far and so deep that some judges think that ''[t]rying to keep the *Wednesbury* principle and proportionality in separate compartments seems [. . .] to be unnecessary and confusing.''[39] They argue that the proportionality principle, although set aside a few years ago,[40] has become part of English law, if only because of the European Convention on Human Rights and that it is likely to replace the *Wednesbury* test. The review exercised by English judges over internment measures decided by the

[34] P. Craig, ''Public Law and Control Over Private Power,'' in M. Taggart (Ed.), *The Province of Administrative Law*, Oxford, Hart, 1997, p. 196.

[35] For instance, in a case concerning a ban of hunting deer with hounds, the court held that, since the land had been acquired under a statute authorizing acquisition of land for ''the benefit, improvement or development of their area,'' the county council was permitted to pursue objects that would ''conduce to the better management of the estate'' only. Since the ban was fueled by the ''ethical perceptions of the Councillors about the rights and wrongs of hunting,'' the purposes it sought were outside that of the governing statute. The ban, which probably would have been sustained under the *Wednesbury* test, could be decided for objective motives, compatible with the public interest, see R. v. *Somerset County Council, ex parte Fewings*, [1995] 1 All ER 513, 524.

[36] *Council for Civil Services Union* v. *Minister for the Civil Service* [1985] AC 374.

[37] R. v. *Panel on Takeovers and Mergers, ex parte Datafin plc* [1987] QB 815.

[38] *Ridge* v. *Baldwin* [1964] AC 40.

[39] R. (*Alconbury Development Ltd*) v. *Secretary of State for the Environment, Transports and the Regions* [2001] UKHL 23 (Lord Slynn of Hadley, § 51), 2 WLR 1389, p. 1406.

[40] R. v. *Home Secretary, ex parte Brind* [1991] 1 AC 696.

governmental authorities for an indefinite period of time against persons suspected of terrorist activities support these views.[41]

Hesitations and uncertainties. The new developments in English public law are a cause of division among legal scholars. Resistance against the introduction of a distinction between public law and private law is still very strong.[42] Behind the scholarly debate, the fear is that the more public law grows, the more private law, and hence private power, dwindles. The debate is both political and legal at the same time.[43] It revolves around the dilemma of deciding whether the judge must stick to *Wednesbury* or free himself from its constraint and move toward a broader power of judicial review that would lay a stronger hand on the exercise of public power. Some believe that, in being more intrusive in the exercise of discretionary powers, the judges go beyond what the doctrine of parliamentary sovereignty authorizes. Others think that the first duty of the judge in the English legal system is to protect individual rights and that this is, indeed, the greatest legacy of the common law. The question is not resolved whether English public law (which in any case does exist today in the British legal system, if only under the procedural forms of public law remedies) will grow inside or outside the common law. If the first possibility carries the day, tradition will prevail, and England will have no public law, at least in a formal sense. If the second prevails, England could develop a true concept of public law.

It is still always possible to say that the distinction between public law and private law is overridden by the fact that the spirit of the common law has always been to forbid abuses of power, whether public or private.[44] Even assuming that this is correct in the light of legal history, public law does not end with the distaste for abuse of power. A ban on the abuse of power is a leading principle among public law's basic tenets; but the end and the object of public law are broader. Public law is the law of the *res publica*, the law of the public good. Its vocation is alternately to protect public authorities in their legitimate vindication of the public interest against private interests or to forbid them to go

---

41 *A (FC) and Others (FC) Appellants* v. *Secretary of State for the Home Department* [2004] UKHL 56.

42 See M. Taggart, "'The Peculiarities of the English': Resisting the Public / Private Law Distinction," in P. Craig & R. Rawlings (Eds.), *Law and Administration in Europe: Essays in Honour of Carol Harlow*, Oxford University Press, 2003, p. 107.

43 See P. Cane, *An Introduction to Administrative Law*, 3rd ed., Clarendon Law Series, Oxford, 1996, p. 362.

44 See the declarations and statements made by Sir Stephen and Sir John Laws in D. Oliver, *Common Values and the Public-Private Divide*, Butterworths, 1999, pp. 249-250

further than they are authorized and exact sacrifices from citizens that go beyond what the legitimate public interest may require. There is no public law without some conceptualization of the public interest; it is not to be ruled out that judges may find this concept in the common law itself. Until this step is taken, there will be no public law in England. Some recent cases, particularly dealing with terrorism, suggest that English judges may be heading in this direction, while remaining adamantly vigilant on the protection of private interests and, in particular, personal freedom.[45]

---

[45] See the opinion by Lord Hoffman, *A (FC) and Others (FC) Appellants* v. *Secretary of State for the Home Department* [2004] UKHL 56, §§ 91-97.

BOOK II
THE REPUBLICAN AGE

New economic and social conditions. The republican age began at the end of the eighteenth century, with the American and French Revolutions. Nowadays, it is possible to say that it has completely replaced the monarchical age. True, some States still exist that are formally monarchies (Belgium, Spain, the Netherlands, and the United Kingdom). However, all these States present social and political characteristics that turned them into ''disguised republics,'' as England already was at the end of the nineteenth century, according to a jest by Walter Bagehot.[1]

At the social level, modern societies no longer have much in common with the societies of the monarchical age that were divided into ''orders'' or ''estates,'' within which social position was hereditary, and thus not freely chosen, and founded on relations of allegiance and faith, and thus personal and based on feelings. The societies of the republican age are made of men free and equal in rights; the equality of conditions being their basic tenet, social relations in them are voluntary, objective, based on interests.

At the political level, equality of conditions ousted the monarchical principle and replaced it with the republican principle, which defined itself by the sovereignty of the people. The *res publica* is no longer the thing of a monarch, it is the thing of a people; it no longer belongs to one, it belongs to everyone.

Transformations of public law. The coming into being of the republican principle transformed public law insofar as it completely changed its significance or, even, its meaning. In the monarchical age, public law was not liked, but feared and even loathed, particularly when it was used to tax people. On the eve of the revolutions of the eighteenth century, experience had taught mankind, rightly or wrongly, that public law had worked only for the benefit of the

[1] W. Bagehot, *The English Constitution*, 2nd ed., 1873, p. 214, note 12. The formula *''disguised republic''* is not to be found in the first edition of 1867.

monarchs who resorted to it to strengthen their power of coercion over their subjects. Everything, it was believed, would be different when the *res publica* should become the thing of everyone, because it was impossible that the people would work against themselves and for their own misery.

The men who in America, as in France, lived through and worked for the passage from the age of monarchies to the age of republics were initially convinced that a new era had started, with the coming into being of the sovereign people, and that henceforth public law could serve only the happiness of the people. "Happiness is a new idea in Europe," said Saint-Just in 1793 while article 1 of the Constitution of Year I proudly asserted: "The aim of the society is the common happiness." Actually, there was nothing new in this affirmation; it had been known for a long time; the whole eighteenth century had been immersed in the philosophy of happiness. The true novelty was that the awaited happiness would no longer be the happiness dreamed up by a despot for his people, but happiness freely conceived by the people, for the people.

On both sides of the Atlantic, the republican principle of the sovereignty of the people raised the same enthusiasm. The times that followed the Declaration of Independence in the United States and the Declaration of the Rights of Man and the Citizen in France produced a spectacle of fervor so exceptional in the history of Western civilization that people can today barely imagine it.[2] The revolutionaries in both the United States and in France embraced the republican principle as the beginning of a new era. Everything was about to begin, to be born again, as before the era of tyrannies. People thought it was a return of the Republic of Ancient Rome, busy on behalf of the collective happiness of the people, and they were convinced that the public good would henceforth always triumph over private interests. Governments would no longer be the exercise of domination of man over man but the exercise of a collective power that would work only for the defense of liberty and the promotion of the public good.

In the United States as well as in France, the great expectations of the Revolution collapsed onto themselves. The Americans and the French discovered that transfer of sovereignty from one person to the multitude neither makes it disappear nor makes the problem it raises easier to solve. Worse, the transfer raises a problem that was unknown under the monarchy.

---

[2] For the United States, see G. S. Wood, *The Creation of the American Republic (1776-1787)*, 1969, reprint New York, W.W. Norton & Co., 1987, and G. S. Wood, "The Origins of Vested Rights in the Early Republic," 85 *Virginia L. Rev.* 1421 (1999). For France, see J. Michelet, *Histoire de la Révolution française* in *Œuvres complètes*, vols. XVII—XXIII, Flammarion, 1897-1898.

Survival of sovereignty. A creation of the monarchical age, sovereignty curiously outlived that period. Such continuity calls for explanation, for it is not self-evident.

The first republicans, that is, chronologically, the Americans, were convinced that sovereignty would die with monarchy. They thought that, in the republican age, it was bound to disappear and would soon be replaced by law. In the pamphlet *Common Sense*, published in February 1776, which inflamed the revolt against England in the colonies, Thomas Paine wrote:

> But where says some is the King of America? I'll tell you Friend, he reigns above, and does not make havoc of mankind like the Royal Brute of Britain. Yet that we may not appear to be defective in earthly honors, let a day be solemnly set apart for proclaiming the charter; let it be brought forth placed on the divine law, the word of God; let a crown be placed thereon, by which the world may know, that so far as we approve of monarchy, that in America THE LAW IS KING.[3]

Paine who would in 1793 be made a "French citizen" by the National Assembly, got it wrong; law has not replaced the king, neither in America nor elsewhere. In the United States, what has replaced the king of England (George III) is not law, but the people ("*We The People*"[4]). Still the aversion Americans cherished to this monarchical concept left a definite mark;[5] none of the founding texts of American public law, whether the Declaration of Independence of 1776 or the federal Constitution of 1787, contains the term "sovereignty."

In Europe, sovereignty followed the same path. Sovereigns have disappeared, or if they have not disappeared, they turned into constitutional icons; sovereignty remained. True, the republican age forbids sovereignty to lodge itself in a physical body and to be dressed in human clothes. Sovereignty can therefore be only a "principle" nowadays, as article 3 of the Declaration of the Rights of Man and the Citizen put it.[6] But it is lodged in the universality of the citizens (the nation, in France; the people, in the United States), and it remains. Sovereignty remains in the republican age the founding principle of public law—of modern public law, of course. What is it that explains this survival?

---

[3] T. Paine, *Common Sense* in *Collected Writings*, New York, Literary Classics of the United States, Coll. The Library of America, 1995, p. 34.

[4] These words are the very first of, and open the U. S. Constitution of 1787.

[5] See J. N. Rakove, "Making a Hash of Sovereignty, Part I," 2 *Green Bag* 35 (1998); "Making a Hash of Sovereignty, Part II," 3 *Green Bag* 51 (1999).

[6] Article 3 of the Declaration of the Rights of Man and the Citizen: "The principle of all sovereignty remains in essence in the Nation."

The explanation lies in this one fact: sovereignty has been historically and still remains the condition of modern liberty. It has freed men from the myriad powers that bore on them in the Middle Ages, the powers of the lords, the power of the monasteries, of the priests, of the guilds—to reduce all of them to one single power, the power of the State, which later was conquered by the people in democratic revolutions. Despite all the efforts made from a theoretical standpoint to negate it, or to make it disappear,[7] sovereignty has remained because it fulfills a function that is key to modern liberty. Sovereignty requires distinguishing between the public power, the only legitimate power, and the numerous private powers that run through the social fabric and that must by necessity be subject to law if liberty is to be preserved. It must, indeed, be remembered, before discarding sovereignty as a useless concept, that all the space that is not filled by statutory law is bound to be filled by private power. The famous aphorism by Montesquieu, ''Every man invested with power is apt to abuse it, and to carry his authority as far as it will go,''[8] may be applied to the holder of any power, whatever its nature, whether public or private; whatever its kind, religious or feudal as before, economic or financial as today. To that extent, the distinction between the State and civil society has been a huge step toward liberty.[9]

The new problem of representation. In the monarchical age, sovereignty was not represented. It did not need to be; sovereignty was an attribute of the sovereign, and the sovereign was the monarch. It was, indeed, society that was represented before the sovereign; and it was represented in its ''estates,'' that is, the three orders that, in France as in England, although under different names, derived from feudal society (the estate of the warriors, which formed the nobility, or the temporal Lords; the estate of the priests, which made the clergy, or the spiritual Lords; and the peasantry, which became the Tiers-État in France and the Commons in England). Only England succeeded in making use of this representation before the king to set up a theory of the king's Two Bodies, which enabled the representatives of society to form together with the king a body politic, distinct from the physical body of the king, and to govern with him. However, this evolution does not change the legal fact that the English Parliament does not represent the sovereign; Parliament *is* the sovereign.[10] This

---

[7] On the efforts of the conservative liberals in the nineteenth century, see J. Ellul, *Histoire des institutions: le XIXe siècle* (1962), PUF, Coll. Quadrige, 1999, p. 360.

[8] Montesquieu, *The Spirit of Laws*, [Translated by Th. Nugent, 1752, revised by J. V. Pritchard], 1748, Book XI, chap. 4, available at http://www.constitution.org/cm/sol.htm.

[9] See the Introduction, Section C.

[10] This odd legacy from the monarchical age obliges the classical British scholars such as Dicey to draw a line between legal sovereignty, which is within the hands of ''King in

is why, from a strictly legal standpoint, England still belongs to the monarchical age, despite the fact that, from a political standpoint, it is possible to say today that the sovereignty of Parliament rests on very different foundations. Today, a better explanation is that the legal sovereignty exercised by Parliament is viewed as deriving its legitimacy from the fact that Parliament's composition is determined by the electorate in whom ultimate political sovereignty resides.[11]

The coming of the republican age drastically changed the tradition of the monarchical age in which sovereignty was personified by a man or a body politic.[12] When sovereignty lies in an immense body made of millions of individuals, sovereignty takes a very novel shape. It is possible that this large body may exercise sovereignty itself, as was true in the past of citizens in the city-state who conducted their common affairs assembled in the agora, and this is true today in some western European States (Switzerland, France); it is also true in many states in the western United States where citizens are called to decide on public issues by way of referenda. In the contemporary world, however, these practices of direct democracy are rare, mostly exceptional; they exist usually for deciding constitutional matters, or occasionally for deciding statutory issues, but always in special circumstances. It is out of the question that they would be exercised on a daily basis. Therefore, the sovereign, in everyday public life, does not act by itself, but by delegation. It is represented. But how should it be represented? Here lies the very first great difficulty of modern public law. If the sovereign today is the whole society, it cannot be represented in the same way society in the monarchical age was for this decisive reason: The orders, or estates, no longer exist. From this disappearance, a second difficulty arises in modern public law: what remedy is there now against abuse of power?

Parliament,'' and political sovereignty, which lies in the hands of the electorate. Parliamentary sovereignty is ''an undoubted legal fact'' (see the explanations by A. V. Dicey, *Introduction to the Study of the Law of the Constitution*, with an introduction by E. C. S. Wade, 10th ed., London, The McMillan Press Ltd., 1959, p. 68, available at http://www.constitution.org/cmt/avd/law-con.htm).

[11] See the lecture given at New York University School of Law by Lord Irvine of Laird (Lord Chancellor in the Blair government 1997-2003), ''Sovereignty in Comparative Perspective: Constitutionalism in Britain and in America,'' 76 *N.Y.U.L.Rev.*1, 12-13 (2001).

[12] No text better explains this complete change than article 3 of the Declaration of the Rights of Man and the Citizen that, after enunciating the axiom of the republican age, ''the principle of all sovereignty remains in essence in the Nation,'' adds ''no public body'' (innuendo, ''no body politic'' as the Parliament in England), ''no individual'' (meaning, no monarch) ''can exercise authority that does not expressly derive from the Nation.''

The enduring difficulty of abuse of power. Whether it be within the hands of one individual, or of thousands of them, or of some chosen among the thousands, sovereignty remains identical and does not change. In its purest form, sovereignty is always the "supreme, irresistible, absolute, uncontrolled authority" referred to by Blackstone.[13]

In the monarchical age, only England succeeded, as we saw it, in fending off the danger and limiting sovereignty by establishing the parliamentary institution of the "King in Parliament," but it could manage to achieve that result only by using the estates of the society of the monarchical age, that is, the orders that organized themselves around the central figure of the king to form with him the mixed government.[14]

The republican age did not make sovereignty inoffensive. Whether it found an expression in the triumph of individual egoisms in the young American republic after the Declaration of Independence, in the populist laws then enacted and in the demagogic measures adopted, or whether it made its terrible force be known by the massive executions, the confiscatory laws, and the expedited judgments that marked the Terror, sovereignty proved to be as dangerous, if not more so, in the republican age as it was in the monarchical age. How do we stay away from such excesses; how do we limit sovereignty and make sure that it will always work for the public good when the resources of the monarchical age (*i.e.*, the social structures), no longer exist? This is the first question to be solved in the republican age.

The res publica *in the republican age.* As in the monarchical age, public law in the republican age has built itself upon the concept of sovereignty, and its object is still the public good. Sovereignty has not disappeared; but the sovereign has changed. It is no longer a monarch who is sovereign, but the

---

[13] W. Blackstone, *Commentaries on the Laws of England, A Facsimile of the First Edition of 1765-1769*, 4 volumes, Chicago & London, University of Chicago Press, 1979, p. 49, available at http://www.constitution.org/tb/tb-0000.htm (edited by St. George Tucker).

[14] The mixed government that constituted the excellence of the British system of government entered into periods of great turmoil when its moderating element, the House of Lords, lost its influence in the interplay of balance of powers, due to the increasing democratization of society and the growing obsolescence of aristocratic forms of government. The reforms of 1911 (loss of the power to reject the budget) and of 1949 (loss of the power to durably oppose bills from the Commons) together with a new constitutional convention, the so-called Salisbury convention, by which the House of Lords in 1945 agreed that it would be constitutionally wrong for it to prevent the manifesto commitments of the elected Government from being enacted into law, marked a gradual, evolutionary, but ineluctable decline of the mixed government.

society, and the entire question under consideration is what to do to ensure that this new sovereign always acts for the public good. The question arises under a much more complicated context than before, for at least two reasons.

The first difficulty is that a modern republic, made of citizens with lots of divergent interests, all of them thrown in the race for a rapid maximization of profits in a highly competitive capitalistic economy, can no longer take refuge in the resources of the small republic of the city-state, which lived under an agrarian economy and which, because of its size, formed a community of men closely united by similar interests and values, in particular the search for virtue and the public good. The second difficulty is that, insofar as it is grounded in the equality of conditions between men, the modern republic can no longer make use of the estates of monarchical society, the moderating factors of the mixed government.

As James Madison, a founding father of the American republic, so well understood, the dilemma of the republican age is to find ways of ensuring the public good in societies that are ''unmixed and extensive republics''[15] : ''unmixed,'' because they are no longer socially mixed, they no longer embody the estates that could be mixed and balanced against each other in the mixed government; ''extensive,'' because these republics occupy large territories, making the direct democracy of the city-state inaccessible to them for practical reasons. The core dilemma of modern public law is that, because of their social fabric and their size, these new republics in their quest to attain the public good have the help of neither the estates that formed monarchical society and the basis of the mixed government nor the virtue that was the soul of the small republic.

Two republican models. Two answers were given to the dilemma; each of them stands for a republican model. The first answer is that of the United States. Quickly found, as early as 1787, only ten years after the war against England, the answer has remained the same for two centuries; the American republican

---

[15] The expression is embodied in Letter no. 14 of *The Federalist. The Federalist* (short name for *The Federalist Papers*) is a collection of eighty-five letters (editorials in modern parlance) written by three authors, Alexander Hamilton, James Madison, and John Jay, and published in various newspapers of the State of New York in 1787-1788. The point of these writings was to convince the people of New York of the excellence of the Constitution adopted the year before in Philadelphia and to incite them to ratify the text. A positive vote by that State was regarded as crucial for the future of the Constitution. We are using the following edition: A. Hamilton, J. Madison & J. Jay, *The Federalist Papers*, C. Rossiter Edition, Mentor Book, N.Y, 1961, p. 101, available at http://www.yale.edu/lawweb/avalon/federal/fed.htm.

model today exercises an exceptional influence throughout the world. The second model is that of France. Invented just two year later, in 1789, it has developed on very different foundations, in particular in the answer it gives to the problem of representation—the opposite extreme of the American model. Of course, in both cases, we are dealing with models only—generalizations that are, of necessity, painted with a broad brush—that is, ideal types, which in the long run have evolved and adapted to various crises in human affairs. However, as models, they still influence how we think about the public good, how to conceive, protect, and maintain the *res publica* that unites men. Both models stand for the benchmarks that help us to understand where contemporary public law comes from and where it is going.

Part C
The American Model

The State and society. In the United States, the State is not "a power in a way external to the body social." The country wanted to break away from the tradition of the monarchical age characterized by a sharp distinction between the State and civil society. The first to have understood it was Tocqueville, when, in *Democracy in America*, he contrasted the United States and these European countries "where a power in a way external to the social body acts on it and forces it to march on a certain track." He added:

> Nothing like this is seen in the United States; there society acts by itself and on itself. Power exists only within its bosom; almost no one is encountered who dares to conceive and above all to express the idea of seeking it elsewhere. [. . .] The people reign over the American political world as does God over the universe. They are the cause and the end of all things; everything comes out of them and everything is absorbed into them.[1]

Because it rejects any distancing between the State and civil society, the American model is characterized by an absence of any formal distinction between public law and private law, and public law does not receive any particular fate. To be sure, in republics with extensive territory, a perfect match between the State and civil society is more an ideal than a reality. That said, there actually is in the United States a distinction between the State and civil society, between the governed and the government, and thus a difference between a public and a private interest. However, the distance between them is small, or at least tends to be minimal. One consequence of this situation is that it is impossible to apply to the United States the theoretical analysis of the French legal scholars in the beginning of the twentieth century who claimed that sovereignty was born in the State and then, subsequently, communicated to the

[1] A. de Tocqueville, *Democracy in America*, [Translated by H. C. Mansfield & D. Winthrop], University of Chicago Press, 2000, I, I, chap. 4, p. 55.

citizens.[2] In the United States, sovereignty was born first in the people and was then communicated to the State, or, to put it differently, in the United States, the people are the State; they make it, so to speak.[3]

The immediate proximity between the people and their government is the bedrock principle of American public law; it derives from the American conception of representation, based on popular sovereignty (Chapter 5). The rather negative consequences of this system of representation for the public good are alleviated by a particular conception of separation of powers, which forms, after popular representation, the second principle of the American system of government and is the backbone of the idea of limited power (Chapter 6).

---

[2] See, for instance, R. Carré de Malberg, *Contribution à la théorie générale de l'État*, 2 vols, 1920, reprint CNRS 1962, vol. II, p. 166.

[3] The United States is, par excellence, the model of the "popular State" described by Sir Henry Summer Maine in his work of the same name: H. S. Maine, *Popular Government: Four Essays*, London, J. Murray, 1890.

Chapter 5
Popular Sovereignty

The American conception of the sovereign. In the United States, the sovereign is the people, the actual people: the people in their everyday reality made of hundreds of millions of men and women living in fifty states; the people made of immigrants coming from all five continents; the people made of all races, all religions, all beliefs, all origins; in short, the people in their entire diversity. As it is conceived in the United States, the sovereign could not be other than these real people. This means, as Justice Jackson put it in *West Virginia State Board of Education* v. *Barnette* (1943), that: "There is no mysticism in the American concept of the State."[1]

As it is conceived in the United States, the State is not the idealized form of the *res publica*, as in the French tradition. The State, at the federal as well as the state level, is first and foremost a government—that is, a group of men who have power and who are thus potentially dangerous for the freedoms of the people. To keep these powerful men from trampling on the liberties and rights of the people, society must be as close to them as possible so that they are carefully watched over.[2] The absence of any mysticism in the American concept of the State explains the very practical and realistic way of thinking about, setting up, and organizing a system of representation in the United States. Representation American-style is popular representation, centered on the real people in every sense of the term (Section A). Its implications must be well understood because the system of representation always determines the status of statutory law within the State (Section B).

---

[1] *West Virginia State Board of Education* v. *Barnette*, 319 US 624, 641 (1943)

[2] The idea, a direct legacy of the British tradition, was the keystone in the building of the institution of king in Parliament. The king remained king only because he consented to reign "in Parliament," that is, with society represented alongside, and sharing the power with him, until society and its representatives eventually absorbed his power completely.

A. POPULAR REPRESENTATION

Representation of all interests. Popular representation aims at giving an image as faithful as possible of the whole body social in all its diversity—that which presents itself as a picture of society at a certain time, as it is composed of a multitude of interests and communities. It purports to represent individuals in their social reality, as they may define themselves by their affiliation with the numerous groups that make society, whatever their racial, ethnic, economic, religious nature, the objective being in the end that all interests, whatever their nature, may be represented in the government.

1. Historical Formation (1776-1786)

Initial doubts about representation. From the very beginning, Americans were doubtful about the virtues of representation for at least two reasons. On the one hand, they were not used to it; on the other, they did not know much about it. The few things they knew about it, they had learned from the English, and these did not inspire much confidence in this device of government, which they viewed as being potentially subject to all kinds of easy manipulations.[3]

The system of representative government did not thrive in the first colonies; it was never regarded as the usual system of government. From the beginning, the colonies practiced self-government, particularly in New England, where direct democracy was widely used. Several factors can explain this phenomenon. In the first place, the absence of any aristocracy greatly facilitated first the transplant, then the extraordinary development of the English system of self-government that represented (and still represents today in certain domains such as local education) a true system of direct democracy. In the second place, the Protestant colonies of New England were peopled, particularly in Massachusetts, by those who were the fundamentalists of Protestantism, the Puritans. Tocqueville appreciated the power of this doctrine: ''Puritanism was not only a religious doctrine; it also blended at several points with the most absolute democratic and republican theories.''[4]

The first American communities, the townships of New England, governed themselves like the Swiss cantons: the citizens themselves, all gathered in a town meeting, discussed the affairs of the community, elected the magistrates of

---

[3] Particularly objectionable to them was the practice of designating courtiers and political friends to sit in the House of Lords so that the balance of power would tilt in the direction wished by the government.

[4] Tocqueville, *Democracy in America*, [Translated by H. C. Mansfield & D. Winthrop], University of Chicago Press, 2000, I, I, chap. 2, p. 32.

the county each year, and assigning them their commissions. It is in these townships, where representative government had not been adopted, that American people learned the basics of democracy.[5] Still today, at the local level, if the majority works through representatives and magistrates when it is dealing with the general affairs of the community, direct participation of the citizens in the deliberation and management of certain public matters, particularly education, remains the rule. The citizens are not only consulted; they decide, themselves, by their votes on the projects and orientations of their community.

These elements of self-government did not prepare the Americans for a representative system of government. However, the reason they became hostile to the representative system of government is closely linked to their dispute with the English about their taxation by the Parliament in London, without them being actually represented in this compound body. This dispute, which triggered the American Revolution, is a turning point in American history that determined many of the political choices made later, after independence.

The fiscal debate with England. In the beginning of the 1760s, England decided to raise taxes on the colonies; the idea was to oblige the colonies to share the burden of providing a military defense for the new possessions won from the French territories in America after the Seven Years War. The new customs duties on the trade of goods caused some irritation, but the true revolt against England began in March 1765, when Parliament by an overwhelming majority passed the Stamp Act, levying a tax on legal documents, almanacs, newspapers, and nearly every form of paper used in the colonies. The amount of the parliamentary tax was modest; what caused alarm in the colonies was its significance for the future of their relations with England. Until then, it was commonly accepted that the colonies in theory were immune from taxation. The customs duties raised by London on their trade were regarded as measures aimed at regulating foreign trade, not at raising revenue. The Stamp Act had nothing to do with foreign trade; it directly touched Americans' everyday affairs; it affected purely internal affairs. The Stamp Act, therefore, was seen as an attempt to raise revenue from the colonies without the consent of their legislatures. The Americans invoked the ancestral right of the Englishmen: "No taxation without representation."

The refusal of virtual representation. In the eyes of the Englishmen, the colonies were subject to the laws adopted by Parliament because they had consented to them; and they consented to them, the English said in essence, because they were virtually represented therein, like any possession of the

---

[5] *Id.* I, I, chap. 5, p. 61.

British empire, even if they had not elected representatives. The idea that Parliament represented the whole society grew out of the correspondence between the political organization of the kingdom and its social organization; the government, that is, the body politic made by the King in Parliament was a perfect mirror of the entire society. Moreover, at the political level, the representative character of Parliament was the keystone of parliamentary sovereignty. The whole society was bound to obey the laws adopted by Parliament because it was presumed that the whole society was virtually represented in this precinct and, thus, had consented to the laws that were debated and voted on.

Virtual representation had important consequences for both the status and the mandate of the representatives. In a speech to the electors of Bristol in 1774, the Conservative Edmund Burke developed these consequences when he insisted on the representative rather than imperative nature of the mandate, meaning that the representative may never be bound by authoritative instructions from his electors. Burke explained to his electors:

> Parliament is not a *congress* of ambassadors from different and hostile interests; which interests each must maintain, as an agent and advocate, against other agents and advocates; but parliament is a *deliberative* assembly of *one* nation, with *one* interest, that of the whole; where, not local purposes, not local prejudices, ought to guide, but the general good, resulting from the general reason of the whole. You choose a member indeed; but when you have chosen him, he is not member of Bristol, but he is a member of *parliament*. If the local constituent should have an interest, or should form an hasty opinion, evidently opposite to the real good of the rest of the community, the member for that place ought to be as far, as any other, from any endeavor to give it effect. I beg pardon for saying so much on this subject. I have been unwillingly drawn into it; but I shall ever use a respectful frankness of communication with you. Your faithful friend, your devoted servant, I shall be to the end of my life: a flatterer you do not wish for.[6]

The theory of virtual representation did not impress the Americans, who answered the English that, as far as they were concerned, their alleged virtual representation in the Parliament was pure fiction. An attempt was made to

[6] E. Burke, Speech to the Electors of Bristol (November 3, 1774), in P. B. Kurland & R. Lerner (Eds.), *The Founders' Constitution*, University of Chicago Press, 1987, vol. 1, pp. 391-392 (emphasis in original), available at http://press-pubs.uchicago.edu/founders/tocs/toc.html.

designate representatives of the colonies who could sit in the Parliament in London, but it did not succeed. The English, then, moved the debate onto a different plane, that of sovereignty, arguing that, even if the Americans were not represented in Parliament, they nevertheless were bound by what Parliament might decide because, being sovereign, Parliament had the power to tax the colonies as it saw fit. The argument backfired; the Americans claimed sovereignty for themselves (*i.e.*, independence). They proclaimed it unilaterally on July 4, 1776.

The triumph of actual representation. Once they proclaimed themselves "free and independent states" according to the terms of the Declaration of Independence, the thirteen colonies had to organize themselves. Many of them did not change their existing legislatures, particularly because of the ongoing war against England, but all felt the repercussions of the dispute with England over representation.[7]

The new States adopted constitutions that provided for assemblies popularly elected on conditions very close to universal (white and masculine) suffrage. Very soon, however, a great gulf lay between those who were inside and those who were outside the assembly. Few Americans believed that their representatives could be a faithful image of the electorate as so many expected them to be. The citizens and their representatives were forming two separate worlds. Some radical elements in the North Carolina convention informed their representatives that they were their delegates only and that political power "is of two kinds, one principal and superior, the other derived and inferior . . . The principal supreme power is possessed by the people at large, the derived and inferior power by the servants which they employ." In the minds of Americans, the people were radically distinct from their representatives. The former natural correspondence between representatives and represented that was the hallmark of representation in the European societies divided into estates, each of them being represented in the State, broke apart in the egalitarian society that prevailed across the Atlantic.

Representative institutions fell under suspicion. The people out-of-doors (the electors), as they called themselves, wanted to legislate with the people indoors (the elected). Among the people, many thought that there was no reason to give away sovereignty to representatives who represented nothing but themselves. Their criticisms became all the more acute in that an elitist, almost aristocratic, party had taken shape among the elected. A few of them resurrected

[7] On the crisis over representation in America in the aftermath of independence, see G. S. Wood, *The Creation of the American Republic (1776-1787)*, [hereinafter *The Creation*], 1969, reprint New York, W.W. Norton & Co., 1987, p. 363.

the privileges of the British MP's, and others, although in small number, even succeeded in having a too vocal critic, William Thompson, a tavern keeper, threatened with banishment and reprimanded by the House of Representatives of South Carolina for allegedly insulting one of its wealthy members, John Rutledge.[8] The trust between the representative and the represented no longer existed. The people were convinced that their representatives had become the straw men of political parties and factions; legislatures were regarded as places of political conspiracies between private interests against the public good. The representatives, prone to like power and the honors it bestows, made their differences of rank and status felt by laymen and became execrated. Some were called the "Nabob members of the legislature." The implicit trust they requested from their electors was of course denied to them. Americans could not accept that a few appropriated the right to decide for all.

The people wanted either to keep or to take into their own hands the power they had delegated. Popular assemblies were spontaneously created in the counties to reexamine the laws adopted by the representatives. People were proud to say that "yes, they legislate at home!" Some demagogues presented themselves as true spokesmen for the will of the people, who exhausted themselves trying to find all possible means by which they could keep their representatives under control. The electors addressed authoritative instructions to their representatives; elections were held at very close dates. The representatives were supposed to be the mere agents and instruments of the will of the people. Samuel Chase went so far as to declare that the people's power "is like the light of the sun, native, original, inherent, and unlimited by human authority. Powers in the rulers or governors of the people is like the reflected light of the moon, and is only borrowed, delegated and limited by the grant of the people."[9] The people entertained a mechanical conception of representation.

Distrust of the representatives. The widespread distrust of elected bodies entailed unexpected consequences. American distrust of the virtues of representation had tremendous fallout for the American approach to the public good and public law in general. If the law made by the legislative assemblies was not in truth a reflection of the will of the people, if it was not an image of the general will, but rather the mere product of the will of corrupt and suspect elected representatives, all kinds of devices then would be necessary to limit the scope of their laws and, in some case, to keep their laws from taking effect.

---

[8] *Id.*, p. 367.

[9] *Id.*, p. 371.

The first remedy sought was the simplest; the people resorted to authoritative instructions addressed to their representatives so that they would be bound in all their words and votes; from there, the electors wondered whether general oversight by the people of all the organs of State was not to be provided for. Everything that seemed to limit, to circumscribe, to restrain the power of the representatives was received with favor by the people. People were obsessed, haunted by the power their representatives might enjoy and the ways they might abuse it. The idea emerged that, if the people could not be truly and honestly represented by their delegates, who would necessarily turn into spokesmen for particular interests, then the representatives of the people deserved to represent the people for certain objects only, not for all conceivable objects of legislation. The powers of the legislature therefore had to be limited. These ideas eventually led to a radical redistribution of powers in society and a shattering of all the set notions that dominated European political thought.

The end of classical politics. The less people trusted their representatives, the more they looked for remedies that would guarantee a representation as faithful as possible of all their interests. Distrust of representation led them to ensure that all interests of the electors were represented in the assemblies. The politics of interest groups made its first appearance in American politics.[10] The electoral mandate was conceived as a means to promote all interests in politics, including private interests.

In a profound article on the origins of this foundational and deciding factor in the American republican model, Gordon S. Wood recalls an event that he regards very rightly as "one of the crucial moments in the history of American politics—maybe the crucial moment." It is the debate that occurred in 1786 in the Pennsylvania assembly over the rechartering of the Bank of North America. Two principals confronted each other in this debate. On one side was William Findley, the defender of the debtor-paper money interests in the State, who had been a schoolmaster, farmer, and militia captain before ending up as a political officeholder. On the other was Robert Morris, the wealthiest merchant in the state, with aristocratic aspirations, who was a major stockholder in the bank and a strong supporter of its rechartering. Findley charged that supporters of rechartering of the bank were themselves interested men; they were directors or stockholders of the bank and thus were acting as judges in their own cause. As Wood says, there was nothing new in these charges. To accuse one's opponent of being self-interested was conventional rhetoric in eighteenth-century debates.

[10] C. R. Sunstein, "Interests Groups in American Public Law," 38 *Stanford L. Rev.* 29 (1985).

What was new—startlingly new—was the following by Findley himself: ''Any others in their situation would do as they did.'' Morris and the other investors in the bank, he pursued, had every ''right to advocate their own cause, on the floor of this house.'' But they had no right to protest when others realize ''that it is their own cause they are advocating, and to give credit to their opinions, and to think of their votes accordingly.'' As Wood says, this debate was indeed ''crucial.'' It meant that ''the promotion of interests in politics was quite legitimate, as long as it was open and above board and not disguised by specious claims of genteel disinterestedness. The promotion of private interests was in fact what American politics ought to be about.''[11] This novel approach to politics completely changed the science of government.[12]

In accepting that the government shall mirror all the interests of society, Americans turned personal interest into the driving force of modern politics. A most unfortunate application of this deleterious principle was the additional representation granted to the particular interests of slave owners in the southern States, in the form of a number of representatives in the House of Representatives, apportioned among the several States according to their respective numbers, with ''all other Persons'' counted as ''three fifths'' of a person each.[13] Although the Civil War and the three constitutional amendments adopted in its aftermath have made these provisions obsolete, the idea that triggered their initial inclusion in the Constitution is still alive. This idea runs as follows: it is commonly agreed that what is made in the legislatures does not necessarily promote the public good, but vindicates in the first place the defense of private interests.[14] A whole chapter of classical politics came to an end; the idea of virtue and disinterestedness in the management of public affairs broke into pieces. The republic moved into an era of jealousy and suspicion.

The coming into being of modern constitutionalism. In accepting the representation of all interests into the legislatures, Americans paved the way to a radically new approach to the notion of Constitution. They had already taken a

---

[11] G. S. Wood, ''The Origins of American Democracy, or How the People Became Judge in Their Own Cause,'' 47 *Cleveland State L. Rev.* 309, 320-21 (1999).

[12] As Gordon S. Wood explained it in Chapter XV ''The American Science of Politics'' of his masterful book: *The Creation, supra* note 7, at p. 593.

[13] Article I, sec. 2(3) of the Constitution [changed by section 2 of the Fourteenth Amendment].

[14] On the coming into being of private interests in public affaires, see G. S. Wood, *The Radicalism of the American Revolution*, Vintage Books, 1993, pp. 241-270. As Wood makes understood as an understatement, promotion of private interests in politics is a mere fact that Americans very early resigned themselves to; this does not mean that a majority of them finds it acceptable, still less desirable.

similar path with the reinvention of federalism. In deeming a ''Constitution'' a document that most contemporaries regarded as a ''compact'' between sovereign people—in other words, a treaty—they already had written a new chapter in the complicated history of the law of mixed or composed State structures, which legal scholars at that time analyzed as pertaining to the law of nations rather than to domestic law.[15] However, the disastrous consequences of the promotion of private interests through popular representation reinforced this particular constitutional feature.

From the day it became clear that nothing good could be expected from representatives driven by the defense of particular interests, trust in their actions vanished. Distrust and suspicion took its place, and a remedy to alleviate them soon became necessary. It was the Constitution that, as early as the end of the eighteenth century, acquired in the United States a radically different meaning than on the European continent where it was understood as an ''assemblage of laws, institutions and customs, derived from certain fixed principles of reason, directed to certain fixed objects of public good, that compose the general system, according to which the community hath agreed to be governed.''[16] The Constitution in the United States turned into a single written piece, contained within the four corners of the document, which soon became the disciplinary charter of the government. In the draft resolution he prepared for the legislature of Kentucky in 1799, Jefferson offered the new meaning for the document as follows:

> It would be a dangerous delusion were a confidence in the men of our choice to silence our fears for the safety of our rights: [. . .] confidence is everywhere the parent of despotism—free government is founded in jealousy, and not in confidence; it is jealousy and not confidence which prescribes limited constitutions, to bind down those whom we are obliged to trust with power: [. . .] our Constitution has accordingly fixed the limits to which, and no further, our confidence may go. [. . .]

---

[15] The idea that the Constitution was a ''compact'' between sovereign States survived for a very long time in the United States, notwithstanding the strong denial by John Marshall as early as 1803; it was definitively crushed only with the Civil War, although, even today, it still keeps feeding certain aspects of the southern confederate thought. On the passage from the treaty to the Constitution, see E. Zoller, ''Aspects internationaux du droit constitutionnel, Contribution à la théorie de la fédération d'États,'' 294 *RCADI* 39 (2002).

[16] Bolingbroke (Henry St John), *A Dissertation upon Parties* (1733-1734), Letter X, reproduced in A. W. Bradley & K. D. Ewing, *Constitutional and Administrative Law*, 13th ed., Harlow, Pearson Education, 2003, p. 4.

> In questions of power, then, let no more be heard of confidence in man, but bind him down from mischief by the chains of the Constitution.[17]

The American conception of the Constitution. The new approach to the Constitution that Americans have spread throughout the world has always been an object of national pride. They regard it as the safest guarantee of liberty that has ever been found. As early as 1803, John Marshall drew a sharp distinction between two models of constitutions—the constitutions that "organize the government, and assigns, to different departments, their respective powers [and that] stop here" (an excellent description of what European constitutions and particularly the English Constitution used to do at that time) and the constitutions that (too) "organize the government, and assigns, to different departments, their respective powers, [but that also] establish certain limits not to be transcended by those departments." And John Marshall proudly adds: "The government of the United States is of the latter description."[18] After John Marshall, James Madison too underlined the specificity of the American Constitution when, commenting upon one "vital characteristic of the political system of the United States," that is, that "the Government hold its powers by a charter granted to it by the people," he added: "Hitherto charters have been written grants of privileges by Governments to the people. Here they are written grants of power by the people to their Governments."[19] The new approach to the Constitution entails the following consequence: "Without a steady eye to the landmarks between these departments, the danger is always to be apprehended, either of mutual encroachments and alternate ascendencies incompatible with the tranquil enjoyment of private rights, or of a concentration of all the departments of power into a single one, universally acknowledged to be fatal to public liberty."[20]

2. The Theory of Popular Representation

Popular representation and public interest. The representation in the government of all interests of the society is one thing; the consequences that derive thereof are quite another. From a public law standpoint, the major and

---

[17] Th. Jefferson, Original Draft of the Resolutions 8 and 9, which he supplied to the Kentucky legislature: October 1798, reprinted in Kurland & Lerner, *supra* note 6, at vol. 5, p. 134.

[18] *Marbury* v. *Madison*, 5 US (1 Cranch) 137, 176 (1803).

[19] J. Madison, Supplement to the letter of November 27, 1830, to Andrew Stevenson, on the phrase "common defense and general welfare."—on the power of indefinite appropriation of money by Congress in Kurland & Lerner, *supra* note 6, at vol. 2, p. 459.

[20] *Id.*, p. 458.

most difficult question to solve is this: how do all these interests work for the public good, and how can it be enunciated?

Ten years of popular representation in the states brought an obvious fact to light: modern politics were plagued with a disease against which no remedy seemed to be available, the triumph of individual egoisms and a complete lack of interest in the public good.

Having become closed precincts of bitter struggle between private interests, the states lost all interest in the confederate Union that they created in 1777 to wage war against England and that enabled them to free themselves from British rule. Once peace was established, each state turned inward and became focused on its own interests only; discord was sown in the Union. Within the States, each interest group struggled to conquer power and to put forward its own interests. In a difficult economic climate, fraught with the consequences of the War of Independence, the individual egoisms of all triumphed over the interests common to all. The States, henceforth deprived of access to the traditional commercial markets of the British empire, struggled to survive by relying on their own means; trade war between the States loomed in the near future. Financial difficulties caused popular dissatisfaction, and even populist unrest, particularly among the farmers whose smallholders, driven to the brink of bankruptcy, voted en masse for the demagogues who promised them debtor relief laws. In order to choke off the financial crisis that threatened to bring the Union to ruin, the Congress of the Confederation passed a Resolution on February 21, 1787, "for the sole and express purpose of revising the Articles of Confederation [to] render the Federal Constitution adequate to the exigencies of Government and the preservation of the Union." After four months of work by the fifty State delegates gathered in Philadelphia, a Constitution for the United States was eventually signed on September 17, 1787. This most important document, which stands as the charter of the American republican model, endeavored to find potent medicine against the sickness of the newborn modern republic, the promotion of private interests in politics. The subtle composition, the proper balance between the ingredients and the beneficial effects of the new medicine have been laid out by James Madison, a most important founding father of the American Constitution, in Letter no. 10 of *The Federalist Papers*.[21]

Factions in the modern republic. Letter no. 10 of *The Federalist* is a decisive text to understand the ins and outs that may explain why and how

[21] A. Hamilton, J. Madison & J. Jay, *The Federalist Papers* [hereinafter *The Federalist*], C. Rossiter Edition, Mentor Book, N.Y, 1961, p. 77, available at http://www.yale.edu/lawweb/avalon/federal/fed.htm.

Americans very early lost all their illusions about what politics and the alleged search for the public good may be in a modern republic. In this letter, Madison draws lessons from ten years' experience of republican government in the new free and independent States of America. He explains the proclivity of popularly elected assemblies to legislate for the sole profit of a few, not for the common profit of all. He sets out the partiality and unfairness of these laws, pointing to the fact that "measures are too often decided, not according to the rules of justice and the rights of the minor party, but by the superior force of an interested and overbearing majority."[22] In other words, power is within the hands of factions that work against the public good, what Madison calls "the permanent and aggregate interests of the community." And he raised the question: can we do away with factions? He implicitly admits that this would be the best solution, but he thinks that such an undertaking is unrealistic and that the cure is worse than the disease.

The impossible suppression of factions. Curing the mischiefs of faction may be done by two methods: by removing its causes or by controlling its effects. Removing the causes of faction may in turn be done by two methods, either by destroying the liberty which is essential to its existence, or by giving to every citizen the same opinions, the same passions, and the same interests. In both cases, Madison believes that these drastic measures would amount to killing liberty. He expounds: giving to every citizen the same opinions amounts to destroying freedom of expression and freedom of religion; giving to every citizen the same passions is tantamount to imposing the civil religion of Hobbes haunted by the search for consubstantiality between the Christian State and the Church,[23] or that of Rousseau, obsessed by the will to reunite "the two heads of the eagle, and the restoration throughout of political unity, without which no State or government will ever be rightly constituted"[24]; giving to every citizen the same interests is equivalent to suppressing property, and this, Madison rejects with all his might, because he is convinced, like Locke, that property is the fountainhead of modern liberty. He also makes the point that there exists "an insuperable obstacle to a uniformity of interests," which is "the diversity in

---

[22] *Id.*

[23] In *De Cive,* Hobbes writes: "In Christian Cities the judgement both of *spirituall* and *temporall matters* belongs unto the civill authority. And that man, or councell who hath the Supreme power, is head both of *the City*, and of *the Church*; for a *Church*, and a *Christian City* is but one thing." T. Hobbes, *On the Citizen (De Cive)* [Edited and translated by Richard Tuck & Michael Silverthorne], Cambridge University Press, 1998, chap. XVII, § 28, available at http://www.constitution.org/th/decive.htm.

[24] J.-J. Rousseau, *The Social Contract*, Book IV, chap. 8 [Translated G. D. H. Cole], available at http://www.constitution.org/jjr/socon.htm.

the faculties of men.'' Madison's conclusion is irrevocably final: factions are inevitable in society; they are ''sown in the nature of man.'' The only way to cope with them is to put up with them.

Remedies to factions. Failing a possible eradication of factions, attention must be focused on the means that may neutralize their effects. Two possibilities are conceivable. If the faction is a minority, nothing is to be feared; relief is in the ballot box, supplied by the republican principle, which enables the majority to defeat its views by regular vote. If the faction is a majority in a position to rally a majority, this is the real danger for individual rights and the public good. Madison believes that there are only two methods to prevent such factions from carrying out their grievous projects. If the majority is not yet formed, one must intervene to prevent its formation by breaking power into several organs so that each of them has only a portion of the power—and accordingly particular motives to resist the encroachments of the others (this is the remedy of the separation of powers). If the majority is already formed, the men who make it are already united in their disastrous identity of passions contrary to the public interest. In that case, Madison wrote, one must make use of their number and local situation to keep them from carrying out their plans of oppression (this is the remedy of federalism).

The objection of the antifederalists. The adversaries of Madison in particular, and to the federalists in general, who were called the antifederalists, did not see the problem in the same light. They, too, regarded factions as the worst threat to the republic, but, unlike Madison, they did not regard factions as inevitable; indeed, they were convinced to the contrary. For them, factions diminished and even disappeared in small communities, and it was possible, in their view, to develop a civic spirit through education and self-government.

The antifederalists thought that unity could be achieved through decentralization. They subscribed to Montesquieu's views that a republic may support itself without any internal factions only if it is small. When there are too many interests, they are too diverse, and it is impossible to reach a common good beneficial to all—a situation in which every citizen may take advantage of political association, where there are no winners and no losers. ''Brutus,'' one of their leaders (Roman first names were fashionable, in remembrance of Ancient Rome), dreamed of a society where no one would lose. In order to achieve this, everybody had to be the same, so that everybody would meet the conditions of winning. In a large unit, representation of all the interests is never perfect, if only because there are groups that lose by dint of being in the minority. Brutus believed in small homogenous republics in which both wealth and power are equally distributed, in which every citizen knows every other, in which every citizen may force his neighbor to be virtuous, and where it is possible to attain a common good that may benefit everyone. According to him, there was no need for the big machinery that was the federal government as provided for in the Constitution; the solution was to bank on the States and to trust governments that would be close to the people.[25] Brutus was a supporter of decentralization.

To these arguments, Madison answered that, in a small republic, the probability of factions is even greater than in a large republic, because the majority will always share common interests and common passions, due to the fact that the form of government will necessarily enable it to unite and work in agreement. Madison very cleverly convinced all those who feared for the protection of their rights against the power of the majority that a great republic provides better protection against factions than the small republic can. The diversity and the multiplicity of the interests that form the great republic minimize the risk that a common desire or passion may be felt by enough people at the same time to oppress a minority.

The Madisonian theory of the public good. Madison provided remedies against faction in the republic, but he was far from thinking that, once all private egoisms were under control, the public good would spring by itself, as if by magic, from a clash between all these private interests then neutralized. He knew that something more was needed. Concretely, he knew that the public good called for honest and upright statesmen who would be in charge of public affairs and work hard to enhance the public interests. To put such virtuous statesmen at the helm, he relied on the same mechanisms that brought about a solution to the religious conflicts. The multiplicity of religious sects in America prevented any one of them from becoming predominant in one State, a result that, in turn, enabled enlightened statesmen such as Jefferson and himself to ensure that the public interest would prevail at the federal level (in the separation between Church and State embodied in the First Amendment).

In Madison's view, the great advantage of the republic over democracy was that it made it possible for talented men, caring for the public good, to come to the fore. By republic, he meant a government in which the idea of representation exists, thus allowing governmental affairs to be delegated to a small number of citizens chosen by the people while avoiding the pitfall of democracy—degeneration into factions, no matter how small the democracy may be. The republic, he insisted, avoids the dangers of democracy precisely because of

---

[25] Brutus, Essay I (October 17, 1787), in *The Anti-Federalist Papers and the Constitutional Convention Debates* (R. Ketcham (Ed.)), New York, Mentor Book, 1986, p. 270.

representation, which makes it possible "to refine and enlarge the public views, by passing them through the medium of a chosen body of citizens, whose wisdom may best discern the true interest of their country, and whose patriotism and love of justice will be least likely to sacrifice it to temporary or partial considerations."[26]

Representation, buttressed by the conviction that elections deriving thereof necessarily send enlightened and responsible statesmen to the helm, is at the heart of the American conception of the public good. This theory operates on the premise enunciated by Madison himself as follows: "I go on this great republican principle, that the people will have virtue and intelligence to select men of virtue and wisdom."[27] There is little doubt that the Madisonian approach to the public good is premised on an elitist conception of politics. The Federalists—Madison chief among them as one of their brightest supporters—were not so much adversaries of power as fierce opponents of the State governments headed by uneducated people of petty low condition. Their fear for the future of the Union lay in the mediocre quality, the short-sighted views, and the narrow-minded projects of those who held power in the States and who seemed to be interested only in parochial disputes. Their dream was less to replace them than to subject them to the liberal, enlightened, cosmopolitan views of the natural aristocracy of society, as they saw themselves.

The virtues of the great republic. In order to do so, they suggested enlarging the field of politics and shifting the most important decisions to a higher level, the federal or national level, with a broadening of the electorate and a diminution of the elected as a result. The combination of a larger electoral basis and a reduced government concentrated on the problems common to all would work as a filter for selecting the best minds to take on national responsibilities. The great republic is bound to be propitious to the public interest, they said, because it will produce more good leaders; the breeding ground for virtuous men is larger by necessity, and, insofar as they would confront a larger number of electors and a wider range of interests, candidates would be more likely to be held to account by a larger public. This calculation was the winning bet of the great republic that the federalists created in Philadelphia. Madison outlined the inner mechanism of the scheme as follows: "In the extended republic of the United States, and among the great variety of interests, parties, and sects which it embraces, a coalition of a majority of the whole society could seldom take

---

26 Letter no. 10, *The Federalist*, *supra* note 21, at p. 82.

27 J. Madison, Virginia Ratifying Convention, June 20, 1788, in Kurland & Lerner *supra* note 6, at vol. 1, p. 409.

place on any other principles than those of justice and the general good.''[28] For carrying out his design, Madison relied heavily on the Senate. In his mind, this chamber of States—which was not originally popularly elected, but rather designated by the State legislatures—would work ''as a defense to the people against their own temporary errors and delusions'' and form ''some temperate and respectable body of citizens, in order to check the misguided career, and to suspend the blow meditated by the people against themselves, until reason, justice, and truth can regain their authority over the public mind.''[29]

Democracy and republic. The antifederalists objected that a system of filtering the electorate was aristocratic, contrary to the republican principle, and undemocratic. The federalists were clever enough to counter the charge by circumventing it and attacking their opponents on their own field. Against the relentless charges of elitism, the Federalists replied that the new system, in complete contrast with the former confederation, would derive its powers entirely and exclusively from the people. The source of power will always derive from the popular will, they kept repeating, an assertion that was perfectly correct since the people not only elected the political organs of the government, but also had to approve the Constitution through constitutional conventions in their states. Their propaganda worked so well that, as early as 1787-1788, the word ''democracy'' in the United States was equated with ''election'' and put on a par with the term ''republic.'' Eventually, representation was identified with election, pure and simple. Once that identification was reached, the old categories of democracy and mixed government that went back to Aristotle became obsolete, failing to describe the new American system of government.[30]

The contemporary variation of the pluralist State. In the twentieth century, Letter no. 10 of *The Federalist* has been understood as having laid down the foundations of the pluralist State. It is true, in one sense, that Madison's genius was to invent a theory of representation free from any need for virtue. Contrary to classical authors, who listed the spirit of sacrifice, devotion to the *res publica*,

---

[28] Letter no. 51, *The Federalist, supra* note 21, at p. 325.

[29] Letter no. 63, *The Federalist, supra* note 21, at p. 384. The Seventeenth Amendment to the Constitution, which imposed popular election of senators by universal direct suffrage in the states eviscerated Madison's hopes of a great part of their substance. See I. Kramnick, ''The 'Great National Discussion': The Discourse of Politics in 1787,'' 45 *Wm. & Mary Q.* 3, 13 (1988) and, in French, R. Dehoussse, ''Le paradoxe de Madison: Réflexions sur le rôle des chambres hautes dans les systèmes fédéraux,'' *RDP*, 1990, p. 643, in particular pp. 646-647.

[30] See G. S. Wood, ''Democracy and the Constitution,'' in R. A. Goldwin & W. A. Schambra (Eds.), *How Democratic is the Constitution?* Washington / London, American Enterprise Institute for Public Policy Research, 1980, pp. 1-17.

renunciation of self-enrichment, and frugality as being the prerequisites for the proper functioning of a republican government, Madison fathered a new system that did away with the need for virtue in that it deprives the personal and egoistic interests of individuals of success in their undertakings. To keep these particular interests from working against the public good and the common interests, they should be allowed to grow and multiply as freely as possible, so that, as Philippe Raynaud writes, "an individual is prevented from defining himself solely by his belonging to *one* group of opinions or interests only."[31] In order to reach such a result, Madison advocated organizing government so as to prevent its organs from uniting into an oppressive majority and, in fact, to instead contrive for them to work for the public good while looking out for their own interests. The Madisonian theory of the State made it possible for all the interests of society to be represented in the government without adverse consequences for the public good; it paved the way for a polity that would later be called the pluralist State.

Although Madison's ideas laid down the foundations of a theory of popular representation that relies on the plurality of interests to better protect individual rights, it would be misleading to say that they directly gave birth to the theory of the pluralist State; at best, they prepared the way for it. Madison is a forerunner of Robert Dahl; but he does not advocate a pluralist vision of politics. In his view, the government is not a public space in which all sorts of interests clash in the hope that mutual concessions by all parties will give rise to a public arrangement satisfying everybody. For Madison, the government was rather a neutral and disinterested umpire, made up of impartial and enlightened men who were called to decide and take sides among the various interests without being co-opted by the most powerful among them. Madison does not defend the pluralist State; he is not a modern political scientist.[32]

Representation of interest and governance. In turning the State into a mirror reflecting all the interests of society, the American conception of representation has made a distinction between the State and the government pointless. In truth, the distinction is no longer necessary, except in external relations, where the concept of the State, as in England, stands through the international legal personhood for the enduring interests of the American nation, as opposed to the transitory character of the various administrations at the helm. By contrast, in

---

[31] Ph. Raynaud, "Préface," in J. M. McPherson, *La guerre de Sécession (1861-1865)*, Robert Laffont, 1991, p. xxiii (emphasis in original).

[32] See R. J. Morgan, "Madison's Theory of Representation in the Tenth federalist," 36 *Journal of Politics* 852 (1974); P. F. Borke, "The Pluralist Reading of James Madison's Tenth Federalist," 9 *Perspectives in American History* 271 (1975).

internal relations, the people being represented in the government or, better, the people being the State itself, the government and the State are two sides of the same coin. The State is completely absorbed in the government, and the government stands for the State; both of them are places of conciliation between all the particular interests therein represented; they stand for a meeting point of all these interests without ever claiming to be in a position to "govern" in the true meaning of the term, that is, to "direct" all these interests toward a goal of common good that would represent a public interest distinct from the aggregation of individual interests.

The principal consequence of the fusion between the State and the government is that the quality of government is no longer measured as before by the ends it pursues (or, at least, is supposed to pursue, that is, the public good). Rather, it is assessed by its aptitude in fulfilling the function of conciliation between all the interests therein represented and its capacity to keep any especially powerful interest from taking over the governmental mechanisms and imposing its own preferences on the other interests.[33] Scholars focus their attention less on the legitimacy of a particular policy than on its effectiveness in satisfying, as far as possible, all the interests represented in the public space. Concern for the ends is secondary; the primary concern is with the means used to reach an agreement that will satisfy all these interests. A good government is judged by the quality of the means it employs to deliver to the citizens what they expect, not by the ends it assigns itself—hence, the importance given to the procedures and mechanisms of dispute settlement in modern politics. The conflict among interests may not be resolved by public authority (the concept of public authority in the United States is hard to grasp), but by negotiation and mutual adjustment among everyone's claims.[34] To make a long story short, government is replaced by governance. Instead of a search for the public good, good governance puts the emphasis on the modalities by which power is exercised, and it downplays the importance of its ends.

---

[33] See F. H. Easterbrook, "The State of Madison's Vision of the State: A Public Choice Perspective," 107 *Harv. L. Rev.* 1328, 1337 (1994).

[34] For a criticism of this "popular State" whose political philosophy is summarized by the expression "interest-group liberalism" and in which the priority of politics is to make the government accessible to all the interests of society without ever allowing it to exercise an independent judgement on the value of their various claims, so that the public interest is nothing more than an amalgam of all these interests, see T. S. Lowi, *The End of Liberalism*, 2nd ed., New York, W.W. Norton & Co., 1979.

B. THE STATUS OF STATUTORY LAW IN THE STATE

Representation and legislation. To a great extent, popular representation determines the status of statutory law in the State. A statute is appreciated less in consideration of a distant and hypothetical public interest that nobody believes in, than in consideration of the tangible and real interests of the individuals represented in the legislatures. The first yardstick of a fair and good law is its aptitude to satisfy the individual interests of the electors. The public interest is envisioned only in reference to the individual preferences of the electors, as they are expressed at the ballot box. In *Brown* v. *Hartlage* (1982), the question was what kinds of promises a candidate may make to his constituency and, in particular, whether he may pledge himself to reduce his salary if elected. The Supreme Court with equanimity decided that there was nothing reprehensible in "the fact that some voters may find their self-interest reflected in a candidate's commitment." The Court added:

> We have never insisted that the franchise be exercised without taint of individual benefit; indeed, our tradition of political pluralism is partly predicated on the expectation that voters will pursue their individual good through the political process, and that the summation of these individual pursuits will further the collective welfare. So long as the hoped-for personal benefit is to be achieved through the normal processes of government, and not through some private arrangement, it has always been, and remains, a reputable basis upon which to cast one's ballot.[35]

The presence, always perfectly legitimate, accepted and even desired, of all the private interests in the government, and in particular in the legislatures, has had a heavy cost on the law-making process. It explains the reserved and suspicious approach of public opinion towards statutory law.

Representation of all interests. A legislature that would represent all the different interests and views of the various classes of the community is obviously an ideal beyond reach. During the debate on the ratification of the Constitution, it was said "to be necessary, that all classes of citizens should have some of their own number in the representative body, in order that their feelings and interests may be the better understood and attended to." In that vein, it was argued that landholders, mechanics, manufacturers, farmers, and men of the learned professions should be represented by members of each class in order to be fairly represented. Hamilton answered these visionary arguments:

---

[35] *Brown* v. *Hartlage,* 456 US 45, 56 (1984).

''This will never happen under any arrangement that leaves the votes of the people free.''[36]

The basic idea of popular representation—the implicit expectation that all interest groups and classes in society have a legislative presence, so that the legislature may be regarded as a mirror of society—does not mean that each citizen has a right to have all his own personal interests taken into consideration in the debate, but this is how this sense of entitlement is operative in practice—even though not established in theory as an actual right. The causes of this phenomenon are diverse. Two of them seem crucial: the extreme brevity of electoral mandates in the lower chambers (no more than two years), which strongly induces the elected to always think about satisfying the preferences of his electors, and, at the same time, the distrust of the voters for the representatives. Scholars, including the Supreme Court, justify the system by recalling Madison's aphorism, ''that the private interest of every individual may be a sentinel over the public rights.''[37]

The result of all these considerations is that the statute, and more generally all legal rules, may be made only in taking scrupulous account of all classes of interests, private and public, general and individual, likely to be affected. This entrenched idea is the reason for the prodigious development of lobbies and interest groups that besiege the legislatures at the federal as well as at the State level. The right of all classes of interests to participate in the making of rules likely to affect them is of general scope nowadays. Since World War II, this right has been extended to include the rule making functions of executive and administrative agencies. A 1946 statute, the Administrative Procedure Act, provides for a mandatory consultation of all classes of affected interests. It forms the very substance of what ''Administrative Law'' stands for in the United States. For example, it compels administrative agencies to publish in the *Federal Register* a general notice of proposed rulemaking and, more particularly, ''[to] give interested persons an opportunity to participate in the rule making through submission of written data, views, or arguments with or without opportunity for oral presentation.'' It must be noted that federal courts have construed the statute as requiring the agency, whenever its rule does not take into account the various representations made during the rulemaking, to give reasons, although ''comments must be significant enough to step over a threshold requirement of materiality before any lack of agency response or

[36] Letter no. 35, *The Federalist*, *supra* note 21, at p. 215.
[37] Letter no. 51, *The Federalist*, *supra* note 21, at p. 322.

consideration becomes of concern.''[38] In the second half of the twentieth century, these techniques have spread all over the world; they penetrated European law and inspired the procedures applicable to the making of directives and regulations in the European Union. Today, these techniques make the substance of what is called ''participatory democracy.'' They developed and coexist next to the ''deliberative'' or ''elective democracy,'' which used to regard both statutes and regulations as the final result of deliberations between unbiased and honest representatives—moved only by the pursuit of the public good, such as was the heart of the republican model envisioned by the Founding Fathers in 1787.

Free communication of ideas and free trade of interests. The system of popular representation has the advantage of allowing representation of all classes of interests that may exist in society, giving each of them a chance to participate in the making of the legal rules that will affect society. All interests expect to be heard and to be represented by the candidates they may have won over to their cause. All these interests compete against each other in the same manner that ideas compete in public debate. From the free trade of interests on the market, the same benefits are expected as from the free trade of ideas.

The free trade of ideas that, due to conservative and puritan prejudices, did not exist in the American society at the beginning of the nineteenth century, was forcefully defended by Justice Holmes as the best means to reach ''the ultimate good desired'' because, in his views, ''the best test of truth is the power of the thought to get itself accepted in the competition of the market.''[39] When it is free, open, and untrammeled, the free competition between ideas is supposed to be the best means to reach truth and to make it prevail. The problem is that, ideas being often shields for interests, the transition from competition between ideas to competition between interests is easy to make, and today, what is true of ideas is held to be true of interests, too.

The free market of ideas and interests is entirely based upon absolute liberty of the will and unlimited trust in the individual judgment. It can work effectively and properly only if it is accompanied and supported by complete freedom of speech. There is therefore little surprise if that freedom is a ''preferred

---

[38] *Portland Cement Ass'n* v. *Ruckelhaus*, 486 F.2d 375, 394 (D.C. Cir. 1973), cert. denied, 417 US 921 (1974). See also A. C. Aman, Jr. & W. T. Mayton, *Administrative Law*, 2nd ed., West Group, 2001, p. 55.

[39] Holmes (dissenting) in *Abrams* v. *United States*, 250 US 616, 630 (1919). ''When men have realized that time has upset many fighting faiths,'' Holmes added: ''that truth is the only ground upon which their wishes safely can be carried out. That at any rate is the theory of our Constitution. It is an experiment, as all life is an experiment.''

freedom'' in American public law, for it is the prerequisite to the smooth functioning of popular representation. There are no limits to the peaceful resources, whether financial or otherwise, that a general or particular interest may mobilize to make itself heard in the market and to win the votes of the electors. True, some laws exist to regulate the role played by money in political campaigns, but their aim is mostly to ensure the transparency of private funding and contributions to candidates.[40] Expenditures are not capped, and there are no limits to the number of interests—whether political, economic, or social, or causes, whether national or local, public, or private—that may enter into the public debate. The goal is to give all interests, whatever they may be, a chance to be represented in the legislature (whether at the State or national level) and to be in a position to be heard—hence, the numerous pressure groups, or lobbies, that revolve around the representatives.[41]

From the theory of domination to the socialization of authority. The system of popular representation, as it evolved in the United States toward the pluralist State, radically transformed both the conception of the public good and the relation of the individual to the latter. It would be wrong to assume that because all interests are represented in one way or another in the government, this means that they all must be satisfied, but the close proximity of all these interests to the centers of power creates a situation that tends toward such a result. The pluralism that characterizes the American republican model has created a State system that cannot be properly explained with the analytical tools given by the so-called ''general theory of the State,'' elaborated in the nineteenth century by German scholarship and introduced in France in the beginning of the twentieth century by Carré de Malberg.

The theory of ''*Staatsgewalt*'' (State power), which analyzes the State as an instrument of domination over the society, never thrived in the United States. As early as the end of the nineteenth century, American political scholars broke away from the German ''general theory of the State.''[42] They steered academic scholarship toward another and completely different theory of political authority

---

[40] See *Buckley* v. *Valeo*, 424 US 1 (1976).

[41] Leaving aside the prohibition of corruption, there are no limits to the means used to be heard. Electoral campaign regulation is not as strict as it may be in Europe, notwithstanding the recent efforts by the Senate to reinforce it; see *Congress and Pressure Groups*, Senate, 99th Congress, 2nd session, S-Prt 99-161 (1986) and *Lobbying Reform, Background and Legislative Proposals, 109th Congress*, CRS Report for Congress (updated March 26, 2006).

[42] See S. D. Fries, ''*Staatstheorie* and the New American Science of Politics,'' 34 *Journal of the History of Ideas* 391 (1973).

inspired by the philosophy of Pragmatism, which has exercised a tremendously important influence not only in the United States, but also overseas. This shift triggered a paradigmatic change in the analysis of social domination. Born in the Progressive Era (1880-1920), this theory, which may be called the theory of social control, endeavored to consider in depth the foundations of a new rationale justifying obedience to law and political power.[43]

According to the theory of social control, the rationale for obedience to law and power does not derive from a transcendental source (such as natural law, in which the social contract is rooted), but from the experience acquired in the intersubjectivity and interdependence of human relations. The reflexiveness of human reality is crucial in this theory; both human ethics and human knowledge are not innate or revealed, but based on intersubjective agreements and forged in social relationships, hence interdependent. Man in the state of nature is a pure fiction (with the implication that the social contract is legal fiction). Rejecting Max Weber's analysis of legal-rational domination, the theory of social control teaches that man obeys authority, not for formal reasons, but because he has acquired through exchanges with his peers a feeling of social responsibility. The social link originates in the reciprocity and responsibility of human relations. Obedience is grounded not in domination, but in the mechanisms of human interdependencies and in the social codes that the individual acquires in his community and social environment. Power is not external to society; it does not take the form of a State external to the social body; it is society itself; or, in other words, authority is socialized.[44]

Social control is therefore a decisive element of the insertion of the individual into the group. It grows out of natural mechanisms such as, for instance, the market, whose rules and discipline are a natural mechanism of socialization. It is also possible to enhance better socialization of the individual through a thorough knowledge of the sciences of organization. It must be said that these last scientific disciplines, which derive from the American approach to power, underwent considerable development in the twentieth century, in particular with management, which is a scientific application of the new theory of obedience based upon social control (where leadership is a modern version of command). The aim of social control theory was originally to build the theory of obedience upon bases other than domination and to demonstrate that the mystery of obedience is not a top-down, but a bottom-up mechanism insofar as it comes

---

[43] See G. G. Hamilton & J. R. Sutton, ''The Problem of Control in the Weak State, Domination in the United States, 1880-1920,'' 18 *Theory and Society* 1 (1989).

[44] See J. P. Diggins, ''The Socialization of Authority and the Dilemmas of American Liberalism,'' 46 *Social Research* 454 (1979).

from the subject himself. The theory was initially born as a revolt against the rigid and dogmatic European formalism that Americans have always regarded as inadequate to explain the specificity of their republican model.

Rejection of majoritarian logic. Unlike the European model, the American governmental model builds itself against majoritarian logic. In the spirit of the Founding Fathers, the criterion of a free government is to be found in its aptitude to put a check on the ambitions of "an interested and overbearing majority."[45] That government was achieved by favoring the multiplicity and multiplication of interests. The Founders, however, never take sides as to how to settle between these interests, leaving to the deliberative process the responsibility for reaching conciliation among them.

Formally, the American model adheres to what Hamilton termed the "fundamental maxim of republican government, which requires that the sense of the majority should prevail," on the condition that this is the sense "of a respectable majority."[46] What is a respectable majority? There is no clear answer to that question, and it would be foolhardy to try to give one. One may, however, suggest this: a majority is respectable if it has taken shape in striving to take into account all opinions, hence all interests, on the question under discussion. This is the reason why, beyond formal appearances, the system actually works in accordance with a different principle than the majoritarian principle: it works in accordance with the principle of compromise.

The principle of compromise. The principle of compromise is a matter of legitimacy, not legality. It would be erroneous to say that it amounts to a veto power for the minority over the decisions by the majority, for this is not the case. But the organizing principle of American politics is this: every major interest in the country—whether regional, economic, or religious—has a right to be heard before any political decision affecting it is to be taken, even to the point of being entitled to request that the decision will not be taken without its consent.

The principle of compromise is a reminder of the principle that John C. Calhoun called "the rule of concurrent majority." Calhoun, a former vice-president of the United States and a senator from South Carolina, fought for the minority interests of the southern states in the 1830s. He developed an ingenious theory arguing that in a truly constitutional government, every political decision must be made with the agreement of at least a portion of the minority with the majority. He thought that a decision could be fair only if it

[45] Madison, Letter no. 10, *The Federalist*, *supra* note 21, at p. 77.

[46] Hamilton, Letter no. 22, *The Federalist*, *supra* note 21, at pp. 146, 148.

combines the majority of the majority and the majority of the minority, that is, a majority of consensus. Although Calhoun's theory may be said to have been defeated by the Civil War, it would wrong to conclude that its spirit has not survived.[47] Europeans, who usually look at history with a sense of fatality, are prone to invoke the irreducibility principle of politics or, in the words of Carl Schmitt's famous aphorism, the view that ''sovereign is he who decides on the exception.''[48] There is no doubt that, in great historical moments, he who decides is sovereign, although it is rare that the sovereign in such exceptional moments decides without the people and their various interests gathered behind, and supporting him. History is not made of exceptional moments only. In the day-to-day life of the American republic, it is true that the majority may carry the day, but it is rare that it does so without having first tried to govern, whenever this is possible, with the consent of the minority.

Consequences. The rejection of majoritarian logic seems to be sown in the fabric of American politics. This can be verified in the numerous usages that bend the techniques and mechanics of the decision-making process toward respect for minority interests. These methods or usages are not made official; but they are regularly followed and tend to make the law-making process into one of mutual concessions that are regarded as necessary for the public good. Among these usages, the following ought to be noted:

(1) The working methods of the Congress—Congress works essentially in committees and subcommittees, in front of limited audiences where a conciliation of all interests present may take place; all interests to be heard are admitted in the course of public hearings; when the bill leaves these committees, the plenary session takes place for appearances' sake.[49]

(2) The absence of any structured political parties—the two major American political parties do not represent ideas, but interests; they have no ideology. Pragmatism is their dominant discourse. They may adjust themselves to circumstances, and their program is very general; they have no other goal than to set up winning strategies that will

[47] See P. F. Drucker, ''A Key to American Politics: Calhoun's Pluralism,'' 10 *Review of Politics* 412 (1948).

[48] Carl Schmitt, *Political Theology: Four Chapters on the Concept of Sovereignty* (1934) [Translated by George Schwab], MIT Press 1985, p. 5.

[49] This was already well noted as early as the beginning of the twentieth century by the future president of the United States, Woodrow Wilson, in *Congressional Government, A Study in American Politics*, Boston, Houghton Mifflin, 1885.

enable them to gain power, thus giving to the multitude of interests that compose them a chance to win the elections.

Popular representation, private interests, and the public interest. Popular representation holds that the representation of interests in the republic is the necessary condition for the public good. According to its supporters, it necessarily works for the good of everyone because it allows all the interests of society to be represented and because, if the public interest exists, it cannot be anything other than an aggregation of all individual preferences. The American conception of the public good is a legacy of the British monarchical age; it holds the public interest to be in nothing more than the protection of every individual's private rights. The whole law-making process is organized to satisfy the private interests of society. Popular representation leads to a system that puts a strong value on a pluralist and interactive approach to collective action.[50] In the American republican model, the laws—and, along with them, the idea of the public good—are the result of a competition and a negotiation between numerous interest groups, whether private (such as those involved in the business world) or public (as those dedicated to the public interest) without either of them being in a position to win over its rival in a lasting and permanent manner. The problem with this approach is that some groups are more powerful than others, and they tend to win over the others more often than the theory predicts. Without a regulation of the role played by money in politics, the system gives a decisive advantage to financially powerful groups. That said, its major and most appealing advantage is to present the protection of individual rights as the *raison d'être* of the State;[51] private interests are not severed and radically distinct from that of the public interest.

On such premises, the distinction between public law and private law has no *raison d'être*. There is one law only, which constantly mixes the State and the society, the public and the private.[52] Its purpose is to defend and promote the

---

[50] See J. Chevallier, ''La gouvernance et le droit,'' *Mélanges Amselek*, Bruylant, 2005, p. 189, especially p. 191.

[51] On that score, American and French philosophers shared the same philosophy. The affirmation of the 1776 Declaration of Independence [''To secure these (unalienable) rights (Life, Liberty, and the Pursuit of Happiness), Governments are instituted among Men''] is echoed by article 2 of the 1789 Declaration of Rights [''The purpose of every political association is the preservation of the natural and indefeasible rights of man (liberty, property, security, and resistance to oppression)''].

[52] See W. J. Novak, ''The Pluralist State, The Convergence of Public and Private Power in America,'' in W. Gamber, M. Grossberg & H. Hartog (Eds.), *American Public Life and Historical Imagination*, University of Notre Dame Press, 2003, p. 27 s., in particular pp. 36-37.

interest of the individuals who compose society. In the United States, when scholars refer to public law values, what they have in mind are values that serve the individual members of the society; they are individual not collective values. Legal scholars interested in them cite one after another: fairness, publicity, transparency, accountability, due process, legality, rationality, participation, and even efficiency. Since these values have in common the fact that they all work to the benefit of the private interests of individuals, they tend to merge with the rights of men, which, as far as Americans are concerned, are the values of the Bill of Rights. Public law in the United States is not the law *of* power but the law *against* power—public power (the State) as well as private power (monopolies).

Chapter 6
Limited Power

Initial distrust of power. No idea is more important to understanding the American republican model than that of limited power. Few people have taken more seriously the admonitions of Montesquieu about the aptitude of every man to abuse power.[1] Extending his observations much further than he envisioned, Americans have invented a republican model that gives all power to the individual, but denies it to the State. Although their theory of popular representation has spread throughout the world, their theory of power and the model of government that emerged from it have remained distinct to them. No other people are governed as Americans are. The constitutional theory of federalism, which they invented "to form a more perfect Union," already, ex hypothesis, implies a limited power because of the distribution of power between the federal government and the states. In addition, their general political theory inherited from the British is that political power must be limited because it is inherently dangerous. The combination of both theories in the Constitution has resurrected the medieval approach to power, where power is treated like a bundle of sticks, so to speak, made of jurisdictions parsimoniously granted and meticulously counted.

The American deep-rooted distrust for power has many origins. Historically speaking, the rejection of State power originates in the hatred for any domination of one man over another, which was regarded as incompatible with liberty. Bernard Baylin related in minute detail the distaste that the colonists had for power; they preferred to call power "dominion," recalling its feudal origins, which they loathed. Power, it was said over and over, has "an encroaching nature"; power is "grasping" and "tenacious"; "what it seizes, it will retain."

---

[1] In *The Spirit of Laws* [Translated by Th. Nugent, 1752, revised by J. V. Pritchard], 1748, Book XI, chap. 4 available at http://www.constitution.org/cm/sol.htm, Montesquieu wrote: "Constant experience shows us that every power invested with power is apt to abuse it, and to carry his authority as far as it will go. Is it not strange, though true, to say that virtue itself has need of limits?"

Sometimes, power was "like the ocean, not easily admitting limits to be fixed in it." Sometimes, it was "like a cancer, it eats faster and faster every hour." Sometimes, it was like "jaws . . . always open to devour." From the power and sovereignty, which they abhorred, Americans have retained their irrepressible tendency to be restless, aspiring, and insatiable, and to invade all that they could subdue. The word most often used in relation to them is trespass, a common law tort that refers to the invasion of something private, privately owned, and hence, sacred. In their view, power was inherently aggressive and always prone to fall on its natural prey—liberty, law, and right.[2]

The effect of popular representation on the legislative process. Practical implementation of the principles of popular representation did not make things better. It even worsened the situation insofar as, once all the interests of the society, from the noblest to the basest, were present in the legislatures, the distrust formerly directed against the laws of the king was extended to the laws of the people. As soon as it became clear, as Jefferson put it, that "173 despots [can] surely be as oppressive as one,"[3] the statutes of popular legislatures were not more gently treated than the statutes of the tyrants. Statutory law was regarded as the result of makeshift coalitions of private interests that eventually succeed only because they have numbers behind them, in particular, the required number of votes. True, the idea that the law must always aim to promote the public good—common to all, not the private good of a few—was never far from sight. However, in the absence of any will (or power) to curtail in any way the right of the people to be actually represented in all their tangible interests within the legislatures, the public interest, or the public good, appears to be in the eyes of many citizens a chimera—a sort of wishful thinking, so to speak. The common opinion is that it is possible that statutes may pursue the public good, but that nothing could be more uncertain, and that this is most likely not the case. On such premises, public opinion tends to hold that the fewer laws, the better. The first requirement of public law in the United States is that it limits power.

Divided sovereignty. In order to limit power, Americans have undertaken, as Justice Kennedy put it so well in *U.S. Term Limits Inc.* v. *Thornton* (1995), "to split the atom of sovereignty."[4] They broke power into pieces; they exploded it; they enervated the State of its power. How? By dividing

---

[2] B. Bailyn, *The Ideological Origins of the American Revolution*, Cambridge, The Belknap Press of Harvard University Press, 1967, enlarged edition 1992, p. 56.

[3] T. Jefferson, "Notes on the State of Virginia," in *Writings*, New York, Literary Classics of the United States, 1984, p. 245.

[4] *U.S. Term Limits Inc.*, v. *Thornton*, 514 US 779, 838 (1995).

sovereignty under an original application of the theory of separation of powers that has remained unique to them (Section A) and leads the American republican model to fit under the paradigm of the liberal State (Section B).

A. THE SEPARATION OF POWERS

The American contribution to the theory of the separation of powers. It would be an overstatement to say that the separation of powers was invented by Americans, but it is true that the theory experienced in the United States is an implementation not experienced elsewhere. In less than two decades, it was elevated to the rank of "first principle of free governments," as Madison said in 1792.[5] That promotion did not take place at once; nobody could imagine in 1776, when the theory was first put into practice, that it would turn into the elaborate doctrine it had become by 1792. It has not ceased to develop since, year after year. Americans came to the building of the theory progressively.

1. Historical Formation

Origins. No other principle of American public law has drawn more scholarly interest than the separation of powers. It is usually presented as a founding principle of the American political system, and this is the correct approach if one construes the principle as implying the splitting of power and division of sovereignty. The principle originates in the classification of functions of the government first undertaken by Aristotle. But the sources that Americans used to establish their theory of separation of powers do not go back further than the seventeenth century in England. During the Revolution and the Interregnum, several English radicals had developed a theory of separation of powers as a means of isolating the legislative function of Parliament from the executive function of the monarch. Locke had pursued this idea, and built a loose theory of separation of powers among the legislative, the executive, and the federative powers (by which he meant foreign affairs). In the beginning of the seventeenth century, the separation of powers was at the center of scholarly disputes between

---

[5] *National Gazette*, February 6, 1792:

> Power being found by universal experience liable to abuses, a distribution of it into separate departments has become a first principle of free governments. By this contrivance, the portion entrusted to the same hands being less, there is less room to abuse what is granted; and the different hands being interested, each in maintaining its own, there is less opportunity to usurp what is not granted. Hence the merited praise of governments modelled on a partition of their powers into legislative, executive, and judiciary, and a repartition of the legislative into different houses.

political theorists. It was often blended with other political theories, in particular that of the mixed government, which represented and balanced against each other the different estates of the society, namely the nobility, the clergy, and the commons. In the 1730s, the separation between the legislative and the executive powers was often assimilated to the mixed government and often absorbed by it.

The contribution of Montesquieu. The genius of Montesquieu was to sort out all these theories and to bring about there complete reorganization through an analysis that has since become immortal. When his work was published in 1748, there was nothing new in his affirmation: "When the legislative and executive powers are united in the same person, or in the same body of magistrates, there can be no liberty." This had been believed for a long time. A little more novel was his remark: "There is no liberty, if the judiciary power be not separated from the legislative and executive." Although Montesquieu also spoke about the mixed constitution, and kept the confusion between separation and balance of powers alive and well, he is the first author who clearly identified a tripartite classification of governmental functions into the legislative, the executive, and the judiciary. The gist of his famous Chapter 6 of Book XI of *The Spirit of Laws*[6] was simply this: political liberty is at risk when these three functions are within the same hands. It is more desirable to distribute the various functions of the State into several hands than to put them all within a single hand.[7] Thus, for Montesquieu, the secret of moderate government is in the sharing of power. In order to understand this and to persuade oneself of the wisdom of this arrangement, it suffices, as Montesquieu reiterated in substance, to take a close look at England, where the King shares power with the Lords and the Commons, and where, as a result, he is firmly kept from abusing power—thus allowing political liberty to "appear in its highest perfection."[8]

a. The Years of Formation (1776-1779)

The separation of powers in 1776. In 1776, Americans agreed that there were three functions of government; but few of them attached great importance to a real and effective division of governmental functions because no one saw clearly how this could be concretely applied in an unmixed republic. Once elected by the sovereign people, legislative assemblies naturally became the

[6] Montesquieu, *supra* note 1, Book XI, chap. 6.

[7] For more details, see the classical analysis by Michel Troper, *La séparation des pouvoirs dans l'histoire constitutionnelle française*, Paris, LGDJ, 1973, new edition, 1989; Michel Troper, "The Development of the Notion of Separation of Powers," 26 *Israel Law Review* 1 (1992).

[8] Montesquieu, *supra* note 1, Book XI, chap. 5.

dominant organs in the new governments; they added other executive and judicial powers to the executive powers already taken from the governors during the colonial period. It should be recalled that all through the eighteenth century, the legislative assemblies in the colonies encroached upon the powers of the governors designated by the king. They cut back on the prerogative powers of the governors, managing to win power in the administration of public finances and even a power of review over monetary appropriations—since they could decide on the use of public money to wage war against the Indians and on the nomination of most public officers. They fought the patronage power of governors in the designation of candidates for executive and judicial functions. Beyond appointment power, they also assumed the right to exercise judicial power, and they occasionally decided cases of a public or private nature. The distinction between the political and judicial functions was blurred. If the colonial assemblies had encroached upon judicial functions, it was because of the extreme politicization of the British judicial system, the fear of judgments handed down by courts under the control of the king, the distrust for the equity decisions made by governors designated by the king, and the lack of professional judges. The legislative assemblies often agreed to hear and decide private cases, and they strove to adjudicate them in a manner agreeable to right and justice.

The Revolution did not change these developments; on the contrary, it reinforced them. The new Constitutions gave to the legislative assemblies not only the powers they had already gained over the governors in the years before the independence, but they also provided some powers that, in British constitutional tradition, could not be labeled other than executive—such as the power to wage war and make peace, to make treaties, to have diplomatic relations, to summon and dissolve the assemblies, or to grant pardons. In the 1780s, the assemblies interfered even more in judicial functions by winning the power to designate judges. What could the separation of powers mean in such a context? The answer is deceptively simple: separation of powers at that time meant a prohibition against a single person occupying multiple public positions, no more, no less. The Constitution of Virginia paid its tribute to the separation of powers in providing that "nor shall any person exercise the powers of more than one of them, at the same time." The separation of powers was understood in the first place as ruling out conflicts of interests.

The first step: Using the separation of powers against executive power. Besides the prohibition against holding more than one office at the same time, the separation of powers meant something more for the colonists. Only the context of eighteenth-century politics makes it comprehensible. What had particularly shocked and disturbed the colonists under British rule was the manner in which governors used to exercise their extensive powers to pressure, to influence, even to bribe the other governmental organs and, in particular, the representatives of the people in the legislatures, in their promises to give them favors that their positions of power put at their disposal. This is how they managed, for instance, to redraw electoral maps or to reapportion electoral districts; they manipulated representatives by luring them into public positions or judicial functions in exchange for their support of the government. Patronage was of general application. Governors cajoled, enticed, and bribed the representatives of the people; they did this so well that they led Americans to believe that they were indeed killing their liberties.

When Americans started to talk about separation of powers in the 1770s, they had in mind these corrupt practices. They sought in the first place to isolate the courts and, especially, the legislature from these manipulative governors and shield them from evil influence. Their priority was to isolate the popular assemblies from any sort of executive influence or impingement. All the revolutionary constitutions drafted in 1776 were emphatic in excluding from the assemblies ''all persons possessed of any post or profit under the Government,'' so that the legislative department might be preserved from its corrupting influence. The absolute prohibition of any executive presence in the assemblies was the consequence of historical experiments in the colonies. As Gordon S. Wood demonstrates, this choice represented one of the greatest American contributions to the science of politics, a great achievement in the building of truly free governments. The principle of isolating legislatures from executive influence, with its assumption of a sharp separation between ruler and people, also represented a clear victory of the traditional Whig conception of the nature of politics.[9] It put into practice the particular conviction of the Whig party that the secret of liberty was to be found in a complete separation between the people and their rulers, so that the latter would no longer be regarded as the depositories and best guardians of the interests common to the former.

The second step: Using separation of powers against legislative power. In the 1780s, the great expectations of the Revolution were on the wane. Americans came to realize that their new rulers were just as intoxicated by power as their former governors and that no matter who is exercising it, power has an encroaching nature The great hopes raised by the republican form of government in 1776 collapsed when it became clear that the republic was no shelter against tyranny. Tyranny actually just changed names; it became the

---

[9] G. S. Wood, *The Creation of the American Republic (1776-1787)*, 1969, reprint New York, W.W. Norton & Co., 1987, pp. 157-159.

modern tyranny, that form of tyranny that Tocqueville would later immortalize as ''the tyranny of the majority.''[10] When this situation was fully understood, public opinion changed. If separation of powers had been successfully used to protect against the executive, why could it not be used against the legislative? As elections on account of popular representation became the normal means of selecting the members of all the organs in the State, they were regarded as representative of the people, and, thus, because of their common source of authority, put on the same level. No particular prerogative, special right, or derogatory status could be granted to one of them, lest the seeds of political war be sown between them.

Once all organs of the State were unified and homogenized, important consequences could ensue. The truth of the matter is that, if all organs of the government must be considered as equal, because all of them emanate from the people and are supposed to work for the people, there is no longer a reason to regard the legislative power as fundamentally different from the other powers and, in particular, from the executive power. And, if it is true that the government must work for the good of the people, then its different organs, whether they be legislative, executive or judicial, must be equally separated and put under scrutiny, so that the powers granted to one are not absorbed by another. If the powers are properly separated, the officers at service in one of them will stand sentinel against any usurping attempt on the part of another. From the moment it was written down in the States' Constitutions and successfully used, the technique of separation of powers could be used against any department, no matter its representative nature. These ideas came to life in New England in response to the difficulties caused by legislative supremacy and the unexpected excesses of the revolutionary constitutions.

---

[10] The expression was coined by Tocqueville, who writes under the paragraph titled ''Tyranny of the majority'' the following: ''I regard as impious and detestable the maxim that in matters of government the majority of a people has the right to do everything [. . .] I shall never grant to several the power of doing everything that I refuse to a single one of those like me,'' in A. de Tocqueville, *Democracy in America* [Translated by H. C. Mansfield & D. Winthrop], University of Chicago Press, 2000. The idea that the majority has all the rights comes straight from Hobbes. The English philosopher justified the rule by the original contract supposed to have been concluded between all the members of society to create Leviathan: ''[B]ecause the major part hath by consenting voices declared a Soveraigne; he that dissented must now consent with the rest; that is, be contented to avow all the actions he shall do, or else justly be destroyed by the rest.'' T. Hobbes, *Leviathan*, Penguin Classics, 1985, Part II, chap. 18, p. 231 available at http://www.constitution.org/th/leviatha.htm.

By the end of the 1780s, the principle of separation of powers had already traveled a long way in America since Montesquieu. In 1778, the report of the Essex County Convention declared: "If the three powers are united, the government will be absolute, whether these powers are in the hands of one or a large number."[11] It is, however, Jefferson who explained better than anybody else, in his *Notes on the State of Virginia* (1781),[12] the secret springs of the new theory of separation of powers. That theory was, as Gordon S. Wood rightly noted, a minor doctrine in the constitutional theory of the eighteenth century that, once exploited to its maximum by the founders of the great republic, became a basic tenet of the American system of government.

b. The Years of Consolidation (1780-1787)

The ideas of Jefferson. In his *Notes on the State of Virginia* (1781), Jefferson denounced the concentration of all the powers of government—legislative, executive, and judicial—in the legislative body as the radical vice of the Constitution of Virginia. The judicial and executive members are left dependent on the legislative for their subsistence and, sometimes, even for their continuance in office. Jefferson remarked: "If the legislature assumes executive and judiciary powers, no opposition is likely to be made; nor, if made, can it be effectual."[13] He also noted that the legislature had in many instances decided rights that should have been left to judicial controversy and that it had often assumed the direction of the executive during the whole period of the legislative session.

His assessment of the situation is harsh, but not radically new: "The concentrating these in the same hands is precisely the definition of despotic government." By contrast, what follows is radically new: "It will be no alleviation that these powers will be exercised by a plurality of hands, and not by a single one." This is the decisive turning point, for, in saying this, Jefferson forgoes the English remedy, which he believes in that case particularly ineffective. The solution he recommends is truly revolutionary; it goes much further than the remedy of Montesquieu. Montesquieu relied on "the very nature of things" for power to check power. In other words, he relied on society (the estates) and the natural inclinations of its members—the wisdom of the aristocracy, the frugality of the people—to moderate power. Jefferson's solution goes much further. He sets up a model, a theory, which does not derive from the

---

[11] *supra* note 9, at p. 451

[12] T. Jefferson, "Notes on the State of Virginia," in *Writings*, New York, Literary Classics of the United States, 1984.

[13] *Id.*, pp. 245-246.

social status of the classes, but from sheer human will. He enunciates his theory as follows:

> An elective despotism was not the government we fought for; but one which should not only be founded on free principles, but in which the powers of government should be so divided and balanced among several bodies of magistracy, as that no one could transcend their legal limits, without being effectually checked and restrained by the others.

Thus Jefferson definitively holds to a system of government in which the powers are distinct and separated, so that none may transcend their legal limits, but he says—and here is the novelty in the analysis—this is not enough, for ''no barrier was provided between these several powers.'' Here lies, in his eyes, the weakest point of the Virginia Constitution. Convinced of the folly of claiming that representatives will not abuse their powers because of their disinclination to do so currently, he adds on a pessimistic note:

> Human nature is the same on every side of the Atlantic, and will be alike influenced by the same causes. The time to guard against corruption and tyranny, is before they shall have gotten hold on us. It is better to keep the wolf out of the fold, than to trust to drawing his teeth and talons after he shall have entered.[14]

The discovery of the barriers to legislative power. Progressively, the barriers to the legislative power, which later will become the famous checks and balances, were discovered by digging into the governmental practices and usages that were familiar to the colonists—the British institutions. Two of them, the first one in the hands of the executive, the second one in the hands of the judges, gave the American conception of separation of powers its distinctive form.

The veto power. The first barrier was the discovery and reinvention of the governor's voice in legislation. The king's signature on the bills adopted by the two houses of Parliament under the form of the royal assent took a very different shape once in the hands of the governor. A limited right of veto by the governor was described as a way of maintaining the necessary separation of powers. The governors were granted a share in lawmaking not because, as in England, the magistracy was a social entity that must consent and thus bind itself and its administration to all laws, but rather because a due balance had to be preserved in the three powers of government. The veto power became a means for the executive to control the legislative power. First, it was conceived as a defense of

[14] *Id.*, p. 246.

the executive against hegemonic undertakings by a legislature that might seek to encroach on and strip it of its powers. Then it was understood that the technique could have a further use; it could be a check against the adoption of bad laws, an additional security against the enactment of improper legislation. As Hamilton later said: ''It not only serves as a shield to the Executive. [. . .] It establishes a salutary check upon the legislative body, calculated to guard the community against the effects of faction, precipitancy, or of any impulse unfriendly to the public good, which may happen to influence a majority of that body.''[15] The limited rather than definite right of veto—it may be overthrown by a two-thirds majority vote in both houses of the Congress—is premised ''upon the supposition that the legislature will not be infallible.'' It represents one of the most important powers of the president.

Judicial review of statutes: The origins. The second barrier was the theory of judicial review of statutes that the Americans did not so much invent as rejuvenate. It must be recalled that in the monarchical age, enforcement of statutes was subject to compliance with existing law. The law and the statutes were two separate and distinct notions; they were not merged as is the case nowadays—particularly in the civil law system, and less so in the common law system because of the survival of the common law. The statutes enacted by the king were supposed to respect the rights and freedoms (privileges and immunities, benefices, franchises) possessed by his subjects and protected by the judges, their natural guardians. The idea that the subjects of the king were legitimately entitled to expect their sovereign to respect their rights was accepted in all European monarchies but applied differently depending on the country. Judicial review over statutes was practiced under different forms. In France, it had a preventive character. Upon registration of royal legislation in the provinces, the *Parlements* had the right to address remonstrances to the king on the ground that they had a right to review the legislation against the fundamental laws of the realm and to draw the monarch's attention to any legislation, whatever its form (edicts, ordinances, *lettres patentes*), which might hurt the customs or the rights of his subjects.[16] In England, by contrast, the review was, in theory, corrective. It was supposed to intervene *a posteriori* after enactment of the statute by way of judicial review. In 1610, Sir Edward Coke, in the famous *Dr Bonham's case*, defined the power of judicial review as being

---

[15] A. Hamilton, J. Madison & J. Jay, *The Federalist Papers* [hereinafter *The Federalist*], C. Rossiter Edition, Mentor Book, N.Y, 1961, Letter no. 73, p. 443, available at http://www.yale.edu/lawweb/avalon/federal/fed.htm.

[16] See Chapter 1, Section B.2.b; Vernon V. Palmer, ''From Embrace to Banishment: A Study of Judicial Equity in France,'' 47 *AJCL* 277 (1999).

implied by the common law in very broad terms: "And it appears in our books, that in many cases, the common law will control Acts of Parliament, and sometimes adjudge them to be utterly void: for when an Act of Parliament is against common right and reason, or repugnant, or impossible to be performed, the common law will control it, and adjudge such an Act to be void."[17] At the end of the eighteenth century in England, the proud assertion of the Chief Justice had long become obsolete because of the coming into being of parliamentary sovereignty at the time of the glorious revolution and the necessity for English judges to recognize the power of Parliament to modify the common law.[18] But the idea embodied in *Dr Bonham's case* had survived in the American colonies, all the more so that it had been enunciated by Sir Edward Coke himself in another landmark case that also outlived the English Revolution in America, the celebrated *Calvin's case* (1608), which asserted: "The law of nature is immutable and cannot be changed."[19] These principles of a paramount, superior, inalterable law had been upheld with fervor in the American colonies, in all likelihood because they corresponded to the most cherished and entrenched religious beliefs of the colonists.

At the end of the eighteenth century, confronted by statutes inspired by egoistic and partial interests, some state judges resurrected the old doctrine of judicial review that had originated in medieval law. Summoned by the "sovereign" (*i.e.*, the people represented in the legislatures by "an interested and overbearing majority") to give effect to its will, these judges issued a reminder, in substance, that the law is above the statute (just as God was above the king in the Middle Ages), that rights exist above power. Also, since no one can be a judge in his own cause, they were entitled, as the oracles of law, to exhort the new sovereign to respect these old, ancient, and venerable principles that came from time immemorial.[20] In short, state judges had recourse to the

---

[17] *Dr. Bonham's case* (1610), 77 Eng. Rep. 646, 8 Co. Rep. 114 a; see also M. R. Redish & L. C. Marshall, "Adjudicatory Independence and the Values of Procedural Due Process," 95 *Yale L. J.* 455, 479-480 (1986).

[18] See Chapter 4, Section A.

[19] *Calvin's case* (1608), 77 Eng. Rep. 377, 8 Co. Rep. 1a.

[20] They were all the more inclined to adopt such a course of action in that the laws in question affected property, and that property at that time was not a political object, but rather a judicial object. Insofar as the laws voted by the popular legislatures dealt with the right of property, Madison was well received in the context of the time when he insinuated that these laws were indeed very similar to "judicial determinations, not indeed concerning the rights of single persons, but concerning the rights of large bodies of citizens." This analysis undertaken in Letter no. 10 of *The Federalist*, *supra* note 15, enabled Madison to assimilate statutes to judgments and to subject the former to compliance with the same principles that apply to the latter. Concretely speaking,

secular rhetoric of the common law, and they began to assert a power of judicial review over statutes as their own.[21] By the end of the eighteenth century, the idea of judicial review was well received. Hamilton struck a sympathetic chord in public opinion when, in Letter no. 78 of *The Federalist*, he turned the courts of justice into ''bulwarks of a limited Constitution against legislative encroachments'' and insisted that the lifelong tenure of federal judges would encourage them to display ''inflexible and uniform adherence to the rights of the Constitution, and of individuals.''[22] Soon after the federal Constitution went into effect, the Supreme Court followed suit and alluded to its power to make statutes conform to the prescriptions of the Constitution.[23] The decisive turning point was taken in the landmark case *Marbury* v. *Madison* (1803).[24] The importance of the case comes from the fact that the Court gave a constitutional status to the power of judicial review so that the legislature can no longer evade it, in the same manner that it cannot evade the veto power of the president. Congress, the house of the American people, is henceforth squeezed between two checks.

Judicial review of statutes: The evolution. With the passing years, the judge has become the decisive figure in the American republican tradition of the check on the sinister designs of an ''interested and overbearing majority,'' with his power to invalidate almost the totality of decisions made by the political organs. The power of judicial review is of general scope; it may be used against executive as well as legislative decisions. It is, however, when the judge uses it against the legislative power that its nature as a countermajoritarian (a euphemism in the United States for undemocratic) institution is the most palpable. True, the judiciary no longer ventures to oppose the legislatures all

---

operating on the premise that statutes could be assimilated to judicial determinations, Madison raised the crucial question: how can this situation be justified in light of a venerable principle from time immemorial such as ''no man is allowed to be a judge in his own cause'' (*nemo judex in re sua*), which is the basis of the rule of law? The underlying assumption to the question is this: if this principle was successfully invoked the monarchical sovereign, why couldn't it be invoked against the popular sovereign too? The principle *Nemo judex* was, and still is, so fundamental in the common law that it is indeed this very principle that was at stake in the illustrious *Dr Bonham's case* (1610) in which Chief Justice Coke confidently affirmed that, should Parliament ignore it, the common law would hold it in check and stop it.

[21] See W. E. Neilson, ''Changing Conceptions of Judicial Review: The Evolution of Constitutional Theory in the States, 1790-1860,'' 120 *U. Penn. L. Rev.* 1166 (1971-1972).

[22] Letter no. 78, *The Federalist*, *supra* note 15, at pp. 469, 470-471.

[23] *Hylton* v. *United States*, 3 US (Dall.) 171 (1796); *Calder* v. *Bull*, 3 US (3 Dall.) 386 (1798); for a general overview, see J. Goebel, *History of the Supreme Court of the United States: Antecedents and Beginnings to 1801*, 1971, pp. 554-568 and 580-584.

[24] *Marbury* v. *Madison*, 5 US (1 Cranch) 137 (1803).

across the board, as it used to do before the New Deal. After the crisis of the court-packing plan initiated by President Roosevelt, judicial review in economic and financial matters exists only for appearance's sake. In other words, the court no longer protects the right of property and the freedom of contract with the same vigilant scrutiny as before. Judicial review of laws infringing on individual rights and, in particular, on the rights of ''discrete and insular minorities,'' is, however, more extensive and intrusive.

Because it developed in a common law system where it is commonly held that there exists positive rights before the statutes (''retained'' rights, also called ''reserved'' rights,[25] that are not put into the social contract), the power of judicial review not only allows the judge to review the statutes against ''the words of the Constitution'' strictly speaking, it also enables him to review the statute against ''the general principles of our political institutions'' as John Marshall put it in 1810,[26] that is, the principles of equality, freedom and justice of the American civilization. In other words, judicial review empowers the judge to substitute his judgment to that of the legislature and to govern in its place. True, there are a few decisions that are left to legislative discretion; they are known under the label of ''political questions,'' but they are in limited number. Brought by the judge himself over the past few years within narrow limits,[27] these questions are mostly related either to the internal functioning or procedures of Congress, or to foreign affairs. With the sole exception of these questions, the majority does not have the right to make its will prevail or, to speak in the metaphoric language of Cass Sunstein, to order its ''naked preferences,''[28] that is, what it wants, when it wants, and how it wants, simply because it is the majority. Such behavior is always regarded as leading to arbitrary and capricious decisions. The majority does not systematically have its right of way; it has it only when, and because, a judge says it does.

---

[25] The retained or reserved rights represent an odd survival in the republican age of the immemorial rights of the monarchical age, the Rights of Englishmen, that for some of them preceded the Conquest and that had been quite effective in the struggle against the pretensions to absolutism of the Stuarts. These rights that are rooted in the common law are expressly provided for, in the Ninth Amendment to the federal Constitution.

[26] *Fletcher* v. *Peck*, 10 US (6 Cranch) 87 (1810).

[27] *Baker* v. *Carr*, 369 US 186 (1962).

[28] C. Sunstein, ''Naked Preferences and the Constitution,'' 84 *Columbia L. Rev.* 1689 (1984).

2. The Theory of the Separation of Powers

Theoretical underpinnings. Originally, the American theory of the separation of powers, with its checks and balances, is nothing more than a practical device, a technique, to remedy a very practical need, the need to contain the consequences of a system of popular representation regarded as limitless in its absolute respect for the liberty of the individual. The question may be raised why Madison never envisioned taking action on the composition of the legislature. The answer is obvious. Taking action on the composition of the legislature probably meant—in Madison's mind—reintroducing the corruption of the British monarchy, which had become a master in the art of manipulating the composition of the chambers in order to find allies. In addition, such a course of action was impossible without resurrecting the feudal traditions as the estates and orders, the guilds and corporations, the honors and titles of ennobled families—all kinds of institutions doomed to obsolescence in the republican age.

Behind the reluctance to tamper with actual representation, there is, however, more than pure opportunism. There is the principled belief that taking action on representation amounts to interfering with the freedom of conscience, the liberty of the individual to think of himself in the State as he sees fit. The American conception of the republic regards as eminently desirable that the individual think of himself with respect to the republic as a virtuous citizen caring for the public good and the public interest. It highly values the citizens who choose to sacrifice for the community (*e.g.*, to serve in the armed forces or to bequeath property for the public rather than private heirs, even if they are in need). But it values as well its commitment not to take action on citizens who refuse to follow suit and choose to give priority to their own interests before those of the community. Nobody can "be forced to be free"[29] in the great republic. The individual has the right "to isolate himself from the mass of those like him and to withdraw to one side with his family and his friends, so that after having thus created a little society for his own use, he willingly abandons society at large to itself."[30] Nobody can be forced "to think well." The call for a responsible citizenship is not absent in the United States; it even may occasionally come from the State.[31] But it runs against the bedrock principle of

---

[29] J.-J. Rousseau, *The Social Contract* [Translated by G. D. H. Cole], Book I, chap. 7, available at http://www.constitution.org/jjr/socon.htm. Rousseau uses the formula to convey the idea that the citizen must subordinate his own preferences to the common good, his own will to the general will, so that he may be free with the community, and the community may be free with him.

[30] Tocqueville, *supra* note 10, at II, 2, 2, p. 482.

[31] Such is the case, nowadays, with the debates over welfare and other social support, resting precisely on such State prescriptions.

American philosophical approach so clearly expounded by Justice Jackson in *West Virginia State Board of Education* v. *Barnette*: "If there is any fixed star in our constitutional constellation, it is that no official, high or petty, can prescribe what shall be orthodox in politics, nationalism, religion, or other matters of opinion or force citizens to confess by word or act their faith therein."[32] In other words, the individual is absolutely free to think what he wants; no public authority may indicate a way to follow.[33] Virtue is a free choice as well as disinterestedness, individualism, and selfishness. On such premises, power must be organized in such a way as to counter the consequences of the most hard-hearted egoisms. And this is precisely what the separation of powers is good for; it is a technique that makes up for an absence of high and uplifting ideas among men by putting into place instead a perpetual competition between their opposed and antagonistic interests.

Madison's theory. First experienced in the States, then codified in the Constitution, the principles of the separation of powers were theorized by Madison in Letter no. 51 of *The Federalist.* These principles boil down to one single idea: "[C]ontriving the interior structure of the government as that its several constituent parts may, by their mutual relations, be the means of keeping each other in their proper places."[34] Two prerequisites must be met.

First, each branch must have a will of its own, independent from the will of another. Their members should therefore be elected at different times and by distinct bodies of electors and means of selection. Madison acknowledges that this condition is bound to be fulfilled with difficulty as far as the judicial power is concerned because that department, to be staffed by competent members, must be designated rather than elected. But he does not rule out a participation of the judicial power in the scheme of separation of powers as a result.

Second, each branch must keep a will of its own, which means that each must be kept from falling under the domination of another. In this respect, the greatest difficulty for Madison is the financial question. In a republican government, legislative authority necessarily predominates and usually has the final say in financial matters. If it may tamper with the emoluments annexed to the offices of other branches, the independence of the latter will be merely

[32] *West Virginia State Board of Education* v. *Barnette*, 319 US 624, 642 (1943)

[33] It is worth noting that the prohibition is addressed to the "public" authority only. It does not affect in the slightest manner the "private" authorities whose power of influence over the individual may be considerable, due in particular to the efficacy of the various means used (more generally, the media) and the unlimited scope of the domains concerned (from religion to morals, including economics and politics).

[34] Letter no. 51, *The Federalist, supra* note 15, at p. 320.

nominal. The Constitution wards off the danger by forbidding Congress to diminish the emoluments of judicial offices while the incumbent judges are in office.[35] But this is not enough; there are also all the means of the departments, whether they concern the personnel or the buildings and, more generally, all the financial appropriations that are necessary for the laws to be enforced and justice to be done. All these means are under the control of popular representation. Nothing would be easier than for the popular assemblies to take control of them and annex all the means necessary for enforcing the laws. Against this danger, Madison follows Jefferson's lead from the *Notes on the State of Virginia*.[36] Like him, he wards off the danger by resorting to ''barriers'' between departments, elaborating as follows: ''The great security against a gradual concentration of the several powers in the same department consists in giving to those who administer each department the necessary constitutional means and personal motives to resist encroachments of the others.''[37] These constitutional means are the veto power of the executive and the power of judicial review. He waxes at length on the veto, probably because it runs contrary to the logic of the republican government (his major defense is that the veto is relative only, not absolute or final). He does not refer explicitly to the power of judicial review, but he implies it underlines the need to distribute the checks to ''each'' department, a language that includes the judiciary.

The federal component and the reinvention of the separation of powers. The theory of the separation of powers could have stopped with the internal structure of the central government. However, in the second part of Letter 51, Madison gave a new dimension to the theory by extending it to the external (*i.e.*, territorial organization of the State). A rather unexpected analysis, since it had never been raised in the debates at Philadelphia, the question is closely tied to the theory of federalism. Having concluded in favor of the separation of powers as an organizing principle of the internal structure of the government, Madison caps his argument by pointing to ''two considerations particularly applicable to the federal system of America, which place that system in a very interesting point of view.''[38]

According to Madison, the federal system of America, the fact that it is a compound republic made of several units, gives it two advantages over a single republic. First, insofar as power is divided between two distinct and separate

[35] The Constitution provides the same prohibition as far as the emoluments of the executive function are concerned [article II, sec. 1 (7)].

[36] See *supra* note 12.

[37] Letter no. 51, *The Federalist, supra* note 15, at pp. 321-322.

[38] *Id.*, p. 323.

governments, the rights of the people are doubly protected. Not only will the different governments control each other, but each at the same time will control itself, giving society better protection against the oppression of its rulers. Second, the federal system of America gives the individual a better protection against the oppression of society and, in particular, against the tyranny of the majority. Insofar as, on the one hand, all authority in the republic is derived from society and, on the other, society is, due to the federal structure of the republic, broken into so many parts, interests and classes of citizens, the rights of the individuals, or of the minority will be in little danger from interested combinations of the majority. A compound republic is therefore the safest possible shield against the tyranny of the majority. Madison elaborates further: "The security for civil rights must be the same as that for religious rights." In the same manner that the multiplicity of sects kept one from gaining predominance over the others, the multiplicity of interests will keep one part of society from becoming a majority and oppressing the minority.

These analyses have acquired great celebrity. They complete the initial theorization of the separation of powers by splitting it in two. The theory of separation of powers is now dual, inasmuch as power may be divided horizontally (contriving the internal structure of government) and vertically (dividing the society into a multiplicity of interests and sects). The so-called "horizontal" and "vertical" separation of powers became part of the common constitutional discourse in the twentieth century.

Adaptation of the theory. From its origins, the separation of powers has always ranked in the first place among the constitutional principles of the American republic. However, its content has not been immutable. Initially, when Madison developed his theory in *The Federalist Papers*, his aim was to explain to his readers its exact import in the new Constitution. His particular concern was to convince them that, by contrast with most States' Constitutions adopted thus far,[39] the republican model established in Philadelphia would effectively guarantee a real separation between powers in the republic in that each department had been given "the necessary constitutional means and personal motives to resist encroachments of the others." He did not, however, envision that the theory would prevent the slightest participation of one department in the functions of another, for in his words: "[T]he political apothegm there examined does require that the legislative, executive, and judiciary departments should be

[39] Letter no. 47, *The Federalist*, *supra* note 15, at p. 300. For the criticism of the States' Constitutions, see pp. 304-308.

wholly unconnected with each other.''[40] A most famous application of this connection is the participation of the executive department in the legislative function as exemplified by the ''information'' that the president is requested by article II, section 3, of the Constitution to give ''from time to time'' to the Congress on ''the State of the Union,'' including the ''Measures as he shall judge necessary and expedient [to] recommend to their Consideration.''

This coordination between departments has never gone very far, if only because the president is actually allowed to enter Congress and to give ''information'' to its members only once a year, for the so-called annual presidential message on the State on the Union. If contacts have developed between the executive and legislative branches, their nature is of confrontation, rather than of coordination, except during these rare periods when the same party holds the White House and the Capitol. But, even so, the spirit of the separation of powers means that the most frequent connection between the two branches is to be found in the constant oversight function of the Congress over the executive branch through the committees process. The possible connections between the departments as Madison envisioned them have never resulted in the affirmation of a governmental power, a real power able to spur the government toward definite goals and to impart a direction to political action. A turning point occurred at the beginning of the twentieth century in the *Myers* case, when the Court for the first time faced the question whether the president had the power to dismiss officers of the United States without the advice and consent of the Senate. The answer was in the affirmative. However, a dissenting opinion by Justice Brandeis read: ''The doctrine of the separation of powers was adopted by the convention of 1787 not to promote efficiency but to preclude the exercise of arbitrary power.''[41] If this phrase deserves to be highlighted, it is for the word ''efficiency,'' a clear reminder, albeit in a disavowing tone, of the intrinsic quality of the parliamentary regime as expounded by Walter Bagehot, the Englishman who portrayed it as inherently superior to the American presidential regime. It is actually in the 1930s that Brandeis's ideas triumphed, probably in reaction to the growing presidential powers under the New Deal, and a fundamentalist approach to the theory of separation of powers ultimately carried the constitutional day for the future. The Supreme Court has been extremely reluctant to endorse delegations by Congress of legislative powers to the executive, and it has subjected them to stringent prerequisites.[42] With the sole exception of foreign affairs, which it considered ''in origin and essential

[40] Letter no. 48, *The Federalist, supra* note 15, at p. 308.

[41] *Myers* v. *United States*, 272 US 52, 293 (1926).

[42] *Schechter Poultry Corp. et al.* v. *United States*, 295 US 495 (1935).

character different from that over internal affairs''[43] and that it viewed as requiring to ''often accord to the President a degree of discretion and freedom from statutory restriction which would not be admissible were domestic affairs alone involved,''[44] the Court relentlessly fought any aggrandizement of presidential powers outside statutory authority.[45]

---

[43] *United States* v. *Curtiss Wright Export Corp.*, 299 US 304, 319 (1936).

[44] *Id.*, p. 320.

[45] This does not mean that the president is powerless; the executive is certainly a very powerful organ, all the more so after the war on terror launched by President George W. Bush. A decade ago, Martin S. Flaherty went as far as to argue that the executive had turned into the most dangerous branch in the American government; see M. S. Flaherty, ''The Most Dangerous Branch,'' 105 *Yale L. J.* 1725 (1995-1996). However, presidential powers in domestic affairs are first and foremost hortatory as illustrated by the metaphor of the ''bully pulpit,'' from which the president may exhort the American people to follow a certain course of conduct. As Robert H. Jackson, J., wrote in a famous concurring opinion, the ''own'' constitutional powers of the President of the United States endow him with an authority that is bound to remain ''at its lowest ebb,'' failing an ''expressed or implied will of Congress,'' in *Youngstown Steel & Tube Co.* v. *Sawyer*, 343 US 579, 637 (1952). Justice Jackson gave the following rationale: ''Presidential powers are not fixed but fluctuate, depending upon their disjunction or conjunction with those of Congress,'' *id.* at 635. *Mutatis mutandis*, in England, the realization of the public good—this common good that was formerly contained in the prerogative, the fountain-head of executive powers in common law tradition—is subject to parliamentary approval (see Chapter 3, Section B.3).

In the beginning of the twenty-first century, due to the legal arguments put forward by the Bush administration to launch a war on terror with sweeping consequences on liberties and civil rights, the question was debated among constitutional scholars whether the president—by sole virtue of his position at the head of the executive branch—is endowed with extraconstitutional, inherent, powers. See M. D. Ramsey, ''The Myth of Extraconstitutional Foreign Affairs Power,'' 42 *Wm. & Mary L. Rev.* 379 (2000-2001). Such ''inherent'' powers—which originate in Justice Sutherland's opinion in *U.S.* v. *Curtiss-Wright Export Corp.*, 299 US 304 (1936), as clearly expounded by D. M. Levitan, ''The Foreign Relations Power: An Analysis of Mr. Justice Sutherland's Theory,'' 55 *Yale L. J.* 467 (1946)—would enable the president in emergency situations to act on his own motion (*i.e.*, outside statutory authority). This theory amounts to considering the president as the Crown in England, that is, as endowed with inherent powers—a legacy of the prerogative—that may be exercised, particularly in foreign affairs, outside parliamentary approval. This is not the place to dwell on this constitutional debate—much influenced by Carl Schmitt's ideas about sovereignty—that eventually goes to decide where sovereignty ultimately resides. Suffice it to say that in the republican age—as opposed to the monarchical age—the government (no matter whether the legislative or the executive branch is concerned) cannot be granted ''inherent'' power, thus ''inherent'' sovereignty, inasmuch as such theory would negate the principle of the sovereignty of the people, the first meaning of which is that, in a republic, the principle of all sovereignty resides essentially in the people (or the nation).

Construction of the theory opposing executive power. In the eighteenth century, Hamilton predicted that only the president could be a guardian of the public interest, "the permanent and aggregate interests of the community" dear to Madison. This is why he advocated for a strong executive, reminding the electors of New York that, if

> it is a just observation that the people commonly intend the public good [. . .], this often applies to their very errors [and that] when occasions present themselves, in which the interests of the people are at variance with their inclinations, it is the duty of the persons whom they have appointed to be the guardians of those interests, to withstand the temporary delusion, in order to give them time and opportunity for more cool and sedate reflection.[46]

These ideas never prevailed.

Except for a few prominent exceptions (Lincoln, Roosevelt, Kennedy), arising at times of national crisis, if not national tragedy (the Civil War in 1860, the Great Depression in the 1930s, the Civil Rights Movement in the 1960s), the president of the United States is not a guardian of the public good; Americans are too vigilant about the risk of tyranny to entrust a single man with responsibility for deciding on a day-to-day basis what the public good requires, and the executive function has never been conceived of in the United States as it has been in Europe. The shadow of George III has always loomed large over American political institutions. Fear of the abuse of power and obsession with the constant possibility of tyranny still weighs heavily on the executive power. The sole domain in which the American political system is a true presidential regime is that of war and diplomacy, foreign affairs—those matters that require the use of armed force. The president is first and foremost a "commander-in-chief." Such is, indeed, his very first function, according to article II, section 2(1) of the Constitution.[47]

In internal affairs, his powers do not have the same legitimacy. True, he is often presented as a "leader," but the checks and balances of a government with divided and separated powers put a brake everyday on his actions. In the twentieth century, Justice Jackson recommended a less rigid interpretation of the principle of separation of powers that would integrate all these dispersed powers into "a workable government" on the ground that the constitutional theory

---

[46] Letter no. 71, *The Federalist*, *supra* note 15, at p. 432.

[47] George W. Bush and his administration relied on the presidential constitutional stature in foreign affairs to obtain from Congress in the war against terror delegations of powers that would have been inconceivable in purely internal matters.

''enjoins upon its branches separateness but interdependence, autonomy but reciprocity.''[48] His appeal has never been heard, nor his construction of the Constitution ever accepted, except in foreign affairs.[49] Still, the problem remains the same. In the beginning of the twenty-first century, Justice Breyer recalls that the whole constitutional history of the United States has been ''a quest for workable government.''[50]

Rejection of all presidential dominance. Fear of arbitrariness always prevails over concern for efficiency. The Court stuck to rigid, almost dogmatic, construction of the separation of powers. It jealously made sure that the president would remain tightly boxed-in by the initial limits of the constitutional framework. It checked any initiative, any construction, or any reform that would have augmented presidential power. It refused to vest the president with a leadership power over the numerous administrative agencies, divesting him of the power to nominate and to revoke their chief executive officers and creating the concept of the ''independent'' administrative agency.[51] It refused to grant him with line item veto over the budget that would have enabled him to cancel budgetary provisions aimed at providing financial advantages to private interests only, and it authorized Congress, with multiple interests represented therein, to make its own budgetary choices prevail over his priorities for the nation.[52]

However it is perhaps in *INS* v. *Chadha* (1983) that the Court best revealed its extreme separation of powers approach in constitutional jurisprudence. Turning its back to realist approaches that recommended interpreting separation of powers in the context of a modern government—either as a separation of functions not hampering governmental action or as the technique of checks and balances itself—the Court stuck to an idealist approach of the first principle of American government. With a comfortable majority of 7 to 2, it held:

> The Constitution sought to divide the delegated powers of the new federal government into three defined categories, legislative, executive and judicial, to assure, as nearly as possible, that each Branch of government would confine itself to its assigned responsibility. The hydraulic pressure inherent within each of the separate Branches to

---

[48] *Youngstown Sheet & Tube Co.* v. *Sawyer*, 343 US 579, 635 (1952).

[49] See *Dames & Moore* v. *Reagan*, 453 US 654, 669 (1981); *Hamdi* v. *Rumsfeld*, 542 US 507, 531, 536 (2004); *Hamdan* v. *Rumsfeld*, 126 S. Ct. 2749, 2774, n.23 (2006).

[50] S. Breyer, *Active Liberty, Interpreting Our Democratic Constitution*, New York, A. Knopf, 2005, p. 34.

[51] *Humphrey's Executor* v. *United States*, 295 US 602 (1935).

[52] *Clinton* v. *City of New York*, 547 US 417 (1998).

> exceed the outer limits of its power, even to accomplish desirable objectives, must be resisted.[53]

It could not have said more clearly that even the public good does not authorize stepping beyond constitutional limits. The president and Congress, therefore, have only the powers delegated to them by the people and, if these powers do not suffice to secure the conditions of public good, this may be a shame, but it is also in some way proof of the excellent work done in Philadelphia: the people are forced to be and remain free.

B. THE LIBERAL STATE

The contingency of power. The American concept of the separation of powers explains why there is no ''State'' in America, comparable to the sense of the word in continental Europe and, in particular, in France: an ideal carried by a political will, a public power in charge of leading society toward a common end defined in a manifesto, a program of government. The American concept of the separation of powers rules out the existence of a strong government that enables each department to exercise its powers ''for its part and under its responsibility to their fullest extent'' such as enunciated in the constitutional law of June 3, 1958, that empowered General de Gaulle to elaborate a new Constitution for France. How did this come about?

A first explanation is that no governmental organ in the United States, whatever the level of state or federal responsibilities, possesses the totality of governmental functions since the United States is a federation, a Union of States. Under such conditions, the ''State,'' at any level, is always exercising only part of its powers. In theory, the vertical separation of powers (federalism) works to limit governmental authority by keeping it from overstepping the ''enumerated powers'' entrusted to it. The principle of ''enumerated powers'' embodied in article I, section 8, of the federal Constitution has not been, however, the check on power initially envisioned. As of 1787, the option was taken to prevent the interpretation of the powers of the Union from being in line with that of international compacts or treaties. By contrast with the Articles of Confederation, which entrusted the Union only with the powers ''expressly'' delegated by the States, the Constitution did not contain the same adverb. As a result, the powers of the federal government have been able to be generously and extensively interpreted, in particular due to clause 18, which closes the above-mentioned provision and considerably increases the scope of the so-called ''enumerated powers'' in giving Congress the power ''to make all Laws which

---

[53] *INS* v. *Chadha*, 462 US 919, 951 (1983).

shall be necessary and proper for carrying into Execution the foregoing Powers, and all other Powers vested by this Constitution in the Government of the United States, or in any Department or Officer thereof.''[54] The true reason for the weakness of power in the United States is therefore not to be found in federalism and the ''vertical'' separation of powers[55] but in the ''horizontal'' separation of powers as construed and put into effect in the United States. This calls for closer examination.

Divided sovereignty. In order to understand the innate contingency of power in the United States and the fact that, except in external affairs, where emergency requires unity of action in the hands of the president, the government in internal affairs is constantly hampered, one must start by looking at the horizontal separation of powers.

Haunted by the fear of a republic tipping over into monarchy or dictatorship and wary about a government of men replacing the government of laws emblematic of the new republic, first the Founding Fathers, then the Supreme Court have plunged into a dogmatic construction of the prudential principle articulated by the political theorists of the eighteenth century. As of the convention of Philadelphia, it became common wisdom that the sovereign, that is, the people, may choose to be represented in any manner, as legislator, as executive, or as judge (at least, where judges are popularly elected, as is often the case in the States), and any level (federal, or state, or local). To each organ and at each level, the people delegate the portion of power that they deem fit. These powers that all, each in its own way, represent the people may be opposed

---

[54] Article I, section 8, clause 18 (the necessary and proper clause) was at the heart of the case *McCulloch* v. *Maryland*, 17 US (4 Wheat.) 316 (1819). To those who argued that if the clause did increase the powers of Congress, it did not actually leave it the free choice of means, John Marshall answered: ''Let the end be legitimate, let it be within the scope of the constitution, and all means which are appropriate, which are plainly adapted to that end, which are not prohibited, but consist with the letter and spirit of the constitution, are constitutional.'' The *McCulloch* case, which invites the Court to exercise a light review over congressional statutes, reached an apex after the New Deal, with the Court's interpretation of the Commerce Clause [article I, section 8(3)]. The generous and expansive construction of the Commerce Clause enabled Congress to increase the powers of the federal government dramatically. If the case *Lopez* v. *United States*, 514 US 549 (1995), does turn back the tide of this jurisprudence and affirms the Court's willingness to come back to a more restrictive interpretation of the Commerce Clause, there is a common agreement among constitutional scholars that the flow is bound to be relatively limited.

[55] This is so true that there are many state Constitutions that provide for a vertical separation of powers and that are not weak States. Such is the case of the federal States with parliamentary regimes (Australia, the Federal Republic of Germany).

to one another, just as they were in the monarchical age. As in the past, they can be used as forces and counterforces in the interplay of the balance of powers that gave birth to the mixed government, that excellent form of government, which had successfully tamed the monarchy. The work accomplished (and Madison was very proud of it) was all the more remarkable in that the social conditions that had made it possible (*i.e.*, the estates) had disappeared.[56]

The difficulty with this elaborate scheme is that in breaking the representation of the people into several organs, the Founding Fathers broke the popular will into pieces. The sovereign no longer has one will, as under the monarchy, but several; the will of the people is split, distributed among at least six organs (both at the federal and state level, there are three powers in the government). In other words, sovereignty is divided. In the case law of the Supreme Court, the terms ''separation'' and ''division'' have become interchangeable, as if the founding principle of American federalism that is, indeed, based on the idea of divided sovereignty,[57] had been drawn into, then eventually encompassed by the principle of separation of powers.[58]

The disembodiment of government. The result of this arrangement of divided and separated powers is that the sovereign people are never represented as a whole, as forming a nation, but always at several levels and in different organs balanced against each other, among which none may lastingly prevail over the others. Even the president of the United States does not represent the American people in all their enduring common interests, only those interests that have been federalized. He therefore speaks in the people's name, in one voice, only on federal matters, where centralization of powers is common law and practice, as in foreign affairs.[59] For the rest, legally speaking, the president represents the sovereign people indirectly and for certain objects only.[60] The

---

[56] On all these points, see the remarkable demonstration by Wood, *supra* note 9, at pp. 561-562.

[57] See *McCulloch* v. *Maryland*, 17 US (4 Wheat.) 316, 410: ''In America, the powers of sovereignty are divided between the government of the Union, and those of the states. They are each sovereign, with respect to the objects committed to it, and neither sovereign, with respect to the objects committed to the other.''

[58] See *Seminole Tribe of Florida* v. *Florida*, 517 US 44, 151 (dissenting opinion Souter) (1996); *Bowsher* v. *Synar*, 478 US 714, 721 (1986); *INS* v. *Chadha*, 462 US 919, 951 (1983); *Goldberg* v. *Kelly*, 397 US 254, 273 (opinion Black) (1970).

[59] See *United States* v. *Curtiss Wright Export Corp.*, 299 US 304 (1936)

[60] There is little surprise if, notwithstanding numerous proposals of constitutional amendments, a revision of the electoral process to choose the president has never succeeded. The president and vice president are not elected on direct universal suffrage; they are elected by an electoral college, an assembly that is elected by the voters in the States. However, today, both of them are regarded by the Supreme Court as ''the only

result of all this is that the sovereign is composed not of one body, but rather "of several connected pieces": it is a "man of several bodies."[61] Being represented never as one body politic, but rather as a composite body made of several pieces, the sovereign is weak; it can never be seen, so to speak. Harvey C. Mansfield said this well: "The essential character of the American Constitution is that while all its parts are *derived* from the people, none of them *is* the people."[62] The State as a personification of the sovereign cannot therefore be an instrument of domination over the society; it is much too contingent, disabled from exercising lasting and permanent efforts, except, as already mentioned, in those centralized matters such war and diplomacy. In internal affairs, society dominates the State in peopling its organs by way of electing representatives of all its interests, who in turn transform the State into a public forum for conciliating these antagonistic interests.

Perhaps the most important consequence of these developments has been to divest the people out of the government, achieving what Gordon S. Wood has called "the disembodiment of the government."[63] The alleged congruence of interests between the representatives and the people, which had made the British representative system in the eighteenth century so successful, was broken into pieces and replaced by an incommensurable divide between the government and the governed. A climate of suspicion and jealousy took hold between them. From the day when election became the only criterion for representation, it was extended to all political organs, and democracy got a better foothold; but it never again brought about that unity of views and interests between the people and their representatives that had been the key to the success of the British system. The logic of the growing distrust between the people and their representatives took the people out of the government and put them outside, and above, the government, in a position where they would watch over it and evaluate its

---

elected officials who represent all the voters in the Nation," *Anderson* v. *Celebrezze*, 460 US 780, 795 (1983); *Bush* v. *Gore*, 531 US 98, 112 (2000). The phrase seems to indicate that they transcend the diversity of interests in the country. But it may also have been used just to indicate that, under such conditions, the Court has jurisdiction in the case, despite the fact that the matter is entirely governed by State law. Whatever the exact meaning of the phrase is, there is no doubt that the actual concept of separation of powers would become obsolete were the president and the vice president to be elected by universal direct suffrage.

[61] Rousseau, *supra* note 29, at Book II, chap. 2.

[62] H. C. Mansfield, Jr., "Constitutional Government: The Soul of Modern Democracy," *The Public Interest*, no. 86 (Winter 1987), p. 53 s., in particular p. 55 (emphasis in original).

[63] Wood, *supra* note 9, at p. 383.

conduct in relation to the Constitution. Disembodied from the government, the sovereign people in America exist as a constitutional entity rather than as a nation. The upshot is that "the people" are actually "represented" in their totality by the Supreme Court, the only organ where they "speak" as a constitutional entity by the mouth of the justices. Paradoxically, only the nonrepresentative branch can claim to speak to, and for, the totality of the constitutional entity that is "the people."

The realization of the public good. In the United States, the principle of the separation of powers took on a meaning very different from that commonly understood in Europe. French constitutional scholars usually draw a line between "rigid" and "soft" separation of powers. As opposed to the rigid separation of powers, which allows no collaboration between legislative and executive powers, the soft separation authorizes, even favors, such collaboration, by entrusting an executive cabinet, originating in the Parliament, with the responsibility of acting on a manifesto—an expression of the public good chosen by the electors when electing Parliament. On such premises, a distinction is made between the parliamentary regime, which ultimately entrusts the Parliament with the responsibility of bringing about the public good (cabinet members are all MPs and accountable before Parliament) and the presidential regime, which vests the same responsibility with the president. This theoretical framework is only partly true. For there is no comparison between the energetic power of a head of government in Europe and the limited powers, sparely distributed and meticulously enumerated, of the president of the United States. Whereas the separation of powers in Europe does not weaken the government, because it is meant as a separation of functions, the same doctrine in the United States has been meant precisely to do this (*i.e.*, to weaken power by turning all questions of public good into questions of power structures). The government—"the State" in the U.S. sense—is a constant, polymorphous object of contention.

In the United States, powers are separated, not, as in Europe, by a mere separation of functions that does not divide the unity of State power; instead, the powers are separated and broken into pieces by a division of governmental power that runs into the very core of governmental action, as if it were aimed at splitting the common will of the people into pieces and keeping it from ever forming a unity. Separation of powers means constant debate over powers. The result of all this is that no political organ in the United States, whether at the federal or at the state level, can claim to be responsible for the public good; the separation of powers forbids it. Consequently, the public good, or the public interest, is taken care of not by the State, but rather by society, and society takes care of the public good with its own rules (*i.e.*, the rules of the market).

Economic theory inevitably prevails over political theory to define the public good.

Prevalence of economic analysis of the law. Two reasons may be put forward to explain the extraordinary success of economic analysis of the law in defining the public good. They confirm and reinforce each other in a reciprocal interplay.

(1) *The disrepute of politics.* From the outset, the presence of individual interests in the government casts into question anything it may decide, for it is impossible to say with certainty if decisions were made for the real benefit of the public good or, as is more likely, for the sole benefit of some private powerful interest. Public opinion holds as common wisdom that public choices are always impure, because politics is by nature impure. The economic theory of legislation assumes that statutory as well regulatory enactments are generally the product of special interest groups.[64] It holds that it is always highly desirable, whenever possible, to trade public for private choices because the individual, taken as *homo economicus*, is a rational human being who always makes decisions for objective and scientifically quantifiable reasons (*i.e.*, the satisfaction of his individual preferences).

(2) *The prestige of economics.* The second reason that seems to explain the scholarly preference of some legal academics for measuring the public good by the yardstick of economic analysis of the law may be enunciated as follows: Since society does not have any other choice but to take charge of the public good by itself, it does so using rules that are familiar to it (*i.e.*, the rules of the market). But, it has been scientifically proved—here is the crucial point in the reasoning—that the rules of the market can in theory do as well, if not better, than the rules of the legislature. Such is indeed the core message of the Coase theorem.[65] The great economist demonstrated in substance that, in a world with no transaction costs, that is, a world in which individuals can meet and talk with each other, rational individuals always choose the most efficient solution for their common problems and always succeed by the

[64] See D. A. Farber & Ph. P. Frickey, ''The Jurisprudence of Public Choice,'' 65 *Texas L. Rev.* 873, 890 (1986-1987).

[65] R. Coase, ''The Problem of Social Cost,'' 3 *Journal of Law & Economics* 1 (1960). See, however, the misgivings of the Nobel prize winner over the extensive application of his theory to noneconomic disciplines such as law in R. Coase, ''Economics and Contiguous Disciplines,'' 7 *Journal of Legal Studies* 201 (1978).

> exchange in bringing about the optimal solution, in economic terms, to their problems. From the day the celebrated theorem became common wisdom among the elites—this happened in the early 1980s—the important legislation of the welfare state, based upon a political approach of the common good (dealing with poverty, civil rights, environment, health and safety), was swept away. Deregulation carried the day, and the public good reversed to the market.

Because it favors the maximization of individual preferences for the participants, the market is allegedly the clearest demonstration that it always provides for the public good. Pragmatic, society knows by experience (this is one of the greatest lessons of liberalism) that the free exchange between people satisfies the individual, at least in most cases.[66] It thus concludes that, in order to bring about the public good, nothing more is necessary than to supply remedies for market failures—in other words, corrective substitutes for everything that free exchange cannot satisfy. Everything that can be claimed as a property right is subject to trade, including body parts, even human tissues, cells, and genome; the concept of inalienable right having no real content in the law currently into force,[67] the concept of property is virtually without limits. In addition to means of redress against market failures, two other problems must be solved: on the one hand, the free rider problem that arises from the impossibility of making everybody pay individually for collective goods (such as security granted by the army and the police), and that justifies taxation and, on the other, the no-seller problem that arises from the impossibility of forcing people to sell, and that justifies appropriation by eminent domain.

The contingency of power in the United States explains the absence of any idea of a public good that could be free from market rules. Indeed, nobody sees interest in such a concept. Priority is given to individual interest because it is commonly accepted that the only legitimate goal of public interest is the satisfaction of private rights and that the public good can be nothing more than the satisfaction of private rights. Economic analysis of the law that derives from the liberal economic theory is influential and pervasive.[68] The jealous suspicion

---

[66] There is, however, a great deal of social science to show that individual negotiations are likely to be encumbered by nonrational factors such as unequal status due to age, race, gender, knowledge, etc. The Coase theorem ''works'' in part because it assumes that participants are already equal. But society pays little attention to these warnings, for it is too convinced that ''all men are created equal.''

[67] This is the direction of modern law in the United States, but earlier law was more reserved.

[68] One of its most distinguished scholar is Richard Posner, whose major work is *Economic Analysis of Law*, 6th ed., New York, Aspen, 2003; for an application of his

that looms over all political decisions, constantly wrapping them in the dark cloth of egoistic self-interest, makes it relatively easy to convince public opinion that economic analysis is in most cases superior to political analysis of the law and can always advantageously replace it.

Conclusion. The American republican model has no public law because it does not believe that private law resides outside the *res publica*. In the United States, the *res publica* is utterly abstract and dreamlike. The government being held to be a mirror of the society, the *res publica* is actually in the mechanisms by which the society controls itself. In other words, the *res publica* is in the separation of powers itself, that is, in a process (and therefore, history), not in a structure. The public interest in the United States is a constant work in progress—a political process, so to speak, not a thing—mixing democracy, participation, and information flows. It cannot be grasped by a single organ elected by the nation as a whole, such that only the nonrepresentative branch (the federal judiciary) can claim to speak for the totality of the constitutional entity that is "the people." And so the battle is constantly pitched between the forces of law and the forces of the market (*i.e.*, heirs to federalism and antifederalism). In the United States, the *res publica* is a distant future—hence the propensity of the country to think of itself as forever young, capable of reinventing itself as the times demands.

As to the real, tangible public good, it is acted on at the local not at the national level; it is to be seen in the community to which everyone voluntarily belongs not in the State. It is, for instance, in the county, in local associations, in churches, in small communities that citizens work for the public interest, always with dedication, often with enthusiasm. True, there are some national institutions expressly in charge of defending tangible public interests. Such is the case with the administrative tribunals that can be found in all administrative agencies; such is also the case with the federal courts without limited territorial jurisdiction, such as the U.S. Court of Federal Claims, in charge of adjudicating private claims against the Union, or the U.S. Tax Court, with jurisdiction over the finances of the Union. However, all these institutions in charge of defending the interests of the Union, that is, the public interest in its strongest expression, are always subject to judicial review of their decisions by the Supreme Court of the United States, the highest authority for the protection of individual rights (hence private interests) and a symbol of this judicial power that, in all common law countries, even a republic, never yields before a statute of the sovereign.

---

analysis to political decisions, see, in particular, chapter 19 on "The Market, The Adversary System, and The Legislative Process as Methods of Resource Allocation," p. 529.

Part D
The French Model

The State and society. In France, the State is radically distinct from society. It forms, as Tocqueville would have put it, "a power in a way external to the body social," which it dominates, influences, and forces to progress in a certain direction. That said, of course, the government broadly understood as including all the organs of the State emanates from society, since "universal suffrage is the sole source of power"[1] in the Republic, and, as a result, election is directly or indirectly the fountainhead of the organs vested with legislative and executive powers. But the government is not, as in the United States, a mirror for the interests of the society. Society has its interests, and the State has others. The first are regulated by private law, the second are governed by public law, and the latter always prevail over the former. In short, the distinction between the State and society, between the government and the governed, is much more underlined and rigid than in the American model. In French law, it would be inconceivable that a private interest could hold the State in check, still more that it could capture it. The *res publica* in France is subject to special treatment. How did this come about?

The reason lies in this single fact: the sovereign is not conceived in the same manner. In their distrust of power, Americans reduced sovereignty to ashes and dispersed it throughout society, so that each member would own a little fragment of it. France never operated on the same premises. Of course, the French people are sovereign; but they are sovereign as a nation. In other words, *vis-à-vis* sovereignty, the United States is a people, while France is nation. This means that the millions of French people residing in the French territory are

[1] The principle that originates in the French Declaration of the Rights of Man and the Citizen of 1789 was recalled in the constitutional law of June 3, 1958, that laid down the terms of reference within which the drafters of the new Constitution were to work. See J. Godechot, *Les constitutions de la France depuis 1789*, GF-Flammarion, no. 228, 1978, p. 423; A. T. von Mehren & J. R. Gordley, *The Civil Law System*, Boston, Little Brown, 1977, p. 228.

sovereign together, not separately, that is, they are sovereign in the interests that unite them, not in those that divide them. The French republican model is based on national sovereignty (Chapter 7). The major, and most important, consequence is that the public interest is not an uncompleted quest, but rather a day-to-day task for the republic. Far from being the limited power of the American model, power in the French model is a complete power, a State power (Chapter 8).

Chapter 7
National Sovereignty

The French concept of the sovereign. In France, the sovereign is the nation, the nation in all its historical depth, its revolutionary past, its emotional component. It may be said, as the Constitution of October 4, 1958, puts it in article 3, that ''sovereignty belongs to the people,'' but the sovereignty in question is still qualified as ''national sovereignty.''[1] By contrast with the American model, sovereignty in France belongs to the people as forming a nation; it is not popular, but national. This entails significant implications that must be clearly understood.

The nation is not the people in all their diversity, but rather the people conceived in their unity. The nation knows nothing of races, of religions, of beliefs, of ethnicities; it knows nothing but men, free and equal in rights, who are citizens of the republic. It defines itself by liberty, equality, and fraternity; it upholds an ideal, and it takes shape only by the values that bind its members. Ernest Renan was quite right when he said that the nation was ''a soul, a spiritual principle.''[2] In complete contrast to the American republican model, the French model is embedded in mysticism.

In French public law, the State is not the government (except in the vernacular language that is not that of lawyers). In law, the State is completely detached from the persons of those who are office holders. When article 5(1) of the 1958 Constitution proclaims that ''the President of the Republic shall ensure [. . .] the continuance of the State,'' this does not mean that he is responsible for watching over the functions of the prime minister and the government, but

[1] Article 3 (1) provides: ''National sovereignty belongs to the people, which shall exercise this sovereignty through its representatives and by means of referendums.''

[2] E. Renan, *Qu'est-ce qu'une Nation ?*, Discours en Sorbonne (March 11, 1882), available at http://ourworld.compuserve.com/homepages/bib_lisieux/nation01.htm. Renan added: ''This soul is made of two components [. . .], a common possession of a rich legacy of memories [. . .], a willingness to keep fructifying the bequest to be held in common.''

rather that the president is in charge of a legacy, the *res publica*, which he is accountable for maintaining in the present and bequeathing unaltered to his successors in the future. The president of the republic exercises today the same functions as the king under the old regime, except for this crucial difference: since there is no longer an ecclesiastical foundation for the State, its head holds his powers no longer from God, but rather from the nation, which is the sole source of sovereignty.[3] National sovereignty is the most important principle of French public law.

Legally speaking, it is the nation that is sovereign, not the people. In other words, the French people as a sovereign are always represented as forming a nation. Representation therefore is not popular, but rather national (Section A); and it is from the concept of national representation that the completely different status of statutory law in the French model, as opposed to the American model, is derived (Section B).

A. NATIONAL REPRESENTATION

Raison d'être. National representation is the keystone of the French republican model. Even before the Revolution, it had been advocated by Emmanuel Sieyès, in two works written as a follow-up to the summation of the General Estates for 1789 and both published in 1788: "*Views of the Executive Means Available to the Representatives of France in 1789*," followed a few months later by the famous "*What is the Third Estate?*."

National representation is poles apart from popular sovereignty. The latter came into being as a reaction to virtual representation. However, it should not be concluded that national representation is the same as virtual representation. National representation has nothing in common with virtual representation; the people are not represented without even having elected their representatives. But the people are represented as forming a nation, not merely as a people. The difference lies in this fact: whereas popular representation aims at being a perfect copy of the social reality, at mirroring society, national representation is an intellectual construction of society that justifies itself only by its goal—to attain a representation entirely committed to promoting the public good. The *raison d'être* of national representation according to Sieyès is this:

> It would be a grave misjudgment of human nature to entrust the destiny of societies to the endeavors of virtue. What is needed instead is for the

[3] Article 3 of the Declaration of the Rights of Man and the Citizen of 1789 provides: "The principle of all sovereignty remains in essence in the Nation. No public body, no individual can exercise authority that does not expressly derive from the Nation."

> nation's assembly to be constituted in such a way as to ensure that individual interests remain isolated and the will of the majority cleaves constantly to the public good even during these long periods when public manners are in a state of decadence and egoism seems to be the universal rule.[4]

True, there is a common point between Sieyès and Madison: both of them are convinced that relying on "the endeavors of virtue" to ensure the public good is unrealistic in the modern age. But the crucial difference between them is this: Madison lets society be represented as it is, with its vices and it virtues, relying only on good fortune to get to the right result ("I go on this great republican principle, that the people will have virtue and intelligence to select men of virtue and wisdom"[5]). Sieyès thinks in a mandatory mode; in his view, action is "needed" to get an assembly that will cleave to the public good, action is called for to reach such a good result. That action is this: one must ensure that "individual interests remain isolated."

Representation of common interests. For "the individual interests [to] remain isolated," one must take into account common interests only; people are therefore represented in what brings them together, not in what separates them. The whole theory of national representation is based on this principle. There are, according to Sieyès, three types of interests to be found in the human heart: first, the common interest, the interest by which citizens resemble one another; second, the factional interest, the one by which an individual allies himself with some number of others; third, the individual interest, by which each individual separates himself from the rest, thinking solely of himself. Whereas the common interests are the general interests, factional and individual interests form the particular interests that keep the representatives from expressing a true general will (*i.e.*, the legal expression of the common good). In order for the representatives to espouse only the public good, only the common interest—that is, only the one by which members of an association decide how to deal with matters of common concern—must lead the will of the legislative body. Therefore, it is necessary to exclude from national representation everything that is relevant to an individual or separate interest. Particular interests have no vocation and no right to be represented nationally; excluding them is the

[4] E. Sieyès, *What Is the Third Estate?* in E. J. Sieyès, *Political Writings* [Translated by Michael Sonenscher], Hackett Publishing Co, Inc., Indianapolis / Cambridge, 2003, p. 154.

[5] J. Madison, Virginia Ratifying Convention, June 20, 1788 [Papers 11: 163] in P. B. Kurland & R. Lerner (Eds.), *The Founders' Constitution*, University of Chicago Press, 1987, vol. 1, p. 409, available at http:press-pubs.uchicago.edu/founders/tocs/toc.html.

prerequisite for ensuring that "the will of the majority cleaves constantly to the public good."

Not only does national representation not reflect a faithful image of the entire people's interests—it does not aspire to do so. It reflects common interests only. These interests are limited, for only few interests are common (*i.e.*, those interests that make the *res publica*).[6] The political association to be created is a re-public, not a re-total.[7] "Only what is needed to fulfill the purpose of the political association ought to be put in common."[8] The common interest comprises not the totality of private interests, but rather an aggregation of only those interests that men decide by an act of free will (*i.e.*, a social contract) to put in common. This common interest is the public interest; it represents the "general good" that Sieyès regards as the fixed star of the representatives. This general good is the *res publica*, no more, no less. It is the "public thing"—it is "the State."

The French theory of representation is intimately connected to belief in the public interest as a concept distinct from a mere aggregation of private interests, made of those interests regarded as common to all the participants in a social contract. Such an approach to the public interest may be found in Sieyès' *Third Estate* ("It is impossible to conceive of a legitimate association whose objects are not common security, common liberty, in short, the public thing [*res publica*]"[9]) as well as in Rousseau's *Social Contract* ("The common element in these different interests is what forms the social tie; and, were there no point of agreement between them all, no society could exist."[10]) In French public law theory, the public interest is not to be confused with the aggregation of private interests; it a political choice, voluntary, made of all the interests held in common in the social contract. The French republican model is based on a political theory of the public interest.

---

[6] See P. Bastid, *Sieyès et sa pensée*, Hachette 1938, New enlarged edition, 1970, p. 381.

[7] See P. Pasquino, *Sieyès et l'invention de la constitution en France*, Paris, Odile Jacob, 1998, p. 73.

[8] The phrase is from Sieyès in a manuscript of 1792, titled *Contre la ré-totale* and quoted by P. Pasquino, *id.*, p. 79.

[9] E. Sieyès, *Qu'est-ce que le Tiers État?* (1788), PUF, Collection Quadrige, 1989, p. 85.

[10] J.-J. Rousseau, *The Social Contract*, [Translated by G. D. H. Cole], Book II, chap. 1 available at http://www.constitution.org/jjr/socon.htm.

1. Historical Formation

Social constitution and political constitution. When the French Estates General convened in Versailles on May 5, 1789, the social constitution of the French realm was very similar to that of England. French society was divided into three estates, or orders: the nobility, the clergy, and the Third Estate. The king having authorized double representation for the Third Estate, the composition of the Estates General was as follows: both the nobility and the clergy had 300 deputies who represented some 200,000 people, while the Third Estate had 600 deputies representing about 26 million souls. The three orders gathered in one single united assembly for the opening session, which was presided over by the king. Then, contrary to the wishes of the Third Estate, the three orders separated to verify the powers of their members; the verification of powers of each deputy was made in separate chambers. On May 12, the nobility declared the powers of its members had been duly verified and instituted itself as a separate chamber, expecting the Third Estate and the clergy to do the same.

On June 15, the Third Estate made it known that, the powers of its members having been duly verified, it was ready to begin working with the other two orders on the great reform project, the regeneration of the realm. Although ambivalent, the clergy was not opposed to working with the popular party. The nobility, however, was strongly opposed to it, in line with a tradition that could be traced far back in time.[11] It was, in its opinion, out of the question to work in

---

[11] In his *Essay on the Privileges* (1788) (annexed as an introduction to his *Qu'est-ce que le Tiers-État? supra* note 9), Sieyès explained how the privileges of the nobility had led members of this order to believe that they formed an order "set apart" from the two others and to regard the "others," that is, the people, as "an assemblage of nobodies, a class of men created especially for the service of others whereas they had been themselves created expressly for command and pleasure," *id.*, p. 9. To better illustrate his argument, he complements it with the following extract from the minutes of the meeting of the Estates General in 1614. Shocked by the suggestion of the Third Estate, which, then, would have liked to be able to present the French realm as "a family made of three brethren," the President of the nobility, Baron de Senecey, objected to this proposal on the ground that the Third Estate held the last rank in the assembly. And he added in graphic language:

> They [the Third Estate] are those who dare to compare themselves to us. . . They claim the clergy to be the eldest, we to be the younger, and themselves to be the youngest. . . . What a miserable condition did we fall into should these words be true! How could so many services rendered from time immemorial, so many honors and dignities, inherited by the nobility and highly deserved by reason of its labor and fidelity have it served so well that, instead of raising the order, they degrade it to the vulgar in the closest union to be envisioned between men, which is fraternity?

Id., pp. 25-26.

common with the other two orders. In its view, the political constitution of the kingdom could not differ from its social one. In the same manner that the three estates in England were represented in two chambers, there should be in France the same representation of the orders in separate chambers. According to the nobility, because it and the clergy were not united, there should continue to be three chambers, each having veto power over the decisions of the two others. The obstinate determination of the nobility and part of the clergy not to work together in a single chamber with the Third Estate left the latter no other option but to constitute itself, too, in an assembly.

Representatives of the people or representatives of the nation. The deputies of the Third Estate were hesitant about the title they should give themselves to be rightly constituted as a deliberative assembly. What name could they choose? In reference to his famous pamphlet ''*What is the Third Estate?*'' Sieyès suggested ''representatives, known and verified, of the French Nation.''

Mirabeau objected on the ground that this could jeopardize a smooth sequence of events in the near future. Anxious about the need to obtain royal assent, he explained to the assembly that it could not do without this substantial formality, were its resolution to come into force. If assent were lacking, the assembly would run the risk, Mirabeau warned, of being dissolved or prorogated, and would eventually be exposed to ''an outburst of vengeance, a coalition of all aristocracies, and the hideous anarchy that always paves the way to despotism.''[12] The concern of the deputy from Aix was understandable. According to the law of French monarchy, it was commonly understood that the nation in France was not an independent body politic, but rather was entirely subsumed within the king's body. There was little doubt, from that standpoint, that Sieyès's proposal was a provocation. Advocating for a more conciliatory

---

The French Revolution was less against the monarchy, the political constitution of the realm, than against its social constitution, namely, the division of the society into orders, each endowed with separate rights. If the concept of nation is so fundamental to French public law, it is because that concept has been the political and legal means by which France left the monarchical age by putting an end to the society of the old regime and its division into orders. The vocation of the nation is to welcome under the same roof a people of free men, equal in rights, and living under a common law. In the French constitutional tradition, the French nation is not an aggregate of people endowed with diverse status and various privileges or immunities; the people are sovereign as forming a nation. There is little doubt that the genealogy of the nation is religious; the nation realizes a unit very similar to the Christian community: ''There are no longer Jews, or Greeks, or slaves, or freemen, or men, or women; in Jesus Christ, you are whole in one,'' *Galatians*, 3: 28.

[12] *AP*, vol. VIII (June 15, 1789), p. 111.

stance, Mirabeau offered the following formula: "representatives of the French people." Drawing on English laws and customs adopted by the Americans, he declared to the Assembly that the word "people" was usually understood as encompassing the greatest part of the nation and that this formula had the advantage of not being a "frightening title."

Between "representatives of the nation" and "representatives of the people," there was no small difference. Choosing Mirabeau's formula would not have political consequences only. The deputy from Aix was, in all likelihood, using the formula in the hope of bringing about a change in French constitutional tradition similar to what had taken place in England. It is probable that, in his view, the representatives of the French people were called sooner rather than later to constitute a counterpart to the low chamber (Commons), while the nobility would turn into a high chamber (Lords), with the clergy (whose members were extremely unequal in wealth) dividing between the two, depending on their fortune. In choosing the title "people," the Assembly would have accepted a sharing of sovereignty between the king, the privileged orders (nobility and clergy), and the people (Third Estate). Had this solution been adopted, history would have taken another course; but it was not. The reason has to do with the fact that in England, as Sieyès had explained it in his pamphlet on "*What is the Third Estate?*," the nobility had privileges only insofar as part of its members participated in the legislative process.[13] In other words, the nobility (although, not the whole nobility, but only that part which had seats in the House of Lords) was distinct and separate from the rest of the English people because of political not civil rights. Englishmen were lucky to be subject to the same law, the common law, and to have their disputes adjudicated by the same courts, the king's courts. Whether criminal or civil, the common law was theoretically the same for all in England; the laws were equally protective. Such was not the case in France where the individual, as such, had no legal existence[14] ; everyone was defined in society by his estate, or social class (*corps*).[15] Each estate, or

[13] Sieyès, *supra* note 9, at p. 60.

[14] Under the old regime, the human being has a legal existence only insofar as he lives in society and is linked and attached to other men; he is defined from social, economic, or legal standpoints by his belonging to communities such as towns, provinces, countries, guilds, religious orders, lordships, universities. The society in the old regime is a society of estates (corporations), and the corporations define themselves by their privileges.

[15] The estate (corporation), under the old regime, is a group of Frenchmen united for the common good. The corporations enjoy legal personality; they may sue, elaborate their own rules, provide for their recruitments; they may also exercise juridical functions and adjudicate cases, tax their members, and provide for a common budget; they are recognized, and reformed when necessary, by the king who exercises general oversight

social class, had its own laws, the privilege being in essence ''dispensation from the common law'' (Loyseau).

The constitution of the Third Estate into a ''National Assembly.'' Accepting Mirabeau's formula amounted to dooming the task of national restoration that the Third Estate had put at the top of its agenda. How could it be realistic to imagine that this agenda could ever be put into practice, if it was subject to the consent of the privileged orders and the assent of the king? To accept Mirabeau's formula meant, as Sieyès had predicted in his pamphlet on the Third Estate, that the will of 26 million souls could be held in check by the will of 200,000 privileged (the nobility and the clergy) and even by that of one individual (the king). Mirabeau's formula did not carry the day. The obsessive will of changing, first, the social constitution of the kingdom before improving its political constitution won over all oppositions.

By a decree of June 17, 1789, the Assembly of the Third Estate, recognizing that it was ''already composed of the representatives sent directly by at least ninety-six percent of the nation,'' that ''the members who compose it are the only representatives lawfully and publicly known and verified,'' and that ''they are sent directly by almost the totality of the nation,'' and recalling that ''the representation is one and indivisible'' declared: ''The denomination of National Assembly is the only one which is suitable for the Assembly in the present conditions of things.''[16] This revolutionary move was the act that gave birth to modern France.

---

over them. The individual is socially respected only insofar as he belongs to an estate (corporation), for he then may enjoy the privileges of the corporation. Corporations have indeed their privileges, each of them different between estates; these privileges may be social (position in the official ceremonies; apparel, for instance, only nobles may wear silk), fiscal (tax exemptions and immunities, the nobility is tax exempted for the ''*taille,*'' a kind of income tax, and the ''*gabelle,*'' a salt tax), or legal (special courts, university members have their own jurisdictions). All Frenchmen, in one way or another, are ''privileged.'' Privileges may apply to the economic sector (corporations enjoy a *de facto* monopoly over making and selling part of the production); the royal manufactures enjoy their own privileges (in particular, monopolies) all of them granted by the king. The nobility has its own privileges: tax exemptions, right to bear the sword, right to wear precious fabrics, right to enter and make a military career (soldiering is exclusively reserved to the nobility as of 1781), special colleges for the education of their children dedicated by their parents to soldiering (four generations of nobility to enter the royal college of La Flèche, but sixteen to enter that of Lure and Saint Claude). Last but not least, privileges regulate the right to access and be presented to the court. See Yves Durand, ''Privilèges, privilégiés,'' in *DAR*, p. 1024.

[16] Frank Maloy Anderson (Ed.), *The Constitutions and Other Selected Documents Illustrative of the History of France (1789-1901)*, Minneapolis, Wilson Co., 1904, p. 2.

The meaning of national sovereignty. Article 3 of the Declaration of the Rights of Man and the Citizen adopted two months later implemented the consequences of the decisions made by the Third Estate. It provides: "The principle of all sovereignty remains in essence in the Nation. No public body, no individual can exercise authority that does not expressly derive from the Nation." The meaning of this text is at least twofold.

First, it puts an end to the fusion that traditionally existed between the king and the nation. The king is no longer the nation; he is separate from it. The law of the French monarchy held that *the Nation is no body politic per se, in France* and that *it remains entirely in the body politic of the King.* To the *Parlement* of Paris, which had dared to speak in the name of the nation and to defend on its behalf the fundamental laws of the kingdom, Louis XV contemptuously replied in the so-called audience of Flagellation of 1766: "The rights and the interests of the Nation, which some dare to envision as a body politic separated from the monarch, are necessarily united to mine, and remain in my hands only."[17] There was not, on the one hand, the nation, and on the other, the king; they were joined in one single body politic. "Without the King, no Nation"[18] affirmed the jurist Jacob Nicolas Moreau, who was also an historiographer of the king. The concept of national sovereignty discards that approach, without, however, imposing the republic. The nation could elect to give itself a king, but the latter, in theory, would no longer rule by the grace of God, but rather by the grace of the nation. One may underline that the terminology "in essence" ("The principle of all Sovereignty remains in essence in the Nation") seems to bear witness to the difficulty the people of this era had in imagining a king who would be "King of Frenchmen," as it would be said later in the middle of the nineteenth century of Louis-Philippe, and no longer "King of France."

The second implication of the article calls for a more complex analysis. No doubt, it withdrew all legitimacy from the pretensions of the *Parlements* that, starting in the 1760s, had claimed to be the "representatives of the Nation" and, as such, to be entitled to defend the fundamental laws of the kingdom, of which they were, incidentally, unable to give a proper definition.[19] But the article also ruled out an evolution English-style, so to speak (*i.e.*, the establishment of a sovereign body politic such as the institution of "King in Parliament" used to be, and still was). This exclusion of a sovereign body politic signaled the end of the monarchical age. National sovereignty calls for one center of power, the one

---

[17] P. Brunet, *Vouloir pour la nation, Le concept de représentation dans la théorie de l'État*, Bruylant / LGDJ, 2004, p. 73. See also Chapter 1, Section A.2.

[18] The formula is quoted by Pasquino, *supra* note 7, at p. 59.

[19] *Id.*, p. 58.

where the nation is represented. Moreover, in ruling out the possibility of an institutional body politic being inherently sovereign, it also rules out a sharing of sovereignty between separate organs, as is the case in England. The principle of national sovereignty belongs to the republican age; it implies the sovereignty of the people, a people forming a nation.

The revolutionary nation. The French Revolution did not invent the concept of nation, which had been in existence since the sixteenth century and was synonymous with "human group" or "community," but it radically transformed it.[20] In the eighteenth century, the term nation tends to be equated with that of State. In 1748, Montesquieu referred to "nations" in relation to the law of nations[21] and, ten years later, Vattel spoke indifferently of nations or States, defined as "bodies politic, societies of men united together for the purpose of promoting their mutual safety and advantage by the joint efforts of their combined strength."[22] What is the new nation made of? The answer is given in article 1 of the Declaration of the Rights of Man and the Citizen. The nation is made of "men [who] are born free and remain equal in rights." The new nation has nothing in common with the old one, which united not individuals, but rather groups of individuals—estates, corporations, and guilds, all of which were bound to each other by sentiments (honor, loyalty, faith, or love).

What does bind these men "born free and remaining equal in rights" together? What is the social link? Sieyès gives the following answer: men are linked to each other by labor, which supplies each nation—as Adam Smith had put it—with "all the necessaries and conveniences of life" and is "the fund" of any wealth.[23] The brilliant idea of the English liberal that economic exchange, in particular trade, is indeed what makes the social link is the cornerstone of Sieyès's essay.[24] The reason why the Third Estate is a self-sufficient "complete nation" is that it undertakes all the activities that support society, that is, all kinds of private employment (work on the land, human industry, occupations of merchants and dealers, most liberal and scientific professions, as well as the

---

[20] See Yves Durand, "Nation, nations," in *DAR,* p. 882; P. Nora, "Nation," *DCRF* (Idées), p. 339

[21] Montesquieu, *The Spirit of Laws* [Translated by Th. Nugent, 1752, revised by J. V. Prichard], 1748, Book I, chap. 3, available at http://www.constitution.org/cm/sol.htm.

[22] E. de Vattel, *The Law of Nations, or Principles of The Law of Nature Applied to the Conduct and Affairs of Nations and Sovereigns* [Translated by J. Chitty], Philadelphia, 1832, Preliminaries, § 1.

[23] A. Smith, *An Inquiry Into the Nature and Causes of the Wealth of Nations*, Liberty Classics, Indianapolis, 1976, vol. I, Introduction and Plan of the Work, p. 10.

[24] It has been proved that Sieyès carefully read Smith's *Wealth of Nations* and embraced Smith's ideas with enthusiasm; see Pasquino, *supra* note 7, at p. 118.

least esteemed domestic services) and most public services (the army, the law, the Church, and the administration), nineteen out of twenty employed in the public services are members of the Third Estate, the chief difference from the other orders being that its members "are required to bear the whole burden of all the genuinely hard work, namely, all the things that the privileged orders simply refuse to do." The Third Estate does indeed contain, within itself, everything needed to form a complete nation. It works like an industrious beehive. The Third Estate is, according to Sieyès, "a strong and robust man with one arm still in chains." He elaborates: "If the privileged order were removed, the nation would not be something less but something more [. . . .] The nobility is not part of our society at all: it may be a burden for the nation, but it cannot be part of it [. . . .] Such a class is, surely, foreign to the nation, because of its idleness." Thus, idleness, formerly a privilege of aristocracy, becomes a dividing line in society. The French nation defines itself as including all those who participate in the making of the nation's wealth. Labor is the criterion that includes or excludes from the nation.[25] If labor is the cement that forms the new nation, there is no doubt that the social link has become, like in America, voluntary, objective, based upon interests.

The modern nation. The nation of the twenty-first century is no longer that of 1789. True, its foundations are still the same. "What does a nation require to prosper and survive?" asked Sieyès. "Private activities and public services," he answered. This is certainly still the case. It is indeed labor that brings men together and makes the foundations of a nation so that the social link is principally interest. But it has never been only that, and it is still less today. From the origins, because it had to assert itself against the monarchical nation, the modern nation has always lived with an obsessive yearning for unity, unity (limited here to public law only) of representation, of power, of legislation, of citizenship, of its secular people enriched today with the children of its former colonies, "the sons and the daughters of the Republic."[26] Haunted by a fear of dislocation that has always loomed large, since it was built on the people united by these abstract concepts of liberty and equality, derided by Burke as "stubble and quicksand,"[27] the revolutionary nation could survive as a collective project

---

[25] *Id.*, p. 61. See also C. Clavreul, "Sieyès et la genèse de la représentation moderne," *Droits*, no. 6 (1987), p. 45, particularly, p. 49.

[26] Jacques Chirac, Speech of December 17, 2003, available at http://www.elysee.fr/elysee/elysee.fr/francais/interventions/discours_et_declarations/2003/decembre/discours_prononce_par_m_jacques_chirac_president_de_la_republique_relatif_au_respect_du_pri ncipe_de_laicite_dans_la_republique-palais_de_l_elysee.2829.html.

[27] E. Burke, *Thoughts on the Cause of the Present Discontents*, continued, 1. 1. 139, in *Select Works of Edmund Burke, and Miscellaneous Writings*, Indianapolis, Liberty Fund,

only. This was, and has remained, "the happiness of all"[28] announced as early as 1789 in the Declaration of the Rights of Man and the Citizen *in fine* and later in the Declaration of Rights of Year I (1793) as "common happiness."[29]

This ambitious project bears witness to the most important and significant difference between the American people and the French nation. There is no doubt that both republican models aim at ensuring happiness (happiness is the lodestar of political thought in the eighteenth century). But, unlike the American model that, from the very beginning, has construed "the Pursuit of Happiness," mentioned in the Declaration of Independence of 1776, as an individual project that eventually turned into the "American Dream," the French model from the beginning interpreted happiness as a collective project. "The libretto was written when the curtain raised, but history set it to music," writes Pierre Nora.[30] The happiness of all was bound to come into being by and in unity only. Carried forward by this perpetual search for unity, the nation excluded from itself all its causes of division (the religion chief among these, with the law of 1905 on the separation of Church and State) and included within itself all the values that could bring it back to what had made the success of the monarchical nation, the "whole-in-one" France. These values are found in the socialist doctrines and the principle of fraternity affirmed in 1848, the hardships of the two Worlds Wars, and affirmation in 1946, reiterated in 1958, that the republic was henceforth "indivisible, secular, democratic and social."[31]

2. The Theory of National Representation

The search for a good legislature. Unlike Madison who, because of his skepticism about human nature, does not think it realistic to expect to elect a legislative assembly of virtuous representatives motivated only by the public

---

1999, available at http://www.econlib.org/LIBRARY/LFBooks/Burke/brkSWv1c1a.html. In E. Burke, *Reflections on the Revolution in France*, Penguin Classics, 1968, p. 122, Burke blamed the revolutionaries for "despising everything that belonged to [them]," and "set up [a] trade without a capital."

[28] The Preamble to the Declaration of 1789 reads in part as follows: "The representatives of the French people [. . .] have resolved to set out, in a solemn declaration, the natural rights, inalienable and sacred, of man so that [. . .] the complaints of the of citizens [. . .] will always resolve around the maintenance of the Constitution and the happiness of all."

[29] Article 1 of the Declaration of the Rights of Man and the Citizen of Year I (June 24, 1793) provided: "The aim of society is the common happiness."

[30] P. Nora, "Nation," *DCRF* (Idées), p. 345.

[31] The phrase is contained in article 1 of the Constitution of October 4, 1958 (it was already mentioned in article 1 of the Constitution of October 27, 1946).

good, Sieyès operates on the premise that "a good representation is essential for a good legislature." To make good laws, one needs a good legislature, motivated by the public good only. The conformity of laws to the public interest depends on the composition of the assemblies. It is thus necessary to require two prerequisites, which may be described as the flying buttresses of the theory of national representation: the deputy is the representative of the nation, and the deputy represents the national interest.

The deputy is the representative of the nation. The first proposition, indeed a basic tenet, insofar as it determines all the rest, is in complete opposition to that accepted by the American theory of popular representation. It is as follows: the French deputy is the representative of the nation; he represents the whole nation, not his electors, not his constituency. The reason for this proposition is to be found in the consequences of the opposite proposition. If a deputy represented his electors only, it would seem, says Sieyès, that each constituency, electing its own representatives separately and having no say in the selection of the others, would be entitled not to recognize as valid law a bill that is not the work of the whole body of representatives and to claim the right to recognize as good law only the work of the majority of its own representatives. Each constituency would therefore have a *liberum veto* on every other, that is, it would have the right to claim not to be bound by any law that had not been adopted by its own representative. A right of this nature, says Sieyès, would sooner or later paralyze the law-making process and make it impossible for the legislature to perform its functions.[32] The French deputy is thus regarded as elected by the whole nation; he represents general, never individual interests; he represents not those who voted for him, not even his constituency, but rather the whole nation.

The deputy represents the national interest. The second proposition that flows from the first is as follows: as each deputy is a representative of the nation, he always represents a national, hence general interest, not particular interests. His will, therefore, is necessarily led by the national interest, hence the public interest, so the law is always the expression of general, not particular will. This result is the logical, quasi-mathematical consequence of the theory of representation envisioned by Sieyès, whose only concern was to set up a system that would enable the assembly of a nation to be composed in such a way that

---

[32] See E. J. Sieyès, *Views of the Executive Means Available to the Representatives of France in 1789*, in E. J. Sieyès, *Political Writings* Including the Debate between Sieyès and Tom Paine in 1791 [Edited, with an Introduction and Translation of *What Is the Third Estate* by Michael Sonenscher], Hackett Publishing Co., Inc., Indianapolis / Cambridge, 2003, p. 12.

"the will of the plurality cleaves constantly to the public good."[33] Sieyès's theory is the opposite extreme of Madison's.[34] In contrast to the latter, who is convinced that the public good is achieved through a multiplication of particular interests, the former believes that the public good is premised on total exclusion of particular interests from national representation. The goal is less to forget these particular interests than to represent them elsewhere than in the national assembly.

Representation of particular interests. It is greatly to the credit of the French system of national representation that its ultimate goal is to extract a general interest rising out of the multiplicity of factional interests in the social fabric. It suffers, however, the drawbacks of its qualities in that it stifles diversity in rolling back everything that could unravel the unity of national representation. The theory is obviously incompatible with the communitarian approach to representation, today so popular, which emphasizes groups' rights in the name of multiculturalism, just as it was at odds at the beginning of the twentieth century with the corporatist doctrine that advocated specific representation for economic and social interests. It is within these contradictions that one may find the exact meaning of the principle of indivisibility of the republic set forth in article 1 of the Constitution.

What the principle of the "indivisible Republic" enunciated in article 1(1) of the Constitution in effect means exactly, seems to be this: the sovereign (*i.e.*, the French people) shall not be represented other than in the national form. It does not mean that the numerous groups, communities, and interests that compose French society may not be represented as such, but that they may not be represented in the national representation, for that would imply that they have a right to take part and have a say in the exercise of sovereignty. The theory of national representation does not rule out any representation for particular interests; rather, it keeps them from being represented in sovereign powers. These interests can be represented outside sovereign powers, as is the case with economic and social interests today represented in the Economic and Social Council, an advisory body in the legislative process.

The national representation may reflect national interests only; particular or individual interests are not part of it. To change this, the Constitution would have to be amended, as was done for the ratification of the Maastricht Treaty in 1992. Since senators were elected by the organs of territorial subdivisions and

[33] Sieyès, *supra* note 9, at p. 86.

[34] See B. Manin, *Principes du gouvernement représentatif*, 1995, Flammarion, Champs, no. 349, p. 12.

local towns, and EU foreigners were admitted to be represented in these organs, some foreign, and thus, particular, interests were henceforth represented in the Senate. A constitutional revision took place to authorize this derogation made inevitable by the ratification of the Maastricht Treaty. For the same reasons, article 3 of the Constitution was amended to enable the legislature, if it chooses to do so, "to promote equal access by women and men to elective offices and positions." It may be noted that the formula rules out any discriminatory quotas in favor of women, insofar as access must always be provided equally (*i.e.*, for "women and men").

B. THE STATUS OF STATUTORY LAW IN THE STATE

Representation and legislation. National representation is conducive to approaching statutory law in a spirit completely different from the Americans. Insofar as it leads to a legislature representing not a multitude of diverse and antagonistic interests, but rather a united nation, charged with attending common interests only, the statute is necessarily the expression of a general will, never that of a (or some) particular will(s); it is therefore not inclined to create injustices. To the extent that the legislature is composed in such a way that, according to Sieyès's wishes, "the will of the plurality cleaves constantly to the public good,"[35] the statute may fairly be described as a true "expression of the general will," not the expression of "an interested and overbearing majority,"[36] prone to impose its "naked preferences."[37] It is the theory of national representation, that is, the idea that general interests only may be represented in the legislatures, that explains why the obsessive fear of the tyranny of the majority was in France never as vivid, almost palpable, as in America.

National representation leads to the public good with great probability but not certitude. In reality, it has not always brought about the expected results. This is not to say that its premises are flawed; they are not. Close observation of American political practices and the role of interest groups and lobbies is convincing enough in this respect. But the theory, a pure product of the powerful reason of the Enlightenment, can produce its beneficial results only upon fulfillment of certain conditions that, in reality, are difficult to meet. The whole theory boils down to the concept of generality. In order for the lawmakers to

---

[35] Sieyès, *supra* note 9, at p. 86.

[36] A. Hamilton, J. Madison, & J. Jay, *The Federalist Papers*, Letter no. 10, p. 77, C. Rossiter Edition, Mentor Book, N.Y, 1961, available at http://www.yale.edu/lawweb/avalon/federal/fed.htm.

[37] C. Sunstein, "Naked Preferences and the Constitution," 84 *Columbia L. Rev.* 1689 (1984).

always legislate for the public good, they must pay attention to, and represent, only general interests. This can be done only by acting on the law-making process as well as the object of legislation. The principles of French public law were built on these premises, but they have had to be adapted from their revolutionary beginnings.

1. The Law-Making Process and the Representation of Interests

"Good representation" and "good legislature." Sieyès's basic idea is to compose a legislature that would be well and truly national, that is, composed in such a way that "the will of the plurality cleaves constantly to the public good." In practice, this can be done only if the deputy is forbidden to represent anything but the nation. Such ambition supposes, as Sieyès himself acknowledges, getting over "the major difficulty that springs from the interest by which a citizen allies himself with just a few others." For as Sieyès explains: "It is this interest that leads to conspiracy and collusion; through it anti-social schemes are plotted; through it the most formidable public enemies are created."[38] These interests that are a danger to the republic are, of course, akin to the factions of Madison. However, where Madison thinks that there is nothing to be done but to accommodate them and minimize their harm to the republic, the Frenchman proposes a much more radical solution. Haunted by the estates, guilds, and corporations that divided French society of his time, Sieyès is certain that they must be kept, in the first place, from forming. He offers the following remedy: "It should not be surprising therefore that the social order should require that no citizens be allowed to organize themselves in corporate bodies."[39] Sieyès follows in the footsteps of Rousseau, who wrote: "It is essential, if the general will is able to express itself, that there should be no partial society within the State, and that each citizen should think only his own thoughts."[40]

Plurality and majority. The great design of Sieyès is to extract from representation, or elections, an assembly composed so that its members always cleave to the public good. Let us ensure, he says in substance, a "good legislature" through "good representation," and its members will naturally promote the public good. They would be inclined to do so, because of both their characters and their working methods. Having no ties to particular interests, their will shall be free; the deputy will think only his own thoughts.

[38] Sieyès, *supra* note 4, at p. 87.

[39] *Id.*

[40] Rousseau, *supra* note 10, at Book II, chap. 3.

True, decisions cannot be required to be unanimous as this would be impracticable, even under such favorable circumstances as an assembly determined by individual wills only. In that respect, Sieyès considers: ''[T]o require for the future that the common will should always be the exact sum of every individual will would amount to giving up the possibility of being able to will in common and would mean the dissolution of the social union.''[41] However, it will not be simple majority rule either, for Sieyès adds: ''It is therefore absolutely necessary to resolve to attribute all the characteristics of the common will to an agreed plurality.''[42] ''Plurality,'' not ''majority,'' says Sieyès. The difference is no trifling matter.

What Sieyès has in mind is not the numerical majority of Hobbes, the mathematical majority that derives from the criterion for decision agreed upon in the initial pact.[43] The plurality Sieyès is referring to is the ''*major et sanior pars,*'' the majority of the Church and the canons, that is, not the strict majority of more than half, but the opinion of the most important part of the deliberative body, the majority that takes shape by exchange and discussion, and that eventually appears to be a reinforced majority. The legislature of the republican age cannot be identical to that of the monarchical age, for as Sieyès put it in terms that should be agreeable to Thomas Paine: ''Everything between men is exchange, and in every act of exchange, there is necessarily on both sides a free act of will; but no man has a right to dominate another; the opposite maxim would open the door to all crimes, all horrors, and to the annihilation of all rights.''[44]

The role of deliberation. In order to reach a plurality of voices, and to get away from the hard-line majority logic—that mechanical majority that is incompatible with liberty—Sieyès relies on the role of deliberation and recommends the test of argumentation and discussion. He is convinced that from a free deliberation, a ''*major sanior pars*'' should necessarily spring, because consensus always comes out of a healthy and robust discussion between free men, free from any allegiance to a particular interest, and motivated solely by their reason and intelligence. A free deliberation in his opinion always leads to a ''single view,'' as he explains in the following excerpt:

---

[41] Sieyès, *supra* note 32, at p. 11.

[42] Sieyès, V*ues sur les moyens d'exécution dont les Représentans [sic] de la France pourront disposer en 1789*, pp. 17-18, Paris, 1789, available at http://gallica.bnf.fr/ark:/12148/bpt6k41688x.

[43] See Chapter 6, Section A.1.a.

[44] Sieyès, *supra* note 42, at pp. 16-17.

> In every deliberation there is a kind of problem to be solved. This is to know, in any given case, what the general interest would prescribe. When the discussion begins, it is not possible to identify the direction it will take to reach that discovery with certainty. Doubtless, the general interest would be nothing if it were not someone's interest. It has to be the one interest among the various individual interests that is common to the largest number of voters, hence the need for a clash and coincidence of opinions. What you take to be a mixture and confusion that serves to obscure everything is an indispensable preliminary towards enlightenment. All these individual interests have to be allowed to jostle and press against one another, to take hold of the question from one point of view, then another, each trying to push it according to his strength towards some projected goal. In this trial, views that are useful and those that are harmful will be separated from one another. Some will fall, while others will maintain their momentum and will balance one another until, modified and purified by their reciprocal interaction, they will end up by becoming reconciled with one another and will be combined together in a single view, just as in the physical universe a single, more powerful movement can be seen to be made up of a multitude of opposing forces.[45]

As Bernard Manin underlines, the discussion does not form in itself a principle of decision; what gives a proposal a decisional value is not its being debated, but rather its ability to obtain consent.[46] True, this is not universal assent; it is the consent of a majority, but a large majority.

The theory of good representation in the face of political parties. As a matter of pure logic, the theory of Sieyès is faultless. Madison followed the same line of reasoning with respect to the Senate, which he envisioned composed of virtuous and wise men who would be able to refine the popular will and lead the people to the public good. The difficulty with that theory is that, in order for the deliberation to be the product of an exchange between authentically free wills, private citizens must not be "allowed to become members of corporate bodies."[47] Concretely speaking, this amounts to restricting the freedom of association. Unsurprisingly, freedom of association was recognized in French law only in 1901 and, still today, French law does not equally protect associations, insofar as full and complete legal capacity is

---

[45] Sieyès, *supra* note 32, at pp. 39-40.
[46] Manin, *supra* note 34, at p. 241.
[47] Sieyès, *supra* note 9, p. 87.

granted solely to those associations recognized as contributing to public utility (*associations reconnues d'utilité publique*). More importantly, the status of political parties is still today uncertain in French law.[48]

In practice, the expected adjustment between "good representation" and "good legislature," which in turn results in "good legislation," has not always been realized. Factional interests, or political parties, in modern language, have defeated elaborated constitutional schemes more often than not. And the statute, instead of being what the Constitution commands it should be, "the expression of the general will," has been sometimes transformed into an expression of particular wills, occasionally aligned against the general interest. Sieyès realized the danger and, without giving up on the necessity of keeping factions from investing legislative assemblies, he eventually decided—five years after his initial writings—to abide by Madison's recommendations. He, too, came to believe that, failing the suppression of factions, controlling their effects was the best option. In 1795, he suggested setting up an assembly of 108 members in charge of reviewing the conformity to the constitution of voted statutes, the so-called "*jurie constitutionnaire.*" His proposal for a legislative, not judicial, review marks the first attempt to establish a system for reviewing the constitutionality of statutes in French law; it did not succeed and was soon forgotten. Although a cause within academic circles, particularly at the end of the nineteenth and beginning of the twentieth centuries, the different idea of a judicial review for statutes never prevailed during the third republic (1875-1940). The fear was that a judicial remedy of this type would introduce into France the same "government by judiciary" criticized by the French scholar Édouard Lambert in a memorable and influential book, a faithful account of the *Lochner* era reigning supreme in the United States at that time.[49] However, after World War II, Sieyès's idea was resuscitated under the form of the Constitutional Committee of thirteen members, a sort of legislative joint committee, since all members came from the legislative assemblies, that was in charge of reviewing actions legislative in form in the Constitution of October 27, 1946.[50] Its activity was nonexistent. In 1958, the French system for reviewing the constitutionality of statutes was brought to a successful conclusion

---

[48] See J.-C. Colliard, "La liberté des partis politiques," *Mélanges J. Robert*, Montchrestien, 1998, p. 81.

[49] É. Lambert, *Le gouvernement des juges et la lutte contre la législation sociale aux États-Unis. L'expérience américaine de contrôle judiciaire de la constitutionnalité des lois*, Paris, Edition Giard, 1921, reprint Dalloz, 2005.

[50] See the debates on the creation of the Committee in the casebook by A. T. von Mehren & J. R. Gordley, *The Civil Law System*, Little Brown, 1977, p. 264.

by the creation of the Constitutional Council, a legislative organ composed of individuals from different fields, charged with exercising a check on the abuse of power by the legislature.[51]

The French model for reviewing the constitutionality of statutes. This developed much more slowly than the American system. By contrast with the American system of judicial review, which modeled itself on the English system as theorized by Sir Edward Coke in the beginning of the seventeenth century, the French system departed from the monarchical system of judicial review as early as the beginning of the Revolution. No principle is more firmly established in French law than the prohibition on the courts to take any part in the legislative function. The prohibition was stated in article 10 of the *Loi* of August 16-24, 1790, as follows: "The judicial tribunals shall not take part, either directly or indirectly, in the exercise of legislative power, nor impede or suspend the execution of the enactments of the legislative body." It is regarded as deriving directly from the principle of national sovereignty. A rapporteur to the law of 1790, the deputy Thouret gave the core justification of the principle when he declared that "a nation which exercises the legislative power through a permanent body of representatives cannot leave to the tribunals, enforcers of its laws and subject to its authority, permission to revise its laws."[52] To this reason of principle, another one may be added, which is more one of common sense and opportunity: conformity between statutory law and the public interest cannot be sought by those who are in charge of protecting private interests. This solution is compelling not only to avoid conflicts of interests, but also to protect the independence and impartiality of the judges.

The French model for reviewing the constitutionality of statutes is an original creation that, unlike the American model, owes nothing to the powers of judicial review the courts enjoyed in the monarchical age. Definitely anchored in the republican age, it is usually regarded as a successful institution because of the broad consensus it enjoys in public opinion, a status far from the apparently endless controversy that exists in America on the existence as well as the exercise of the power of judicial review. The success of the French model comes from the fact that it is not exercised by a judicial body, but rather by an organ, the Constitutional Council, which, on the one hand, is not composed of judges, and which, on the other hand, does not adjudicate cases. It does not address itself to the actual material interests of private persons, and it is not interested in

---

[51] See G. Vedel, "Excès de pouvoir administratif et excès de pouvoir législatif [I et II]," *Cahiers CC*, no. 1 (1996), p. 57 and no. 2, 1997, p. 77.

[52] *AP*, vol. XII (March 24, 1790), p. 344.

their sufferings or their losses; in other words, it does not dispense justice. The Constitutional Council addresses abstract questions only.

The Constitutional Council is an advisory body that, in those activities relevant to our present demonstration,[53] belongs to the law-making process, as does the Council of State (*Conseil d'État*) when giving an advisory legal opinion on bills before their being put forward before Parliament. The most important differences between the former and the latter are two: First, unlike the Council of State, which intervenes before a bill goes to Parliament, the Constitutional Council comes into play after the bill has been debated but before its promulgation by the president, which is followed by enactment. As a result, the Constitutional Council does not review statutes, strictly speaking, but rather actions that are legislative in form.[54] Second, unlike the Council of State, whose opinion is always advisory, so that the government is free to abide by it or not, the Constitutional Council's opinion is binding, and a bill's provision that has been declared contrary to the Constitution may not be promulgated. Beyond these characteristics, which by themselves distinguish the Constitutional Council from a Supreme Court, the spirit in which it performs its functions is not the same as in the United States. The Council is not a piece of the mechanism of the separation of powers as that theory is understood in the United States; it is not conceived as a counterweight to the legislative power. Its role is not to put a check on the will of the legislature and to oppose its ambition to the latter's, but rather to make sure that the text to be promulgated will conform as far as possible to the general interest. In that respect, the Council has the power to raise *ex officio* arguments that have not been invoked by critics of the bill, if it thinks that the public good so requires, a prerogative that would be inconceivable if it were a true judge or court. Last but not least, the role of the Council is not even to protect the rights of "discrete and insular minorities" insofar as the organs that may refer bills to it (*i.e.*, the president of the republic, or each president of both chambers, or sixty deputies, or sixty senators) are not the spokespersons or representatives of minority groups, but rather are all representatives elected at the national level and thus, necessarily, representatives of the nation.

---

[53] Besides reviewing the constitutionality of actions legislative in form, the Constitutional Council exercises an oversight function over the presidential and legislative elections; it also reviews the compatibility of treaties with the constitution before ratification.

[54] This is the rightful terminology, in our opinion, adopted by von Mehren & Gordley, *supra* note 50, at p. 264.

Reviewability of statutes against treaties. The absence of judicial power to review statutes against the Constitution in the French legal system does not mean that courts may never go beyond a mechanical application of the legislative enactment to the case at hand. After World War II, an important novelty was introduced into the French constitutional tradition, due to the influence of the monist doctrine of international law, represented by Georges Scelle. Operating on the inherent superiority of international law to domestic laws, the constituent power in 1946 imposed an important limitation on the "exaggerations" (the word is from Talleyrand) of the legislature. Article 26 of the Constitution of October 27, 1946, laid forth the principle of an automatic superiority of treaties duly ratified or approved over laws, without, however, formally giving the courts the power to enforce the provision (*i.e.*, to make the treaty prevail over the conflicting statute by effectively setting aside the statute and applying the treaty instead). The same provision reappeared in Article 55 of the Constitution of October 4, 1958. Treaties, when duly ratified or approved, were declared to have "an authority superior to that of laws," save for the slight difference *vis-à-vis* the 1946 text that their superiority is no longer automatic, but rather "subject, for each agreement or treaty, to its application by the other party." It took almost thirty years in the case of the judicial courts[55] and more than forty years in the case of the administrative courts[56] to resolve that they were empowered to enforce the constitutional provision. Nowadays, French courts review statutes against international treaties binding on France, chief among these the European Convention on Human Rights, on a regular basis.

The fact that today courts are reviewing the compatibility of statutes with international treaties is often invoked to argue that the distance traditionally separating French and American legal systems has narrowed and that the former has come very close to the latter. It is said that review of "constitutionality," which is the core of judicial review American style, is not very different from review of "conventionality" (by reference to the European Convention on Human Rights), which is the substance of judicial review, French style. The assimilation of the two systems of judicial reviews seems ill-conceived. The superiority of treaties over statutes as set forth in Article 55 of the French Constitution does not fit within the logic of checks and balances that accompanies the principle of the separation of powers, but rather derives from a quasi-federal logic that defends and promotes the superiority of universal and humanist values over nationalistic preferences. The superiority of universal

---

[55] Cour de Cassation, *Société des Cafés Jacques Vabre* v. *Administration générale des douanes*, [1975] 2 CMLR 336.

[56] Conseil d'État, *Nicolo*, [1990] 1 CMLR 173.

values, as enshrined especially in the Declaration of the Rights of Man and the Citizen of 1789, has been a permanent feature of French legal tradition since the Revolution of 1789, which never adhered to the dualist theory erecting a wall of separation between international law and domestic law.[57]

Originally, article 26 of the 1946 Constitution, then article 55 in the 1958 Constitution, was introduced to protect the foreigners lawfully settled and engaged in business in the French territory against the xenophobic laws adopted during the period of economic hardship that followed the Great Depression of the 1930s. In particular, the French National Assembly had adopted discriminatory laws that withdrew the rights of establishment of the foreigners (mostly Italians and Spaniards) in violation of the bilateral treaties that protected them. With the conclusion of large universal and regional treaties on human rights, the provision ended up applicable to nationals, too. But, no matter how broad the protection of the constitutional provision may be, its aim is solely to protect the individual in his rights. It has never been, like judicial review in the American legal system, a technique that enables the judicial power to oppose its ambition to that of Congress and impede the government in its policies.

When a judge makes a treaty prevail over a statute, he no longer acts exclusively as an organ of enforcement of national laws. Rather, upon express constitutional authorization, he acts as an agent of international law enforcement, following a technique of "functional dual enforcement authority" that empowers the judge to enforce both international and domestic law. That technique, which was theorized in the interwar period by Georges Scelle,[58] has today become a means commonly used for enforcing international law. International treaties, particularly in the field of human rights, often give a cause of action to the individual to have his rights duly enforced and protected by national courts. The technique, today, plays a crucial role in European law, not only in ensuring the primacy of EU law over national laws, but also in

[57] This permanent and enduring feature of French legal thought is recalled in the Preamble to the Constitution of 1946 by the incise "faithful to its traditions" in the phrase: "The French Republic, faithful to its traditions, abides by the rules of international law." That phrase has important consequences on the principles governing relations between international law and domestic law.

[58] The technique is known in French as "*dédoublement fonctionnel.*" G. Scelle, who coined the expression, explains it as follows: "When a national judge delivers a judgment in a case between nationals and foreigners or between foreigners, he ceases to be a national judge and becomes an international judge," in *Précis de droit des gens, Principes et systématique*, Sirey, 1932, vol. I, p. 56; see also, vol. II, p. 317.

guaranteeing the effective application of the European Convention on Human Rights.[59]

2. Object of Statutory Law

The generality of the statute. No concept is more important than generality in understanding the privileged position of statutory law in French law. If the statute enjoys in French law a highly respected position in public opinion beyond all comparison with its usually inferior status in the American model, it is principally because its object must be always general. A *loi* (*i.e.*, a statute in French law) cannot address a particular situation or individual as its object. Under the old regime by contrast, the sovereign could address any object and legislate on anything; his will had no limits; the essence of sovereignty in the monarchical age was, indeed, to be unlimited. In the republican age, when liberty comes before sovereignty, the statute has a supplementary character. It may regulate all rights without exception (from this standpoint, there can be no ''reserved rights'' in a republic, all citizens having the same rights); however, to regulate does not mean to forbid. The statute may not forbid all rights insofar as ''the *loi* has the right only to prohibit actions harmful to society'' (article 5 of the Declaration of the Rights of Man and of the Citizen of August 26, 1789).

The principle of the necessary generality of the statute was developed by Rousseau in the *Social Contract.* Rousseau gave a crucial role to the principle of generality, insisting on the fact that ''there can be no general will directed to a particular object.''[60] In his view, the *loi* is ''the expression of the general will'' if, and only if, it pursues a general object. Only when this prerequisite is met, may a statute be regarded fair, nondiscriminatory, and to have been adopted for the public good. In the theory of the *loi* as the ''expression of the general will,''

---

[59] For those familiar with the evolution of American federalism after the Civil War, the ''functional dual enforcement authority'' theory seems to have been inspired by American techniques. Its core meaning, which is to rely on the individual to have his own rights protected by the judge, is exactly the same as that found to protect civil rights after the Civil War. Curiously enough, the United States has reserved the technique for domestic law enforcement purposes and has not extended its benefit to the enforcement of international law, most human rights treaties binding on the country being expressly declared non-self-executing in domestic law.

[60] Rousseau, *supra* note 10, at Book II, chap. 6. For a profound scholarly exposition of the principle of generality of the *loi*, see R. Capitant, ''Principes du droit public,'' Paris, Cours de droit 1951-1952, reprinted in *Écrits constitutionnels*, Paris, Éditions du CNRS, 1982, pp. 98-99.

all classifications between people, not only those "which curtail the civil rights of a single racial group," are "immediately suspect."[61]

The principle of the necessary generality of statutory law entails important consequences, which were developed by Portalis in his famous Preliminary Address on the First Draft of the Civil Code (1799). The fundamental principle is enunciated as follows:

> The office of the statute (*loi*) is to lay down, with high views, the general maxims of the law: to establish principles fertile in consequences, not to dwell on the details of the questions that may arise on every subject. [. . .] The statute (*loi*) rules everyone: it considers men as a mass, never as individuals. It must not involve itself either in individual events, or in the disputes that divide citizens.[62]

Therefore, a *loi* cannot be the work of a jurisconsult (*i.e.*, a jurist, an expert in law), but that of a legislator, who must not be driven into details; drafting a *loi* is not like writing a bill of particulars. Portalis explains:

> There is a science for the legislators, just as there is one for the jurists; and the one does not resemble the other. The legislator's science consists in finding on every subject the principles most favorable to the common good. The jurist's science consists in applying those principles, ramifying them, extending them, through wise and reasoned application, to private hypotheses.[63]

These ideas fostered in French law an approach to statutory law very different from that prevailing in the United States, both in the states and even in Congress.[64] In French law, a statute, in principle, may not have a particular

---

[61] *Korematsu* v. *United States*, 323 US 214, 216 (1944).

[62] Portalis, *Discours préliminaire au premier projet de Code civil*, reprint, Paris, Collection "Voix de la cité," Éditions Confluences, 1999, pp. 19 and 23. There is an English translation of the Preliminary Address to the First Draft of the Civil Code prepared by The International Cooperation Group, Department of Justice of Canada, available at http://www.justice.gc.ca/en/ps/inter/code/index.html#note1.

[63] *Id.* pp. 23-24.

[64] Private bills, which exist in the United States as well as in all common law systems, are inconceivable in French law; see, "Private Bills in Congress," 79 *Harv. L. Rev.* 1684 (1966). They stand for a legacy of the monarchical age, when the sovereign could pay attention to everybody and everything. When a law in the French legal system pays attention to a private situation or a private person, this is always for a reason of public interest (such is the case of a statute that orders national mourning for a deceased person or that orders the transfer of the ashes of a great man). True, private laws in the United States are today extremely rare. However, their mere existence bears witness to the concept of representation, which is very different from the French approach. They are

object or be addressed to a particular situation. For, should this be the case, Portalis warns: ''The legislator, bogged down in the particulars, would soon be no more than a jurisconsult. The legislative power would be besieged by private interests, distracting it, at every turn, from the general interest of society.''[65]

As Portalis explains, the necessary generality of the statute makes it that ''rare and exceptional cases cannot fit within the framework of a reasonable legislation.'' The legislator must not occupy himself with ''the too-volatile and too-contentious particulars, nor with all the subjects it would be futile to try and foresee, or whose hasty prediction could not be free of risk.''[66] A subject that does not come within the framework of a *loi* is a matter for regulation or a matter for judgment. Both of them are the responsibility of the executive power, since they call into question administrative or judicial functions.

The birth of regulatory power. An important consequence of the principle of the generality of the statute in French law is a sharp distinction between the statute (*loi*) and the regulation (*règlements*). The distinction was already in force before the Revolution, but it did not have the same scope or the same meaning.[67] Under the old regime, the king made the laws, then called ordinances or edicts, and the ''*Parlements*'' (courts of law) were in charge of making regulations within their respective territorial jurisdiction. The judges were then considered the traditional organs for enforcing the laws; besides enforcing the law by adjudicating private disputes, the courts were also in charge of functions that today are regarded as administrative; in particular, they were in charge of taking all the measures necessary to ensure public peace (*repos public*), public order, and tranquility, a task that they performed by drafting, enacting, and enforcing regulatory decrees (*arrêts de règlement*). Such *arrêts* stemmed from their broad jurisdiction over justice and police matters; they might deal with the prevention of fire, public health, regulation of public markets, surveillance of inns and cabarets, maintenance of public order, and even policing prostitution.

The *loi* of August 16-24, 1790, abolished this system of regulation in its article 12: ''They [the courts and tribunals] shall not make regulations, but they shall have recourse to the legislative body, whenever they think necessary, either

---

anecdotal features that may better illustrate a fundamental principle of the French theory of statutory law: the national characteristic of representation means that statutes may only have a general object.

[65] Portalis, *supra* note 62, at p. 23.

[66] *Id.*, p. 24.

[67] See M. Verpeaux, *La naissance du pouvoir réglementaire (1789-1799)*, Paris, PUF, Les grandes thèses du droit français, 1991; A.-M. L.-B., ''Pouvoir réglementaire,'' *Dictionnaire constitutionnel* [Duhamel (O.) & Mény (Y.), Dir.], PUF, 1992, p. 782.

to interpret a law or to make a new one.'' Once regulatory decrees (*arrêts de règlement*) were forbidden, they certainly had to be replaced, because statutes, unless they address the minute details of particulars, must be followed by measures of enforcement. The *arrêts de règlement* were replaced by the regulatory decrees of the National Assembly, which eventually turned into a legislative body of unlimited powers, the concentration of all powers, legislative and executive.

Regulatory power, conceived as a power distinct from legislative power, and henceforth attributed to executive power, came into being under the Directoire in the Constitution of Year III (August 22, 1795). It was systematized in article 44 of the Constitution of Year VIII (December 13, 1799): ''The Government proposes the laws (*lois*) and makes the regulations necessary to secure their execution.''[68] Since then, this distinction has been part the French legal system, and it must be considered as a fundamental characteristic of the French conception of legislation.

The distinction between the statute and the regulation. In the history of French public law, regulatory power has been a decisive factor in the transformation of executive power. It is thanks to its existence that the executive power ceased to be considered as a mere faithful executor of the laws, in line with the fate that had become its lot after the Revolution, under the influence of English constitutional ideas. The regulatory power very clearly comes into being under the Directoire (1795-1799) and is consecrated under the Consulate (1799-1804). Two distinct kinds of regulatory decrees are identified: (1) the regulations of police that are made of all the texts necessary to secure public peace, public order, public tranquility and security, and that fall within the jurisdiction of several national or local authorities; (2) the regulations necessary to secure the execution of the statutes that, because of the principle of generality of statutes, are indispensable to concretely enforce the laws.

Contrary to a well-received, though ill-conceived set notion, the regulatory power did not develop at the expense of legislative power, as is too often said by those who invoke the republican tradition that allegedly authorized the National Assembly to occupy itself with any object of its own choice. The relation between legislative and executive powers is not a zero sum game; all that is gained by one power is not lost by the other. Legislative power gains in authority and legitimacy when it confines itself to general subjects. The principal advantage of a regulatory authority, complementary to a statutory authority, is that legislative power, forced to limit itself to general objects, may

[68] Anderson, *supra* note 16, at p. 276.

legitimately claim that, because of the generality of its object, which precludes granting particular advantages to specific groups, the statute is truly the expression of the general will and thus conforms to the general interest.[69]

From theory to reality. The distinction between statutes and regulations was explicated by Portalis in a lofty view of the legislative process as follows:

> Statutes (*lois*), strictly speaking, differ from mere regulations. It is the function of statutes to set down, in every sphere, the fundamental rules and to determine the basic legal forms. The particulars of enforcement, the provisional or incidental precautionary measures, the transitory or inconstant objects, in a word, anything that requires far more the vigilance of the administering authority than the intervention of the instituting or creating power, is the concern of regulations. Regulations are acts of magistracy, and statutes are acts of sovereignty.[70]

In practice, the distinction between statutes and regulations had many trials and tribulations. It was enshrined with great force in the Constitution of October 4, 1958, with the distinction between article 34, listing all the subjects in which Parliament was called upon to lay down either "rules" (*règles*) or "fundamental principles" (*principes fondamentaux*), and article 37, cursorily stating that "matters other than those that fall within the domain of statutes shall be of a regulatory character." The idea behind these subtle distinctions was to oblige Parliament to remain at a sufficient level of generality and abstraction in order to avoid getting into the minute details of legislation that usually give rise to discrimination or unequal distribution of wealth through classifications between

---

[69] In *Railway Express Agency* v. *New York* (336 US 106, 112-3 (1949)), Justice Jackson established a clear connection between the generality of a statute and the fairness of its content:

> I regard it as a salutary doctrine that cities, states and the Federal Government must exercise their powers so as not to discriminate between their inhabitants except upon some reasonable differentiation fairly related to the object of regulation. This equality is not merely abstract justice. The framers of the Constitution knew, and we should not forget today, that there is no more effective practical guaranty against arbitrary and unreasonable government than to require that the principles of law which officials would impose upon a minority must be imposed generally. Conversely, nothing opens the door to arbitrary action so effectively as to allow those officials to pick and choose only a few to whom they will apply legislation and thus to escape the political retribution that might be visited upon them if larger numbers were affected. Courts can take no better measure to assure that laws will be just than to require that laws be equal in operation.

[70] Portalis, *supra* note 62, at p. 26.

people. This was particularly true in the domain where Parliament was invited to lay down ''fundamental principles'' as opposed to that where it was invited to adopt ''rules.''[71] The problem is that the distinction between ''rules'' and ''fundamental principles'' has never worked well. After the bitter experience of the Code of Civil Procedure being amended by the regulatory authority and subsequently invalidated in part by the Council of State on the ground that it conflicted in some provisions with general principles of law that are left to the legislative power for restriction or modification,[72] the government seems to have chosen to put forward its major projects before Parliament and to label them as ''bills'' (*projets de lois*).

Still, the idea of a Parliament that must limit itself to laying down the general maxims of the law, leaving to the regulatory authority the details of legislation, is alive and well in French legal thought. Even if the initial design of the 1958 Constitution has not been carried as far as it could have been, with the result that the so-called ''autonomous regulatory authority'' granted to the government by article 37 is in practice less broad than originally foreseen, the fact is that, in most cases, the statute is not self-executing in French law and is usually supplemented by regulatory decrees setting down the details necessary for its proper enforcement.

Generality of the statute and equality before the law. The principle of the generality of statutory law has close connections to that of equality before the law. Under the old regime, the fact that the statute could deal with any subject is precisely the reason for so much discrimination. Statutes were unequal; in particular, they could exempt the so-called privileged orders; thus, they were

---

[71] In respect to the domain of ''fundamental rules,'' article 34 provides:

> Statutes shall determine the fundamental principles of:
>
> The general organization of national defense;
> The self-government of territorial unites, their powers and their resources;
> The preservation of environment;
> Education;
> The regime governing ownership, rights *in rem* and civil and commercial obligations;
> Labor laws, trade-union law and social security.

There is little doubt that the original intent of the Constitution was to make these fields a privileged domain for the regulations, save for the ''fundamental principles,'' a wording reserving on its face anything that could deal with political and/or civil rights, but probably too loosely formulated.

[72] See, in particular, Conseil d'État, Assemblée, *Dame David*, *Rec. Lebon*, 464, Conclusions Gentot; D. 1975, 369, note J.-M. Auby; *AJDA*, 1974, 525, chr. Franc & Boyon; *JCP*, 1975, II, 19967, note R. Drago.

arbitrary. At the Revolution, the principle of statutory generality was regarded as a prerequisite to effective equality of citizens before the statutes and, more generally, before the laws.

The principle of equality in statutory law is embodied in article 6 of the Declaration of the Rights of Man and the Citizen as follows: "The statute must be the same for all, whether it protects or punishes." The statute may not grant privileges to anyone; it may not use economic or social distinctions between citizens and bestow a particular status on some of them while refusing it to others. The prohibition is of general application and applies both to the statutes that "protect," such as civil laws, and to the statutes that "punish," such as the penal laws. Fiscal laws, however, are not covered by the principle of equality in the same manner. Article 13 of the same Declaration that sets down the indispensable character of "a communal contribution," in order to maintain a public force and to defray the expenses of the administration, adds an important caveat: "It (the contribution) must be equally apportioned among all the citizens, according to their abilities." It is thus plainly clear that fiscal matters do authorize discrimination based upon factual situations. Fiscal law in the French republican model aims at real not formal equality.

When it was proclaimed in 1789, the principle of equality before the law marked a breaking point with the past. It took decades, however, before it was effectively applied as a principle of actual, not merely formal equality. The "social question" in the nineteenth century, the economic upheavals triggered by World War I, and the Great Depression played a role of first importance in the change of mentalities and thus of interpretations of the legal rules. Nowadays, it is commonly established that the legislature may, if not must, take into account, and legislate with due consideration for the factual differences of situation between people. Today, a paragraph routinely used by the Constitutional Council in its jurisprudence provides: "The principle of equality does not preclude the legislature from treating different situations in different ways or from departing from equality for reasons in the general interest, provided, in both cases, the resultant difference of treatment is directly related to the purpose of the statute generating it."[73] In fiscal matters, the Constitutional Council is more flexible, and the legislature is empowered with a discretion that would be inadmissible in other domains. In this particular domain, the legislature may bestow some advantages on certain classes of taxpayers while refusing them to others, provided that the legislature decides, for "reasons in the general

[73] CC, 2004-507 DC, December 9, 2004, para. 5, Rec. 219; 2004-511 DC, December 29, 2004, para. 11, *ibid.* 236; for an English summary, see *ibid.* 421.

interest,'' a formula, which means that the advantages directly granted to some are compatible with the law if they also indirectly benefit the entire nation.

Chapter 8
State Power

Trust in power. No idea is more foreign to the spirit of the French republican model than that of limited power. The American model will never be at rest until power is limited in its exercise by being split into so many pieces that it can never be formed as a whole again, and sovereignty can be held to be rooted out from the government. By contrast, the French model has always understood power as a will put at the service of the nation for one purpose, the preservation of the enduring common interests of the people. As the Conseil d'Etat put it in 1999, what underlines the French political tradition is a ''preeminent inclination for a volontarist approach'' to the relationship between power and society.[1] Far from being limited, the French republican power is a complete power, a ''State power.''[2] If the American idea is that limiting arbitrariness must be sought as a first priority because individual liberty comes before efficiency, the French idea is that the nation must be, first and foremost, able to govern itself. The American model has consistently developed on the basis of a principle of distrust of the governed for the government, while the French model has developed around an idea of trust between the nation and its organs.

The reasons for the striking differences between the spirit of the American model and that of the French model are diverse. There is little doubt that all of them are related to the respective histories of both people, to their ideas, their beliefs, and all the prejudices deposited by history in their collective memories. The American model was built in Philadelphia on the basis of English institutions as they were in the middle of the eighteenth century, and it has not developed since, so to speak. Frozen on the model of limited, or constitutional

[1] See Conseil d'État, *Rapport public 1999*, Etudes et Documents no. 50 (*L'intérêt général*), Paris, La Documentation française, 1999, especially pp. 265-269.

[2] The expression ''State power'' (*pouvoir d'État*) is borrowed from M. Hauriou, *Précis de droit constitutionnel*, 2nd ed., Sirey, 1929, reprint CNRS 1965, p. 103.

monarchy, which had been achieved in England as early as 1689, it operates on the premise of a necessary protection for the individual against tyranny.[3]

In the late 1770s, Turgot, Comptroller-General of the Finances of France from 1774 to 1776, took the view that the free and independent States of America had modeled their institutions after "an unreasonable imitation of the usages of England [. . .] Instead of bringing all the authorities into one, that of the nation, they have established," he said, "different bodies, a House of Representatives, a Council, a Governor, because England has a House of Commons, a House of Lords, and a King. They undertake to balance these different authorities as if the same equilibrium of powers, which has been thought necessary to balance the enormous preponderance of royalty, could be of any use in republics, formed upon the equality of all citizens."[4] In a few sentences, Turgot said everything that needs to be said about the second crucial cleavage that, after representation, separates the French model from its American counterpart. The French have never thought it either possible or realistic to govern the commonwealth in the republican age with the forces and counterforces of the separation of powers dating from the monarchical age. The French republican model was built on this firm belief. Its principle is therefore the exact opposite of that governing the American model. Its principle, exactly as Turgot forecast it in the eighteenth century, is not to separate the powers, but rather "to bring all the powers into one, that of the Nation." This is the necessary implication of the principle of national sovereignty.

The nation as the source of all powers. The principle of national sovereignty, as conceived by Sieyès, enabled France to escape the old regime and the society divided into orders, a legacy of the feudal society. Sieyès's affirmation, "the nation is prior to everything; it is the source of everything,"[5] paved the way for modern France in establishing the "constituent power"

---

[3] See R. Capitant, "Régimes parlementaires," *Mélanges Carré de Malberg* (1933) reprinted in R. Capitant, *Écrits constitutionnels*, "Les transformations du parlementarisme," Ed. CNRS, Paris 1982, p. 238.

[4] Letter written by Turgot on March 22, 1778, to Dr. Richard Price in London, reprinted in R. Price, *Observations on the Importance of the American Revolution and The Means of Making It a Benefit to the World*, London, 1778, p. 71. R. Price passed Turgot's letter onto John Adams who responded to Turgot's criticism in a vibrant *Defense of the Constitutions of Government of the United States of America*, 1787-1788, available at http://www.constitution.org/jadams/john_adams.htm. Adams takes the defense of the American conception of the separation of powers without saying much about the sovereignty of the people that, in his views, cannot mean something other than tyranny and oppression.

[5] Sieyès, *Qu'est-ce que le Tiers État?* (1788), PUF, Collection Quadrige, 1989, p. 67.

(*pouvoir constituant*)—the highest power, the supreme power, that which gives a country both its social and political constitution. Thanks to the constituent power, the National Assembly changed, first, the society, in establishing natural liberty and equality between all men and, second, the government, in making the nation the source of all powers (articles 1 and 3 of the Declaration of the Rights of Man and the Citizen).[6]

The nation is not a people that would be represented next to power; the nation is power itself, the supreme power, and all the powers derive from the nation. The direct relationship that unites the nation and power is a key element to understanding both the relationship of trust existing between the nation and its representatives and the justification for the authority it gives them. Once it is accepted that representation is national, not popular, and that representatives are elected so as to be bound to cleave always to the public good, the nation is naturally inclined to trust its representatives. There is no reason to anticipate a likely tyranny on their part nor to contrive the interior structure of the government in such a way that its constituent parts can impede each other by mutual entanglement. It is enough to watch out that they do not exceed the limits fixed to their authority by organizing a separation of functions (Section A). As for the rest, the will of the nation is one. It must be carried out by one single center of power, where the nation is represented and where the charge of realizing the republican State can be fulfilled (Section B).

A. THE SEPARATION OF FUNCTIONS

From separation of powers to separation of functions. The separation of powers was enshrined in the very first text that laid down the foundations of French public law, the Declaration of the Rights of Man and the Citizen. Article 16 of this text provides: ''Any society in which neither the protection of rights is guaranteed nor the separation of powers established has no constitution.'' Before an article 17 was adopted at the last minute,[7] article 16 was supposed to

---

[6] Article 1 of the Declaration: ''Men are born and remain free and equal in rights.'' Article 3: ''The principle of all sovereignty remains in essence in the Nation.''

[7] Article 17 of the Declaration provides: ''As property is an inviolable and sacred right, nobody may be deprived of it, except in those cases where public necessity, legally established, obviously requires it, and provided that just and prior compensation has been paid.'' It was put forward by some representatives of the privileged orders who feared for their property rights, in particular their feudal rights, which were obviously doomed to disappear and for which they hoped to receive some compensation. The link between this provision and the feudal rights was clearly underlined in the very first version of the text, which referred to property in the plural form (properties, not property, in the second word); it was later modified and is now in the singular.

close the Declaration and announce the forthcoming Constitution. At the time, the article was a reminder of a long-established experience since Montesquieu: the reunion of the three powers in one single hand is the very definition of despotism.[8] In linking the protection of rights to the separation of powers, the article suggested, in line with a widely held opinion, that a good constitution with separated and wisely distributed powers is the guarantee of political liberty.[9]

The specificity of the French republican model is that it has never been able to function with the "auxiliary precautions"[10] added to it by American constitutional and political practice. In particular, the famous "barriers" between the different powers on which Jefferson insisted to guarantee the effectiveness of the theory—that is, the checks and balances—either have never been applied, or, if applied, have precipitated the country into crisis. The absence of checks and balances between the powers underlines a fundamental difference between the French and the American models. The reason is that, if checks and balances may well be opposed to the power of the people, the same counterpowers may not be opposed to the power of the nation because the concept of nation, with its inclusiveness, rules out not only the idea, but even the need for counterpowers (Section A.1). As a result, the separation of powers is not at all understood in France as it is in the United States; it does not cut power into pieces given to different organs, as one cuts a cake into slices to distribute them, and it does not guarantee maintenance of the separation by interplay between forces and counter forces. Power is one; it is that of the nation, and it cannot be divided. However, if this is the case, what remedy does the French republican model provide against abuse of power? How does it prevent the arbitrariness that the Montesquieu's theory specially aimed to avoid? The answer is quite simple—by a separation of functions. Power, or sovereignty, implies functions (all kinds of functions such as to defend the country, to legislate, to enforce the law, to adjudicate disputes, to raise and collect taxes, to spend, all inherited from the ancient prerogative rights), and the remedy against the risk of their being abusively exercised is found in their distribution among several organs instead of their concentration into one single hand (Section A.2).

---

[8] See Chapter 6, Section A.1.

[9] See S. Rials, *La Déclaration des droits de l'homme et du citoyen*, Hachette, Collection Pluriel, 1988, p. 373.

[10] A. Hamilton, J. Madison & J. Jay, *The Federalist Papers*, C. Rossiter Edition, Mentor Book, N.Y, 1961, Letter no. 51, p. 322, available at http://www.yale.edu/lawweb/avalon/federal/fed.htm [hereinafter *The Federalist*].

1. Absence of Checks and Balances

Relations between the executive and the legislative powers. By contrast with the American model, which has turned the presidential veto over congressional bills into a key element of the separation of powers, the French system rebels at any conflict between the legislature and the executive power. The examples are manifold; they mark French constitutional history, consistently repeating the same teaching: the nation is one and longs to be governed by one and one power only. Any antagonism, any conflict between the legislative and the executive is generative of political crises that end with the victory of one power over the other. The system is unable to remain in this balanced equilibrium of divided government that, from an historical standpoint, is the common lot of the relations between powers in the United States. Depending on the circumstances, it is one or the other power that prevails, but they do not remain opposed during long periods of stasis.

Sometimes, it is the legislative power that prevails. Such is the lesson that may be drawn from the sad experience of the royal veto exercised by Louis XVI, in full compliance with the Constitution of 1791, against two decrees of the legislative body. The effect of his veto was, in short order (within a few weeks), to precipitate the downfall of the monarchy, immediately followed by a toppling of the Revolution into extremes. ''If the Constitution empowers the King with a right of veto, the Declaration of Rights gives the people a right of resistance to oppression'' wrote a journalist in a widely read newspaper.[11] The second example took place during the crisis of May 16, 1877, triggered by the dismissal of the moderate republican Jules Simon, head of the government, by MacMahon, president of the republic, and his replacement by a hard-line conservative. The Chamber refused to accord its trust to the new government, thus forcing the president to dissolve Parliament. Léon Gambetta, the opposition leader, famously said: ''When France will have let its sovereign voice heard, then one will have to submit or resign.'' Indeed, when the nation sent back to Parliament a republican majority, the executive had to submit. Yielding to the ballot box, the president had no other choice but to appoint a moderate republican, Jules Dufaure, as president of the Council of Ministers (equivalent to prime minister). Disavowed by the nation, he subsequently resigned and was replaced by the republican Jules Grévy. The crisis bore witness to the preference of the nation for a parliamentary system, sealed the victory of the legislative over the executive power and paved the way to a system of ''Parliamentary

[11] See M. Morabito & D. Bourmaud, *Histoire constitutionnelle et politique de la France (1789-1958)*, 5th ed., Montchrestien, 1998, p. 77.

Sovereignty,'' French-style, with an omnipotent Parliament, which lasted for more than seventy years, until 1940.

Sometimes, it is the executive that prevails. Such was the rule in the late eighteenth and nineteenth centuries when France experienced Constitutions with a strict separation of powers, American-style (*i.e.*, with checks and balances), the functioning of which eventually led to a paralysis of the government, resolved in every case by a *coup d'état*. Such sad experiences occurred under the Directoire (1795-1799) and the II Republic (1851-1852).

The so-called ''cohabitation''—equivalent of a divided government in the United States—inaugurated by President François Mitterrand in 1986, indirectly confirmed once more the radical incompatibility of a system of checks and balances with the national temper. The three cohabitations experienced by the country between 1986 and 2002 duplicated in every respect the American system of divided government that illustrates so well the interplay of checks and balances between powers. The system had not been experienced twice before it was clear that the French would not rest until it was changed. Their impatience in the circumstance was a splendid confirmation of the veracity of De Gaulle's remarks on the expectations of the nation regarding its government: ''One could not accept a diarchy at the top.''[12] The constitutional reform of 2000, which reduced the length of the presidential term to five years, followed by a public law setting the date for the legislative elections no later than two weeks after the presidential election, in the avowed hope of giving a parliamentary majority to the president so that he may govern, runs contrary to the spirit of the American separation of powers with its checks and balances.

Relations between the judicial and legislative powers. In the French republican model, the judiciary is not a ''power,'' but rather an ''authority.'' This status is expressly provided for in Title VIII of the Constitution of 1958, ''On Judicial Authority,'' and it must be regarded as implied by the principle of national sovereignty. The nation is the source of all powers, and the judiciary does not proceed from it because it is not elected by it.[13] Like the administration, the judiciary is not anointed by popular suffrage; like the former, the latter is an ''authority.'' This does not mean that the judiciary is bestowed with an inferior

---

[12] Ch. De Gaulle, Press Conference of January 31, 1964, reproduced in D. Maus, *Les grands textes de la pratique constitutionnelle de la Ve République*, La documentation française, 1998, p. 43.

[13] True, some judges in the French system are elected, such as the professional judges who compose commercial or labor courts. But these elections are limited to the interested professions; as a rule, no judge is elected by the nation. This is the decisive reason in French law why the judiciary cannot be a power.

status. On the contrary, the judiciary holds great authority; it is even ''sovereign'' in its jurisdiction (the *Cour de Cassation*, for instance, is sovereign regarding the interpretation of the statutes that come under its competence). What this means is this: the judiciary in the French legal system cannot play the role of the judicial power in the American system; it cannot hold the legislative power in check and thwart the will of the nation.

Due to the prestige enjoyed by the American constitutional system in Europe and, in France particularly, the impossibility of the judicial power acting as a check on the legislature is often presented as outdated. It is argued that, when reviewing a statute against a treaty, courts do exercise a power of judicial review that is, as a matter of fact, identical to that exercised by United States courts when they review statutory laws against the Constitution. Such a view is mistaken; judicial review of statutes against the European Convention on Human Rights or against EU law does not fall within the logics of separation of powers. As noted above,[14] the superiority of treaties over statutes is not identical to the supremacy of the Constitution over the laws; it does not square with the checks and balances of the separation of powers. The point in such a review is less to hold the legislature in check than to defend and promote the superiority of universal and humanist values over nationalistic preferences. In addition, the interplay of forces in the American system between the judicial and the legislative powers is supported by a legal reality that is missing in the French legal system. That legal reality is the common law.

The reason why American courts may stand fast against legislators and, occasionally, venture to set aside their laws can be explained by their being able to implicitly rely on a rich legacy of rights and liberties, dating from time immemorial and standing behind them, so to speak. These ancient rights and liberties have never been abrogated; on the contrary, all of them were received by the legislatures in the states, and they are still in force when courts decide on their cases. This wealth of rights and liberties is the common law, and this common law is the fulcrum, so to speak, that allows the lever of judicial review to rise so high. As in England,[15] the common law means that there exists in the legal system a thick and large bundle of rights and freedoms, coming from the depths of history, still in force, which have not been put in the Social Contract, but rather which have been ''reserved,'' that is, protected, from legislative encroachments. And the role of courts is to dig into this endless wealth of rights, as needed, and recall their existence to the legislator.

[14] See Chapter 7, Section B.1.

[15] See Chapter 4, Section B.

In the civil law system, which originates in the principles laid down by the French Revolution, courts do not have these resources. There are no "reserved rights" in this model; there are just natural rights, which have all been put into the Social Contract. The genuine characteristic of the political association created by the nation is that everyone gives himself entirely to it, so that the conditions are equal for all. For, as Rousseau put it: "If the individuals retained certain rights, as there would be no common superior to decide between them and the public, each, being on one point his own judge, would ask to be so on all; the state of nature would thus continue, and the association would necessarily become inoperative or tyrannical."[16] Under such circumstances, only a statute may regulate rights, to the exclusion of a court's opinion. This is actually what the Declaration of the Rights of Man and the Citizen of 1789 precisely provides for, in article 4: "The exercise of the natural rights of any man has no other limits than those which guarantee to the other members of society the enjoyment of these same rights. These limits may be defined *only* by statutory law." The idea of a judiciary—counterforce in the Republic, which would regulate (in lieu of the legislature) the boundaries and the content of the rights and liberties among citizens and between the citizens and the Republic—is not a complement, but rather a distortion of the French republican model.

2. The French Conception of the Separation of Powers

The separation of powers understood as separation of functions. The French conception of separation of powers is not identical to the American approach. On the one hand, it takes into account not three, but just two powers, the legislative and the executive. On the other hand, it does not balance these two powers against each other through an interplay of checks and balances. The two powers are separated as in the United States; they are not in a state of fusion as in England. What is the exact relation between them?

One thing is certain: the "two" powers in question actually exercise "one" power only—the power of the nation. They are not true "powers," strictly speaking, but rather "organs" of the nation, and the term "separation of powers" does not have the same meaning in French and American law. Thus, the problem is to explain how a system of government that does not rest on the traditional tripartite interpretation of the separation of powers, as envisioned by Montesquieu, may nevertheless be regarded as protecting political liberty (*i.e.*, this "tranquility of mind arising from the opinion each person has of his

---

[16] J.-J. Rousseau, *The Social Contract* [Translated by G. D. H. Cole], Book, I, chap. 6, available at http://www.constitution.org/jjr/socon.htm.

safety''). The answer may be as follows: if Montesquieu is still relevant to explain the French republican model, it is because the one and indivisible power of the nation is not concentrated in the hands of a single organ, but rather because the functions it implies are distributed and exercised by different and separate organs—the president of the republic, the government, and the Parliament. The French republican model divides the power of government only insofar as it distributes its implied functions to distinct organs.

The functions of power. Montesquieu distinguished in every government three sorts of functions, which he called ''powers'':

(1) the legislative, by virtue of which ''the prince or magistrate enacts temporary or permanent laws, and amends or abrogates those that have been already enacted'';

(2) the ''executive in respect to things dependent on the law of nations,'' that is, the executive in respect to international affairs, by which the prince ''makes peace or war, sends or receives embassies, establishes public security, and provides against invasions,'' and which he proposed to call simply the executive power of the State;

(3) the executive ''in regard to matters that depend on the civil law,'' in other words, judicial power, by which ''he punishes criminals, or decides the disputes that arise between individuals.''[17]

His exposition of the three powers in every government is the origin of the tripartite classification of the State functions widely in use today.

Although well established in all contemporary legal systems, the tripartite classification of the functions of the State is very much of its epoch. Tailored for the power of the monarchical age, it refers to a government ruling over a static society, frozen in an order established from time immemorial. It refers to a period where the State legislates, certainly, but sparingly, because the peculiarity of the law at that time is to be ''already here,'' rooted for most of its rules in customary usages coming from the past. It calls to mind a time when the State defended the kingdom in aggrandizing the realm whenever possible to the detriment of its neighbors. It evokes a time when the State limited itself internally to securing public peace and ensuring proper justice in civil and criminal matters. These three functions still exist today, in the republican age, but their content has experienced profound changes with the codification of the

[17] Montesquieu, *The Spirit of Laws* [Translated by Th. Nugent, 1752, revised by J. V. Prichard], 1748, Book XI, chap. 6, available at http://www.constitution.org/cm/sol.htm.

law (which revolutionized legislative and judicial functions) and the evolution of international law, which deeply affected the conduct of foreign relations. Additionally and more importantly, the traditional tripartite functions of the State have been supplemented by two other functions that barely existed in the eighteenth century of Montesquieu, but that have since undergone tremendous development. These two functions are those of government and administration.

The governmental function consists in leading the society towards a common goal that, in the republican age, cannot be anything else than "common happiness."[18] During the monarchical age, this function had grown in continental Europe in the form of the Police-State. The complete destruction of the society of the monarchical age caused by the French Revolution, and the subsequent necessity to build a new society based on the new principles of the republican age, has elevated the governmental function. The revolutionary experience demonstrated that, in order to build a society all over again and to put into place the "masses of granite" that hold it together such as legislation, justice, an administration and a police, there was a need for an "intelligent authority" (Cicero) or, as De Gaulle said, "a level-headed man at the helm" (*une tête à l'État*). This transformation in the traditional methods of government was initiated by Bonaparte, who, as early as 1799, in the Constitution of Year VIII, introduced a new State power, the governmental power. An essential means of efficiency in the modern State, the governmental function has greatly modified the executive power insofar as it has attributed to it part of the legislative power: not just any part, but the most important, that which sets the whole governmental machine into motion, the power to initiate laws. Article 44 of the Constitution of Year VIII simply stated: "The Government proposes the laws." Once vested with the governmental function, the executive power has ceased to be a faithful executor of the laws, a clerk-in-chief, so to speak, as was commonly held at the beginning of the Revolution. At the political level, the governmental function turned the executive into a "real" power, endowed with a will of its own, a force on the move, in charge of conceiving and carrying out a governmental program. The task of the executive nowadays no longer consists only in "tak[ing] care that the laws be faithfully executed";[19] it consists in

---

[18] Article 1 of the Declaration of Rights in the Constitution of Year I (1793), which established in French public law the first republic: "The aim of society is the common happiness."

[19] The formula is, of course, borrowed from Article II, Section 2 of the Constitution of the United States: "He [the President] shall take Care that the Laws be faithfully executed." Interestingly enough, the governmental function in the United States has found its place in American constitutional law, and it is nowadays well illustrated by the presidential address on the state of the Union.

governing, in steering society to "common happiness," in "solving crises that call into question the national unity and taking care of major national interests";[20] in other words, in "foreseeing," as Pierre Mendès-France put it.

The administrative function consists in executing the laws; it is however only one side of the executive function, the other being the judicial function. At the time of Montesquieu, the administrative execution of the laws was still modest, particularly in England—the country he used as a point of reference for his theoretical model of separation of powers—but also, if less so, in France. The greatest change to the executive function in the late nineteenth century was a shift in the nature of law enforcement methods in the modern State, which changed from a system of judicial enforcement to a system of administrative enforcement of the laws.

In the monarchical age, the execution of the laws was mostly judicial in nature. The problem of the application of the laws was within the hands of lawyers, and it arose occasionally, on a case-by-case basis. As modern societies advanced further into new technologies and became increasingly complex, they came closer to "societies of a higher type" as Emile Durkheim put it; judicial enforcement of the law—so simple in its principle—tends to become increasingly differentiated.[21] Concretely speaking, the problem of executing the laws no

---

[20] Such is the definition of the governmental function given by Maurice Hauriou in *Précis de droit administratif et de droit public*, Paris, Sirey, 1933, reprint Dalloz 2002, p. 15.

[21] One must refer here to the analysis made by Emile Durkheim in his criticism of Spencer who, in the second half of the nineteenth century, became the champion of the market against the State. By contrast with the British economist, who was convinced that the exchange between people, that is, the contract, would diminish the need for a regulatory apparatus and reduce the functions of the State solely to the organization and functioning of courts of law, the French sociologist objects that regulation, hence administrative law, is all the more developed in societies that are technically and industrially advanced and that the more we go back in history, the more modest regulation is. For Durkheim, as new technologies come into being, regulation can no longer be rudimentary. In his opinion:

> The state's attributions become ever more numerous and diverse as one approaches the higher types of society. The organ of justice itself, which in the beginning is very simple, begins increasingly to become differentiated. Different law-courts are instituted as well as distinctive magistratures, and the respective roles of both are determined, as well as the relationship between them. A host of functions that were diffuse become more concentrated. The task of watching over the education of the youth, protecting health generally, presiding over the functioning of the public assistance system or managing the transport and communications systems gradually falls within the province of the central body. As a result that body develops. At the same time it extends progressively over

longer arose occasionally, but permanently. It no longer concerned particular cases only, but rather a large number of cases identical in their nature and calling for common solutions. Occasional judicial resolution of disputes limited to specific cases no longer sufficed. It became necessary to anticipate possible future conflicts, to prevent them by prior, precise definition of the conditions of the application of the laws—no longer on a case-by-case basis only, but rather at a higher level, presupposing a large number of identical legal situations. In other words, it became necessary to regulate—or to administrate. This point is subtly underlined by Laferrière when he says: "To administrate means to secure a *daily* application of the laws"[22] —as opposed to "adjudicate," which, as is exemplified by the existence of judicial terms, consists in securing the application of the laws during certain periods delimited in the course of the year. As a result of these developments, in most industrial countries, the end of the nineteenth century witnessed a formidable development of administrative bodies and institutions that, for obvious reasons of fairness (equal application of the laws to all citizens) progressively evolved toward acquiring a status close to that of the courts (*i.e.*, independence).[23]

Guarantees of separation of functions. The French concept of separation of powers consists of separating the functions of government, distributing them among distinct organs, and making sure that each of them stays within the limits of the function entrusted to it. The major difference from the American approach is this: the encroachment of one organ over another is not remedied by the counterforces represented by "the necessary constitutional means and personal motives [given to those who administer each department] to resist encroachments of the others,"[24] but rather by independent organs. Three organs play a crucial role in separating legislative, governmental, judicial, and administrative

---

> the whole area of its territory an even more densely packed, complex network, with branches that are substituted for existing local bodies or that assimilate them. Statistical services keep it up to date with all that is happening in the innermost parts of the organism. The mechanism of international relations—by this is meant diplomacy—itself assumes still greater proportions. As institutions are formed, which like the great establishments providing financial credit are of general public interest by their size and the multiplicity of functions linked to them, the state exercises over them a moderating influence.

E. Durkheim, *The Division of Labor in Society*, [Translated by W. D. Halls], The Free Press, 1984, pp. 167-168.

[22] E. Laferrière, *Traité de la juridiction administrative et des recours contentieux*, vol. II, 1896, Paris, LGDJ, reprint 1989, p. 33 (emphasis added).

[23] This was achieved with the development of a civil service recruited through a merit system instead of a spoils system.

[24] Letter no. 51, *The Federalist*, *supra* note 10, pp. 321-322.

functions: the Constitutional Council (*Conseil Constitutionnel*), the Council of State (*Conseil d'État*) and the *Tribunal des Conflits*. Their in-depth analysis pertains to the field of constitutional law. Suffice it to say that the Constitutional Council is in charge of monitoring Parliament,[25] the Council of State oversees organs in charge of executive functions, whether governmental or administrative (president of the republic and government),[26] and the *Tribunal des Conflits* watches over the judicial authority.[27]

The technique of separation of functions as a guarantee against the abuse of power has been used extensively in French public law; it is not limited to the constitutional distribution of powers between State departments. It is also applied within the administrative functions as a means of preventing abuse of authority. For instance, the separation of functions pertain to the following techniques: in matters of public accounting, the separation between the officials who spend and those who pay; in police matters, the separation between the judicial police that assists the judicial department and, thus, is in charge of individual liberty, which is under the protection of ordinary courts as a matter of constitutional rule,[28] and the administrative police in charge of regulation and

---

[25] The Constitutional Council makes sure that Parliament limits itself exclusively to the legislative function and does not encroach upon judicial functions (for instance, in retroactively giving effect to State actions invalidated by the courts; CC, Dec. 80-119 DC, July 22, 1980, *Validations d'actes administratifs*, Rec. 46) or abandon its legislative function, but rather exercise it in its plenitude (legislative delegations are subject to strict conditions). It also makes sure that Parliament does not displace the limits between judicial and administrative functions; the judicial authority has reserved powers, it is in charge of individual liberty, and Parliament may not delegate to the police the determinations to be made on confinements; conversely, Parliament may not attribute to the judicial authority review of State actions that call into question the exercise of prerogatives of public authority (CC, Dec. 87-224 DC, January 23, 1987, *Conseil de la concurrence*, Rec. 8).

[26] The Council of State exercises its power of review over executive action either as an advisory body when it vets the bills drafted by the government before they are sent before Parliament, or as a court of law, when it adjudicates between individuals and the State. In both cases, the Council of State makes sure that the executive does not encroach upon legislative or judicial functions.

[27] The *Tribunal des Conflits* is in charge of keeping the judicial authority from adjudicating disputes involving the exercise of functions reserved to the administrative authority and to remain within the limits of its function.

[28] Article 66(2) of the Constitution of October 4, 1958, constitutionnalized a general principle of law in recalling that "the judicial authority" (*i.e.*, the ordinary courts) is "guardian of individual liberty," a wording that means (1) that no one can be imprisoned except by a regular sentence handed down by a ordinary court of law, and (2) that criminal law is necessarily part of private law since it is adjudicated by ordinary courts. It is worth noting that article 66(2) addresses individual "liberty," not "property,"

public services; in matters of justice, the separation between two kinds of judges, the seated magistrates (also called *magistrats du siège*, because they remain seated at trial) who are in charge of adjudicating the case, and the standing magistrates (also called *magistrats du parquet*) who stand up when speaking and who are in charge of suing the accused. All these techniques are applications, in various degrees, of the precepts enunciated by Montesquieu, originally developed for the monarchical age, and subsequently reinvented to fit the needs of the republican age yet without fragmenting the power of the nation, such that the nation remains free to govern in a republican State.

B. THE REPUBLICAN STATE

The entrepreneurial State. The republican State is an enterprise,[29] "a sort of agency enterprise" said Maurice Hauriou,[30] at the service of one client, the nation, and in charge of one business, the realization of a social contract. Hauriou is the French scholar who best underlined this quintessential characteristic of the French republican model. The idea of the State conceived as enterprise helps to highlight the key difference separating it from the American model. It illustrates the two completely opposite views of the relationship between the State and the civil society—views so different that the idea of the State as an enterprise is totally foreign to the American model, which regards the enterprise, if any, as the province of society, not the State.

The French republican model as an enterprise entrusted to the State has been built since the Revolution. It is the Revolution that imprinted on the State this characteristic—one that it did not previously possess and that was not in accord with its spirit, at least until the middle of the eighteenth century. Under the old regime, the State had neither the will nor the means to be an enterprise. The will of the monarchical age was "to maintain everything in its existing order." When—due to economic growth, social developments, and the evolution of public opinion—the French monarchy realized the amplitude of reforms to be accomplished, it discovered that it had neither the legal means (the statutes of the king had to respect the law) nor the financial means (the revenue did not defray the costs) to carry out such projects. The royal State was certainly a paternalistic State, as Pierre Legendre accurately noted, and the myth of the father more than that of the policeman is indeed "the integral myth" of French

---

meaning that, when the public interest is involved and pursued with public authority (as in fiscal matters), property rights may be adjudicated by administrative courts.

[29] I use the term not in the capitalist sense of a business, but to mean any undertaking that is accomplished efficiently by collective action.

[30] See Hauriou, *supra* note 20, at p. 17.

society.[31] But it remained a myth and did not find a concrete expression before the Revolution. Under the old regime, no matter how paternalistic governmental intentions may have been, the truth of the matter is the State did not have the means to put them into practice. Here was the crucial difference between the French monarchy and all the monarchies of Central Europe that had built the well-ordered Police-State. In France, this evolution had barely taken place, because the State was constantly bumping into society and its law of privileges and immunities, each more unequal than the next. In destroying these institutions and tearing apart the feudal structures that enabled them to grow, the Revolution could write on a clean slate. But it was unable to design the State model that would best fit the new civil society it established. It is with the Empire established by Napoleon that the State built itself, or rather, that it rebuilt itself and eventually became—due to the destruction and reconstruction imposed by the Revolution—the enterprise it has never since ceased to be. Since the Revolution, the idea of the State as an enterprise has never been absent from French public law. However, since it came into being, the enterprise has profoundly changed in its objectives, and it is currently undergoing great changes in its methods.

1. Objectives

Original objectives. The French republican model was based on theories of social contract, drawn from different sources, although clearly favoring the theory developed by Rousseau. Rousseau prevailed in the circumstance over Locke because of the absence, in Rousseau's social contract, of reserved rights for the associates—a fact that marks a sharp difference with the English author who inspired the American model. The first form taken by the French republican model in the nineteenth century was that of the liberal republic, which in its own way was also an enterprise, although at the service of limited objectives such as public peace and order and ensuring basic public utilities.

Even when liberal, the republican State has always been characterized by a touch of authoritarianism inherited from the Napoleonic experience. It owes this to the means chosen for rebuilding French society destroyed by the Revolution. Everything happened as if the ends of the enterprise overdetermined the means selected to achieve them. The first objective of the State built after the Revolution was public peace, and even, as Mona Ozouf noted, "an obsession

[31] P. Legendre, *Histoire de l'administration de 1750 à nos jours*, PUF, Thémis, 1968, p. 204.

with public peace.''[32] This cannot be understood without taking into account the terrible legacy of the Terror, ''that lawless regime, [. . . . .] that anarchy in the strictest sense of the term, which was the dictatorship of Year II,''[33] a national tragedy that ''has poisoned the entire political life in the nineteenth century,''[34] until the consolidation of the republican regime in 1875. These tragic events, the memory of which severely hampered the development of labor unions in France, originally left no choice to the French republican model but to be authoritarian. They stood for the backdrop against which Napoleon established a powerful, coherent, and rational administration, the backbone of French centralization.[35]

Modern objectives. The French republican model is today fully emancipated from its initial authoritarian characteristics, which became less and less necessary as the republican regime was more and more accepted. Satisfaction of the public interest always starts with ensuring public peace; however, it progressively extended to other objectives, particularly at the end of the nineteenth century, and today it embraces great ambitions. The public interest that two centuries ago confused itself with public necessity (what the State decided to carry out had to be necessary and even absolutely necessary) has turned into a much broader concept, social utility.[36] The twentieth century witnessed a prodigious development of public utilities and the coming into being of a so-called public sector so large that its limits became indistinct. It became customary to refer to the ''general interest''[37] instead of the ''public interest.'' This shift in the meaning of ''public interest'' had the effect of downgrading the satisfaction of ''private interest'' in public opinion—private interest being henceforth suspect on account of both public or general interests. As the dividing line between public and private activities became blurred, and the sphere of private autonomy was invaded by public laws, new values emerged, such as real (as opposed to formal) equality,[38] or dignity;[39] others were

---

32 M. Ozouf, ''Esprit public,'' *DCRF* (Idées), p. 179.

33 P. Nora, ''République,'' *DCRF* (Idées), p. 404.

34 F. Furet, ''Terreur,'' *DCRF* (Evénements), p. 307.

35 See J. Ellul, *Histoire des institutions—Le XIXe siècle* (1962), PUF, Quadrige, reprint 1999, p. 164.

36 See the foreboding analysis of Hauriou, *supra* note 20, at p. 58-59.

37 See D. Truchet, *Les fonctions de la notion d'intérêt général dans la jurisprudence du Conseil d'État*, Paris, LGDJ, 1977; Conseil d'État, *Rapport public 1999, supra* note 1, at p. 237.

38 G. Calvès, *Les politiques de discriminations positives*, PPS no. 822 (1999).

39 D. Roman, *Le droit public face à la pauvreté*, Paris, LGDJ, 2002.

awakened from deep sleep.[40]

The apex in this evolution occurred in 1946, with the unsuccessful attempt to substitute a new Declaration of Rights for the Declaration of the Rights of Man and the Citizen 1789. Instead of a new Declaration, the French people decided to adopt a new text—the Preamble to the Constitution of 1946—which incorporated by reference the Declaration of 1789, and ''further proclaim[ed] as particularly necessary to our times, [some sixteen] political, economic and social principles'' that modified the original conditions of the republican compact in depth (gender equality, right of asylum, duty to work and right to employment, union rights, right to strike, right to collective bargaining, right to education, etc.). Unlike the American model, which is still a liberal model, the Preamble of 1946 changed the French republican model into a social model. Such is precisely what the current Constitution of 1958 provides in article 1 when it defines France as ''an indivisible, secular, democratic and social Republic.'' Being a ''social'' republic, the French model necessarily implies a certain kind of State, the republican State endowed with the means, in particular the means of public authority, necessary to attain the objectives outlined in the social contract.

2. Means

The public authority. The French republican model is that of a strong State, a State asserting itself as a State power and thus ''very naturally'' (as Hauriou noted) called a public authority (*puissance publique*). It is customary in France to designate the State as ''the public authority'' without any other qualification. The term has no equivalent in English. In French, it evokes a vital energy, an irresistible force aimed at one single objective, the common good. The idea of ''public authority'' derives from a broader concept—power. Both terms are obviously very close but need to be distinguished inasmuch as they do not operate within the same fields in public law.

''Power'' is a notion of constitutional law, usually associated with the State. To refer to the power of the State is the same as referring to sovereignty, ''the principle of principles,'' as Olivier Beaud underlines.[41] Insofar as sovereignty implies the power to lay down positive law as an initial lawgiver or, to use a more ancient vocabulary, ''to make law binding on all his subjects in general and on each in particular,'' it is not severable from the power of the State; sovereignty is indeed the signature of State power. And, as there is neither State

[40] M. Borgetto, *La notion de fraternité en droit public français*, Paris, LGDJ, 1993.

[41] O. Beaud, *La puissance de l'État*, PUF, Collection Léviathan, 1994, p. 11.

without sovereignty nor sovereignty without a State, power is inherently possessed by each State. In French law, the power of the State to enact law as an initial lawgiver is exemplified by the legislative power (article 34 of the Constitution) supplemented, when needed, by the power to enact ordinances (article 38).

"Public authority" is a notion of administrative law that comes into play with enforcement not enactment of the laws. "Public authority" is the term usually used in French law to refer to the administration whose function is to ensure the application of laws to all. Why is it referred to as a "public authority"? The answer lies in this simple fact: the French administration is completely independent from the other authority in charge of the application the laws (*i.e.*, the judicial authority). In France, administration is a public authority because its action is free from any preliminary judicial review by courts of law. By contrast with the common law tradition, in which the individual whose rights are affected may usually invoke equitable remedies in the courts of law to stop the State in its course, the civil law tradition requires individual obedience to the administration (*i.e.*, the decisions of the public official). The ability to command immediate compliance is the true mark of the public authority. Of course, there are remedies—chief among these, judicial review of administrative action—but, as a rule, such remedies always follow after compliance (except in case of emergency procedures)[42] and are never actionable before ordinary courts.

The coming into being of the "public authority." Under the old regime, administrative power was no public authority at all; it was indeed so far from being one that the French kings were fighting endless battles to have it recognized as one. In the provinces, king's representatives (*intendants*) were under the surveillance of the *Parlements* and reviewed with a zeal that put a halt to any administrative action and a check on any attempt to reform the legal system. Every time a right was abridged or a privilege ignored, the victim could sue to be redressed in his rights. As the *Parlements* claimed to be the guardians of the rights and freedoms of the subjects of His Majesty, the laws of the king stumbled everywhere and on everything.

The Revolution was barely one year old when the National Assembly, anxious not to permit its projected reforms to be absorbed and lost in the maze of the judicial procedures, hurried to adopt a law that put an end to the

---

[42] The most important reform in the principles governing French administrative contentious procedures over the past half century has been a drastic change in the emergency procedures and the possibility for the administrative courts to grant stay orders against administrative determinations whenever it appears that the individual liberty is likely to be seriously and permanently affected.

prerogatives of the judicial power and replaced them with those of the administrative power—henceforth called upon to become the new ''public authority.'' This was the object of article 13 of the *Loi* of August 16-24, 1790, on judicial organization which provides: ''The judicial functions are distinct and shall always remain separated from the administrative functions. The judges, under penalty of forfeitures, shall not disturb in any manner whatsoever the operations of the administrative bodies, nor cite before them the administrators on account of their functions.''[43] The provision was so new, so revolutionary in the French legal system that the judges, ignoring its spirit, did not yield to it, particularly in the fields of national domains, emigration, and especially, taxation.[44] A second attempt was called for. Such was the object of the Decree adopted in 1795 (16 Fructidor of Year III), which prohibited courts from acknowledging any case involving an administrative function under any circumstances. Three years later, Bonaparte locked the system all the way up. Courts and tribunals were forbidden to acknowledge any case involving functions or acts by administrative authorities but also any case involving a public officer. Article 75 of the Constitution of Year VIII (1799) provided: ''The agents of the Government, other than the ministers, can be prosecuted for acts relating to their duties only in virtue of a decision by the Council of State; in that case, the prosecution takes place before the ordinary tribunals.''[45] For three quarters of a century, this provision gave public officers what amounted to blanket immunity from legal suits as a complement to the principle of separation of judicial and administrative functions. The so-called system of ''guarantee of public agents'' was abolished by a legislative Decree of September 19, 1870—unlike the two other texts, which have never formally been repealed from French law.

Separation of administrative and judicial functions: Genealogy of a principle. Since the Revolution, the principle of separation of administrative and judicial functions has been part of French law, notwithstanding all the changes of regimes—including the temporary return of the monarchy after 1815. In 1987, the Constitutional Council made it a constitutional rule by turning it into a fundamental principle recognized by the laws of the republic.[46] The principle of

---

[43] F. Maloy Anderson (Ed.), *The Constitutions and Other Selected Documents Illustrative of the History of France (1789-1901)*, Minneapolis, Wilson Co., 1904, p. 35.

[44] See G. Bigot, *Introduction historique au droit administratif depuis 1789*, PUF, Coll. Droit fondamental, 2002, pp. 36 and 39.

[45] Anderson, *supra* note 43, at p. 280.

[46] CC, Dec. 87-224 DC, January 23, 1987, *Conseil de la concurrence*, Rec. 8.

separation of administrative and judicial functions is a founding and foundational principle of the French republican model. How did this come about?

In order to justify the principle that was about to be enshrined in article 13, on March 24, 1790, Thouret (the rapporteur of the bill for reorganizing the judicial system) said,: ''Let's say that, now that this Nation elects its public officers, the ministers in charge of distributive justice must not interfere with the administration of the functions which are not entrusted to them.''[47] Popular election, thus, was apparently the decisive factor for withdrawing cognizance of administrative cases from ordinary judges, in the same manner that it then justified and still today justifies the prohibition on them to review the constitutionality of the laws. Public officers are no longer elected (actually, they have almost never been elected, except for brief periods of time, when election was the norm at the local level), but they have kept the judicial immunities, which, protect them against the judiciary whenever they are exercising prerogatives of public authority. If this means anything, it is that the principle of separation was indeed justified by something other than election.

At the end of the eighteenth century, the principle of separation of administrative and judicial authorities had been known for a long time. It was a pillar of the ''strong State,'' the backbone of enlightened despotism, which was carrying reforms out at a gallop. Maria Theresa of Austria (1740-1780) had made separation of justice from the administration (*die Trennung der Justiz von der Verwaltung*) her pet idea. Put into effect as early as 1749, with a complete reorganization of the administrative machinery of the Habsburg Empire, the idea had nothing to do with the theory of separation of powers advanced by Montesquieu. Its design was not to slow power down, but rather to speed it up. As Werner Ogris explains it,

> Maria Theresa would not have ever dreamt of creating a system of checks and balances that could impose restrictions or limitations on her absolute power. In separating the judiciary from the general administration, she tried to accomplish two things: first, to simply improve efficiency and promptness of jurisdiction, which at that time presented a picture of misery; and secondly (and most importantly) to secure herself more freedom in exercising governmental power outside the judiciary. Why was this? Jurisdiction was thought to be very conservative and excessively reliant on custom.[48]

---

[47] *AP*, vol. XII, p. 344.

[48] W. Ogris, ''The Habsburg Monarchy in the Eighteenth Century: The Birth of the Modern Centralized State,'' in A. Padoa-Schioffa (Ed.), *Legislation and Justice*, European Science Foundation, Clarendon Press, 1997, p. 313 s., especially p. 325.

Both in Austria and in France, separation of the judiciary from the administration has been the key, the necessary prerequisite for the entry of old feudal societies into modernity.

Separation of administrative and judicial authorities: A condition of the entrepreneurial State. In removing all the obstacles that the application of the laws used to run into everyday, in freeing the execution of the laws from all the exacting checks aimed at protecting privileges and immunities—all those private rights, in particular property rights, usually held to be vested and often sources of abuses—the principle of separation of administrative and judicial authorities made it possible to carry out the Revolution that overwhelmed French society. It is indeed the Revolution that, on account of both the magnitude of the reforms and the coercion necessary to implement the principles deriving from them, obliged the administration to turn into a ''public authority.'' In order to so, it had to be freed from the judges and endowed with the power necessary to enforce the needed reforms. This latter condition was realized when the Jacobins won over the Girondins, a victory that gave the administration, after its emancipation from judicial oversight, the second springboard of State power—that is, centralization.[49]

The building of State power was pursued by Napoleon Bonaparte and achieved once he was Emperor, with the establishment of a two-tiered administration at the national and local levels—still the backbone of the republican State, although today it is more flexible and less rigid and authoritarian, particularly following the broad reforms carried out in the second half of the twentieth and beginning of the twenty-first centuries (laws of decentralization of 1982 and the constitutional amendment of 2003, which proclaimed the decentralized organization of the republic).[50] It is under the Napoleonic era and with the reforms then implemented that the administration—henceforth a real ''public authority''—turned the State, as Maurice Hauriou has noted it, into an ''enterprise,''[51] a term that conveys the idea of both a design (securing public order, being at the service of the public interest by

[49] On the necessity of centralization to implement the reforms of the Revolution in the best manner, uniformly and all over the territory, together with the prestige gained by this technique all over Europe at the end of the eighteenth century, see J. Godechot, *La grande Nation, l'expansion de la France révolutionnaire dans le monde de 1789 à 1799*, 2nd ed. enlarged., Paris, Aubier-Montaigne, 1983.

[50] Article 1 of the Constitution of 1958, which defines France as ''an indivisible, secular, democratic and social Republic'' now provides at its very end as follows: ''Its organization is decentralized.'' The formula was added by Article 1 of Constitutional Law No. 2003-276 of March 28, 2003.

[51] Hauriou, *supra* note 20, at p. 57.

relying on the police and public services), and the means necessary to carry it out (a powerful administration, free in its course and uniform in its action).

Insofar as the concept of ''enterprise'' as applied to the State at both the national and the local level paves the way to a ''public authority'' in charge of exercising a sort of ''protectorate over civil society,''[52] that concept may be considered in some ways (although for different reasons) a reminder of the well-ordered Police-State that was the cradle of German public law. This is the reason why, in public law, French and German lawyers speak the same language and think the same way. A notable illustration of this common thought is to be found in the European Community treaties that, from the beginning, in the Paris Treaty (1950),[53] then in the Rome Treaty (1957),[54] and eventually in the Maastricht Treaty (1992),[55] made of ''the general interest'' of the Community a lodestar for every initiative and every decision of the members of the European Commission.

The separation of administrative and judicial authorities: Implementation and follow-ups. In removing all obstacles that the application of the laws ran into under the old regime, and in ensuring immediate enforcement of the laws of the republic, the principle of separation of administrative and judicial authorities has securely established the power of ''public authority,'' but it has less happily rendered the individual powerless before the State. The citizen found himself without remedies against the public authority, which inevitably was made its own judge in cases against individuals. ''Nobody can be a judge in his own cause'' being the very first principle of the Western legal tradition; a solution had to be found.

It was eventually found in the Council of State, an institution originally created to exercise legislative functions, and subsequently directed towards adjudicatory functions; the ministers decided that a body principally made of lawyers was the most appropriate place to hear disputes arising between their respective departments and citizens. Thus, the administrative judge was born. Initially, the solutions suggested to the ministers were merely advisory opinions, and the ministers had the final say. Then, on the return of the republicans to power in 1872, the opinions were made mandatory, and they became true decisions, binding on the ministers, in line with the so-called principle of

52 *Id.*, p. 57.

53 Article 9(2) of the ECSC Treaty.

54 Article 157(2) of the EEC Treaty.

55 Article G(48) of the Maastricht Treaty.

"delegated justice" (justice was delegated to the Council of State by the law of May 24, 1872).[56]

The administrative judge naturally applied to the administrative enterprise a law tailored to its objectives. This is how the great adventure of French administrative law began, growing with its own body of principles derogatory from the "common law" (*droit commun*), a notion that, in the French legal system, means civil law (*droit civil*) as codified in the Civil Code. The administration called for a law fitted to its ends; conversely, the existence of a jurisdiction separated from the judiciary called for a special law. In the end of the nineteenth century, thanks to the return of the republicans to power, the pervasive influence of the notion of solidarity in French national history, and a notable influence of socialist thought in a country nurtured by Catholicism,[57] scholars came to teach that public authority no longer explained the law and, particularly, public law. True, said some scholars, the administration has the privilege not to be subject to the Civil Code and to be subject instead to a special law, outside the common law, for the particular purpose of empowering it to carry out its enterprise. However, the rationale for its exorbitant privileges, the criterion that triggers the application of a status exempt from the common law, applicable as a rule to all other social activities, is not to be found in the concept of power or public authority, but rather in that of the "public service" the administration renders to the nation. For scholars, such as Léon Duguit,[58] the concept of "public service" had replaced that of "power" or "public authority" as the criterion of administrative law.

From the standpoint of political and moral philosophy, they were on very solid ground. For it is only too obvious that, in the republican age, the power of the State is meaningful only in relation to its ends, which cannot be anything other than the common interest or the general interest. From the standpoint of legal analysis, however, the problem is that identifying administrative law by the criterion of public service became unmanageable with the growing involvement of the administration in the economic, social, and cultural life of the country. If the criterion was to be applied as a rule to distinguish between judicial and administrative cases (*i.e.*, between the cases to be adjudicated by ordinary courts and those to be decided by administrative courts), it would have meant that a large part of the national economy was henceforth within the jurisdiction of the

---

[56] See J. Chevallier, *L'élaboration historique du principe de séparation de la juridiction administrative et de l'administration active*, Paris, LGDJ, 1970, p. 17.

[57] See Ph. Jourdan, "La formation du concept de service public," *RDP*, 1987, p. 89.

[58] See L. Duguit, "The Law and the State," 31 *Harv. L. Rev.* 1, 184-185 (1917); L. Duguit, "The Concept of Public Service," 32 *Yale L. J.* 425, 431-435 (1923).

administrative courts. This situation would have been ridiculous, for the administration need not be always armed with a law outside the common law, even if it is clear that, whatever it does, the administration must always work for the benefit of the nation and, thus, always deliver services that are by nature public. The whole administration, in one sense, is nothing but a bundle of public services; but it need not always be subject to special rules derogatory from the common law (*i.e.*, administrative law). The real question is to identify the situations when this must be the case. After much scholarly debate, agreement was eventually reached that these situations were those where the administration needed to be endowed with prerogatives of "public authority." Thus, public authority became the criterion of administrative law.

The prerogatives of public authority. The concept of the prerogatives of public authority plays a central role in French public law; however its importance must not be overstated. The prerogative of public authority is not a definition of public law, but rather a criterion triggering the jurisdiction of administrative courts. These courts are called upon to adjudicate only the cases that call into question a prerogative of public authority; all other cases fall under the jurisdiction of ordinary courts. Prerogatives of public law are attached to the legal personhood of public law; these are two sides of the same coin; their unity in the concept of "legal person of public law" draws a line between the groups that possess that personhood (such as the state, the regions, the cities, or public establishments such as universities or public foundations) and those that do not and have only the simple, ordinary legal personhood (*i.e.*, the legal personality of private law).

The expression "prerogatives of public authority" is not crystal clear. It suggests the image of a nebulous sphere inside which common agreement identifies a "hard core," such as tax power.[59] However, no one is able to draw the exact circumference of the circle. For instance, does it include disciplinary

[59] The European Court of Human Rights qualified the fiscal procedures deriving from tax power as the exercise of public authority, involving public law, and, thus, according to the Court, excluding the right to a fair trial in *Ferrazzini v. Italy*, no. 44759/98, in particular § 28. It also applied the same reasoning on the concept of public authority to controversies over the right to stand for election to the National Assembly (*Pierre-Bloch* v. *France*, October 21, 1997, *Reports of Judgments and Decisions* 1997-VI, p. 2223, §§ 50-51) and to disputes between administrative authorities and those of their employees who occupy posts involving participation in the exercise of powers conferred by public law (see *Pellegrin* v. *France* [GC], no. 28541/95, §§ 66-67, ECHR 1999-VIII). In all these cases, the Court decided, in a very controversial manner, that the victim could not invoke the right to a fair trial as laid down in article 6 of the European Convention on Human Rights.

power? One thing is certain: the prerogatives of public authority have the particular characteristics of affecting the rights of private persons (or public persons, such as local collectivities) without their consent, unilaterally and immediately, without a prior hearing before a court. Whenever prerogatives of public authority come into play, the citizen does not lose his right to a day in court, but he cannot expect to have it before the decision is implemented. As a matter of redress, the judicial remedy of course exists (before the administrative courts), but it comes after execution of the laws. Prerogatives of public authority are not the monopoly of public persons; they may occasionally be granted to private persons, under certain conditions.[60] Insofar as they enable their possessors, whether public or private persons, to affect the liberty or property of citizens, they are unanimously regarded as exemplifications of ''the power of domination of the State,'' as the French scholar Carré de Malberg wrote, drawing on the analysis by the great German jurist Jellinek.[61]

According to Jellinek (1850-1911), the true, genuine and exclusive, attribute of the State is not sovereignty, but rather the power of the State (*Herrschaftsgewalt*), the essence of which is domination. To dominate, Jellinek said, is to command in the most absolute manner, with an irresistible power of coercion. It means to coerce, possibly by force, the execution of the given orders without any other limit than self-limitation on the part of he who possesses the power of the State. Jellinek's ideas had a tremendous influence on German public law thinking at the end of the nineteenth century.[62] They crossed the

---

[60] Whenever private persons are granted prerogatives of public authority, they may enjoy the whole gamut of these prerogatives. The Constitutional Council has decided that the State may not invest private persons with a ''mission of sovereignty'' (CC Dec. 2003-473 DC, June 26, 2003, *Loi habilitant le gouvernement à simplifier le droit*, cons. 19, Rec. 386), a terminology that rules out delegation to the private sector of prerogatives of public authority such as the tax power, the judicial power (prisons cannot be privatized under French law), and probably the power of eminent domain.

[61] R. Carré de Malberg, *Contribution à la théorie générale de l'État*, *op. cit.*, vol. II, p. 25.

[62] In particular, they have influenced German administrative law, noticeably the theory of special relationship of public authority (*besonderes Gewaltverhältnis*), which applied to the specific relations between the State and the citizen and which was grounded in the voluntary or coerced integration (*Einordnung*) of the latter in certain services of the former (schools, prisons, army, etc.). The special relationship of public authority was regarded as exclusively pertaining to the internal structure of the administration and, thus, not subject to law, even less to judicial review. The dismantling of the special relationship of public authority became inevitable with the new constitutional foundations of German legal order after World War II. The fundamental rights (*Grundrechten*) that now form the ideological basis of the German legal order necessarily give priority to the individual over the State and, thus, have rendered this old theory obsolete. See 33 BVerfGE 1 on

border and were introduced into France by authors such as Louis Le Fur, Raymond Carré de Malberg, and Hauriou who, despite their criticisms of the ideas' foundations, relied heavily on them in their own disciplines. In particular, the concept of State power was reinvented by Hauriou through the theory of the institution—which was nothing, in his opinion, but a theory of objective self-limitation.[63] It has developed in French law inasmuch as it served as a matrix from which a proper criterion of administrative law was eventually elaborated, administrative law being nowadays defined as the special law that is applied to those administrative activities that are carried out by means of public authority. However, it would be wrong to infer from these developments that the concept of authority subsumes the totality of the means by which the republican State is carrying out its enterprise (*i.e.*, securing the public good).

Res publica*, public law and public authority.* If public law must still be defined as it has been since its Roman foundations (*i.e.*, as the law of the *res publica*), it is too simplistic to define it as the law of public authority. True, in line with Hauriou's theory, it is possible to say that in the republican age, the *res publica* has become an enterprise, provided that it is also concurrently said that the enterprise need not to be as large as it was envisioned after World War II. At that time, the republic created a huge public sector due to the nationalization of all property or enterprises having the character of a national public service or a monopoly in fact. Recent developments in the laws and regulations of the European Union—in particular, the obligation to open the public services to competition—run along these lines. The public sector need not cover almost half of the national economy, as was at one time the case, in pursuance of the ideas of Léon Duguit (leading French advocate of public service) and those of Hauriou (leading advocate of the prerogatives of public authority), but their idea remains sound.

In French public law, the State, the *res publica*, remains an enterprise, the design of a nation, always with great projects to be accomplished, great designs to be fulfilled. What is currently undergoing transformation is the means by which the enterprise is carried out. On the one hand, the system of natural liberty calls for recognition of the fact that private initiative may contribute to the *res publica* and that, consequently, public authority need not be as extensive as was once thought. On the other hand, the State need not be an entrepreneur and may

---

execution of criminal penalties; H. Maurer, *Droit administratif allemand* [Translated by M. Fromont), Paris, LGDJ, 1992, p. 173.

63 Hauriou, *supra* note 20, particularly the foreward written by the author to the eleventh edition of his work and published in 1926, ''La puissance publique et le service public,'' pp. xv-xvi.

either delegate part of the enterprise to the private sector, for the delivery of merchant goods, for example, or enter into partnership with the latter in development plans to revitalize economically distressed areas, for example. These evolutions prove that the concept of public authority is now quite dated as an explanation for the totality of public law. Let us repeat it once more, the concept of public authority explains one side of public law only, that is, the jurisdiction of administrative courts over contentious cases involving the prerogatives of public authority. Law cannot be reduced to cases only, but it is also true that legal cases, because of their particular nature, are still privileged means for discovering the basic trends of a legal discipline insofar as, when properly analyzed, they always allow the principles and main themes that form the fabric of the discipline to emerge. So far as French public law is concerned, there is a main theme that runs like a red thread through the whole fabric. This red thread is the exemplary persistence of the French nation in refusing to let ordinary courts adjudicate public law cases or decide cases involving the *res publica*, even through judicial review.[64]

The cause of this constant refusal has to do with the manner in which the French people think of themselves as sovereign; as explained above, they are sovereign together, not separately. The duality of courts has no justification other than the deep belief that the cases dealing with the *res publica* are not of the same nature as those concerning the multitude of private interests. It exists only because of the belief in a public interest distinct from an aggregation of private interests, a national interest distinct from the numerous private interests of the people. This means that there is something beyond the technicalities of the cases adjudicated by administrative courts. There is the idea that the French people form a nation; and this idea is not without merit, even for an American.[65]

---

[64] See the following articles by French leading scholars, D. Truchet, ''Mauvaises et bonnes raisons de mettre fin au dualisme juridictionnel,'' *Justices* no. 3 (1996), p. 53; R. Drago & M.-F. Frison-Roche, ''Mystères et mirages des dualités des ordres de juridictions et de la justice administrative,'' *APD*, 1997, p. 135; Y. Gaudemet, ''Le juge administratif, une solution d'avenir ?'' *Clefs pour le siècle*, Dalloz, 2000, p. 1213.

[65] Commenting upon the duality of ordinary and administrative courts in the French legal system and comparing it to the unitary approach of the American system (the duality, if any, in the United States is between federal and state courts), Robert H. Jackson, far from disapproving of the existence of courts separated from ordinary courts to adjudicate on cases involving the public interest, surprisingly enough expressed the following views:

> The painfully logical French went about the controlling of official action where it affected the rights of the citizen in exactly the opposite manner. They recognized from the beginning that controversies between the citizen and an official, in the performance of his duty as he saw it, involved some different

From any perspective, one is always sent back to the principle that forms the irreducible basis of the French republican model, the principle of national sovereignty. A public law justice distinct from a private law justice cannot be understood as anything other than a direct consequence of this principle, which must henceforth be regarded as the defining characteristic of the French republican model.

> elements and considerations than the contest between two private citizens over private matters. They invested the Conseil d'État with jurisdiction over regulatory bodies and recognized that *droit administratif* was a different matter than private law, as to which the Cour de Cassation was the high court.

R. H. Jackson, *The Supreme Court in the American System of Government*, Harvard University Press, 1955, p. 46.

Conclusion

The irresistible rise of statutory law. For a long time, statutes remained at the margin of the law. No matter how numerous, most statutes did not interfere or interfered very little with the law. In civil law as well as in common law countries, statutes were concerned only with the relations between private persons and public authorities by way, for example, of taxation, health regulations, or police powers. In accordance with a well-established practice, the core of law—that is, the ordinary law that applies between private individuals—was made by the judges held to be "the oracles of law."[1]

Contrary to appearances, the Napoleonic codification did not alter this tradition. In casting the foundational rules of private law—particularly in matters of property and contracts, in the mold of statutory law—the codification changed the status of some basic rules (*e.g.*, in family law) from *jus dispositivum* to *jus cogens* (imperative law)[2] thereby unifying the basis of private law made henceforth mandatory for all French citizens. However, at the beginning of the nineteenth century, that statutory framework supported a host of provisions that were optional or additional, not mandatory, especially in the domain of contracts and wills insofar as they applied only failing contrary provisions decided by the parties.[3] In other words, notwithstanding its legislative base, civil law was governed by the so-called principle of the autonomy of will. It was pervaded with a spirit of liberty that was applicable to the whole spectrum of relations between private individuals. Concretely speaking, provided that he did not cause any tort to any one—the notion of "tort" was then narrowly construed—the individual was free to do as he chose.

[1] John P. Dawson, *The Oracles of Law*, University of Michigan, 1968.

[2] Public law means in the first place mandatory law, or rules that may not be discarded at will; see L. Ehrlich, "Comparative Public Law and the Fundamentals of its Study," 21 *Columbia L. Rev.* 623, 632 (1921).

[3] On the distinction between mandatory and optional or additional provisions in the Civil Code, see René David, *Le droit français*, vol. I (*Les données fondamentales du droit français*), Paris, LGDJ, 1960, p. 73.

Beginning in the late nineteenth century, statutes and regulations multiplied outside their traditional domain, that is, the police powers of the State (economic and administrative matters). They entered the domain of relations between private individuals. In every legal system of industrialized States, regardless of whether the law was codified, the "autonomy of the will" shrank to an increasingly narrow field. Freedom of contract dwindled (the work contract and the insurance contract were most affected). The movement accelerated in the United States with the Great Depression, and it assumed even greater proportions in France after World War II, with the implementation of "the political, economic and social principles [. . .] particularly necessary to our times," as stated in the Preamble to the Constitution of 1946.

It did not take long before private law lawyers sounded the alarm and denounced the invasion of private law by public law.[4] Public law and legislation appeared to them as an incoming tide making its way up the estuaries and into the remotest riverbeds of the private law landmass.[5] They calmed down when they understood that while the flood of public law may well enter the smallest of streams, the private law landmass is not submerged as a result. Even if public law irrigates it as a whole, private law does not disappear, but remains firm and solid as a legal domain, distinct and separate from public law. Neither in the United States nor in France have the numerous public laws (or *lois*) that deal with labor law, consumer law, or banking law turned these legal fields into branches of public law. The same can be said of the public laws that legislate on matters of property, leases, or mortgages, or those that apply to relations between debtors and creditors: none of them has made property or contracts migrate to public law. How does this come about?

The explanation lies in this one fact: the commonly received definition of the distinction between private law and public law is mistaken. It is an error with high stakes to define public law as the law that applies to the relations between the State and the citizens when public laws regulate the everyday relations

[4] See, for the United States, Roscoe Pound, "Public Law and Private Law," 24 *Cornell L. Q.* 469 (1939), and more recently, Grant Gilmore, *The Ages of American Law*, Yale University Press, 1977 p. 95, also G. Calabresi, *A Common Law for the Age of Statutes*, Harvard University Press, 1982, p. 5; for France, where the debate focused on the relation between the statute and the case-law in the sources of law, see Henri Mazeaud, "Défense du droit privé," D. 1946, chronique, p. 17; more recently, *La création du droit par le juge*, A.P.D., no. 50 (2007).

[5] In the same way, so to speak, that Lord Denning was to describe much later the effect in England of European law, which he compared to an "incoming tide making its way up the estuaries and into the remotest riverbeds of the British isles," in *H.P. Bulmer Ltd.* v. *J. Bollinger SA* [1974] 1 All E.R. 1226, 1231.

between citizens. The distinction between public law and private law must necessarily have another meaning than one that is purely formal, or organic, that is, based upon the quality of the persons or organs involved. A return to the origins of the distinction in Roman law may shed some light and unfold the contradiction.

The original meaning of the distinction between private law and public law. As enunciated in the Digest, the distinction between public law and private law was never intended to divide law into two domains, public law and private law, opposed to each other in practice, if not enemies by nature. When Ulpianus reminded the freshly made Roman citizens that there was, on the one hand, public law, and on the other, private law, he was referring not to rules, but rather to positions, stances, or viewpoints, in the study of law. ''Of this subject [*i.e.*, the study of law] there are two positions, public and private law,'' he said (''*Hujus studii duae sunt positiones, publicum et privatum.*'') In other terms, the distinction between public law and private law was originally meaningful only for the purpose of studying the law. In order to understand the true meaning of the distinction, it is necessary to go back to the Roman concept of law.

Law, for the Romans, was not a matter of rules but of art. Law was the art of goodness and fairness (*ars aequi et boni*); in other words, law was justice. The word justice (*justitia*) came from *jus*, and *jus* for the Romans was not the rule, but the fair share attributable to every one, the *id quod justum est.* Attribution to everyone of his fair share—said Ulpianus in substance above—requires that the student of law always take into account two positions, or view points, the public and the private. The distinction recalled Aristotle's classification of the kinds of justice: (1) general justice and (2) justice as a particular or specific virtue. The first is a complex of rules formulated by the city-state as legally mandatory for the members of the community; the second is the set of rules that govern relations between the members of the community.[6] The distinction made by Ulpianus sounds quite natural if one keeps in mind its historical context. The problem for him was to justify a tax, that is, in legal, not financial terms, the fair share that had to be given to the *res publica* of imperial Rome: religious affairs, the priesthood, and the affairs of state.

[6] P. Vinogradoff, *Outlines of Historical Jurisprudence*, 1920, p. 45. Vinogradoff adds: ''Justice as a particular or specific virtue [. . .] falls into two classes (a) Distributive justice and (b) Corrective justice or legal redress: (a) covers all cases in which an answer is given to the question as to what one person can claim on the ground of just distribution as against others; (b) covers all function of justice directed towards redressing wrongs as between members of the State.''

Loss of meaning of the distinction between public and private law. Everything in Ulpianus's memorable words that founded the distinction between public law and private law can be reduced to this: real justice will never be reached if the two positions, public law and private law, are not considered in studying the law. True justice requires the taking into account of the distinction between that which belongs to everyone, as a matter of public interest, and that which belongs to each one in particular, as a matter of private concern. The necessity of taking into account the two points of view when studying the law bears witness to the importance of religion in Roman society. Like all ancient societies, Roman society made no distinction between public and religious affairs. Christianity, with its separation between religious and political affairs, and the much later-Reformation, accompanied by individualism and the secularization of societies, radically changed the meaning of the distinction. One can take a measure of the transformation by the simple fact that where the Romans used to consider public and private law as complementary terms, moderns tend to view them, rather, as radically antagonistic.

The idea of natural complementarities between public and private law, of a natural harmony between the community and the self, collapsed in the monarchical age, for reasons that form the backbone of the first book of this work. Logic would have called for their reunification in the republican age, but this did not happen, or happened only partially, as the second book of this work indicates in counterpoint. One of the two terms is always under suspicion: either it is public law or it is private law. The American model is inclined to take the statute as usurping individual freedom, whereas the French model tends to regard private rights as obstacles to the full realization of public rights. Resolving the inevitable tension between the two, as Beccaria said, is the task of the public law lawyer.[7]

The separation between public and private goes back, as previously said, to the Renaissance, when, due to the revolution of Protestantism, a new mode of thinking carried the day. The autonomy of the self asserted itself through the right to freedom of conscience, the individual emerged as a "thinking self" out of the undifferentiated medieval community, and the right to a private sphere, distinct and separate from the public sphere, marked the entry into modernity. The unity of the common good was replaced by a duality between the public good and the private good (or rather, the multitude of private goods). Common

---

[7] "It is for the student of law and the state to establish the relationship between political justice and injustice, that is, between what is socially useful and what is harmful." Beccaria, *On Crimes and Punishments and Other Writing,* "To the Reader," Cambridge University Press, 1995, p. 5.

interests were on the wane; instead, private interests, distinct and separate from the public interest, asserted themselves and demanded to be detached from it, due to individualism, the modern form of liberty.

The separation between the private and the public was a landmark in the evolution of Western philosophy. As a prerequisite to freedom, that separation represents the distinctive criterion of modern society. It is, therefore, particularly unrealistic to advocate a return to the former medieval ''community'' that preceded it (*Gemeinschaft* as opposed to *Gesellschaft*).[8] In the modern age, men are bound to form a *societas*, not a *universitas*. Otherwise, men would no longer form a ''modern'' society, so to speak. Separation between public and private marks a point of no return. This is set forth in simple, albeit illuminating, terms in article 5 of the Declaration of the Rights of Man and the Citizen: ''The *loi* (statute) may prohibit only those actions which are harmful to society.'' In other words, what has no harmful effect on society, what is purely internal to the self, the ''secret garden'' of the individual, is not an object of legitimate concern for the public or the State. The difficulty is that what was originally (and should have remained) a principle of sound separation between private and public law has turned into opposition, if not a principle of antagonism. The upshot is that public law and its quintessential expression, the statute, are regarded as enemies of private law. The paths toward this complete denaturation of the meaning of the separation between private and public law started in the nineteenth century, but they followed quite different courses in Europe and in United States.

The European path. In Europe, the conquest of parliamentary assemblies by the popular classes gave formidable impetus to the statute. In the nineteenth century, public law was turned into a great offensive because the statute was considered as an instrument of social change, a tool for achieving the public good in line with the traditions of the monarchical age. At the same time, the defense of private law took the form of a counteroffensive against this movement with, on the continent, the theory of subjective rights born out of the work of Savigny as a reaction against objective law (the statute), and, in England, the judicial canonization of the precedent (*stare decisis*), which the House of Lords opposed to legislative invasions of the common law by a sovereign Parliament. Although carrying out different legal techniques, the two defensive reactions shared the same spirit. Both were the veiled but resolute expression of the resistance of private rights to the statute (*loi*), the instrument of

[8] The celebrated opposition between community (*Gemeinschaft*) and society (*Gesellschaft*) made by the German sociologist F. Tönnies [*Gemeinschaft und Gesellschaft* (1887)] was intended to serve as a scientific criterion in the study of order in societies over the ages, not to be used as a political manifesto.

public law. To use more political terms, both expressed, in the domain of law, the conservative ideas of the counterrevolution launched in Germany and England against the ideas of the French Revolution.

Today, the resistance has come to an end; the fight of the subjective right against the objective law has only an historical interest.[9] The key factor in the pacification of relations between private rights and public law seems to have been the development of judicial protection for subjective rights by way of judicial review of statutes against a "higher law." Sometimes, this higher law is of a constitutional nature—judicial review of statutes against the constitution is not, however, very developed in Europe (at least, in comparison with the United States) insofar as, when it is effective, parliament often has the last word. Sometimes, this higher law is treaty law—European States are more open to international treaties than the United States (they more readily accept an effect on domestic law, as all European States are parties to the European Convention on Human Rights, and subject to the jurisdiction of the Court). The crux of the matter is that, in Europe, the statute is no longer regarded as the enemy of the public good because it is "sovereign" only in the respect of universal values. Insofar as this element allows reconciliation between the private and the public sphere, it enables the idea of *res publica*—the idea that certain things must be held in common and be subject to a law special to it, that may imply sacrifices—to take shape and, thus, to be legitimate.

The American path. In the United States, the statute never enjoyed the privileged status of its European counterpart because, by contrast with the European tradition, it was never considered as an instrument of public good. From the outset, Americans chose to trust private rather than public initiative to bring about the public good.[10] To exploit the resources of their immense country, they bet on the individual not the State; they sanctified the contract not the statute.[11] The choice was made early, at the end of the eighteenth century, when they rejected taxation as a means to promote national wealth. Public good in the United States was realized through private, not public, law.

---

9 The terms of the struggle between subjective rights and objective law are clearly reported by J. Ghestin, G. Goubeaux & M. Fabre-Magnan, *Droit civil, Introduction générale*, LGDJ, 1994, pp. 126-155.

10 This is the running theme of the great classic by Morton J. Horwitz, *The Transformation of American Law: 1780-1860*, Harvard University Press, 1977.

11 The landmark case on the sanctity of the contract is *Trustees of Darmouth College* v. *Woodward*, 17 US (4 Wheat.) 518 (1819), by which the Supreme Court, in refusing to allow a legislature to modify a contract in force in the slightest manner, operated a sharp distinction between the private and the public, forbidding the latter to interfere with the former.

In turning private law into an instrument of public good, Americans put it on a pedestal where it remains. Still today, recourse to private law—especially, the principles of property law—to promote economic growth is regarded as key to success.[12] What must be clearly understood at this point is this: private law in the United States is the common law, that is, the unwritten law deriving from the principles of reason and enunciated by judges in the cases brought before them. In the face of this private law—largely freed from the English common law to better serve the economic interests of the country—public law makes a poor showing, not only because it comes from a politics that is never above suspicion of corruption, but also because it is considered as inherently unable to do as well as private law. The latter is actually entirely subordinated to the former by means of judicial review, which amounts to an evaluation of the public good not with universal values, but rather with what Marshall termed ''the general principle of *our* political institutions.''[13] Here, the possessive pronominal adjective is a key element insofar as, among the general principles of American political institutions, there survives the medieval idea of a ''higher law,'' a law originating ultimately in God, securing everyone's right, reigning above the power, enunciated by the judges in the cases submitted to them. That higher law has nowadays found a secular replacement with the Constitution.[14] Like the common law, the Constitution originates in a higher power (The People); it secures everyone's rights, it reigns over the government, and it is ''what the judges say it is.''[15]

The judge and the public good. Immersed in a ''legal consciousness''[16] nurtured with idealism, the statute in the United States never triumphed over the old medieval mysticism of an eternal law, unsullied by the act of man. By

---

[12] See World Bank *Doing Business 2004: Understanding Regulation*, in particular p. 93 ''Focus on Enhancing Property Rights,'' available at http://www.doingbusiness.org/Main/DoingBusiness2004.aspx.

[13] *Fletcher* v. *Peck*, 10 US (6 Cranch) 87, 139 (1810).

[14] On the tradition of higher law in United States Law, see Edward S. Corwin, ''The 'Higher Law' Background of American Constitutional Law,'' Part I and II, 42 *Harv. L. Rev.* 149-185, 365-409 (1928-29).

[15] In the Middle Ages, Englishmen could have said of the common law exactly what Charles Evans Hughes said once of the Constitution in a much famous quote: ''We are under a Constitution, but the Constitution is what the judges say it is, and the judiciary is the safeguard of our liberty and of our property under the Constitution,'' in *Addresses and Papers of Charles Evans Hughes*, New York and London, 1908, pp. 139-140; 1916, pp. 185-186.

[16] On the concept of ''legal consciousness,'' see Duncan Kennedy, ''Toward an Historical Understanding of Legal Consciousness: The Case of Classical legal Thought in America, 1850-1940,'' 3 *Research in Law and Sociology* 3-24 (1980)

contrast to the unity achieved in Europe between law and statute, due to the concept of sovereignty, the statute in the United States remained separated from the law. The reason is that the somber and disillusioned attitude Americans entertain *vis-à-vis* power—assimilated to sin and the fall—makes it inevitable that the only ''true'' law is not, cannot, and will never be human law, but rather the higher law, that law formerly given by God (in the colonial age, the Bible was an extraordinarily fecund source of inspiration for New Englanders in the drafting of their laws)[17] and today ordained by the people (''*We The People*''). In the legal culture of the United States, religion never completely separated from the law.[18] The upshot is that the public good, if it exists, can come only from that higher law close to God, which, just like the common law in the Middle Ages, can only be enunciated by a court of law.

The question is obviously whether the judge can enunciate the public good. Clearly, there are two positions on this question as exemplified by the crucial fault between the French and the American models on the role of judges in ''extensive and unmixed,'' or modern, republics. In proclaiming that ''limits [to liberty] may be defined *only* by the statute (*Loi*)'' (article 4 of the Declaration of the Rights of Man and the Citizen, 1789), the French abandoned the old medieval tradition of the judges as sovereign expounders of the law.[19] By contrast, the Americans—as early as the Philadelphia Convention, and without paying the slightest attention to the fact that the British had abandoned that tradition at the glorious revolution[20] —kept in line with the ancestral tradition of the common law, based on the idea of a law ''higher'' than positive law and pronounced by the judges. Mesmerized by the blindfold over Themis's eyes, which they apparently construed as living evidence of impartiality, they chose ''to entrust the keeping of the equilibrium of the Federal Union to a court rather than to the Congress.''[21] The result is that the United States has ''the most legalistic system of government in the world with the judicial power penetrating

---

[17] A. de Tocqueville, *Democracy in America* [Translated by H. C. Mansfield & D. Winthrop], University of Chicago Press, 2000, p. 38, Tocqueville refers to ''the strange idea of drawing from sacred texts'' to compose penal laws.

[18] See C. Greenhouse, *Praying for Justice*, Cornell University Press, 1986; C. Greenhouse, B. Yngvesson, & D. Engel, *Law and Community in Three American Towns*, Cornell University Press, 1986.

[19] See J. H. Merryman, ''The French Deviation,'' 44 *AJCL* 109 (1996).

[20] See Chapter 4, Section A.

[21] R. H. Jackson, *The Struggle for Judicial Supremacy, A Study of a Crisis in American Power Politics*, New York, A. Knopf, 1941, p. 9.

and legal philosophy governing [the] whole national life.''[22] In choosing the courts to define the public good in the last resort, Americans have fated themselves to an indefatigable legal idealism about the capacity of the judicial branch to bring about common happiness—an idealism that has caused them many disappointments in the course of their history.

In the beginning of the twentieth century, the school of legal realism initiated by Oliver W. Holmes put American legal idealism to rest, at least for some time. Starting with the Great Depression and the New Deal crisis, American judges acquiesced in the common sense idea that forms the backbone of positivist legal thought, namely, that, in the republican age, law is not—and cannot be—as Holmes forcefully said, ''a brooding omnipresence in the sky, but the articulate voice of some sovereign or quasi sovereign.''[23] In other words, for Holmes, law is the voice of the sovereign people and their representatives. By the end of the 1930s, the statute thus overthrew the judicial opinion in the enunciation of the public good, becoming recognized as the best instrument to bring it about. Better, judges consented to put themselves at the service of lawmakers, so to speak, passing along the entire legal system the consequences of the will of the sovereign people. In short, American judges converted themselves to positivism. But this period did not last.

As early as the 1950s, believers in the traditional methods of adjudication charged that legal realism empowered the courts to carry out the achievement of political ends by judicial means—effectively legislating from the bench. A search for ''neutral principles,'' buttressed by the deep conviction that they were discoverable—in a nutshell, the spirit of idealism—came back at full gallop.[24] Disguised under various schools of thought emanating from diverse inspirations and methods,[25] legal idealism can be encapsulated by a single idea: ''true'' or ''fair'' law is not, and cannot be made by man. The upshot is that the statute, which is ''human'' law, fallible by nature, has been gradually sent back to its

---

[22] *Id.*, p. 10.

[23] *Southern Pacific Co.* v. *Jensen*, 244 US 205, 222 (1917).

[24] The leading article that started the movement of dissatisfaction with legal realism—which culminated in the leading case *Brown* v. *Board of Education of Topeka*, 347 US 483 (1954) in which the Court for the first time decided a case entirely upon a principle of reality (''Separate educational facilities are inherently unequal,'' p. 495)—is by H. Wechsler, ''Towards Neutral Principles of Constitutional Law,'' 73 *Harv. L. Rev.* 1 (1959).

[25] To name a few, such is the case with the following movements in legal interpretation: critical legal studies of Marxist inspiration, law and economics driven by ultra liberalist economists, if not libertarians, and originalism inspired by conservative philosophy.

traditional inferior and subaltern position in American legal culture, and the United States still ignores public law as the law of the *res publica*. Hegel was right when he said that the United States formed a ''constantly evolving State.''[26]

The American peculiarity with the res publica. The logic of transition from the monarchical age to the republican age was to transform the basis of public law. Concretely speaking, it was to lead legislatures to legislate only for the public interest and to incite courts to adjudicate disputes always by taking into account both dimensions of public and private law. This did not happen or happened only partially. A divide between two legal systems has nowadays taken place. It does not run, as explained by those who advocate recourse to private law as the test for good governance, between civil law and common law systems,[27] but rather between, on the one hand, the United States and, on the other, Europe, if not the rest of the world. In Europe, public law, that is, the law of public interest that comes under the form of statutory law—the law of the *res publica*—has now found its place in the legal system. Its enforcement is organized more or less strongly depending on the States. Courts make it their duty to apply it, as far as possible, in a manner agreeable to both public and private interests. Its existence is not called into question on a daily basis.

In the United States, public law is still struggling for legitimacy. Statutory law is regularly put into question; public action stumbles every day. In other terms, belief and confidence in the public interest comes and goes. The *res publica* is neither stable, nor permanent. There are times in history where it glows as a shining sun, that is, periods when the Constitution is not construed as limited to the protection of certain basic liberties and, instead, is interpreted as having created ''a representative form of government capable of translating the people's will into effective public action.''[28] The New Deal or the Civil Rights eras are cases in point. In many ways, Reconstruction, too, may be an example of a very strong *res publica*, but not in its representative form. During these periods, the federal government passed important legislation dealing with emancipation, poverty, civil rights, the environment, health and safety, etc. But

---

[26] Georg W. F. Hegel, *La raison dans l'histoire*, Bibliothèques 10/18, Plon 1965, p. 240.

[27] As argued in the famous article by R. La Porta, F. Lopez-de-Silanes, A. Schleifer & R. Vishny, ''The Quality of Government,'' 15 *Journal of Law, Economics and Organization* 222 (1999).

[28] *Federal Maritime Commission* v. *South Carolina State Port Authority*, 535 US 743, 787 (2002) [dissenting opinion of Breyer, J., with whom Stevens, Souter, and Ginsburg, JJ., joined]

these periods do not last. Sooner or later, they come to a close and turn into mere parentheses in American history. Private interests then win the day and the idea of the public interest fades away. In other words, the *res publica* in the United States is cyclical. What is it that sustains these cycles?

The common explanation—the most widely held—is to link the intermittent nature of the *res publica* in the United States to the uniqueness of its governmental structure conducive to a conception of public interest as being a constant work in progress. In the United States, the *res publica* is not a thing but a process, so to speak; the public interest is not the result, but rather the political process made possible by the ever whirling wheels of federalism and the nuts and bolts of the separation of powers. The problem with this systemic approach is that it begs the question, for it fails to explain why governmental structures were purposively built like this, that is, with a view toward turning the *res publica* into ''the American uncompleted quest.''[29] The answer, I believe, has to do with the nature of the sacred. There is no such thing as a *res publica* in a society where the sacred remains a matter of purely private concern. In the modern republican age, freedom of conscience and religion compels us to recognize that the sacred is of such a nature; but the crux of the matter is that it cannot be only that. Rousseau captured this well: ''No State has ever been found without a religious basis.''[30] The French republican model reconstituted this religious basis—what Rousseau called the ''civil religion''—with the concept of ''*laïcité*,'' an untranslatable concept that is the cement of the French *res publica*. What *laïcité* means in the first place is a sharp division between the private and the public: the Sovereign—''We, The People'' or the Nation—has no authority beyond the limits of public expediency, nor does the citizen have authority beyond the limits of private conscience. In the United States, where this separation is unstable,[31] the public interest compels the citizens to eternal debate about the nature of the sacred.

The future of public law. At the beginning of the twenty-first century, public law is on the wane. The global age is driven by private law and private interests,

[29] R. N. Bellah, R. Madsen, W. M. Sullivan, A. Swindler & S. M. Tipton, *Habits of the Heart, Individualism and Commitment in American Life*, University of California Press, 1985, p. 252.

[30] J.-J. Rousseau, *The Social Contract* [Translated by G. D. H. Cole], Book, IV, chap. 8, available at http://www.constitution.org/jjr/socon.htm. For an application of Rousseau's idea to the United States, see Robert N. Bellah, ''Civil Religion in America,'' 96 *Daedalus* 1 (1967).

[31] See C. Greenhouse, ''Separation of Church and State in the United States: Lost in Translation,'' 13 *IJGLS* 493 (2006).

as exemplified by the extraordinary success of the jurisprudence of law and economics, that is, the calculation of the cost of everything to the exclusion of more unquantifiable values. In the United States, the *res publica*—alive and well only a few decades ago—has become an increasingly abstract concept, first, with deregulation the effect of which was to transfer to the private sector large pieces of the *res publica* patiently put together since the New Deal, and, second, with the ongoing debate over federal powers against which member States claim the ''umbrage'' of private law to protect themselves (sovereign immunity, and core governmental functions). In France, public law is likely to undergo transformations as the new government elected in 2007 engages in globalization to a much greater degree than before.

The decline of public law at the domestic level coincides with the rise of globalization. The latter is indeed as much a cause as it is an effect of the former inasmuch as the more global the world goes, the more private it goes. This does not mean that no good will ever come from a globalized world. Rather, with so many common dangers, especially in environmental matters, it is unrealistic (if not irresponsible) to expect that ''international peace and security''—the very basic substance of the *res publica* at the world level, as actually enunciated in the first article of the Charter of the United Nations—will arise as by magic from private law principles (*i.e.*, the market). No society can endure without ''some'' public law, even—and, perhaps, even more—if it is not a State.

Bibliography

Adams, J., *Defense of the Constitutions of Government of the United States of America*, 1787-1788, available at http://www.constitution.org/jadams/john_adams.htm (last viewed March 26, 2007).

Alland, D. & Rials, S. (Eds.), *Dictionnaire de la culture juridique*, Lamy / PUF, 2003.

Allison, J. W. F., *A Continental Distinction in the Common Law, A Historical and Comparative Perspective on English Public Law*, Oxford, Clarendon Press, 1996.

Aman, A. C. Jr. & Mayton, W. T., *Administrative Law*, 2nd ed., West Group, 2001.

Anderson, F. Maloy (Ed.), *The Constitutions and Other Selected Documents Illustrative of the History of France (1789-1901)*, Minneapolis, Wilson Co., 1904.

Archives parlementaires de 1787 à 1860, Première série, 1787 à 1799, vol. VIII (5 mai 1789 au 15 septembre 1789), Paris, 1875, available at http://gallica.bnf.fr/ark:/12148/bpt6k495230 (last viewed March 26, 2007).

Archives parlementaires de 1787 à 1860, Première série, 1787 à 1799, vol. XII (2 mars au 14 avril 1790), Paris, 1875, available at http://gallica.bnf.fr/ark:/12148/bpt6k49527c (last viewed March 26, 2007).

Auby, J.-B. & Friedland, M. (Eds.), *La distinction du droit public et du droit privé: regards français et britanniques*, Éditions Panthéon-Assas, LGDJ, 2004.

Auby, J.-B. (Ed.), *The Public Law / Private Law Divide: Une entente assez cordiale*, Oxford; Portland, OR, Hart, 2006 [previously published in 2004 by LGDJ, Paris].

Bagehot, W., *The English Constitution*, 1867, Oxford World's Classics, Reed, 2001.

Baker, K. M., ''Souveraineté,'' *DCRF* (Idées), p. 483.

Bailyn, B., *The Ideological Origins of the American Revolution*, The Belknap Press of Harvard University Press, 1967, enlarged edition 1992.

Baranger, D., *Parlementarisme des origines*, PUF, Coll. Léviathan, 1999.

——, ''Angleterre (Culture juridique),'' *DCJ*, p. 58.

Barbey, J., ''Le sacre'' in S. Rials (Ed.), *Le miracle capétien*, Paris, Librairie académique Perrin, 1987, p. 79.

——, ''Droits régaliens,'' *DAR*, p. 445 s.

Bastid, P., *Sieyès et sa pensée*, Hachette 1938, New enlarged edition (1970).

Beaud, O., ''Préface, Carl Schmitt ou le juriste engagé,'' Introduction to the work by C. Schmitt, *Théorie de la Constitution*, PUF, Coll. Léviathan, 1993.

——, *La puissance de l'État*, Coll. Léviathan, PUF, 1994.

——, ''La théorie générale de l'État (*Allgemeine Staatslehre*) en France, Quelques notations sur un dialogue contrarié'' in O. Beaud & E. Volkmar Heyen (Eds.), *Eine deutsch-französische Rechtswissenschaft? / Une science juridique franco-allemande?* Nomos Verl.-Ges., 1999, p. 83 s.

——, ''La distinction entre droit public et droit public: un dualisme qui résiste aux critiques'' in J.-B. Auby & M. Friedland (Eds.), *La distinction du droit public et du droit privé: regards français et britanniques*, Ed. Panthéon-Assas, 2004, p. 29.

Beccaria, *On Crimes and Punishments and Other Writings*, Cambridge University Press, 1995.

Bellah, R. N., Madsen, R., Sullivan, W. M., Swindler, A. & Tipton, S. M., *Habits of the Heart, Individualism and Commitment in American Life*, University of California Press, 1985.

——, ''Civil Religion in America,'' 96 *Daedalus* 1 (1967).

Bély, L. (Ed.), *Dictionnaire de l'Ancien Régime*, PUF, Quadrige, 2002.

Berman, H. J. & Witte, J., ''The Transformation of Western Legal Philosophy in Lutheran Germany,'' 62 *South. Calif. L. Rev.* 1573 (1989).

Berman, H. J. & Reid, C.J., ''Roman Law in Europe and the *Jus Commune*: An Historical Overview with Emphasis on the New Legal Science of the Sixteenth Century,'' 20 *Syracuse J. Int'l L. & Comm.* 1 (1994).

Berman, H. J., ''The Origins of Historical Jurisprudence: Coke, Selden, Hale,'' 103 *Yale L. J.* 1651 (1994).

Bigot, G., *Introduction historique au droit administratif français*, Coll. Droit Fondamental, PUF, 2002.

Birstch, G., ''Reform Absolutism and the Codification of the Law, The Genesis and Nature of the Prussian General Code (1794),'' in J. Brenner & E. Hellmuth (Eds.), *Rethinking Leviathan, The Eighteenth Century State in Britain and Germany*, Oxford University Press, 1999, p. 343.

Blackstone (Sir W.), *Commentaries on the Laws of England, A Facsimile of the First Edition of 1765-1769*, 4 volumes, Chicago & London, University of Chicago Press, 1979, available at http://www.constitution.org/tb/tb-0000.htm (edited by St. George Tucker) (last viewed March 26, 2007).

Bluche, F., *Le despotisme éclairé* (1969), Hachette, Pluriel, 2000.

Bobbio, N., *Democracy and Dictatorship* [Translated by P. Kennedy], Minneapolis, University of Minnesota Press, 1989.

Böckenförde, E.-W., *Le droit, l'État et la constitution démocratique* [Translated by O. Jouanjan], Bruylant / LGDJ, 2000.

Bodin, J., *The Six Books of the Commonwealth* [Abridged and translated by M. J. Tooley], Barnes & Noble, New York, 1967, available at http://www.constitution.org/bodin/bodin_.htm (last viewed March 26, 2007).

Borgetto, M., *La notion de fraternité en droit public français*, Paris, LGDJ, 1993.

Borke, P. F., ''The Pluralist Reading of James Madison's Tenth Federalist,'' 9 *Perspectives in American History*, 271 (1975).

Boucher d'Argis, ''Droit public'' in M. Diderot & M. D'Alembert (Eds.), *Encyclopédie raisonnée des arts et des métiers*, Paris, 1751-1780, vol. v [Discussion—Esquinancie], 1755, p. 134, available at http://gallica.bnf.fr.ark:/12148/bpt6k50537q.

Boucher d'Argis, ''Police,'' in M. Diderot & M. D'Alembert (Eds.), *Encyclopédie raisonnée des arts et des métiers*, Paris, 1751-1780, vol. XII, p. 905, available at http://gallica.bnf.fr/ark:/12148/bpt6k505440/f906.chemindefer.

Bossuet, *Politique tirée des propres paroles de l'Ecriture sainte*, Paris, Pierre Cot, 1760, Book V, available at http://gallica.bnf.fr/ark:/12148/bpt6k103256m.

Bracton, Henry de, *Bracton De legibus et consuetudinibus Angliæ* (George E. Woodbine ed.), Yale University Press 1915-1942.

Bracton, Henry de, *On the Laws and Customs of England*, 4 volumes [Translated by S. E. Thorne], Cambridge, MA, Belknap Press, 1968.

Bradley, A. W. & Ewing, K. D., *Constitutional and Administrative Law*, 13th ed., Harlow, Pearson Education, 2003.

Braudel, F. & Labrousse, E., *Histoire économique et sociale de la France*, vol. I/ 1450-1660, Quadrige, PUF, 1993.

Breyer, S., *Active Liberty, Interpreting Our Democratic Constitution*, New York, A. Knopf, 2005.

Brunet, P., *Vouloir pour la nation, Le concept de représentation dans la théorie de l'État*, Bruylant / LGDJ, 2004.

Burke, E., *Reflections on the Revolution in France* (1790), Penguin Classics, 1968.

——, *Thoughts on the Cause of the Present Discontents*, continued, 1. 1. 139, in *Select Works of Edmund Burke, and Miscellaneous Writings,* Indianapolis, Liberty Fund, 1999, available at http://www.econlib.org/LIBRARY/LFBooks/Burke/brkSWv1c1a.html (last viewed June 15, 2007).

G. Burness, ''The Divine Right of Kings Reconsidered,'' 107 *English Historical Review* 827 (1992).

Burchell, G., Gordon, C. & Miller, P. (Eds.), *The Foucault Effect: Studies in Governmentality*, Chicago, University of Chicago Press, 1991.

Burdeau, G., *Traité de science politique*, vol. 2: L'État, LGDJ, 1966.

Caillosse, J., ''Droit public-droit privé: sens et portée d'un partage académique,'' *AJDA* 955 (1996).

Calabresi, G., *A Common Law for the Age of Statutes*, Harvard University Press, 1982.

Calvès, G., *Les politiques de discriminations positives*, *PPS*, no. 822 (1999).

Cane, P., *An Introduction to Administrative Law*, 3rd ed., Clarendon Law Series, Oxford, 1996.

Capitant, R., *Écrits constitutionnels*, Paris, Éditions du CNRS, 1982.

Carré de Malberg, R., *Contribution à la théorie générale de l'État*, 2 volumes, 1920, reprint, CNRS 1962.

Carty, A., ''Conservative and Progressive Visions in French International Legal Doctrine,'' 16 *EJIL* 525 (2005).

Chaunu, P., ''L'État de finance,'' *Histoire économique et sociale de la France, I/1450-1660* (F. Braudel & E. Labrousse (Eds.)), PUF, 1993, pp. 129-191.

Chayes, A., ''The Role of the Judge in Public Law Litigation,'' 89 *Harv. L. Rev.* 1281 (1976).

——, ''Public Law Litigation and the Burger Court,'' 96 *Harv. L. Rev.* 4 (1982).

Chevallier, J., *L'élaboration historique du principe de séparation de la juridiction administrative et de l'administration active*, Paris, LGDJ, 1970.

——, *Science administrative*, 3rd ed., Paris, PUF, Collection Thémis Science politique, 2002.

——, ''La gouvernance et le droit,'' *Mélanges Amselek*, Bruylant, 2005, p. 189.

Chevrier, G., ''Remarques sur l'introduction et les vicissitudes de la distinction du '*jus privatum*' et du '*jus publicum*' dans les œuvres des anciens juristes français,'' *APD* 5 (1952).

Cicero, *De la République* (A. Fouillée (Ed.)), Paris, Delagrave, 1868.

Clavreul, C., ''Sieyès et la genèse de la représentation moderne,'' *Droits*, no. 6 (1987), p. 45.

Combe, C., ''Prérogative,'' *DCC*, p. 1187.

Coase, R., ''The Problem of Social Cost,'' 3 *Journal of Law & Economics* 1 (1960).

——, ''Economics and Contiguous Disciplines,'' 7 *Journal of Legal Studies* 201 (1978).

Colliard, J.-C., ''La liberté des partis politiques,'' *Mélanges J. Robert*, Montchrestien, 1998, p. 81.

Congress and Pressure Groups, Senate, 99th Congress, 2nd session, S-Prt. 99-161 (1986).

Conseil d'État, *Rapport public 1999: Jurisprudence et avis de 1998, L'intérêt général*, Etudes & Documents, no. 50, La Documentation française.

Constant, B., *Écrits politiques*, Paris, Gallimard, Folio Essais, 1997.

Coquillette, D. R., ''Mosses from an Old Manse: Another Look at Some Historic Property Cases About the Environment,'' 64 *Cornell L. Rev.* 761 (1979).

Corwin, Edward S., ''The 'Higher Law' Background of American Constitutional Law,'' Part I and II, 42 *Harv. L. Rev.* 149-185; 365-409 (1928-29).

Cottret, M., ''Absolutisme,'' *DAR*, p. 8.

Craig, P., ''Public Law and Control Over Private Power'' in M. Taggart (Ed.), *The Province of Administrative Law*, Oxford, Hart, 1997, p. 196.

David, R., *Le droit français*, vol. I (*Les données fondamentales du droit français*), Paris, LGDJ, 1960.

——, ''Introduction,'' *International Encyclopedia of Comparative Law*, vol. II: The Legal Systems of the World, Chapter 2: Structure and the Divisions of the Law, JCB Mohr / Mouton, Tübingen / Paris, pp. 2-19.

Dawson, J. P. ''The Codification of the French Customs,'' 38 *Mich. L. Rev.* 765 (1940).

——, *The Oracles of Law*, University of Michigan, 1968.

Dehoussse, R., ''Le paradoxe de Madison: Réflexions sur le rôle des chambres hautes dans les systèmes fédéraux,'' *RDP*, 1990, p. 643.

Delamare, N., *Traité de la police*, Paris, J. & P. Cot, 1705.

Denoix de Saint Marc, R., ''Allocution d'ouverture,'' *RA*, 2001, Deuxième centenaire du Conseil d'État, p. 535.

Descimon, R. & Guery, A., ''Justifications: la 'monarchie royale''' (1989) in A. Burguière & J. Revel, *Histoire de la France: La longue durée de l'État* (J. Le Goff (Ed.)), Seuil, 2000, p. 253.

Desmons, E., ''Droit privé, droit public,'' *DCC*, p. 520.

Deswarte, M.-P., ''Intérêt général, bien commun,'' *RDP*, 1988, p.1289.

Dicey, A. V., *An Introduction to the Study of the Law of the Constitution*, with an introduction by E. C. S. Wade, 10th ed., London, The McMillan Press Ltd., 1959, available at http://www.constitution.org/cmt/avd/law_con.htm (last viewed March 27, 2007).

Diderot & d'Alembert (Eds.), *Encyclopédie ou dictionnaire raisonné des sciences, des arts et des métiers*, 1755. 1780, 33 volumes, available at http://gallica.bnf.fr/ (last viewed March 26, 2007).

Diggins, J. P., ''The Socialization of Authority and the Dilemmas of American Liberalism,'' 46 *Social Research* 454 (1979).

Domat, J., *Les lois civiles dans leur ordre naturel*, 1689.

Drago, R. & Frison-Roche, M.-F., ''Mystères et mirages des dualités des ordres de juridictions et de la justice administrative,'' *APD*, 1997, p. 135.

Drucker, P. F., ''A Key to American Politics: Calhoun's Pluralism,'' 10 *Review of Politics* 412 (1948).

Duguit, L. ''The Law and the State,'' 31 *Harv. L. Rev.* 1, 184-185 (1917).

——, ''The Concept of Public Service,'' 32 *Yale L. J.* 425, 431-435 (1923).

——, *Traité de droit constitutionnel*, 5 volumes, 1927.

Dupuy, P.-M., *Droit international public*, Précis Dalloz, 6th ed., 2002.

Durand, Y., ''Nation, nations,'' in *DAR*, p. 882.

——, ''Privilèges, privilégiés,'' in *DAR*, p. 1024.

Durkheim, E., *The Division of Labor in Society*, Introduction by Lewis A. Coser, [Translated by W. D. Halls], The Free Press, 1984.

Dworkin, R., *Taking Rights Seriously*, Harvard University Press, 1977.

Easterbrook, F. H., ''The State of Madison's Vision of the State: A Public Choice Perspective,'' 107 *Harv. L. Rev.* 1328 (1994).

Ehrlich, L., ''Comparative Public Law and the Fundamentals of its Study,'' 21 *Columbia L. Rev.* 623 (1921).

Ellul, J., *Histoire des institutions, Le moyen âge*, PUF, Coll. Quadrige, 1999.

——, *Histoire des institutions, Le XIXe siècle* (1962), PUF, Coll. Quadrige, 1999.

Esmein, A., ''La maxime *Princeps legibus solutus est* dans l'ancien droit public français,'' in P. Vogradoff (Ed.), *Essays in Legal History Read Before The International Congress of Historical Studies Held in London in 1913*, Oxford University Press, 1913, p. 201.

——, *Eléments de droit constitutionnel français et comparé*, 1914, Reprint 2001 Éditions Panthéon Assas, Diffusion LGDJ.

Farber, D. A. & Frickey, Ph. P., ''The Jurisprudence of Public Choice,'' 65 *Texas L. Rev.* 873 (1986-1987).

Flaherty, M. S., ''The Most Dangerous Branch,'' 105 *Yale L. J.* 1725 (1995-1996).

Forsthoff, E., *Traité de droit administratif allemand* [Translated by M. Fromont], Bruxelles, Bruylant, 1969.

Fortescue, Sir J., *On the Laws and Governance of England* (S. Lockwood (Ed.)), Cambridge University Press, 1997.

Foucault, M., *Dits et écrits II, 1976-1988*, Paris, Gallimard, Quarto, 2001.

Foulquier, N., *Les droits publics subjectifs des administrés. Emergence d'un concept en droit administratif français du XIXe au XXe siècle*, Paris, Dalloz, 2003.

Friedrich, C. J., "The Continental Tradition of Training Administrators in Law and Jurisprudence," 11 *Journal of Modern History* 129 (1939).

Fries, S. D., "*Staatstheorie* and the New American Science of Politics," 34 *Journal of the History of Ideas*, 391 (1973).

Fromont, M. & Rieg, A., *Introduction au droit allemand*, vol. I: Les fondements, Paris, Éditions Cujas, 1977.

Fromont, M., "Regards d'un juriste français sur la juridiction administrative allemande," *RA*, 2001, Deuxième centenaire du Conseil d'État, p. 560.

Furet, F., *La Révolution en débat*, Gallimard, Folio, 1999.

——, "Terreur," DCRF (Événements), p. 307.

Furet & Ozouf (Eds.), *Dictionnaire critique de la Révolution française*, Collection Champs no. 264-267, Flammarion, 1992, 4 volumes: Acteurs, Institutions et créations, Événements, Idées.

Fustel de Coulanges, N. D., *La cité antique*, Paris, Durand, 1864.

Gaudemet, Y., "Le juge administratif, une solution d'avenir?" *Clefs pour le siècle*, Dalloz, 2000, p. 1213.

Georget, "Les caméralistes allemands: du principe de réalité à la théorie codifiée," available at www.lameta.univ-montp1.fr/PEA/pages_composantes/Communications/georget.pdf (last viewed April 7, 2006).

Ghestin, J., Goubeaux, G. & Fabre-Magnan, M., *Droit civil, Introduction générale*, LGDJ, 1994.

Gilmore, Grant, *The Ages of American Law*, Yale University Press, 1977.

Girard, P-F., *Manuel élémentaire de droit romain*, Rousseau, 1918, reprint Dalloz, 2002.

Godechot, J., *Les constitutions de la France depuis 1789*, GF-Flammarion, no. 228, 1978.

——, *La grande Nation, L'expansion de la France révolutionnaire dans le monde de 1789 à 1799*, 2nd ed. enlarged., Paris, Aubier-Montaigne, 1983.

Goebel, J., *History of the Supreme Court of the United States: Antecedents and Beginnings to 1801*, New York, McMillan, 1971.

Gordley, J.-R. & Mehren, A. T. von, *The Civil Law System*, 2nd ed., Boston, Little Brown, 1977.

Greenhouse, C., *Praying for Justice*, Cornell University Press, 1986.

——,Yngvesson, B. & Engel, D., *Law and Community in Three American Towns*, Cornell University Press, 1986.

——, "Separation of Church and State in the United States: Lost in Translation," 13 *IJGLS* 493 (2006).

Grewe, C., "L'État de droit sous l'empire de la Loi fondamentale," in O. Jouanjan (Ed.), *Figures de l'État de droit*, Presses Universitaires de Strasbourg, 2001, p. 385.

Guglielmi, G.-J., & Koubi, G., *Droit du service public*, Paris, Montchrestien, 2000.

Gutteridge, H. C., "Abuse of Rights," 5 *Cambridge L. J.* 22 (1933).

Hamilton, A., Madison, J. & Jay, J., *The Federalist Papers*, C. Rossiter Edition, Mentor Book, N.Y, 1961, available at http://www.yale.edu/lawweb/avalon/federal/fed.htm (last viewed March 27, 2007).

Hamilton, G. G. & Sutton, J. R., "The Problem of Control in the Weak State, Domination in the United States, 1880-1920," 18 *Theory and Society* 1 (1989).

Harouel, J.-L., "La monarchie absolue," in S. Rials (Ed.), *Le miracle capétien*, Paris, Librairie académique Perrin, 1987, p. 101.

Hauriou, M., *Précis de droit constitutionnel*, 2nd ed., Sirey, 1929, reprint CNRS, 1965.

——, *Précis de droit administratif et de droit public*, Paris, Sirey, 1933, reprint Dalloz, 2002.

Hayek, F., *The Constitution of Liberty*, University of Chicago Press, 1960.

Hegel, Georg W. F., *La raison dans l'histoire*, Bibliothèques 10/18, Plon, 1965.

Held, V., *The Public Interest and Individual Interests*, New York, Basic Books, 1969.

Heuschling, L., *État de droit, Rechtsstaat, Rule of Law*, Paris, Dalloz, 2002.

Hobbes, T., *Leviathan*, Penguin Classics, 1985, available at http://www.constitution.org/th/leviatha.htm (last viewed March 26, 2007).

——, *De Cive, On the Citizen* [Edited and Translated by R. Tuck & M. Silverthorne], Cambridge University Press, 1998, available at http://www.constitution.org/th/decive.htm (last viewed March 26, 2007).

Holmes, C., "The Legal Instruments of Power and the State in Early Modern England," in A. Padoa-Schioffa (Ed.), *Legislation and Justice*, European Science Foundation, Clarendon Press, 1997, p. 269.

Hood Philipps, O. & Jackson, P., *Constitutional and Administrative Law*, 8th ed. [Paul Jackson & Patricia Leopold], London, Sweet & Maxwell, 2001.

Horwitz, Morton J., *The Transformation of American Law: 1780-1860*, Harvard University Press, 1977.

——, "The History of the Public/ Private Distinction," 130 *U. Penn. L. Rev.*, 1423 (1981-1982).

——, "Republicanism and Liberalism in American Constitutional Thought," 29 *Wm. & Mary L. Rev.* 57 (1987-1988).

Hughes, Charles Evans, *Addresses and Papers of Charles Evans Hughes*, New York and London, 1908.

Humboldt, Wilhem von, *The Limits of State Action* (1852) (ed. J. W. Burton), Liberty Fund, Indianapolis, 1993.

Hummel, J., *Le constitutionnalisme allemand (1815-1918): le modèle allemand de la monarchie limitée*, Paris, PUF, Léviathan, 2002.

Huntington, Samuel P., "Political Modernization: America vs. Europe," 18 *World Politics* 378 (1965-1966).

Irvine of Laird (Lord), "Sovereignty in Comparative Perspective: Constitutionalism in Britain and in America," 76 *N.Y.U. L. Rev.* 1 (2001).

Jackson, Robert H., *The Struggle for Judicial Supremacy, A Study of a Crisis in American Power Politics*, New York, A. Knopf, 1941.

——, *The Supreme Court in the American System of Government*, Harvard University Press, 1955.

Jacqué, J.-P., *Droit institutionnel de l'Union européenne*, 3rd ed., Dalloz, 2004.

Jefferson, T., *Writings*, New York, Literary Classics of the United States, 1984.

Jouanjan, O., "Carl Friedrich Gerber et la constitution d'une science du droit public allemande," in O. Beaud & P. Wachsmann (Eds.), *La science juridique française et la science juridique allemande*, 1997, p. 11.

——, "État de droit, forme de gouvernement et représentation," in O. Jouanjan (Ed.), *Études de droit théorique et pratique*, Presses Universitaires de Strasbourg, 1998, p. 279.

——, *Une histoire de la pensée juridique en Allemagne (1800-1918)*, Paris, PUF, Collection Léviathan, 2005.

Jouannet, E., *Emer de Vattel et l'émergence doctrinale du droit international classique*, Paris, Pedone, 1998.

Jourdan, Ph., "La formation du concept de service public," *RDP*, 1987, p. 89.

Kantorowicz, E. H., *The King's Two Bodies, A Study in Medieval Political Theology*, Princeton University Press, 1981.

Kennedy, Duncan, "Toward an Historical Understanding of Legal Consciousness: The Case of Classical legal Thought in America, 1850-1940," 3 *Research in Law and Sociology* 3-24 (1980).

Keir, D. L. & Lawson, F. H., *Cases in Constitutional Law*, 6th ed., Oxford, Clarendon Press, 1979.

Ketcham, R. (Ed.), *The Anti-Federalist Papers and the Constitutional Convention Debates*, New York, Mentor Book, 1986.

Koenigsberger, H. G., "Monarchies and Parliaments in Early Modern Europe: *Dominium Regale et Dominium Politicum et Regale*," 5 *Theory and Society* 191 (1978).

Kramnick, I., "The 'Great National Discussion': The Discourse of Politics in 1787," 45 *Wm. and Mary Q.* 3 (1988).

Kurland, P. B. & Lerner, R. (Eds.), *The Founders' Constitution*, The University of Chicago Press, 1987, 5 volumes, available at http://press-pubs.uchicago.edu/founders/tocs/toc.html (last viewed March 26, 2007).

La Boétie, E. de, *Le discours de la servitude volontaire*, Paris, Payot et Rivages, 2002.

La création du droit par le juge, A.P.D., no. 50 (2007).

Laferrière, E., *Traité de la juridiction administrative et des recours contentieux*, vol. I (1887), LGDJ, reprint, 1989.

Lambert, É., *Le gouvernement des juges et la lutte contre la législation sociale aux États-Unis. L'expérience américaine de contrôle judiciaire de la constitutionnalité des lois*, Paris, Edition Giard, 1921, reprint Dalloz, 2005.

La Porta, R., Lopez-de-Silanes, F., Schleifer, A. & Vishny, R., "The Quality of Government," 15 *Journal of Law, Economics and Organization* 222 (1999).

Larrère, C., *L'invention de l'économie au XVIIIe siècle*, PUF, Coll. Léviathan, 1992.

Larsen, C., "The Future of Comparative Law: Public Legal Systems," 21 *Hastings Int'l & Comp. L. Rev.* 847 (1998).

Lauvaux, Ph., ''Le principe monarchique en Allemagne,'' in O. Beaud & P. Wachsmann (Eds.), *La science juridique française et la science juridique allemande*, Strasbourg, Presses Universitaires de Strasbourg, 1997, p. 65.

L.-B., A.-M., ''Pouvoir réglementaire,'' in O. Duhamel & Y. Mény (Eds.), *Dictionnaire constitutionnel*, PUF, 1992, p. 782.

Le Bras, G., ''Les origines canoniques du droit administratif,'' in *L'évolution du droit public. Études offertes à Achille Mestre*, Sirey, 1956, p. 395.

Legendre, P., *Histoire de l'administration de 1750 à nos jours*, PUF, Thémis, 1968.

Lepsius, O., ''Faut-il au droit constitutionnel une théorie de l'État? Point de vue allemand: de la théorie de l'État à la théorie des formes de domination,'' 15 *RUDH*, no. 3-6, 30 Octobre 2003, p. 86.

Levitan, D. M., ''The Foreign Relations Power: An Analysis of Mr. Justice Sutherland's Theory,'' 55 *Yale L. J.* 467 (1946).

Lilla, M. (Ed.), *New French Thought, Political Philosophy*, Princeton University Press, 1994.

Linditch, F., ''La réception de la théorie allemande de la personnalité morale de l'État dans la doctrine française,'' in O. Beaud & P. Wachsmann (Eds.), *La science juridique française et la science juridique allemande*, p.179.

Lobbying Reform, Background and Legislative Proposals, 109th Congress, CRS Report for Congress (updated March 26, 2006).

Locke, J., *Two Treatises of Government, Second Treatise*, Cambridge University Press, 1988.

Loughlin, M., ''The State, the Crown and the Law,'' in M. Sunkin & S. Payne (Eds.), *The Nature of the Crown*, Oxford University Press, 1999.

Lowi, T. S., *The End of Liberalism*, 2nd ed., New York, W.W. Norton & Co., 1979.

Machiavelli, N., *The Prince* [Translated by W. K. Marriott] 1908, available at http://www.constitution.org/mac/prince00.htm (last viewed March 26, 2007).

Maine, Henry Sumner, Sir, *Popular Government: Four Essays*, London, J. Murray, 1890.

Maitland, F., *The Constitutional History of England* (1908), Cambridge University Press, reediting 1946.

Manin, B., *Principes du gouvernement représentatif*, 1995, Flammarion, Champs, no. 349.

Mansfield, H. C., Jr., ''Constitutional Government: The Soul of Modern Democracy,'' *The Public Interest*, no. 86 (Winter 1987), p. 53.

Maulin, E., ''Souveraineté,'' *DCC*, p. 1435.

Maurer, H., *Droit administratif allemand* [Translated by M. Fromont], Paris, LGDJ, 1992.

Maus, D., *Les grands textes de la pratique constitutionnelle de la Ve République*, La documentation française, 1998.

Mazeaud, Henri, ''Défense du droit privé,'' D. 1946, chronique, p. 17.

Merryman, John Henry, ''The French Deviation,'' 44 *AJCL* 109 (1996).

Michelet, J., *Histoire de la Révolution française* in *Œuvres complètes*, vols. XVII-XXIII, Flammarion, 1897-1898.

Möller, H., *Furstenstaat oder Bürgernation? Deutschland 1763-1815*, 4th ed., Berlin, Verlag Gruppe Random House, Bertelsmann, 1998.

Mommsen, Th., Krueger, P. & Watson, A. (Eds.), *The Digest of Justinian* [5 volumes] University of Pennsylvania Press, 1985.

Montesquieu, *The Spirit of Laws,* 1748, [Translated by Th. Nugent, 1752, revised by J. V. Prichard], available at http://www.constitution.org/cm/sol.htm (last viewed March 26, 2007).

Morabito, M., & Bourmaud, D., *Histoire constitutionnelle et politique de la France (1789-1958)*, 5th ed., Montchrestien, 1998.

Morgan, R. J., "Madison's Theory of Representation in the Tenth Federalist," 36 *Journal of Politics* 852 (1974).

Napoli, P., *Naissance de la police moderne: Pouvoir, normes, société*, Paris, La Découverte, 2003.

Neilson, W. E., "Changing Conceptions of Judicial Review: The Evolution of Constitutional Theory in the States, 1790-1860," 120 *U. Penn. L. Rev.* 1166 (1971-1972).

Nora, P., "Nation," *DCRF* (Idées), p. 339.

——, "République," *DCRF* (Idées), p. 404

Note, "Private Bills in Congress," 79 *Harv. L. Rev.* 1684 (1966).

Novak, W. J., "Common Regulation: Legal Origins of State Power," 45 *Hastings L. J.* 1061 (1994).

——, "The Pluralist State, the Convergence of Public and Private Power in America," in W. Gamber, M. Grossberg & H. Hartog (Eds.), *American Public Life and Historical Imagination*, University of Notre Dame Press, 2003, p. 27.

Ogris, W., "The Habsburg Monarchy in the Eighteenth Century: The Birth of the Modern Centralized State," in A. Padoa-Schioffa (Ed.), *Legislation and Justice*, European Science Foundation, Clarendon Press, 1997, p. 313.

Oliver, D., "The Underlying Values of Public and Private Law," in M. Taggart (Ed.), *The Province of Administrative Law*, Oxford, Hart, 1997, p. 217.

——, *Common Values and the Public-Private Divide*, London, Butterworths, 1999.

Olivier-Martin, F., *L'absolutisme français* followed by *Les Parlements contre l'absolutisme traditionnel au XVIIIe siècle*, LGDJ, Reprint 1997.

——, *Les Lois du Roi*, LGDJ, reprint 1997.

Ozouf, M., "Esprit public," *DCRF* (Idées), p. 179.

Padoa-Schioppa, A., (Ed.), *Legislation and Justice*, European Science Foundation, Clarendon Press, 1997.

——, "Hierarchy and Jurisdiction in Medieval Canon Law," in A. Padoa-Schioppa (Ed.), *Legislation and Justice*, European Science Foundation, Clarendon Press, 1997, p.1.

Paine, T., *Collected Writings*, New York, Literary Classics of the United States, Coll. The Library of America, 1995.

Palmer, V. V., "From Embrace to Banishment: A Study of Judicial Equity in France," 47 *AJCL* 277 (1999).

Pasquino, P., *Sieyès et l'invention de la constitution en France*, Paris, Odile Jacob, 1998.

Passerin d'Entrèves, A., *The Notion of the State*, Oxford University Press, 1967.

Pfister, L., ''Réforme (La) et le droit,'' *DAR*, p. 1311.

Picard, E., *La notion de police administrative*, Paris, LGDJ, 1984, 2 volumes.

Pollard, A, F., *The Evolution of Parliament*, London; New York, Longmans, Green, 1920.

Portalis, *Discours préliminaire du premier projet de Code civil*, Paris, Editions Confluences, Voix de la cité, reprint 1999; English translation of the Preliminary Address to the First Draft of the Civil Code prepared by The International Cooperation Group, Department of Justice of Canada, available at http://www.justice.gc.ca/en/ps/inter/code/index.html#note1 (last viewed March 26, 2007).

Posner, R., *Economic Analysis of Law*, 6th ed., New York, Aspen, 2003.

Post, R., ''The Challenge of Globalization to American Public Law Scholarship,'' 2 *Theoretical Inquiries in Law* 323 (2001).

Pound R., ''Public Law and Private Law,'' 24 *Cornell L. Q.* 469 (1939).

Price, R., *Observations on the Importance of the American Revolution and the Means of Making It a Benefit to the World*, London, 1778.

Questiaux, N., ''Administration and the Rule of Law: The Preventive Role of the French Conseil d'État,'' 1995 *Public Law* 247.

Raeff, M., ''The Well-Ordered Police State and the Development of Modernity in Seventeenth- and Eighteenth-Century Europe: An Attempt at a Comparative Approach,'' 80 *American Historical Review* 1221 (1975).

——, *The Well-Ordered Police State, Social and Institutional Change through Law in the Germanies and Russia (1600-1800)*, Yale University Press, 1983.

Rakove, J. N., ''Making a Hash of Sovereignty, Part I,'' 2 *Green Bag* 35 (1998).

——, ''Making a Hash of Sovereignty, Part II,'' 3 *Green Bag* 51 (1999).

Ramsey, M. D., ''The Myth of Extraconstitutional Foreign Affairs Power,'' 42 *Wm. & Mary L. Rev.* 379 (2000-2001).

Rawls J., *A Theory of Justice*, Harvard University Press, 1971.

Raynaud, Ph., ''Préface,'' J. M. McPherson, *La guerre de Sécession (1861-1865)*, Robert Laffont, 1991.

——, & Rials, S. (Eds.), *Dictionnaire de philosophie politique*, PUF, 3rd ed. 2003.

Redish, M. R. & Marshall, L. C., ''Adjudicatory Independence and the Values of Procedural Due Process,'' 95 *Yale L. J.* 455 (1986).

Renan, E., *Qu'est-ce qu'une Nation?*, Discours en Sorbonne (March 11, 1882), available http://ourworld.compuserve.com/homepages/bib_lisieux/nation01.htm (last viewed March 26 2007).

Rials, S., ''La dévolution de la Couronne,'' in S. Rials (Ed.), *Le miracle capétien*, Paris, Librairie académique Perrin, 1987, p. 93.

——, *La Déclaration des droits de l'homme et du citoyen*, Hachette, Collection Pluriel, 1988.

Roman, D., *Le droit public face à la pauvreté*, Paris, LGDJ, 2002.

Royer, J.-P., *Histoire de la justice*, Coll. Droit fondamental, PUF, 2001.

Rousseau, J.-J., *The Social Contract* [Translated by G. D. H. Cole, public domain], available at http://www.constitution.org/jjr/socon.htm (last viewed March 26, 2007).

Rovan, J., *Histoire de l'Allemagne: des origines à nos jours* (1994), Paris, Seuil, Coll. Points Histoire, 1999.

Saint-Bonnet, F., *L'état d'exception*, Paris, PUF, Collection Léviathan, 2001.

——, ''Loi,'' *DCC*, p. 959.

Scheiber, H. N., ''Law and Political Institutions,'' *Encyclopedia of American Economic History: Studies of Principal Movements and Ideas* (Glenn Porter (Ed.)), 3 volumes, New York, Charles Scribner's Sons, 1980, vol. II, p. 487.

Scelle, G., *Précis de droit des gens, Principes et systématique*, 2 volumes, Sirey, 1932.

Schmitt, C., *Political Theology: Four Chapters on the Concept of Sovereignty* (1934) [Translated by George Schwab], MIT Press, 1985.

Senellart, M., *Les arts de gouverner, Du* regimen *médiéval au concept de gouvernement*, Paris, Seuil, Collection Des Travaux, 1995.

——, ''Gouvernement,'' *DCJ*, p. 768

——, ''Gouvernement,'' *DPP*, p. 293.

Sieyès, *Vues sur les moyens d'exécution dont les Représentans [sic] de la France pourront disposer en 1789*, Paris, 1789, available at http://gallica.bnf.fr/ark:/12148/bpt6k41688x.

Sieyès, E. *Qu'est-ce que le Tiers État?* (1788), PUF, Collection Quadrige, 1989.

Sieyès, E. J., *What Is the Third Estate*? [Translated by M. Blondel], and edited with historical notes, by S. E. Finer, Praeger Publishers, New York, 1964.

——, *Views of the Executive Means Available to the Representatives of France in 1789*, in *Political Writings: including the debate between Sieyès and Tom Paine in 1791* [Translated by Michael Sonenscher], Indianapolis / Cambridge, Hackett Publishing Co., Inc., 2003.

Smith, A., *An Inquiry into the Nature and the Causes of the Wealth of Nations*, 2 volumes, Oxford University Press 1976, reprint Liberty Classics, Indianapolis, 1979.

Stein, P., *Roman Law in European History*, Cambridge University Press, 1999.

Stephenson, C., & Marcham, F. G., *Sources of English Constitutional History, A Selection of Documents from A.D. 600 to the Interregnum*, 2 volumes, New York, Harper & Row, 1972.

Stolleis, M., *Geschichte des öffentlichen Rechts in Deutschland,* 3 volumes, Verlag, C. H. Beck München-Erster Band: *Reichspublizistik und Policeywissenschaft, 1600-1800,* 1988; Zweiter Band: *Staatsrechtslehre und Verwaltungswissenschaft, 1800-1914*, 1992; Dritter Band: *Staats- und Verwaltungsrechtswissenschaft in Republik und Diktatur, 1914-1945*, 1999.

——, *Histoire du droit public en Allemagne, Droit public impérial et science de la police (1600-1800)* [Translated by M. Senellart], PUF, 1998.

——, *Public Law in Germany (1800-1914)* [Translated by Pamela Biel], New York, Berghahn Books, 2001.

——, *A History of Public Law in Germany (1914-1945* [Translated by Thomas Dunlap], Oxford University, 2004]

Stubbs, W., *The Constitutional History of England*, 3 vols, Oxford: Clarendon Press, (1883-1887), Buffalo (New York): Hein Reprint (1987).

Sunstein, C., "Naked Preferences and the Constitution," 84 *Columbia L. Rev.* 1689 (1984).

——, "Interests Groups in American Public Law," 38 *Stanford L. Rev.* 29 (1985).

Taggart, M. (Ed.), *The Province of Administrative Law*, Oxford, Hart, 1997.

——, *Private Property and Abuse of Rights in Victorian England: The Story of Edward Pickles and the Bradford Water Supply*, Oxford University Press, 2002.

——, "'The Peculiarities of the English': Resisting the Public / Private Law Distinction," in P. Craig & R. Rawlings, (Eds.), *Law and Administration in Europe: Essays in Honour of Carol Harlow*, Oxford University Press, 2003, p. 107.

Thomas Aquinas, Saint, *On the Governance of Rulers* (De Regimine Principium) [Revised edition, translated from Latin by G. Phelan], Institute of Medieval Studies, Sheed & Ward, London & New York, 1938.

Tocqueville, A. de, *Democracy in America* [Translated by H. C. Mansfield & D. Winthrop], University of Chicago Press, 2000.

——, *The Old Regime and the Revolution* [Translated by Alan S. Kahan], University of Chicago Press, 2 vols, 1998.

——, *Voyage en Suisse*, in *Œuvres*, vol. I, Gallimard, Bibliothèque de la Pléiade, 1991.

Tönnies, F., *Community and Society*, New York, Harper Torchbooks, 1957.

Tribe, K., "Cameralism and the Science of Government," 56 *Journal of Modern History* 263 (1984).

Troper, M., *La séparation des pouvoirs dans l'histoire constitutionnelle française*, Paris, LGDJ, 1973, new edition, 1989.

——, "The Development of the Notion of Separation of Powers," 26 *Israel Law Review* 1 (1992).

Truchet, D., *Les fonctions de la notion d'intérêt général dans la jurisprudence du Conseil d'État*, Paris, LGDJ, 1977.

——, *Le droit public*, PUF, Coll. Que Sais-je?, 2003.

——, "Mauvaises et bonnes raisons de mettre fin au dualisme juridictionnel," *Justices* no. 3 (1996), p. 53.

Van Horn Melton, J., "Absolutism and 'Modernity' in Early Modern Central Europe," 8 *German Studies Review* 383 (1985).

Vattel, E. de, *Le droit des gens ou Principes de la loi naturelle* (1758), (Translation Joseph Chitty, 1883), available at http://www.constitution.org/vattel/vattel.htm (last viewed March 26, 2007)

Vedel, G. & Delvolvé, P., *Droit administratif*, PUF, Collection Thémis, 12th ed. 1980.

——, "Excès de pouvoir administratif et excès de pouvoir législatif [I et II]," *Cahiers CC*, no. 1 (1996), p. 57, and no. 2 (1997), p. 77.

Verpeaux, M., *La naissance du pouvoir réglementaire (1789-1799)*, Paris, PUF, Les grandes thèses du droit français, 1991.

Villey, M., *La formation de la pensée juridique moderne*, Paris, PUF, Coll. Léviathan, reprint 2003.

Vinogradoff, P., *Outlines of Historical Jurisprudence*, 1920.

Wade, H. W. R. & Forsyth, C. F., *Administrative Law,* 9th ed., Oxford University Press, 2004.

Weber, M., *Le savant et le politique,* Plon (1959), Collection 10/18, no. 134.

——, *Economy and Society*, 2 vols., G. Roth & C. Wittich (Eds.), University of California Press, 1978.

Wechsler, H., ''Towards Neutral Principles of Constitutional Law,'' 73 *Harv. L. Rev.* 1 (1959).

Weis, E., ''Enlightenment and Absolutism in the Holy Roman Empire: Thoughts on Enlightened Absolutism in Germany,'' 58 *Journal of Modern History* (1986), Supplement: ''Politics and Society in the Holy Roman Empire, 1500-1806,'' S181-S197.

Wieacker, F., ''Foundations of European Legal Culture'' [translated and annotated by E. Bodenheimer], 38 *AJCL* 1 (1990).

Wilson, W., *Congressional Government, A Study in American Politics*, Boston, Houghton Mifflin, 1885.

World Bank Report, *Doing Business 2004: Understanding Regulation*, available at http://www.doingbusiness.org/Main/DoingBusiness2004.aspx.

Wood, G. S., *The Creation of the American Republic (1776-1787)*, 1969, reprint New York, W.W. Norton &Co., 1987.

——, *The Radicalism of the American Revolution*, Vintage Books, 1993.

——, ''Democracy and the Constitution,'' in R. A. Goldwin & W. A. Schambra (Eds.), *How Democratic is the Constitution?* Washington / London, American Enterprise Institute for Public Policy Research, 1980, p. 1.

——, ''The Origins of Vested Rights in the Early Republic,'' 85 *Virginia L. Rev.* 1421 (1999).

——, ''The Origins of American Democracy, or How the People Became Judge in Their Own Cause,'' 47 *Cleveland State L. Rev.* 309 (1999).

Young Seek Choue, *World Encyclopedia of Peace*, 2nd ed., Oceana Publications, Dobbs Ferry, N.Y., 1999.

Zippelius / Würtenberger, *Deutsches Staatsrecht*, 31. Auflage, Verlag C. H. Beck, München, 2005.

Zoller, E., *Droit des relations extérieures*, Coll. Droit Fondamental, PUF, 1992.

——, ''Aspects internationaux du droit constitutionnel, Contribution à la théorie de la fédération d'États,'' 294 *RCADI* 39 (2002).

Index

www.ingramcontent.com/pod-product-compliance
Lightning Source LLC
Chambersburg PA
CBHW061201240926
51846CB00006B/1083
* 9 7 8 9 0 0 4 2 0 5 8 4 0 *